RED LEGS

Red Legs

JOHN GREENE

Dedication

Red Legs is dedicated to all the 157 men of 35th Battalion 'A' Company who served at Jadotville, The Congo 1961 - the greatest defence in Irish military history.

You deserved so much better.

About the author

John Greene was educated at Dulwich College (London) and the University of Hull. He retired from a career in Fund Management in October 2007 to concentrate on writing and other projects. He lives in London with his wife Kate and daughters Lilia-Mae and Shoshanna.

First published in 2012 on behalf of the author by
Scotforth Books (www.scotforthbooks.com)
ISBN 978-1-904244-83-7
Typesetting and design by Carnegie Publishing, Lancaster.
Printed in the UK by Short Run Press, Exeter

Contents

Acknowledgements

It was always a dream of mine that I would one day write a book but I had no idea that I would require so much help along the way. What started as musings with my father Mick and mother Nancy soon turned into volumes of source material detailing their memories and experiences. To mention each individual who helped would involve another volume of work but as the book began to take shape, I was given invaluable support in 'how does this read?' type discussions. Richard Dinham, James Rennie and Andrew Johnson all took time to set me back on track whilst family members like my brother Tom, his wife Nicky, niece Aine, mother-in-law Enid Slimm and Uncle Philip all provided additional observations through endless early versions that provoked further amendments.

Anecdotes to an author are like sweets to a child. Without the stories, photographs, factual corrections and memories of Sean Dowler, Phillip Sweeney, Franco Greene, Kitty Murray, Leo Quinlan, Tiernan Dolan and Kevin Greene, the book would have been much less authentic.

Anna Goddard, Penny Hayashi, Lucy Frontani and Cat Bond at Carnegie Publishing all provided help way beyond their professional remit, moulding the book into the readable version you have in front of you and I thank them for their time and patience.

Throughout the whole process my wife Kate listened, challenged, corrected and sometimes even provoked a change of direction but her honesty and insights drove me on and were without doubt the biggest help any author could have wished for.

Lastly I would like to thank two little ladies who endlessly remind me what writing is all about; my baby daughters Lilia-Mae and Shoshanna. The future is yours 'little-ones' and one day you will hopefully read with great pride the story about how your granddad Mick and many others like him enjoyed growing up in the 50s and 60s but ended up fighting for their own and their fellow peacekeepers lives for the only cause that is truly worthy of soldiering: world peace.

A note from the author

Every anecdote recounted is subject to the storyteller's opinions and emotions, especially when it is recounted some fifty years after the event. Personal experience may be influenced at the time by circumstance and hearsay – and later on by the wonderful advantage of hindsight and the vagaries of memory. One man's vivid observations may be recalled and retold very differently by another, and while all stories should be treasured and remembered, each one based on real life will have many unique versions.

To remain as true as possible to both the storyteller and the listener, real events and names are used throughout this book, but it should be remembered that portrayals of them are inevitably subjective not definitive, and therefore shouldn't be regarded as the basis for judgements about those involved.

John Greene

Michael Greene

Foreword

WHAT ARE THESE WOODEN LIONS on the mantelpiece dad?' I asked as a young boy to my father.

'They are the magnificent black-maned lions of Katanga son,' he replied proudly, 'the finest lions in all of Africa.'

'Wow,' I gasped, and reverently returned the lions back to their familiar place on the mantelpiece next to a memorial card of John F. Kennedy.

'What other animals did you see in the jungle, dad?' I continued, as my childish imagination began to run riot. He responded by telling me about the great African elephants, red river hogs, bongo antelopes, leopards, monkeys, gorillas, colourful toucans and the still beauty of a hummingbird flittering effortlessly in the reeds above a two-ton crocodile.

In his accounts he would also briefly mention the presence of native warriors dressed in big cat headgear, soldiers of fortune, tribal wars, being a prisoner of war, facing execution by firing squad and perhaps most alluringly for a youngster like myself, deadly boy soldiers.

I could have listened to him for hours, but the epic tales were almost always cut short with,

'Yer too young to understand all of this son, I'll tell ye when ya get older.'

I was determined that as I grew older he would tell me more about his journey to Africa but as the years passed the anecdotes became less frequent, the preserve of Christmas day reminiscences as we sat idly watching 'Only Fools and Horses' on the television. We would tease my father that he was like Uncle Albert talking about his experiences 'back in the woar' and sure enough the epic tales from his journey to Africa were no longer recounted.

Daily life had taken over and conversations always reverted back to work, weather, football, and politics, everyday topics that ensured the magnificent black mained lions of Katanga, looking out imperiously from their vantage point on the mantelpiece, were becoming a fading memory.

I busied myself in a career, a hectic social life and keeping abreast of the latest news but ultimately putting off chasing my own boyhood dreams as time was so scarce. I convinced myself that when I had more time I would retrieve those ambitions of one day photographing those majestic animals in Africa I had heard about as a child, maybe writing a book, and even making a film.

Life was good, but another groundhog day went by and nothing really changed.

But then one day it did. It was on the 19th October 2006 and I was enjoying a well earned holiday in Sardinia when I received an unexpected call from my brother Tom.

'Hello mate,' he opened brightly, 'how's the holiday going?'

I instinctively knew something wasn't right.

'Yeh fine,' I replied brusquely. 'Is there something wrong?'

'Well yeh there is,' he answered. 'Dad's had an accident.'

'How bad?' I asked anxiously.

'He's in a bad way alright,' my brother explained 'he's fallen 20 foot off a ladder at work and he's broken his neck and back, and his skull has been smashed in. He's in intensive care.'

I caught the next flight home.

Two days later, I stood with my mother and brother at his bedside as a doctor explained the full extent of his injuries.

'Although he has serious injuries to his neck, head and back, none are life threatening,' the doctor explained. 'Importantly his spine wasn't injured in the fall but he will however take a very long time to recover, and we can't tell yet if there will be long term damage from his head injury.'

It was such a relief to hear that he would survive but we were still unsure what would be left of the father, husband and grandfather we had all known and what kind of quality of life he could expect.

The first few weeks in hospital were very difficult as my father remained unable to move in a neck brace, barely conscious and heavily sedated. We were told that he had amnesia; that he remembered nothing about the accident and was barely communicating with us.

The doctor explained that this was 'normal' with such an injury and that head trauma often resulted in significant memory loss. He advised us to keep talking to him, reminding him of stories which may stimulate his recovery.

I told him about my daily life, about what was happening at work, the weather and how Manchester United were doing but each story seemed to tail off as his concentration would lapse, returning him to his weary state.

'Keep talking to him,' the doctors advised, 'it will help him.'

Of course we all persevered but each time the result was the same and I began to fear that he wouldn't recover his precious memory, that we had lost a cherished part of him.

Then one afternoon, completely unplanned, I happened to mention the magnificent black maned lions of Katanga on the mantelpiece at home.

His eyes opened, alerted by their very mention. The sedatives ensured that the reaction didn't last long, but the momentary glimpse into his eyes had sparked something inside him with vigour and excitement. Although it would take a long time, I immediately knew he would make a full recovery as I had found the precious key to his treasure. What I didn't realise was that I had also found the key to mine.

That night I researched information on the Katangan lions and about the other jungle animals he had told me about as a child so that I could run them by him in hospital the next day.

'Tell me what you saw dad,' I pressed. 'What did you feel at the time you saw the lions, what was going through your mind?'

'I never actually saw a real Katangan lion,' he replied out of the side of his mouth as the rest of him lay motionless. 'I just saw a boy soldier wearing a lion headdress who was immediately mown down by a machine gun.'

I was astounded both by the story and by his ability to articulate such a long sentence, visibly recovering in front of my eyes.

'I just bought them wooden lions off a poor owld fella in Elizabethville,' he finished.

I could tell his energy was sagging and the sedatives were taking effect so I reverted back to stories about my daily life, the weather and football which I knew neither of us had much interest in. My own mind was buzzing with ideas though and that night all sorts of questions kept popping into my head.

Tomorrow I must ask him what he was doing in Africa, I thought to myself. Why was the boy wearing the head-dress mown down by a machine gun?

Each day his answers would open another Pandora's box of questions, often far too many to answer in his injured state so I started reading books, archived newspapers, old military records – anything that could provide more detail as I sought to fill in the gaps.

By the spring of 2007, the neck brace was off and he was at home but still suffering the effects of head trauma. The story of the Katangan lions had grown into an encyclopaedia of research ranging from the African slave trade to Elvis Presley. Sometimes he would hesitate when we spoke about the living conditions of the African natives or the holocaust of the Congolese, the vigour in his eyes turning to anger and sadness. I too found some of the details truly distressing, even at times emotional but I pressed him to continue nonetheless.

Other times he would seem to digress into stories about home and family, to the films he had watched down at his local Picture House or even just stories about having the craic.

'Can you stick to the story?' I asked in frustration.

'But you asked me what I was feeling and thinking about at the time,' he countered, 'and this is it.'

I realised then that this was not going to be a typical 'war story', so I just wrote it down as he would tell me.

I lost track of when my father's full recovery from the accident happened, caught up in the catalogue of memories he was sharing with me, but the most important thing was that he did recover. It also allowed me to finally hear about his remarkable adventure, a story that I found enchanting, heartbreaking, sometimes infuriating but ultimately uplifting; I hope you do too.

CHAPTER ONE

How in Hell's name did I end up here?

Date: October 1961
Location: Jadotville, The Congo
Status: Prisoner of war

I HAD TAKEN THIS GAMBLE, I'd dealt and played the hand that led me to this grisly predicament but I could only make sense of it all now that I was a prisoner of war. As I continued piecing together my young life up to that point, a life whose future now seemed to hang so precariously, it all seemed so ridiculous for it to end almost before it had really begun.

It had started out as the thrill of an adventure, an idealistic young Irish soldier representing the United Nations volunteering for a peace-keeping mission in Africa's Heart of Darkness in the midst of its post independence civil war in 1961. At the time, it sounded so tempting for a young man to travel to a far-flung destination to bring about peace between warring factions while getting the chance to witness an actual war; that revered world of chivalry and desperadoes that I had watched so keenly as a child, acted out at my local Picture House back home by matinee idols.

When I joined the army at just 15, I was three years too young, but my enthusiasm and naïvety were lost in my own deception of a forged birth certificate. I had bluffed and lied like all the great imposters, signed up, been accepted as one of the lads and had volunteered alongside them for a six month tour of duty to The Congo. The soldier's uniform and blue UN helmet may have belonged to someone of more mature years but I had made it my own. I had never wanted one of those distinguished military careers; I just needed the money for my next adventure; to make it over to a swinging London of the early '60s. Films and music had been the future I had envisioned, but instead ahead of me lay the prospect of something far more menacing: execution by firing squad.

It was impossible to imagine anything worse but I chastised myself, like a strict schoolmaster, that it was still only one of a few possible outcomes. Maybe the war will end, I reasoned, or they could try to rescue us. But ongoing doubt makes even the most optimistic young mind fear the worst, and it was the firing squad that occupied my thoughts – supposedly an honourable end for any soldier humiliated by prisoner of war status. I gulped and shook my head despondently. Or, they may be able to swap us for enemy prisoners, I told myself convincingly. After a month in this very African prison-hell, I should have been past worrying about dying as I had already twice received the last rites for my earthly sins but what I cared most about was my family back home in Ireland, my wailing mother wondering if she would ever see her boy again. She had begged me not to volunteer.

'Please don't go Mickey... Please,' was ringing like tinnitus in my ears. I had heard about The Congo's many threats even before I volunteered but young men somehow find enjoyment at the prospect of danger and the challenge of overcoming hardship, and my desire for adventure was only heightened with the wager of unknown perils. As I sat back on the bare prison floor, it was the terrible guilt I felt to those at home that was the most difficult to overcome. I knew it was far too late for me to do anything to ease their suffering.

Before being taken prisoner, we were under siege for eight days, cut off from the rest of the UN forces, vastly outnumbered and surrounded by a mercenary led professional army intent on retaining white colonial control of The Congo's vast mineral resources. Just three days into the siege, the hell of war had abruptly unfolded and an all-out attack was waged against us with constant gunfire, mortars bombs and machine-gun jet fighters strafing our positions for the next five days. We were dug-in in a shallow trench, with little food, even less water and no sleep, fighting for our lives, with the only special gift we had all seemingly been blessed with; an intense desire to stay alive.

The siege in the town of Jadotville in The Congo's southern province of Katanga was all still fresh in my mind – the dizzying sound of whistling bullets, carrying the shot and wounded through no-man's land, the terror of being strafed, the intense day-time heat, the parched throat, uncontrollable vomiting at the sight of death and the vivid hallucinations. I had never imagined the reality of war, the utter devastation of bombs, or the cordite smell of a bullet that pierced the peak of my own helmet as death passed within an inch of my brow. I resigned myself to the fact that sooner or later there had to be one bullet out there with my name on it or, just as conceivably, I could get in the way of someone else's. Those who are fortunate enough to survive war are sometimes called a 'hero' but for me, the initial fear was unimaginable and simply descended into an unfeeling trance-like state in a macabre game of desperate survival, where the most intense hatred was sometimes the only thing that could keep a man alive. If that makes a man a hero, then I didn't want to be one.

The odds we faced during the battle weren't great no matter how we played them, 157 of us against more than 3,000 of them: a hotchpotch of rebel soldiers; highly-paid bloodthirsty mercenaries; drug-crazed tribal warriors and armed civilians. We were told there were over 300 casualties of the siege including at least 150 dead but incredibly all 157 of us UN soldiers were still alive. Most of us couldn't believe it, having been that outnumbered and with all those bullet wounds and serious injuries. The sight of blood-soaked clothing, bandaged legs, arms, and chests just made it more implausible. We agreed that it must have been the slit trenches that had been our saviour or that God himself had been watching over us. But even in that most dire circumstance there was also the camaraderie and the absolute trust we had in the men around us. Perhaps most surprisingly, the craic was mighty.

One fellow prisoner, who had been confined to the medical room since the end of the siege, had been hit by two stray bullets. He was joking that before he came to The Congo he only had one hole but now he had three.

'Jaysus,' he deliberated, 'they'll never be able to get me out of the jacks now.'

'Aye, but ya always spoke shite anyway,' replied another. 'And if ya had died when ye were supposed to, ya would have been better off than ye are now, ye'd just be a little stiff the next morning.'

'I'd rather die than be stuck in that medical room,' he continued. 'They have no medicine anyway. Everyone is feckin sneezing and the smell of shite from dysentery would outlive religion itself.'

It wasn't the kind of medical summary that would be read about in the Lancet, but gallows humour was the best medicine that any prisoner could have wished for.

We laughed like free-men, deep hearty laughs that pinched our idle lungs. Some immediately stood up to let the humour spread through their whole body as arms, legs and faces were visibly renewed with life. It was the same basic human characteristics of humour and survival that had enabled us to overcome the battle of Jadotville itself despite the ongoing disillusionment of how it all ended.

As the siege entered its eighth day, the ferocity of the fighting may have receded but we were in no doubt that this would be a 'bataille du jour' – a duel to the death, after we had run out of supplies two days beforehand.

'We're not long for this world,' I remember Dowler commenting on the final morning of the siege as we wearily returned another bout of gunfire. 'So I'll see yiz in heaven soon, after ye sinners have spent a bit longer than me in purgatory!'

My main regret was that I hadn't sinned more, and listening to older soldiers stories of drinking and dirty women just made me realise how young I really was. Neither, it seemed, would I ever achieve my dream of making it over to the excitement of London Town.

'Purgatory is a place ye go to before ye make it over to London Sean!' I replied, remembering a phrase that I had often heard back in Ireland as we again took cover in the trench from the anticipated return of fire from the distant bushes.

We knew the exchanges would die down for a while before inevitably sparking off again but our dwindling supplies of bullets meant we could only fight on for another couple of hours at the most. We had no other way out, and the thought of being slaughtered for fun if we surrendered was unthinkable. The mercenaries had attacked us for no apparent reason, and were not the kind of honourable soldier who took prisoners and adhered to the Geneva Convention – not in this part of Africa anyway.

But suddenly we were told that the siege was over, that the battle had ended with a ceasefire agreement. We wondered if it could be true, that the 110 hours of continuous combat, of unremitting gunfire and bombing would finally stop and most notably the incessant beating of the Lumba tribe's ominous war drums would abate for a while at least. We were told it was an opportunity to attend to the injured and wounded and for the enemy to retrieve their dead from no-man's land and maybe a chance for us to finally get some sleep.

It was never going to be that straightforward. We were awoken abruptly by forceful orders as the sun shone like a giant searchlight over Jadotville. It was the unmistakably abrasive voices of our NCOs: the company sergeant Jack Prendergast and John Monahan our platoon sergeant.

'Get up lads, ye have to get yerselves over to the Purfina garage,' ordered Prendergast. 'There's tea being made for ye, then fall in for parade.' His once harsh and indomitable commands seemed a little subdued and I sensed something was wrong.

Away from the shade of the trench I was blinded by the intense daylight. Without any food, water or sleep I found the sun's dazzling brightness disorientating and I stumbled to my feet, shielding my eyes like a sleepwalker facing oncoming headlights. Despite the warming sunshine, my whole body started to shiver from dehydration and exhaustion and I went into a cold sweat but I stumbled towards the Purfina petrol garage which had been our HQ during the siege. Ahead of me stood a line of ashen faced and downcast comrades each covered in blooded clothes and red dust. We were handed cans of tea by the company cook, Bobby Allen, but he too seemed unusually downcast, a stark contrast from his normal jovial outlook which was even apparent at the height of the siege.

'How are ya Bobby?' I asked, but this morning Bobby wasn't chatting, and he just handed me back a can of tea then looked at serving the next in line. Perhaps, I thought, we were all just exhausted or maybe he was maudlin over news that some of our injured might not pull through.

We were then directed towards our platoons for what we presumed would be a casualty count. I was in the anti tank gun unit and lined up alongside the other two in the section: Sean Dowler and John Conway, with whom I had shared the same trench for the previous five days. Everyone was looking around counting heads to check who was still alive:

'There's Hegarty walking towards the garage,' I noted, 'and behind him is Sweeney, and there's the Tiger over next to Delayney and there's Ready. Jaysus, thank God he's alive. I was sure that bullet had claimed him.' My muddled tallying-up through squinted eyes was suddenly interrupted.

'You look like shit!' uttered a voice from behind us. It was Pakie Monahan (no relation of our platoon sergeant John Monahan), who I knew from my home town of Edgeworthstown but he was barely recognisable. His once mischievous and boyish face was a dark red clay colour, the encrusted soil caked over him clearly distorting his features.

'Jaysus, is that you Pakie?' I asked, 'howya doin?'

'Ahh, I could do with a couple more hours in the hay but fine otherwise,' Pakie replied 'and how are ye all, I saw a few mortars landing a bit close to yer trench, did yiz get hit?'

'No, we're grand Pakie,' I replied. 'A few close shaves,' I noted, pointing at the bullet hole in the peak of my helmet, 'but just some cuts and bruises is all we have. We'd eat a scabby horse though if ya know where we could find one?'

'Ye won't find any horses in prison,' Pakie blurted out. 'We'll be lucky to get turnips.'

'You fuckin what!' Dowler and I both roared almost simultaneously. 'What in bollocks' name would we be doing in prison?'

Then came Pakie's ominous answer: 'A little while after the ceasefire had been called, we were told they had forced us to surrender.'

We stood motionless for a moment before Prendergast called the whole company to order.

'Attention men of 'A' Company,' he began in his typical matter-of-fact abrupt style. 'A conditional surrender agreement was signed this morning and we are now prisoners of war under the charge of the Katangan gendarmerie.' Behind him stood our adversaries of the last week: a patrol of older looking, craggy mercenaries, still heavily armed and clearly instrumental in the instructions they had given to our officers which in turn were being relayed to us by Prendergast.

'You are required to yield all military apparatus you have in your possession including guns, any remaining ammunition, knives, helmets, transmitting devices and fire equipment. You will be directed to your secured billet accommodation once you have handed over your weapons, where fresh water and a meal will be provided. Those are your orders. That is all.'

I thought for a moment I could make a run for it – somehow scrambling to the safety of the distant dense shrubbery but as my eyes darted 360 degrees all around, the 'mercs', as we called them, were readying their arms, poised for any sign of individual recklessness.

Any escape route had already been heavily guarded and cut off. So that was it, we were prisoners of war, but I was bewildered as to what might have happened after the ceasefire had been called. The last thing I could remember was the mayor of Jadotville meeting our commander Pat Quinlan a few hours before down by the road block to agree the terms for a ceasefire which the enemy had initiated. We were told everything had been agreed, the mayor had raised a flag of truce by the road block and both sides were ordered to disengage their weapons. Then we were told we could stand down and take some rest. We had all been so relieved to think that the eight day siege had finally ended and that for the first time in five days we could rest and wouldn't be shot at or bombed.

It emerged that the ceasefire had been a ruse, a plan devised by the mercenaries, in which the mayor had collaborated. Once they discovered we were out of supplies, the value of the agreement evaporated. They immediately discredited and subsequently re-wrote the old agreement renaming the document an honourable surrender in which, staring down the barrel, we had agreed to become their prisoners.

We knew we had no choice, some of us still had a little ammunition and dog biscuits to survive on, but two days beforehand we had run out of the most important resource in the unforgiving heat of The Congo – water. Had our commanding officer Pat Quinlan refused to sign the re-worded agreement we would probably have died in the trenches from dehydration or been killed within the hour. What provisions we had at the outset, had been rationed to last a maximum of three days in the hope that we would be re-supplied should the siege continue. But the agreed supplies never appeared; neither did re-enforcements, ammunition or the equipment that had been promised from our main base 80 miles away in Elizabethville. Just the day before, I had collapsed from the heat in the trench and had to be given our last ration of water. Others too had fainted or were going delirious from lack of sleep, but despite the hunger and thirst we understood we had to carry on defending ourselves and following our orders.

'Aim well lads, stay low and look out for one another,' was what John Monahan had told us only the previous evening. Fighting to the death is how soldiers believe all battles are expected to end, but then the ceasefire came, the incessant blasts of guns, bombs, mortars and most notably the war drums had finally fallen silent. The battle of Jadotville was supposedly over and we could start thinking of home.

Instead, I was tossing my trusted FN automatic rifle and what ammunition I had left into a worthless pile of metal and I stood outside the Purfina garage waiting for my name to be called out for the casualty count.

'Greene!'

'Yes Sir!' I begrudgingly called back.

With adolescent bravado I could think of nothing honourable in being a prisoner. We had been stripped of our soldierly identity and maybe, I thought, it would have been more credible to have been shot in the same trench where we had fought night and day rather than the humiliation and uncertain future of an enemy prison. I looked at the faces around me: Sean Dowler, Pakie Monahan, John Conway; all forlorn and motionless like they'd being kicked hard in the stomach and were just pretending it didn't hurt.

Although we were told we would be protected by our agreement, the armed mercenaries and Katangan Gendarmerie ahead of us now held all the cards. Our diminished status drained the colour from our faces, our unblinking eyes coldly awaiting our next instruction. Below the surface my blood was boiling with rage, but as a prisoner I instinctively knew I had to keep quiet to stay alive.

We stood there for a few minutes until the others were rounded up, them too dishevelled and weary as they were encouraged into line, by the increasingly impatient Gendarmerie.

Within a short while, we were making our way to the prison. Some were boarded onto army transports to drive the mile or so towards the centre of Jadotville town but we, the unwounded were paraded on foot along the dusty road. Our once neatly pressed army uniforms were now shredded, dragging along behind us like rags as they hung limply from our skeletal frames.

The route was initially lined by crowds of mercenaries in their distinctive khaki shorts, bush hats and veldskoens boots. Prendergast marched out front, straight-backed, unwaveringly proud and solely focused on our intended destination. It was difficult to retain our self-control and we stared pointedly back in the eye at each and every merc as they stood victoriously within two or three feet of the roadside deliberately creating a narrow gauntlet of intimidation. The stench of whisky from their breath wafted across our faces, only abated by the dust being kicked up from those marching ahead of us.

The mercs were giants compared with us: most of them well over six foot tall with stuffed ruddy cheeks, overfed bellies and big puffed out barrelled chests, but most strikingly of all, there were hundreds of them, maybe even thousands. The Katangan gendarmes also stood by the roadside along with the local tribal warriors some still adorning their traditional battle attire – grand big-cat headdresses. Although many mercenaries, gendarmes and tribal troops lay dead in no-man's land, it was becoming clearer that against these vast numbers we had never stood a chance. We knew we had been heavily outnumbered; perhaps 5:1 but we had no idea there were probably 20 of them for every one of us. Most of our adversaries remained angrily silent but others fingered their guns menacingly whilst muttering obscenities and gawking back at us; hateful, bolting stares through bloodshot and intoxicated eyes. A few of the mercs; like typical dogs of war were still agitating for action but they knew their wages would be docked if they took out their revenge on us there and then. Some seemed a little disappointed that such a small number of ragged youngsters had been their adversaries for such a relentless and keenly contested battle, as if their hunt of big game cats had yielded mere cubs. We were clearly not worthy battle trophies that could be bragged about in mercenary drinking dens especially as we had accounted for so many of their dead fellow fortune-seekers.

As we got closer to the town of Jadotville, we caught sight again of makeshift posters that had been pinned onto telegraph poles a few days before the siege with the clear message:

UN

X

NON
ENTRE!

We had never been welcome in this town and we certainly weren't welcomed now, but it hammered home the absurdity of our predicament. We had been sent to protect these very same white residents of Jadotville. The Belgian government had insisted that the UN guard its former citizens as civil war threatened to break out between supporters of Katanga's independence and Congolese nationalists. Other towns and villages in the region inhabited by Europeans colonials had no such protection but Jadotville was also the headquarters of Belgium's richest mining company, the Union Miniere du Haut Katanga, UMHK. The reality was that the Belgian authorities were trying to carve-out for themselves a financial fiefdom by covertly backing Katanga's independence demands and it was the UMHK's bank vaults we had been sent here to protect. More suspiciously, Jadotville had also become the headquarters of Katanga's illegal army of mercenaries bankrolled by UMHK. Luring a company of UN peacekeeping soldiers to Jadotville, it seemed to us, had been a well prepared trap to ensnare a valuable bargaining counter should the UN authorities forcefully impose the demands of the international community to end Katanga's independence and white rule in central Africa.

As we were paraded though Jadotville, the rows of mercenaries and gendarmes gave way to the town's ex-pat Belgian civilian population, many still armed and jeering in our direction. These were the very people we were supposedly protecting, who had instigated the bloody siege against us and were now mocking us as we walked unarmed towards prison. We were sickened by their treachery: vile, disgusting people who had tricked us into helping them in their selfish pursuit of continuing white power and exploitation of The Congolese people. Pakie Monahan suddenly feigned a lunge in their direction with clenched fists and snarled teeth. A few of them seized their guns, stunned into defending themselves against the possibility of being attacked but Monahan said nothing and returned into line, his snarl turning into a crafty smile as if they had fallen for his bait. The panicked civilians slowly re-aimed their guns back towards the ground, slightly embarrassed by their perceived over-reaction of drawing a weapon on an unarmed man, but Monahan had unnerved them, quickly putting an end to their cowardly taunts.

Our prison was once an old-style colonial hotel and restaurant, largely disused since The Congo won its independence from Belgium a year earlier, and was situated on the main boulevard on the other side of the town. Seven of us were assigned together in a low-ceilinged room off the main corridor that was once used as the main storeroom. Pakie Monahan walked in ahead of me along with Sean Dowler and John Conway who had both given me their own ration of water on the second last day of the battle, as I was overcome by the heat.

'By the way Sean, thanks for the water the other day,' I said, as we walked into the storeroom; the first words I had been able to utter since finding out we were prisoners of war.

'Yer alright Michael,' replied Dowler. 'Ya were looking a little thirsty.'

I remembered thinking that single cup of water in the sweltering heat of the trench meant more to me than anything I had ever owned. In this land of such incredible riches, of gold fields and diamond mines, it was water which was the most valuable commodity, without which we were unable to continue fighting.

We were joined in the store-room by two other privates: The Tiger – Mick Tighe from Roscommon, who had joined the army at the same time as me and PJ Sweeney, originally from Leitrim and who had manned a machine gun during the siege. The NCO placed in charge of us in the storeroom was our platoon sergeant John Monahan, a hardened career soldier who was equally subdued at the prospect of being someone else's prisoner.

The prison had the name 'Le Hotel de l'Europa', clearly written above the entrance. Under Belgian colonial rule this was a clear enough statement in segregated Africa that black people were not welcome. Its previous name however, etched into the concrete pillars and window frames was however far more sinister, as it had once been called 'Prince Leopold's', an infamous name in The Congo's distressing past. It would no doubt have had the same resonance with the most of the native population as naming a hotel 'Hitler's' in the middle of Jerusalem. Leopold's was not only a reminder of one of the most painful episodes in human history, it was also a reminder of a bygone era of Belgian colonial rule and a lifestyle for the privileged white community of afternoon tea, playing croquet on the lawn, followed by cigars and sundowners. What had vanished from our new accommodation however, were the façades of grandeur; the velvet curtains, crystal chandeliers and wall-to-wall carpets, replaced with a bare, splintered wooden floor and a few sparsely distributed metal chairs and tables. Some of the dilapidated windows were protected by wrought iron railings long since rusted by the equatorial climate and anything of value had been moved out before we arrived. There were no beds, no blankets nor anything that would have made our imprisonment more comfortable. Only vague traces of a once opulent lifestyle remained. Chipped and broken tile mosaics with elaborate designs lined the bathroom walls, and large cracked mirrors with peeling gold-painted frames were stacked up gathering dust in the entrance hall. The ornate mirrors had once reflected images of eminent guests enjoying splendid luncheons; discussing the hunt for lucrative elephants or rhino tusks, and how they had become masters of Africa. If the mirrors had kept a log of conversations they would recount a life of unrivalled luxury in Belgium's glorious past but also, albeit discreetly, they could chronicle a multitude of its appalling sins.

The Hotel de l'Europa's prominence had abruptly ended when The Congo gained its independence a year beforehand and the bespectacled, stiff collared white gentlemen sporting curly moustaches were left scurrying back to their European capitals in their cream linen suits complaining about the terrible injustice of it all.

Just a year or so later in September 1961, the hotel was ushering through its now shabby entrance hall a very different type of guest – prisoners of war, as we were now known. We weren't the vacuous bankers or mining magnates who had travelled down from Brussels, London or Paris looking to exploit The Congo's riches. Instead we were supposed to be peacekeepers from the UN, most just average Irish country lads from unfamiliar addresses like Athlone, Longford, Leitrim or Roscommon, mainly underage adventure seekers who had volunteered to keep the peace. The grand hotel mirrors that were once so triumphantly regaled with tales from those erstwhile masters of the universe were now listening to harrowing accounts of our experiences during the Jadotville siege as we relived the bloody battle and trauma of what we had been through.

We preferred to call our prison by its former name of Leopold's and in its former store-room, our beds were thin ply-board shelves previously used to stack the hotel's supplies of food and drink, barely two feet wide and just four and a half feet long with ply-wood splinters cutting in at our overhanging legs. They had never been intended to be used as a bed, only to hold a few bottles of wine or beer although Pakie Monahan noted, they were left 'as bare as Brigitte Bardot's arse,' which seemed to spark the Tiger's memory into life and he started to sing one of his familiar songs to which we all slowly joined in the last couple of lines:

It's lonesome away from your kindred and all,
By the campfire at night where the wild dingoes call;
But there's nothing so lonesome, so morbid or drear,
Than to stand in a bar of a pub with no beer.

Slim Dusty. Original *A Pub With No Beer* 1957

Sweeney laughed whilst shaking his head in disbelief 'Of all the times I have sung that song,' he said, 'I never thought I would actually end up in one.'

Pakie too began to laugh at the irony 'I feel like one of dem owld alcoholics that hasn't had a drink since Christmas. Ye must have chosen this bar Sean?' he charged Dowler, the only teetotaller amongst us.

Dowler didn't get a chance to respond as our platoon sergeant John Monahan walked back into the storeroom having attended an officers briefing and he had some important news for us.

'The Secretary General of the United Nations: Dag Hammarskjöld, is dead,' he announced suddenly. A deathly pall of stunned silence immediately enveloped the old-store-room, but Monahan continued explaining. 'We've heard he flew out to The Congo three days ago in a bid to negotiate an end to the Jadotville siege but,' he noted shaking his head, 'he has been shot down and killed.'

It turned out that Hammarskjöld had died just the day before, the last day of the siege, shot down from the skies above us en route to ceasefire negotiations. No-one in the store-room had kept hold of their radios after we were told to hand them in at the end of the siege so we were cut off from a regular source of news but word soon filtered through from those with smuggled radios that the world's media was now focused on this little corner of Africa, gasping at the apparent murder of a revered world-statesman.

John Monahan made no mention of who was accused of his killing but we were sure that it was the same mercenary pilot in the Fouga jet that had been strafing us continuously during the siege. Like us and everyone else that represented the UN, Hammarskjöld was considered an enemy by the Katangan independence forces for not supporting their succession. In this brutal post colonial war, non-cooperation with one side was sufficient reason to be targeted, giving the former colonial supporters every motive to have him killed.

The next day, the grapevine within Leopold's was abuzz with speculation after President John F. Kennedy addressed the Western World on Hammarskjöld's death over the airwaves:

> It is tragic and ironical that his death came during a mission he was undertaking in order to bring about a ceasefire in Katanga. I am hopeful that the members of the United Nations recognising his untiring labours will attempt in the coming sessions and in the years to come to try to build the United Nations into the effective instrument for peace which was Dag Hammarskjöld's great ambition.
>
> John F. Kennedy. September 1961

But perhaps more worryingly, Kennedy's address made no mention of who was replacing Hammarskjöld in his mission to come to our aid. With Hammarskjöld now dead many assumed that our position in prison had become more precarious. As the civil war and bloodshed continued throughout the country, the probability of the worst possible outcome for us was becoming more and more likely. As time ticked by we wondered that if Hammarskjöld had remained alive we surely wouldn't be sitting on our arses in this African prison weeks after the siege had ended, still facing the prospect of a firing squad. But with Hammarskjöld's death it seemed we had not only lost the Secretary General of the UN but also our main negotiator and probably our best hope of survival.
Even if we weren't going to be shot dead by firing squad, none of us had any idea how long we would remain in prison. After a few slow, repetitive days, optimism waned and another set of gates was chalked up onto the bare prison walls. Stories were recounted about the POW camps in World War Two where the prisoners weren't released until long after the war finished.

'It took 15 years for some German POWs to be released from Stalin's Gulag,' Pakie Monahan described glumly 'and those were considered the lucky few that survived.'

Our outlook wasn't helped by the rising tensions in the Cold War. Both the US and Russia manoeuvred their influence to try and gain control of The Congo's resources and fill the vacuum of power that had emerged after Belgium had declared The Congo's independence in June 1960. In an era when most African nations were looking to shake off their colonial pasts, the Belgian government finally succumbed to a nationalist movement led by Patrice Lumumba, who was himself assassinated here in Katanga just six months later. Apparently that execution caused many independent observers to point the finger at the Head of the Katangan succession movement and the leader of the enemy forces imprisoning us, Moise Tshombie.

Not long before the Jadotville siege began, Cold War anatagonism had reached new heights as the communists in East Berlin built a wall dividing the East and West of the city. It was called the 'Berlin Wall' but soon became known as the 'Iron Curtain' and suddenly divided the world into East and West; communists versus capitalists. Even without our radios we knew the world was a tinderbox ready to explode with both sides desperate to gain control of the most precious Cold War resource, uranium. This vital nuclear ingredient had been supplied from the Shinkolobwe mine just a few miles up the road from us here in Jadoville when the Little Boy bomb was used on Hiroshima. Both the US and Soviets needed Uranium for increasingly destructive nuclear deterrents or at least to stop the other side from getting their hands on it.

With the horror of World War Two still fresh in many minds, we were reminded that it was sparked into confrontation by colonial imperialism but fuelled by an underlying principle of racial superiority and domination. The Congo had all of the same ingredients in abundance, a retreating colonial power with precious Cold War commodities and a place where colour of skin was the key determinant on how long you lived or how quickly you died. Some even suggested that World War Three actually may have been sparked off with the Jadotville siege as threats finally gave way to armed combat.

Pakie Monahan spoke up again.

'And remember what President Kennedy said to Khrushchev just a few weeks ago after the stand-off in

Berlin.' He paused and put on his best Boston accent. '"Then, Mr. Chairman, there will be a war. It will be a cold, long winter."'

'Ye must have written the book of Job,' Dowler told Pakie. 'Ye know more miserable stories than a priest!'

If we were going to survive at all, it seemed as though we would have to wait a long time to be freed. Over the first few weeks in prison the mood ebbed and flowed, lifted by rumours of possible release or crushed with suspicions of impending doom. As a diversion, we spoke about what other people our age would be doing at home: going to dance-halls, listening to Elvis Presley, dancing the boogie-woogie and just generally having the craic. Elvis and Johnny Cash had both served time in the army but, since returning to civilian life, had made the most notorious prisons almost acceptable with songs like Jailhouse Rock and Folsom Prison Blues. We also swapped stories about films we had seen back in Ireland and I described fondly how the army had enabled me to climb the social ladder of the Picture House, elevating me to afford the most comfortable seats in the hall to get the best view of films. I was always very careful however to avoid any clue that would have caused others to suspect I was underage, recounting the stories I had been told by my older sisters of films from the forties and early fifties and the great film-stars of that era like Rita Hayworth, Humphrey Bogart and Jane Russell.

On one of the shelves in the store-room was a tattered rope that had probably once been used in one of the main hotel bedrooms, and used to be attached to a bell to call waiters:

'Tell Stanley the bell-boy that I will take the evening meal in my quarters this evening,' quipped Dowler, pulling at the rope. Then he gave it a second pull saying, 'and could you ask him to turn up the fans as it's getting a little warm in here.'

The injection of more humour gave me the impetus to stand up and look out of the small sash window for a breath of cooler air and relief from the tedium of baking hot imprisonment. The celestial blue sky and the uniquely African chorus of bwaking monkeys, shrieking cockatoos and whistling birds bristling with vibrant colours provided a tantalising glimpse of what freedom held in abundance beyond the confines of Leopold's prison. At the beginning of the century, all of The Congo had been King Leopold's private property, a contemporary Garden of Eden where millions of years ago, humanity had first learned to use tools and walk upright. There were more species of plant, animal and birdlife here than anywhere else on earth, but more immediately, only a few yards directly ahead, standing behind rolls of barbed wire, some local Congolese tribes-people had gathered and were gesticulating toward us that we would be killed and eaten if they had their way.

They were members of the Lumba tribe, immediately identifiable by three permanent scars, slashed in precise parallel stripes on each cheek. Under Belgian rule the Lumba had been rewarded with some legislative power and lower admin positions in return for their assistance in the subjugation of the majority Baluba tribe who were effectively used as slave labour. It was a typical colonial 'divide and rule' strategy that was used throughout The Congo, particularly in areas where labour was needed to mine lucrative diamonds, gold or copper. In the vast diamond fields in the north of The Congo, the minority Lulua were rewarded at the expense of the Simbas and, in the Eastern Congolese regions of Rwanda and Burundi, the minority Tutsis were favoured at the expense of the Hutus.

Immediately after independence a year before, the downtrodden tribes had revolted against their former tormentors and vicious tribal wars ensued. We had heard on the news back in Ireland that these uprisings became known as 'the winds of destruction', as the oppressed tribes sought revenge on their oppressors who had collaborated with their Belgian masters. The bloodshed continued and just before the Jadotville siege there were reports of thousands being slaughtered. The once exploited Simbas, Hutus and Balubas looked to take back their land and possessions resulting in thousands of displaced people. To protect themselves, the smaller collaborationists tribes like the Lumba, backed by the mining companies and mercenary soldiers, sought to ethnically cleanse southern Katanga of its Baluba population, burning down villages whilst killing, raping and torturing its former inhabitants. Commando units comprised of Lumba warriors and led by Belgian funded mercenary officers were formed and given the menacing Swahili titles of Chui [Leopard] or Kinguwa [hyena]. Their units' intentions for the Balubas were unequivocal, summed up with one Swahili word – kifo [death]. As Baluba villages and communities were systematically wiped out, massive refugee camps had begun to form around Katanga's major cities, whose only means of defence was the United Nations. Had the UN not been prepared to defend the Balubas, the slaughter could have been counted into the millions.

As a result, the Lumba regarded us, the UN, as their enemy for protecting the Balubas whose young men were counter raiding Lumba villages, with similar levels of viciousness. Although our role was to keep the peace, nobody was considered neutral in this tribal war. It was the same mercenary and Lumba commando units that attacked us during the siege, the tribal warriors incited to lead the attack by their witch doctors with a combination of a black magic potion called maji and by smoking wild dhagga, a type of cannabis. The concoction, they believed made them invincible, even capable of overcoming the all powerful white man, who they called the 'Bula Matari' or 'breaker of rocks' after The Congo's so-called founder, Henry Morton Stanley. The natives believed the maji enabled them to walk through bullets which would just evaporate like water when it came into contact with their immortal bodies and they believed the dhagga was provided by their gods to make them fearless warriors. During the siege, as the war drums built up to a feverish rhythm at dawn and dusk, they attacked us, charging in waves of 10-15 men. The young warriors would roar like the lions, tigers and leopards they were named after although some were so drunk they would just stagger towards us firing guns from both hands. The mercenaries too were fuelled by cases of whisky but similar to the Lumba, most were eventually cut down by our machine gunners within 50 yards of our trenches spewing blood and coughing up maji. If the bullets didn't kill them, the savage heat of the African sun in no-man's land, where even the vultures wouldn't dare to dwell, would mean they would just be a bag of bones within days.

There were apparently 30 white mercenaries killed during the siege, easily totted up by counting the number of cheap plywood coffins that were stacked up outside the Jadotville town hall. But the Lumba people believed that coffins would prevent the release of their spirits which was regarded as bad ju-ju for the superstitious natives, so the exact number of dead Lumba from the siege was unknown. I must have counted at least 60 dead just in the no-man's land in front of our trench, but some said the total number of dead Lumba warriors was closer to 250.

I looked out the window ahead of me and standing behind the barbed wire were, I presumed, the families of those dead Lumba warriors. Even women and children were ominously taunting us through gritted teeth that our throats would be slit as they slid their long razor-like fingers slowly along their tautened necks. As captives we would be at their mercy if our release could not be secured and they wanted revenge for their dead men-folk. It wasn't just an idle threat; here in The Congo, cannibalism was a trophy of battle, a macabre feast that represented the ultimate victory for one human over another. Their contorted faces told a story. Even in the eyes of young children was the unmistakable hate and mistrust they had inherited from their elders. Although French had been the language imposed on them from Belgian colonialism, they knew enough English to shout at us above the barbed wire:

'Fuck off home white man!'

'Are them fellas still looking forward to their dinner Michael?' asked Dowler almost cheerfully.

'Aye, I think they are Sean,' I replied. 'They have the pot ready, they just need the fatted calf'

'Well there's not much fat on any of us,' continued Dowler as he tossed the bell rope back onto an empty shelf. 'The service in this hotel isn't what it used to be!'

As prisoners we were given a chicken stew every day but I had only eaten bread and some boiled vegetables for the last few weeks, no amount of hunger could make me eat white-man's meat after the stories I had heard.

Pakie Monahan stood up to join me next to the window.

'I think they will free us tomorrow Michael,' he said, his eyes still bright with optimism. 'They will have to find their dinner somewhere else.' Then he shouted towards the guard room. 'Will ya bring us some boiled bacon and cabbage with some big flowery spuds, and while yer at it, will ya bring us a few of dem dirty women!'

The guards looked up from their sentry point by the main entrance but paid no more attention and just carried on playing cards amongst themselves. They had been warned by their senior officers not to beat us any more after one discovered a radio at the bottom of a kit-bag and proceeded to kick and punch the offending private, Jack Peppard, repeatedly until his body nearly went limp. Our officers in charge of 'A' Company cited the honourable surrender agreement they had signed and the Geneva Convention principles for proper treatment of POWs; telling their senior commandant this was a war crime to assault us. The regular guards weren't bothered about European conventions but they did understand that disobeying their own officers would mean no pay – so they stopped the beatings and luckily for Peppard, he survived.

'Aye, when they free us tomorrow Michael' Pakie continued 'they'll be waving little Irish flags and we'll have lots of beer, sandwiches and cakes waiting for us.'

I wanted to believe him as I always had and I allowed my mind to wallow in the tempting images of platters of sandwiches laid out on a table, with kegs of beer waiting at the end as we gorged ourselves on fatty platefuls and slapped each other on the backs like celebrating fathers of new-born babies. In those brief moments when the world felt well again, my spirited mind conjured up yet more naïve and unanswerable questions: why did everyone want to interfere in this vast and beautiful land called

The Congo and surely those poor wretched people ahead of us could appreciate that we had just been defending ourselves. Like most idealistic teenagers I struggled to comprehend many of the motives that contributed to this Congo conflict and viewed through my innocent eyes of youth, the world had indeed gone mad.

I carried on peering out at the crowd wondering whether the Lumba's savage threats were plausible but they knew no better. Before the Europeans discovered The Congo, the native people thrived in a culture of close communities in round huts, with open fires, colourful clothes and living a bountiful existence that nature amply provided for. All that had been replaced by a European colonial way of life, which had first brought slavery, then a holocaust and finally famine and extreme poverty, an existence where Europeans in their pursuit of colonial domination knew only how to live off the fruits of the planet by exploiting or eradicating it, either for greed or sheer enjoyment.

The result was a Congo society left with nothing: no homes, no culture, no food, no clothes and no hope. They probably couldn't appreciate why some people should be allowed to simply walk away from this war back to their peaceful homelands, when they were permanently locked-in and had no idea how to get themselves out. They were probably asking themselves why we, another group of white men, couldn't have stayed at home in our own countries and looked after our own families rather than bring weapons and death to theirs. In prison, we often asked ourselves the same question. But this was a country full of hatred, of hearts hardened by decades of misuse of power, of dictatorship and exploitation. What they could not see was that we had unbiased sympathy for the plight of the innocent civilians of The Congo. As part of the United Nations we had been sent to help all of them. Some of their leaders, though, heavily influenced by colonial diplomats, had told them a different story; that we were their enemies. But it was the civilians who were this particular war's real victims, they who had watched the arrival of the great white hunter for the last century devastating the land of their birth. Their anger and desire for revenge was understandable but what I still couldn't understand was how shooting dead 157 UN peacekeepers would change anything for the better.

This war in The Congo was the culmination of a series of wrongdoings where the repressed finally had no other way out. Over the previous five or so years back in Ireland I had heard a constant build up of tensions in Africa on the wireless; stories of independence struggles starting with the Suez crisis which had spread throughout the African continent. I recalled vividly being at home sat around the parlour table whilst my father tried to explain the significance of the news headlines. Even young Irish children could not avoid the regular articles about the 'winds of change blowing through Africa' and the ever present threat of a Cold War. Like me, most paid little attention to it, as places like Algeria and The Congo seemed far too distant to disturb the life of a young boy whose free time was spent enjoying the craic, ceileidh dancing and storytelling, and whose future ambitions lay firmly rooted in the more glamorous pursuits of film and music.

These were the thoughts I wrestled with, as the long silence of night once again approached. I carried out my regular prison bed-time rituals: kneeled down, bowed head: a sign of the cross, one Hail Mary and one Our Father. I had never been a great one for religion or church but I was praying now, as Dowler wryly pointed out:

'Prison provides God with a captive audience.'

So I repeated the same prayers I had been saying for the last month, in the desperate hope that there would be a happy ending to this epic tale. I prayed that it wasn't one of my bullets that had accounted for one of the many dead, that all of the injured would survive and that we would be delivered back home to Ireland safely. I also prayed that we would all be forgiven even if our judgement day of facing a firing squad came too soon, but that should the worst happen I would be buried in Ireland and that my mother wouldn't be too distressed by my foolish decisions. I sighed deeply and blessed myself again, resigned to the certainty of another tormented and sleepless night.

Next to my bed I kept a picture of my parents: my father standing proudly in his Sunday best suit next to

My treasured picture of The County and Katleen Greene

my mother squinting in the unexpected sunshine. It conjured up images of childhood: flashbacks to happier times which may have belonged to the past but with a future so precarious, the vision of a previous life is all that's left. It wasn't that long ago that my mother had wanted me to carry on studying for a profession, 'to have hands like a gentleman' she used to say.

I had other ideas however, I wanted big, tough hands, just like my father, who had been a famous football player in the 1930s and '40s and had been given the prestigious nick-name of 'The County' after he led the previously unaccomplished County of Longford to the semi-final of the All Ireland 10 years beforehand. When I was a boy, I would proudly tell everyone that 'I was the Son of The County', and volunteering for The Congo was my chance to emulate him. Like every young boy I wanted to be my own man and as they say in Ireland 'it doesn't matter how big your daddy was, you have to do your own growing.'

As the dreaded night-time darkness descended, I remembered very clearly my life back home, the innocence of childhood, and what may have influenced me to volunteer for war. I thought about Sunday evenings at the Picture House watching films about daring adventures and great battles. It was undoubtedly a child-like view of war, a perception fuelled by epic tales and film-stars that filtered out the courage and glory, and discarded the gruesome reality of what bullets and bombs are capable of. Before I arrived in The Congo, I would escape into my fantasy world to enjoy an image of what a battle in The Congo might be like: being fired on by mercenaries, fields of gold and diamonds, dodging poisoned arrows and even being chased by rampaging elephants. But what happened in the reality of war was beyond even that most fertile imagination, and those Hollywood images which were once so enticing are nothing like the reality of what soldiers are stuck with when the madness eventually ends. As I sat there in prison, all I could see was the utter devastation that war causes in the minds of men; reliving the senseless and needless killing, the intense fear, and the ongoing unbearable nightmares. Sometimes it is only possible to make sense of what really happened when you have time on your hands and maybe only a little time left.

I had been taught many lessons by The County when we were children. As we gathered round for dinner he would talk about right and wrong and about Ireland's own history, which in some ways so resembled The Congo's buried past. He had forewarned me, as guarded parents do, about the world and its various dangers but like many young idealists I believed all of those bad things would only influence the lives of others. Now, it all made sense as I began wallowing, like only a condemned prisoner knows, in the memories of the life I used to have and all those dreams and ambitions that would remain unfulfilled. And what an irony it seemed that back in Ireland I had once been sent to military prison for laughing too much. Every aspect of that life, the characters, the job opportunities and the hard realities of post war Ireland now had a relevance to our current predicament. I had been given all the information and the best advice of wiser folk but had gone from leaving school at 12, to collecting glasses in a pub to being a teenage prisoner of war in Africa's darkest place.

As the memories flooded back, I paused on those boyish influences and crucial moments which could have led me to take a different course. There was a great deal happening to the world in the late 1950s and early '60s which I blithely interpreted as a jumble of seemingly unrelated events, with a few chance incidents that I had blagged my way through. My mind flicked through a collage of significant events of the time, great political leaders making famous speeches, iconic photos of film-stars, famous sportsmen, pioneering astronauts and moments of major historical significance that all had their place in my cluttered album. There was also an obscure mix of circumstances peculiar to that post-World War era that had helped contribute to our predicament; a world that was driven by centuries-old attitudes towards race and human worth against a backdrop of a new decade and a generation of hope. It all seemed to culminate in the Jadotville siege. As my imagination tied it all loosely together, it seemed inappropriate that what was once such a wonderful adventure could take its final bow in an African prison but I still couldn't help wondering, 'how the fuck did I end up here?'

I may have been the youngest of the 157 that endured the Jadotville siege; too young for love, sensible rationale or soldierly respect but old enough to fight for my country, the UN and to see with my own eyes what really happened. It wasn't however the end of the story and in many ways the difficult part was only just beginning.

Up until then, it certainly hadn't been a normal adolescence that resulted in me becoming involved in the build up to and outbreak of Ireland's first active engagement in an overseas war, its first ever involvement in a world crisis and about Ireland's place in global politics at a time when the Cold War threatened its very existence.

For years after, the events that A company endured were whispered about in the upper echelons of Ireland's military and political hierarchy, becoming known as the Jadotville Affair, actions that were judged and deliberated on by supposedly more privileged, better-educated and highly empowered men.

The battle of Jadotville could have been remembered in the history books as the Irish army's finest achievement, a military defence that would rank alongside revered boyhood stories like the Alomo, Sebastopol and Rourke's Drift. But instead it was swept under the carpet by complicit military leaders and self-interested politicians during an era in Ireland where abuse of power and covering up wrongdoing was commonplace.

Like most who lived through Jadotville I have thought about it every day ever since. At first it was the bolt upright awakenings, drenched pillows and terrifying nightmares followed by the inevitable bitterness, anger and resentment against an enemy that a soldier fears most: those supposedly on his own side. As the decades went past, the pain began to heal but the memories never faded; naïve memories from an underage soldier that over time I have sought to piece together and articulate into the story that today you have in front of you. Thankfully most people these days remember their adolescent years free from the horrors of war and imprisonment but the story that I vividly remember is one where everyday people are proved capable of the most incredible acts of bravery and humanity.

My story is from the perspective of a young Irish boy's journey to adulthood and how I ended up fighting for my life in a slit trench; the people, books and films that influenced me and the things I witnessed. It may not be glamorous or sensational but the reality of what happens in war rarely is. Maybe I was just another one of those foolish youngsters who took a chance that didn't come off – or maybe just another expendable soldier who is not supposed or expected to have a voice.

It would have been an epic adventure for any journeyman, but I viewed this war through the unbiased eyes of youth, a harsh lesson about life and about growing up fast in the turbulent '50s and '60s. While it may have been corruptly dismissed by some of the most powerful men in Ireland, the Jadotville Affair lived long in the memory of those who took part. What took place may have shattered my belief in the idealism of war, but not of the belief there are always ideals that are worth fighting for. One of those ideals was embodied in the UN charter to maintain peace and international security. Fighting to keep the peace may be a contradiction, but so is an army that refuses to defend either itself or the civilian population it is serving. In war, there can be no winners but in telling the truth, we should all gain something. Some say truth is a noble trait for the naïve and is just a romantic endeavour, but without the truth, our hearts would be abandoned and our memories would fade. Oscar Wilde once remarked:

> The truth is rarely pure and never simple
>
> Oscar Wilde: The importance of Being Earnest 1895

An inaccurate version of events may have suited some who wanted to cling on to their powerful status, but the truth of what really happened at Jadotville deserved so much better than that.

CHAPTER TWO

Growing up

Five years beforehand – 1956
Location: Edgeworthstown, Ireland

When I was as young as twelve, I could remember that it was the highlight of the week to go to the Picture House. Just a decade after the end of World War Two, it seemed that war and fighting had again become fashionable and anyone carrying a gun could be part of the action with soldiers, gangsters, rebels and cowboys captured every week on the big screen fighting for their cause.

As a boy, they were the only battles I was ever likely to witness and whilst I may have been too young to appreciate what war was really about, over in Hollywood, they had made conflict into a sensational adventure, it was how boys became men, a world of heroic fantasy, far removed from the peaceful perspective of rural Ireland where I was growing up. I was gripped by the tension and uncertainty amid the furore of the final shootout but all of us knew that over in Hollywood, the good guys always won in the end and lived happily ever after.

Each Sunday evening I would head off with two of my brothers; Kevin and Franco and our jovial neighbour, Pat 'the Dolly' Dolan when the money had arrived from his father working away in England. Even the half hour queue spent in line outside the theatre in anticipation of my next film could make my heart beat with excitement. 'The Picture House was my church' I would say, and Hollywood it seemed, just made the world a better place. As the curtains went back and the lights went out, sweet wrappers or cigarette butts would fill the air. Some would hit us on the back of the head, but the pitch darkness kept the culprits' identities a mystery. Better still, the darkness provided a camouflage allowing us to smoke and swear as much as we liked, two of the most popular habits of many Irish kids, and there would be no priests or mothers around to stop us. With the protection of anonymity, everybody was called a fecker, an eejit or a gobshite.

The Picture House itself could hold about 200 people and we would sit on the wooden benches down at the front, the cheapest seats available, our heads tilted backwards looking up at the flickering images. In the middle rows, the seats were cushioned and covered in velvet, but were twice the price of ours at 1*s.* 6*d.* At the back were the most expensive seats at 2*s.*, but came complete with arm rests and the best view looking down on the giant screen.

Before the film started there would be adverts for some of the larger shops in the area: Shaw's of Mullingar or Connacht Cleaners of Galway with its catchy slogan: 'Delivering dry cleaning to your door.' Nobody was interested in watching adverts and the strange missiles kept flying. After being hit again by another cigarette butt, we'd look around accusingly, but in the darkness could only just make out the outline of faces in the seats directly behind us who would pretend to be totally engrossed in the adverts. The secret world of the Picture House posed many mysteries. But being on the wooden seats sometimes had its advantages as spindles of wood that bound the seats together could be removed, a spiky but not too heavy missile. A quick flick of the wrist and I had sent the spindle soaring through the air landing about five rows back. I smiled smugly and waited for the inevitable argument.

A voice erupted out of the darkness.

'Ow! Did you throw that Poppy?' wrongly accusing Poppy Farrel, one of the usual suspects for throwing spindles, 'ya little fecker!'

No I feckin didn't, I haven't thrown anything!' replied an innocent Poppy, not knowing who the irate victim's voice was.

'Well fuck off then!' came the wounded voice again.

'You fuck off, it was probably Jimmy McDonagh!' alleged Poppy. He may have been unaware of his accuser's identity but knew that diverting the blame was his best form of defence.

Don't be feckin blaming me Poppy', stated an equally innocent and invisible Jimmy 'just because you're a feckin eejit.'

As I laughed to myself, the Dolly whispered next to me:

'Will ye quit throwing feckin spindles, before they beat the livin Jaysus out of all of us?'

As the blaming and accusations continued in the darkness, there was suddenly a loud 'Shuuushhh!' sound from the rest of the audience; tonight's film was about to start. It was *Around The World In 80 Days,* from the famous Jules Verne novel, with David Niven playing Phileas Fogg alongside his ingenious but equally regal valet; Passepartout. They went everywhere in a hot-air balloon from the mysterious beauty of India to the exotic Far East, and from bullfights in Spain to the Wild-West. I loved the scenic shots from the balloon, of elephants in Africa and escaping from India with Princess Aouda played by Shirley MacLean as she's about to be put on a funeral pyre.

We were told the film would last three hours for which I figured out I would need three cigarettes or woodbines and a bag of broken biscuits between the four of us, all of which we would buy beforehand from Maggie Canavan's corner shop. The woodbines were a tuppence each, and the broken biscuits just a penny. She also sold a huge array of sweets; fizzballs, toffee blocks, red and yellow bonbons, fruit drops, nougat – she had everything. My favourite were the Hennessy balls but the red sugar coating would make it look like you were wearing lipstick so I reverted to bulls-eyes, a kind of aniseed gob-stopper, to avoid the inevitable piss-taking. A single bulls-eye would last about 25 minutes so about six of them I calculated should last me the whole film.

As I sat back to enjoy the film, I'd savour the sweet syrupy flavour of a bulls-eye, sucking loudly to extract the most sugar. After half an hour, it was time for my first woodbine.

'Ahh just like James Dean,' I thought, as I puffed away contentedly in the darkness, though not fully inhaling for fear of coughing and looking like a right eejit.

At the end of the film, Phileas Fogg wins his wager for £20,000 after arriving just before 8.45 p.m. at his Gentleman's club in London having completed their journey in under 80 days.

'Incredible! What an adventure!' I thought. 'Wouldn't it be great to be one of those upper class gentlemen, dressed in fine clothes and travelling round the world.' I also wondered whether, after three hours on the wooden spindle seats down at the front of the hall, if I would ever feel my arse again.

As the lights went on and my eyes adjusted to the unaccustomed brightness, I thought that one day I would enjoy the luxury of a velvet-cushioned seat at the back of the picture house.

'Jaysus, that was feckin brilliant!' stated the Dolly rubbing his eyes, his mouth and cheeks bright red from the drool off his toffee apple. 'Them elephants were feckin huge ... and I wouldn't have fancied being chased by one of those Spanish bulls either. I wanna see that again.'

We all knew however, that we could only afford the Picture House once a week: and next week they were showing our favourite film of them all: the unrivalled cowboy western.

The 'rough 'n' tough' cowboys of the wild-west were a regular showing at the Picture House with great characters like Hoppalong Cassidy or the singing cowboy Roy Rogers and his trusted golden Palomino, Trigger. I would be totally captivated, as the Lone Ranger and Tonto helped innocent townsfolk fix an injustice against powerful but greedy villains, the mystery heightened by their eye-masks that concealed their true identity. Like the citizens that had watched them face-up to the danger and overcome the wrongdoing, I would be equally in awe as they enquired as to the identity of the 'masked man', who had come to the aid of an unknown stranger. We all knew the answer but were thrilled each time we heard it.

'Why, that's the lone ranger of course!' we would all mime in unison. Dramatic music would then mix with the sound of thundering hooves as our heroes gallantly rode off to settle another dispute in a distant town: but that was an episode for another week.

After watching our favourite westerns we would emerge like four of the hottest gunslingers in the wild-west, the kings of the wild frontier, with bowed legs and arched arms, 'ready for the draw.'

Dramatic gunfights and exotic locations may have all been childish fantasies but it was a wonderful escape from the monotony of growing up in rural Ireland after weekdays at school, Saturdays spent picking spuds at Barney Farrel's farm and a seemingly endless Sunday morning of washing and Mass.

Whilst many of the films featured legends of yesteryear, Hollywood in 1956 was going through an era of transformation, a golden age of major productions and glamorous film stars that sparked my imagination with actors like John Wayne, Marlon Brando and James Dean, all iconic role models of a masculine post-war America where real men fought and died for their cause. As I had reached the mature age of 12, I was busy moulding a more grown-up character and used to mimic the brash and surly demeanours of John Wayne and Brando, letting a cigarette hang casually from my top lip like James Dean. 'Every girl' I thought, 'loves a rebel without a cause.'

I wanted admiration and I wanted my own adventure, and I wasn't going to get either of these by watching films from the cheap wooden seats down at the Picture House. Unlike my father The County, I was never going to make it as a footballer but I wanted to do something as heroic as him and I would never do that by being skint and continuing to study.

'The wild-west wasn't tamed by schoolteachers!' I would say with childish bravado but every Monday I would set off for school with a head full of dreams that were so big, they seemed almost impossible.

One morning I had a flash of inspiration: 'I will be a teenager soon,' I thought, 'and it is about time I left school and got a proper job.'

The reality was that Ireland in 1956 was poor but I convinced myself that it was only the fat-arsed farmers daughters who were staying on in school, everyone else was working, trying to find work or emigrating.

My first full-time job on the road to emulate The County's great achievements was in the sophisticated surroundings of Tommy Doyle's Pub, the third biggest pub in Edgeworthstown and I was responsible for collecting and cleaning glasses, and shifting beer barrels.

The County asked me how much I was getting paid.

'10 shillings and 5 pence!' I proudly announced.

'I'd rather eat stones,' he said dismissively.

I felt deflated, but I tried to reassure myself that the money would now enable me to buy a new black shirt like that of Johnny Cash, when he sang, 'Don't take your guns to town'.

All the clothes I had up to then, I shared with my brothers Kevin and Franco, which meant on Sundays, washday in our house, we had no clothes to wear at all. We had a single Sunday-best suit between the three of us and as it was the only thing available on Sunday mornings we took it in turns to wear it to mass while the other two waited patiently in bed. As one would come home, having left mass immediately after communion, my mother would work feverishly with safety pins and tape to fix the suit to the appropriate size. Then one of us would run back into town for the start of the next service. My mother's ability at tailoring was mesmeric, neatly tucking and pinning the rough wool suit, her fingers flicking in and out with spellbinding speed, but it still had the effect of making my younger brother Franco, look like Charlie Chaplin and the elder, Kevin look as if he had robbed the suit off a dwarf.

The County had the same Sunday best suit for 20 years, which he kept meticulously, neatly hanging it away each time mass was over. He usually wore it with his county Longford GAA tie, his proudest possession. He was now in his early-forties and his great foot-balling days had become only the legend of travelling story-tellers or, as they were known in Ireland, the 'Seanchai' ['shanakee'].

Gather round good people of the town
To hear a tale so wondrous and gay
He was Edgeworthstown's finest son, The County
Our very own Cuchlain against Ireland's finest

The Seanchais were the neat and smartly dressed men, with a tweed tie and a distinguished walking hat that would perch on an old stool with both hands held out ceremonially in front resting on a wooden cane. Storytelling like dancing was considered an art-form in Ireland and Edgeworthstown had its fair share of would-be Seanchai's.

Come closer with yer drink (aside: and place
mine on this stool, thank you kind sir)
I'll tell ye of the man called The County Greene
From Clover View to Terenare
In our very own parish of St. Mary's of the
Assumption
Erin's green fields knew no equal

The Seanchai

Although the tales of The County were now only pub folklore, I would listen attentively as the Seanchai recounted re-cycled anecdotes of his great achievements. My back would straighten with pride when I heard of the time he led the tiny county of Longford to beat the mighty Meath in the Leinster championship or when he took on, almost single-handedly, the invincible Dubs at Croke Park for the Sam Maguire. It was Edgeworthstown's version of David versus Goliath. 'The County', they said, 'was afraid of no man' and as they took another gulp of Guinness, they affirmed menacingly: 'but there was no man that did not fear The County'. He was my hero and I used to love hearing the stories of how he inspired his team and everyone around him which seemed to get more exaggerated and even more incredible with age.

The County himself would prefer to teach us about the Gaelic language which he spoke fluently, or wax lyrical about the celebrated Irish poets and writers, like W. B. Yeats, George Bernard Shaw, James Joyce and his favourite, Oscar Wilde. Being the father of eight children, the eldest of whom were now young adults, he would often quote Wildes' more philosophical sayings:

> the old believe everything; the middle-aged suspect everything and the young know everything.
>
> Oscar Wilde

Most of The County's observations were too obscure for my young mind to appreciate but they always would seem to lift his spirits. Ten years after he retired from football, he was working for the CIE: the national transport authority, as a ganger man fixing rail lines; not a bad job in those days but although he worked 12 hours a day, his wages would barely cover the food bills, let alone rent. Feeding a large family on low pay had never been easy, so my mother would often have to buy food 'on tick'. The grocer's shops in the town would allow us to get food on the understanding that they could tick off the bill at the end of the week, on payday. Throughout Ireland, people had become very familiar with meagre wages and there were many times we did not have enough money to settle our bills so we would just change our grocer until we had enough money. We knew from our mother not to go near the old shopkeeper as she told us 'there was a dog tied there'.

One place however, where we always paid our bills was to Father Curran, the priest of Edgeworthstown. It was 5*s*. twice a year and 1*s*. every Sunday. If we didn't pay our dues to the church, the shame would be too much as the family names of the non-payers would be read from the pulpit. Father Curran would almost humiliate the offenders announcing:

'And I've seen the very same families drinking in pubs and having a fine old time.'

Paying the priest was obligatory which sometimes meant going without food, not that they ever thanked us for it.

Edgesworthtown itself was a small rural market town in the Midlands of Ireland, named after the Edgeworth family, the most famous of which being Maria Edgeworth the celebrated Irish poet. It was a quiet, mainly agricultural town with not an 'Injun' in sight and consisted of a few pubs, some shops and an undertaker. Our home was a little stone house next to a railway crossing, about ten minutes' walk from the town and my favourite retreat of the Picture House. We had one kitchen/living room, and two small bedrooms, each with a double bed, the girls in one room and the boys in the other. There was a bucket underneath a bench to the side of the house that was used as a toilet but more often than not we would just use the field or a hedge. The floor of the house was made of stone and in winter the rain seemed to sit in shallow pools on the bare floor while the damp was felt throughout. Two

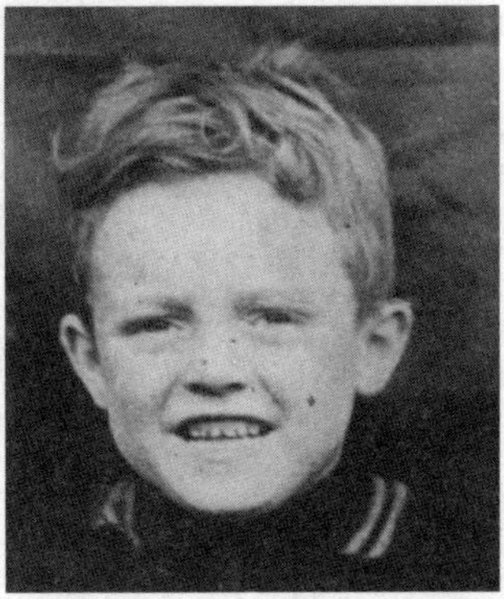

Mickey the Bun

little square windows faced onto the railway crossing which rattled loudly when a train went by.

I was the sixth of eight children, with four older sisters. Mary at 19 was the eldest and was by now engaged to a grand lad from Navan called Paddy; then came Kitty (17) and the twins Lizzette and Gretchen (15). I also had three brothers: one older; Kevin (13), and two younger; Franco (11) and the youngest: Philip (7). I was known in the family as Mickey the Bun because, when I was born, I weighed a staggering 12.5lbs. The midwife described me as the biggest dote she had ever seen while my sister Kitty said I looked like a big juicy current bun that had risen too much in the oven.

I had long since reverted to normal size and by now had lots of freckles and blue eyes but unusually for my family I had a big bushy head of fair curls. We may not have had much money but the one thing that The County always made sure that we had was a football perhaps with the forlorn hope that one of his sons would have inherited his great footballing ability. My mother however, told us 'to pay no attention to all that football shite', and that 'playing football did not put meals on the table.'

The County (Frank Greene) with my brothers form Left: Franco (with ball), Kevin and young Phillip

As far as we were concerned, we had everything we needed. It was however one of the most exciting days of our lives when The County put in our first source of electricity, which provided one light outside, one in the kitchen and a plug, although we still needed to buy turf and coal for the open-fire. The first appliance that my mother bought was an electric iron, prior to which she used two fire-irons interchanging them as one would cool down. The only other appliance we had that could use electricity was our old Pye radio or wireless, which up until then had used batteries.

I wanted to save up for my own radio and even though it was low paid, my new job at Doyle's Pub would also help with the food bills. I could also give my mother some money to untie a few dogs in town and help with the rent but most importantly I could now go to the Picture House twice or even three times a week, although still only on the hard wooden seats down at the front.

The shift at Doyle's was from 10 in the morning til 3 in the afternoon, then again from 5 p.m. until midnight. During the break I would return home to our house on the outskirts of town next to the railway line. My mother's job was the gatekeeper for the railway crossing and to operate the signals. Her job meant she could only leave the house if there was someone to operate the crossing, an 18 hour-a-day job, so my arrival home allowed her to go shopping in town to prepare for her other job of raising a family. Typically, there was a smell of burning turf from the open hearth, the sound of bubbling pots accompanied by the persistent background hum from the wireless. As usual it was tuned into Radio Eirann, a mainly news channel with occasional breaks for religious announcements, births, deaths and marriages and 6 o'clock evening Angelus or daily prayers.

As soon as my mother went out, I would quickly tune the wireless onto the music channel. It was the incomparable Elvis Presley, playing 'You aint a nothing but a hound-dog, ah, a-crocking all the time.' I sang along, curling my top-lip and pointing threateningly at our dog, Nasser: 'You aint never caught a rabbit, and you aint no friend of mine.' As a bemused Nasser pricked up his ears and coiled his head to listen, I would slick back my hair with spit in my hands, pulling a quiff forward, go up on my toes and grind my hips in tune with the music.

My mother always told us not to turn on the music channel after a mishap the previous year, which nearly cost her, her job and us, our home. One Saturday evening she left as usual to go to confession in town. All eight of us kids were in the house so we tuned the wireless onto our favourite show: The Ceilidh House with its cheerful presenter Denjo, pronounced Dinjo.

'Good evening everyone, this is Dinjo, inviting you to…Lift the lock, Open the door, Step right in, And Take the floor!'

Then the sound of clapping and tapping feet would start as the fiddles, flutes and tin-whistles fired up for a night of ceilidh dancing. We cleared all the chairs and tables off the stone floor to create our own ceilidh room. Then we would line up, my bare-footed four sisters lining up opposite the four boys. 'It was like *Seven Brides for Seven Brothers*' pointed out my sister Kitty standing in front of me. However, it was a good job there were no more of us as there would be no room to dance. The voice over the wireless then instructed us:

> Line up now and hold up your arms
> Are you ready for the Siege of Innes?

Dinjo was the compere who would guide you through the steps of the ceilidh dances, his often nonsensical rhyming lyrics always in time with the music.

> In a row, you'll be there
> Look across to find your pair
> Offer your arm and face the band
> Gentle lady, give your hand
> Over and under the arch you go
> Then fall back-in, in a row

We danced up and down, exaggerating the clapping and yelping along with the instructions from Dinjo, then back into line opposite my sisters:

> Take your lady by the arm
> Not too fast, to do no harm
> Then take your ladies round and round
> At the end put her down

We reeled each other round the room, the nails in our untied boots sparking off the floor as my sisters skipped nimbly around us. We'd swing each other round in huge circles, then back into line waiting for the next direction from Dinjo.

> Pretty ladies, listen to me
> Stay in tune, one, two,
> SMAAAAAASH!!!...

'What the fuck was that!!?'
We all ran out of the house to find a goods train had smashed through the level crossing gates and was belatedly slamming on the breaks, the thunderous noise of the smash echoing throughout the countryside. The gates lay strewn across the road and surrounding hedges, broken into about six different parts. This was my mother's job on the level crossing, to ensure that the gates were opened for trains, and we rented the house off her employer, the CIE. We all stood there with gaping mouths, the youngest Philip already in tears. Surely, this couldn't have happened!

We had no sooner got back into the house when our breathless mother arrived home. My sisters tried to explain how they had forgotten to move the gates for the 21.30 goods train from Sligo to Dublin because we were listening to Dinjo's Ceilidh House. Me, and my brothers had already began edging slowly towards the safety of our bedroom.

'We are really in the shit now,' whispered Franco.

As much as my sisters tried to justify what happened, citing 'that eejit Dinjo' was never going to help and my mother was fuming. But as me and my retreating brothers knew; being boys, we were the only ones likely to get slapped.

It took three weeks to replace the gates, during which time we used small red candle-lit lamps to stop the cars crossing the railway, which had to be gathered up and re-set every time a train went past. But more importantly, my mother managed to keep her job and we kept our home.

After that, she laid down a new rule 'there would be no more music in this house!' From that point, our old copper gramophone player with its big flower-like speaker sat redundantly gathering dust on a corner table along with our small collection of 78rpm records of the big band and swing music of the '40s. Even the little Jack Russell pictured listening to HMV [His Master's Voice] on the side of the gramophone box seemed to be waiting impatiently for one of the Duke Ellington or Glenn Miller tracks to burst him back to life. Although we adhered to my mother's rule for a while, the thought of rock n roll and Elvis Presley on the wireless was too much to resist. I would take my opportunity when she went out shopping to hear the latest sounds being belted out. 'Might as well,' I thought 'they keep telling us at mass that Jesus loves a sinner'.

The news on the radio in 1956 was all about political upheaval, from all corners of the globe. I didn't even know where most of the places were but there was a constant update of coups, movements and standoffs anywhere from Hungary to Guatemala.

With such a complex political history of their own, Irish people at the time were eager to hear more about politics wherever in the world it was. The regular stream of news meant our family, particularly The County, became captivated by politics and current affairs. He was widely read about Ireland's own history and a photograph of Michael Collins sat proudly on our mantelpiece next to the picture of the sacred heart and the Virgin Mary, so Fianna Gael, or the 'Free-Staters', was the party of choice in our house. When we were growing up, The County had told us about the 1916 Easter uprising, the civil war between the Free-Staters and the Republicans, and the bravery of the freedom fighters who had fought and died for Ireland. I thought that if I had been around during the uprising, I too would have died for my country such was the reverence everyone seemed to have for the rebels, the leaders of which later executed by the British rulers in Kilmaynon gaol, Dublin. Death seemed a heavy price to pay, but The County would tell us proudly: 'If the country is good enough to live in it is good enough to fight for.'

Although we voted Fianna Gael, Fianna Fáil were the other major political party in Ireland and was led by the only one of the rebel leaders who had escaped execution in 1916: Eamon De Valera. Whilst he was an icon of Irish nationalism because of the uprising, De Valera wasn't very popular in our house because, as The County often told us, he never helped the working man. 'Aye, free beef for the farmers!' he used to say mocking De Valera's perceived bias towards Ireland's landowners. My four older sisters also thought that he acted more like a 1930's old fashioned dictator who had deceived Michael Collins into 'the trap' of negotiations with the British that resulted in Ireland being partitioned: 'he likes to take the credit, but lets others take the bullets' they used to say.

Like football, my mother didn't care much for politics. She had been the oldest of four kids when her mother died when she was 13, so she spent her teenage years bringing up her siblings until she embarked on having eight kids of her own. Her whole life it seemed had been about caring for kids; feeding them, cooking, cleaning and washing. When we were growing up she would regularly go without meals to avoid any of us going hungry and her 18 hour work-days were often supplemented by sleepless nights as she tended to sick babies or coughs brought on from a damp house.

'One day,' I thought, 'I'll have enough money to buy a grand house, with lots of bedrooms and she can come to stay in her own fine bed.'

The priests in Ireland were complaining about the immorality of pop music and Elvis in particular on the minds of young people with his gyrating hips 'encouraging sins of the flesh'. My sisters however loved Elvis. They said that like everything in Ireland, if there was enjoyment in something, it would be called a sin.

Sins of the flesh in a predominantly catholic country was especially frowned upon if you were a woman, who rather like cows in an agricultural economy were treated as if they were not worth as much as bulls. Some old farmer once said to The County that he must have had a 'desperate fright' when he had his four daughters first, and then the relief he must have enjoyed when he finally had four sons. The County would just laugh. Sexism did not exist in our house; he knew that my mother and sisters worked as hard and were the equal of any man in Edgeworthstown; and as for my twin sisters, Lizzette and Gretchen, they could probably out-fight most of them as well.

I pondered why they didn't play more pop songs in church, as some of Elvis' lyrics sounded almost spiritual: 'Don't be cruel to a heart that's true!' Maybe Buddy Holly's 'I love you Peggy Sue' would be too much for the priest on a Sunday but would be great craic for a wedding. 'Or maybe,' I thought 'they should play Johnny Cash and one his gravelly, moral redemption songs like

'Walk the line'. I could then be moody and mysterious during mass rather than having to listen to the boring old bollocks hymns that they usually came out with.

'I'll now have to go to confession' I deliberated to myself 'bless me Father Curran, for I have sinned ... erm I thought the hymns at mass were bollocks and I wanted ye to play some Elvis.'...I laughed – and reckoned I'd be saying a few Hail Marys for my thoughts.

I switched the news channel back on as I could see my mother arriving home with some shopping: a couple of cabbages, a bag of spuds, some sausages for The County and some boxty or potato bread for me and my two younger brothers.

As she unpacked the evening's dinner, our dog Nasser began excitedly to thump the floor with his tail. Nasser was a small black mongrel, a bit of Labrador and a bit of terrier who we had been given the previous year. We joked that he must have been a butcher's dog, as he was so thin when we got him. He didn't come with a name but the 1956 Suez crisis meant he was named after the president of Egypt, Gamal Abdel Nasser.

We had heard over the wireless that the French and British governments had conspired with the Israelis to regain control of the Suez Canal after President Nasser of Egypt had pledged to nationalise it. I didn't understand words like 'conspired' and 'nationalise' so I asked The County to explain: The County would never miss the opportunity of giving his political opinion to anyone but especially to his sons, so he seized his opportunity. He gathered me and my two younger brothers, Franco and Philip round the table as he always did when he thought he had something important to tell us. He then explained that the British and French did not want to let Egypt control a waterway called Suez even though it was in Egypt, as they were using it to transport oil. He went on to explain that Britain and France liked to take over other countries which would become their colonies enabling them to get more money. 'It was how they had operated for hundreds of years, building up empires' he said 'and how they had exploited other countries all around the world.'

None of what The County was saying made any sense to me but as I was the eldest of the three he had positioned around the table I felt that I had to at least look interested, even though my fixed gaze was just scrutinising an old football scar on his left cheek. My mother said that he was trying to teach us to read between the lines before we could even read as my brother Franco; himself nick-named after the infamous Spanish dictator, was already kicking his heels and studying his bootlaces. The youngest Philip had also reverted to drawing a picture of a motor car on his school jotter but being only seven he had a perfect excuse for the tedium of politics and current affairs which my mother claimed on his behalf; 'he's far too young to understand.'

So, with just me and the dog Nasser still looking attentive, The County went on explaining that the conspiracy, called operation Musketeer, was to start a war against Egypt and take control of the Suez Canal. On hearing this, I perked up as I had seen the film *The Three Musketeers* at the Picture House with Gene Kelly and Lana Turner, but the version given by The County made no mention of the daring d'Artagnan or swashbuckling rescues of Lady Constance, crying out, 'All for one, and one for all!' in romantic sounding French towns like La Rochelle.

As I eagerly anticipated a cavalier swordfight or the hero entering the fray from a swinging chandelier, The County explained that Egypt won the support of the

United Nations and the British and French were ordered by the UN to withdraw. Hollywood had taught me to expect a happy ending and that the great British empire always won a magnificent victory but The County I concluded, could not have seen enough war films to make his account more convincing. However, from the passion with which he spoke about politics I knew that it meant as much to him as me going to the Picture House. The grand finale he was building up to was that Egypt's victory at Suez meant the demise of colonialism and freedom for the masses – hardly the momentous ending I was expecting.

I asked him what this freedom meant and why did we have to name our dog after Gamal Abdel Nasser, both of which I thought were intelligent enough questions and would prove I was listening. Franco looked up from his bootlaces and rolled his eyes as if pleading to me not to ask another question.

'Nasser has ended years of colonial domination' The County explained 'which means that people in the colonies are now free son.' Then he went on: 'just as the Southern Irish people were freed in 1922 from colonial British rule, they can now vote and not be ruled by a foreign government and be a nation for themselves.'

I still didn't understand but his obvious satisfaction with the outcome of Suez and its link to the heroic rebels of Ireland had me intrigued. I didn't want to risk asking any more questions, but decided I should pay more attention to the news in the future, although I still preferred to listen to pop music.

During the day at Doyle's Pub we would sometimes play the music channels on the wireless, although the pubs in those days had no young people and no women would ever dare come through the entrance. The clients at Doyle's were almost exclusively men aged from about 25 and upwards, most smoking pipes in flat caps and complaining that the weather was not good enough to draw turf. As they sat supping pint after pint of Guinness, they would often talk of others 'affliction for the drink'. My mother called them hypocrites saying: 'spending all their family's money on porter while their kids ran around without an arse in their trousers.'

Whilst shining glasses, I liked to play the Top 10 chart hits. The Number One single in the charts at the time was sung by a 14 year old boy called Frankie Lymon, singing 'Why Do Fools Fall in Love' – not a subject often spoken about, let alone sung about in a pub. Because I could listen to music and earn my own money I liked my new job at Doyle's, and in just a few weeks had managed to buy my new Johnny Cash shirt. After a quiet November we were looking forward to a busy Christmas, the best time of year in Ireland as many who were working abroad would return home, with stories of their great achievements and lots of money.

A few days before Christmas, Tommy Doyle made what he called the best decision of his life, he bought a new television. He placed it as prominently as he could, on the top-shelf behind the bar. It would be great for business; a 'real attention grabber' and he wanted everyone to see it. I had heard that there were some bars in bigger towns that had televisions but this was the first in Edgeworthstown. The television was a brown colour with speakers built in on either side. The black and white picture was barely visible due to all the snow-like interference but that didn't matter, as we could still make out some famous people. The first programme we tuned into was Pope Pius XII waving to crowds in Rome. I was surprised by how old he looked and almost expected him to look like the photo I had seen of him when he was first elected in 1939, but couldn't wait to tell my mother that I had seen the pope, whom she called the representation of God on earth.

Christmas Eve was the busiest night of the year. I had the glasses all polished and we had ordered extra barrels of Guinness and Smithwicks, the two most popular drinks, along with extra bottles of Gin, Whiskey, Brandy and lots of minerals: cokes, orange, we had everything. The pub was full by 7 o'clock but we still would not turn anyone away. One of the big topics of conversation was the advert in the window of 'McBride's', a clothes shop four doors along from Doyles, which was also trying to grab the attention of those home for Christmas with its slogan:

Knickers Down!
Now's your chance!

One man called Johnny McInerney was home from England just for Christmas. He was working in an asbestos factory in Luton and I couldn't believe it when he ordered a round of drinks for everyone in the pub. The round came to nearly £5. It was the biggest round of drinks I had ever seen and was as much as we would sometimes take in a fortnight. I thought that the money he was earning over in England must be incredible.

As midnight approached, many left to go to mass, some singing and dancing all the way as many believed their prayers for prosperity would be answered if they saw Christmas in whilst in church. Tommy Doyle didn't like to see them leaving on his biggest night of the year to give away his cherished revenue in the collection and commented that it was the only time since last Christmas they had darkened a church door. As the last customers left, we eventually closed at about 2 a.m., totted up the takings in the till which came to an incredible £95! The new television had certainly done the trick.

As Johnny MacInerney settled his enormous bar bill, he said that purgatory was the place ye lived in before ye made it over to England, as he happily handed over pound notes like they were sweets.

It was that night that I decided I too had to get to England, there just seemed to be so much opportunity over there, plenty of jobs, lots of money and so much life. I had even heard Harold MacMillan on the wireless telling the people 'you've never had it so good;' as the UK economy thrived. Conversely, the Irish economy was still in the doldrums. De Valera's Fianna Fail government finally acknowledged that their isolationist trade policies had not worked but, to The County's disappointment, they still went on to win 53 per cent of the seats in the Irish parliament, the Dail Eirann, in the election of 1957. The County explained to me that Ireland should trade openly with Europe and America to create jobs, and that de Valera at 75 was still bitter against the English for the war of independence, partition and everything else that had gone wrong in Ireland for the last 500 years. 'Aye. Burn everything English except their coal!' he'd quote,* ridiculing de Valera's trade policy which, he said, hadn't changed since the Anglo Irish trade war of the 1930s.

The New Year as usual sobered everyone up. Christmas was over and there were the inevitable bills that needed to be paid not least for the over-extravagance of drink at Christmas. Doyle's was quiet and within a couple of months the novelty of just watching anything on television was over. People were only interested in watching

* Dean Swift's famous phrase of 1720

the evening news. I could play music at lunchtime or when I was working on my own, but everyone who came into the pub in the evenings wanted to watch the TV and listen to the news. It was one evening when I was watching the television through the snowy interference that I first heard of a country called The Congo. At first, I thought it might be some kind of exotic drums as it sounded like 'Bongo' and I certainly hadn't heard anything about it in school and not even on the radio. The world fair of 1958 was taking place in Brussels, the centrepiece of which was the Atomium building, which many called 'Brussels' version of the Eiffel Tower.' The Atomium was set up like a giant atom probably over 300 feet high with huge suspended globes held together by walkways. It was the most unusual structure I had ever seen. Being the world fair, other countries were invited to have an exhibition displaying the culture of their home nation.

The commentator spent some time explaining about the competing exhibits and that the World Fair was dedicated to: 'Man and his mission in a peaceful and humane world'. He then explained about the exhibit of The Congo which featured prominently in the exhibition, describing it as Belgium's colonial property in Africa. Amazingly they said it was about 75 times the size of Belgium itself and I wondered why such a massive country should be owned by a little country like Belgium. In The Congo exhibit there were straw and grass huts, and they even had native Congolese people dressed in traditional grass skirts and beads. Unfortunately they had to close The Congo exhibit, we were told, as the local Belgians threw bananas at the African natives. I thought this was funny, calling people apes and monkeys, almost like we would call each other eejits.

Racism did not really exist in Ireland at the time as nearly everyone had white skin, or 'only different shades of blue' as the Dolly noted. There were plenty of petty rivalries about politics, religion, football etc but these were generally just debates in the pub and with no real foundation. The Irish republic had originated with a philosophy of equality, and The County would often recite to me, word for word, the declaration of Patrick Pearse from the GPO in 1916

> The Republic guarantees religious and civil liberty, equal rights and equal opportunities to all its citizens, cherishing all the children of the nation equally, and oblivious of the differences carefully fostered by an alien government, which have divided a minority from the majority in the past.

I had only seen African people in the Hollywood films, with such greats as Sidney Poitier who I had watched escaping from prison chained to a racist convict in *The Defiant Ones*. I also watched Harry Belefonte in the film *Carmen Jones* and remembered a great moment when Dorothy Dandrich who played the title character says to the young teetotaller 'soldier Joe' (Belefonte):

> Boy, if the army was made up of nothin' but soldiers like you, war wouldn't do nobody no good,

a comment I often said to people in Doyle's bar if they told me they weren't drinking.

The darkest skinned people I had seen in Ireland were those who I presumed were of Spanish descent who had been sent from King Philip III to help the Irish rebels at the battle of Kinsale and the aftermath which became known as The Flight of the Earls, but I had never seen anyone non-European.

At mass we were always compelled to give a penny in the collection for the poor black babies in Africa, the cost of a package of broken biscuits I calculated, so I just assumed that countries like The Congo must have lots to eat with everyone sending them their food. In other parts of the world, we heard, being non–European meant discrimination and poverty. We were told about segregation policies in the American south, and the resettlement of blacks or apartheid in South Africa restricting the wealth to whites only. The 'free world', as it liked to call itself, did not seem that free to me if your skin was a different colour.

It had only been 13 years since the end of World War Two, and at school we had been taught about the holocaust of people that had been referred to as 'untermenschen' or sub-human by the Nazis, who stole all the money, even the gold from their victims teeth and then poisoned them with gas. As I began to hear more and more about policies of segregation and racism I remembered in school reading the diaries of Anne Frank, the teenage girl who hid with her family in an Amsterdam attic but was eventually betrayed for money and sent to a concentration camp. One of the entries she made was:

> It's difficult in times like these; ideals, dreams and hopes rise within us only to be crushed by grim reality. Yet I cling to them because I believe, in spite of everything, that people are truly good at heart.
>
> Diary of Anne Frank

Hearing about apartheid in Southern Africa and segregation in the American south, it seemed to me that the grim reality of racism was still with us despite everyone's disbelief at the horrific reality of the Holocaust.

Even though I was still too young to understand fully, I reasoned that the ruling whites in America and South Africa were only interested in safeguarding their money despite their vocal revulsion at what happened to the Jewish people. We were often reminded by Father Curran at mass:

'We are all God's children' as he would continue paraphrasing from the bible: 'and like Jesus himself, who was betrayed for 12 pieces of silver, it is easier for a camel to pass through the eye of a needle than for a rich man to enter the kingdom of heaven.'

My attention was snapped back to the newscast about the world fair when the cameras moved onto the competing exhibits of the US and Russia, the so-called 'Cold War' adversaries. The commentator seemed enthused that the 1925 Russian film *Battleship Potemkin* had been voted the greatest film of all time as the Russian ambassador picked up the award. Despite being a regular down at The Picture House, I hadn't even heard of the film as the only silent movies they ever played were comedies with actors like Charlie Chaplin. The only other silent film actor I had heard of was the great Douglas Fairbanks so I wondered how a silent film about rebellious Russian sailors could be voted the best film ever. To me, silent films had been outdated by the silver screen which in turn had been outdated by the advent of colour in the '30s and '40s. And I wondered what could be better than John Ford's 'cavalry trilogy' of *Rio Grande, Fort Apache* and *She Wore a Yellow Ribbon* set amid the breathtaking scenery of Utah's Monument valley. I sensed that the propaganda of the Cold War was beginning to extend its influence way beyond Brussels' World Fair.

Under communism we were being told, people were all treated equally, which seemed to many Irish people the fairest system. Khrushchev's communism in the late '50s, after the dark days of Stalin, was now being presented as a kind of utopia, of wealth distribution and fairness. Khrushchev advocated the teachings of Karl Marx that described capitalism as a state where people are forced into wage slavery into any job to avoid poverty and starvation under a free market economy. Crime and racism, the communists argued, were the by-products of bourgois elitism that is fostered under capitalism, where riches are made through exploitation of the people.

There were plenty of films about British and American victories in various wars but there were very few movies about the Russians. The atrocities committed under Stalin in the '40s and early '50s were only now being told, five years after he died, disclosed by Khrushchev in his 'secret speech'. We heard on the wireless that Russia's new president had surprised everyone when he denounced the severe repression under the Stalin era. He spoke out against the Gulags, the forced labour camps in the most extreme, most dismal and forgotten outposts of the Soviet Union where alleged enemies of the state were subjected to live in horrendous and often violent conditions. It was said that you could be sentenced to three years in the Gulag if you were late for work three times. I concluded that my brother Franco would surely end up in the Gulag if we lived in Russia, and as for the Dolly he would probably be late for the Gulag as well.

It seemed to me that both the free world and communism had a terrible past, but each now offered competing hopes' for a better future. However, on the wireless and on Doyle's television, the rising antagonism between the American and Soviet ideals suggested a mutual desire to see the other destroyed; there could be no place for both as the Cold War intensified.

I began to enjoy spending time at home as it gave me the chance to discuss all these political topics with The County, which made me feel more grown up and I knew he would appreciate a political debate. He always seemed able to look beyond the short term swings of public opinion and give a down-to-earth perspective on the major political figures. 'Churchill was a great man', he would say 'but de Valera's policies are a bollocks' although his deputy at Fianna Fáil; Sean Lemass 'was decent enough'. The County said he was neither a capitalist nor a communist; he was a working man who believed in a socialist welfare state. To me, this sounded about right and being that I was now a mature working man of 14, my political leanings had been formed.

The great City of London still sounded ideal to me, a multicultural bustling city of music and opportunity. They had a socialist government and we heard stories that people from all over the world were moving there. They were coming from the Caribbean, India, Bangladesh, Pakistan, Kenya, Uganda; everyone it seemed wanted to move to London. In England, many industries had been nationalised and its welfare state provided what The County called the 'Five Adequates': income, healthcare, housing, education and employment.

'Something that de Valera', he said, 'had not given the people of Ireland.'

However, politics and racism all became very personal to me one day when I was watching a television news report in Doyle's.

'De ye see that?' blurted one of the regulars while pointing up at the television 'the feckin bastards!'

I looked up at the television to see what had caused such outrage.

The Irish correspondent was reporting from the UK on the anger felt by English people that foreigners were taking jobs belonging to them. The camera then zoomed in on a sign outside a boarding house in London that said:

> No blacks!
> No dogs!
> And No Irish!

It was not the only bad news I received that day. Tommy's brother, Brendan had returned from Wicklow and needed a job. Tommy said to me that he would help me find something else but he would have to give my job to his brother. I didn't mind, I would have done the same for my brothers 'and besides', I thought, 'I would never make it to London if I didn't move on.'

Tommy told me about a job he heard was being advertised in Mullingar 14 miles up the road towards Dublin, in a pub called the Bridge Bar, which meant that I would have to leave home during the week. There was no other work in Edgeworthstown and the Bridge Bar paid better wages: £1 5*s*., over double what I was getting at Doyles and which included board. I told my mother I could come home once a week to see the family and go to the Picture House. I got the job at the Bridge Bar and moved to Mullingar the next week with a good word from Tommy Doyle. The clients in Mullingar seemed different to those in Edgeworthstown, there were very few farmers or manual workers, what The County called 'decent working class people'. Instead there were some nurses or orderlies from the local Mullingar hospital and soldiers from the nearby barracks. The people here seemed more serious when they spoke to each other and, unlike Edgeworthstown, there didn't seem to be as much craic.

After a while, I started talking to some of the soldiers, who told me about life in the army which sounded great compared to the 14 hour days I was doing. I'd see them going into the barracks reporting for duty at 8.30 a.m., then home for lunch, then back until only 4.30 p.m. in the afternoon, the rest of the time they could do as they pleased. They were even advertising in newspapers and magazines for young men to sign up, with the headline:

Join the Army....Protect your future!

And the money was great too, £3 a week during basic training going up to £4 a week as a regular soldier.
I remembered what the Dolly said to me back in Edgewothstown 'money can't buy you happiness but it does put a feckin big smile on yer face!' With those wages I reckoned I could save nearly £2 a week and it would be no time before I would be smiling all the way over to London. My only problem was the minimum age for the army was 18 and I was four years too young.

I stood there whistling my favourite tune 'All I have to do is Dream' by the Everly Brothers pondering how I could become four years older in as many days so that I could get a good job in the army earning decent money, then mouthed the rest of the song 'only trouble is, gee whiz, I'm dreaming my life away!'

The Bridge Bar also had a television, the reception was still snowy but as many homes could not afford a TV yet, they remained popular with the regulars. On the news, there were two very important stories to report. First, they had 'white smoke' from the cardinals sitting in the conclave in St. Peters; the new pope would be called Blessed John XIII. All of Ireland was delighted but the second thing we heard was that the US and UK economies had gone into a deep recession or as Eisenhower called it 'a breather', after the stock market had crashed.

People in Edgeworthstown could speak for hours about the new pope but never spoke about things like stock markets. The only markets we had were the cattle marts, which I always thought were terrible places that stank and had shit absolutely everywhere. But in Mullingar it was different; the stock markets they spoke of seemed far more civilised but had suddenly lost a third of its value. Many recalled that it took 25 years after the great crash of 1929 for the markets to regain their value, with second-hand accounts of trying to find work during the Great Depression and life in the Hoovervilles, although it only seemed like yesterday since Macmillan had made his 'you've never had it so good speech'. The newscasters explained that prices had become inflated and that people were living exuberantly, spending too much money and enjoying rich lifestyles. I wondered where I had been during all this spending and exuberance, this so-called boom, I concluded, had not reached Ireland and certainly had not reached Edgeworthstown. More importantly they predicted, there would be far fewer jobs available for me to make my fortune. My dreams of moving to London began to fade.

At the Picture House the following weekend I went to see *The Cocoanuts* starring the Marx brothers or 'the feckin eejits' as my mother called them. The film was also made in 1929, and showed Groucho Marx trying to sell grand Florida homes, as rich people stood around with gaping mouths:

> Sunshine, sunshine, perpetual sunshine
> all year round, lets get the auction started
> before the tornado hits.
>
> Groucho Marx

I was beginning to like the capitalist idea that if you were willing to work hard enough, then you could make yourself a fortune. When I got back to Mullingar I impersonated Groucho Marx, just as I had seen the Dolly doing, talking out of the side of my mouth whilst holding a cigar in the other. But back in the more serious town of Mullingar people were not watching comedy films. Instead they were talking about Karl Marx ideology, recounting that after the 1929 crash or black Thursday, the US president had realised that 'all men are equal before fishes'. 30 years later in the late '50s, as people began to feel the effects of the economic downturn, many perceived capitalism was collapsing again and communism was becoming more and more popular.

The build up of the Cold War heightened further when it was announced in January 1959 that Fidel Castro had taken control of Cuba and would implement Marxist ideals with the announcement that the exploitation and inequalities of the former Batista regime 'were finished'. Ireland always had sympathies with rebellion and many thought that socialism brought about a more equal society, but just as Castro was describing his egalitarian vision as 'green as the palm trees of Cuba' he announced something that was unforgiveable in Ireland: he would stop his people from gambling. Whilst many regarded the redistribution of wealth under socialism as fairer, Irish people saw gambling on horses or cards as an enjoyable social pastime that allowed them to dream, and be entertained. They liked the chance to be lucky and the hope of a better future but with one decision Marxist ideals or 'the threat' of communism became despised.

Radio reporters in Ireland interviewed bookmakers and punters at racecourses up and down the country with leading questions:

'What do you think of Castro's ban on gambling in Cuba?'

While the answer may have been different had the question been asked just outside the confessional, people everywhere were incensed that their favourite pastime was being threatened.

'It's like prohibition in the US' said one of the interviewees 'if people want to have a drink, let them have a drink, there's no harm in it, and we all like a flutter on the horses.'

I then read an article left on the bar by one of the punters that pointed out that Richard Nixon, who was in his second term as vice president of America, had funded his political campaigns from his poker winnings. The article noted that to get the things we want, we sometimes have to take a gamble and that the Castro regime now denied the Cuban people their dreams. I knew that I too had dreams and that if I had to take a gamble to achieve them, I surely would.

I didn't like staying in Mullingar on my day off, and would return home to Edgeworthstown, where the people were better craic and where I could catch up with the family. The Dolly Dolan would come round to the house when he heard I was coming home. We always knew he was coming because you could hear him whistling from what seemed like miles away; he was the loudest whistler I ever heard, and louder than most people could sing.

The County used to tease him when he arrived at the door,

'Jaysus, ye must be an awful coward Dolly, whistling so loud?'

But the Dolly was too quick witted to be caught on the back foot.

'That's right Frank,' he used to say. 'I thought youz would make me play feckin football with ye, and I was scared I might hurt ye.'

The County just laughed.

The best thing about the Dolly is that he seemed oblivious to the accepted Irish protocol that in the company of elders you should never swear, blaspheme or call them by their Christian names.

'So anyway Micky,' he returned to me. 'Have ye any craic to tell us, any old lies or anything?'

Before I had the chance to answer he had already shot off into his next story.

'Oh Jaysus! Did I tell ye I went round to Joe Murray's?' he started to explain, 'and herself, Maggie Murray answers the feckin door. "Is Joseph at work?" Says I. "Ah, how would he be at work", she says, "and his eye up there on the mantelpiece!"' Without pausing for breath he asked me, 'Did you know Joe Murray had a glass eye?'

I didn't know, but the Dolly was off again.

'A feckin glass eye!' he roared. 'Left up on the mantelpiece! Apparently he lost it breaking stones in the quarry, and there was I thinking he was just givin' me a quare look!'

My parents liked the informality and light-heartedness of the Dolly, and often use to mimic the way he whistled: 'it's a long way to Tipperary', 'Danny Boy' or 'The Irish Rover'.

My mother would then set the table for tea. As the plates and cups were laid out the Dolly was strangely quiet, you could see him counting the place settings and then counting how many of us were round the table. He smiled when he realised that the one extra cup meant he would be getting an extra tea and a slice of currant bread.

'Jaysus tanks Katleen, yer a topper!' he said to my smiling mother. Nobody else except The County and Father Curran had called her Katleen in 20 years.

Although he was sometimes hungry the Dolly was always happy, and almost as soon as he arrived he'd be off whistling down the road.

'I'll see ye at the Picture House Mickey?' he asked

'Aye, I'll see you in there,' I shouted back.

Along with the Picture House and seeing the family, the thing I used to look forward to most when I returned home was discussing politics with The County. I would overhear the conversations of the more serious regulars of the Bridge Bar and would jot things down so that I could discuss them with him to gain his insights. He seemed to understand the real motives of politicians which he said 'were normally about greed and money' and what it meant for everyday people. Whilst there were many political commentators in the Bridge Bar, especially vocal if they had a few pints, his was the perspective I respected most since it understood the historical context of why decisions were made and the likely upshot of resultant policy. He also understood the rationale and the implications for Ireland.

He told me that the world was in a very precarious position due to the nuclear threat between the two superpowers; the US and USSR, saying that we were in a similar situation to what happened in the build up to World War Two or 'The Emergency', as it was known in Ireland.

'Then,' he explained, 'in 1936 the League of Nations couldn't reach agreement over sanctions against Italy's aggression in Ethiopia and subsequently collapsed which precipitated the rise of fascist imperialism and the Second World War.'

'The UN,' he said, 'is our only hope' and, 'if the UN fails then we'll all be in a nuclear war which will finish everything.'

I was alarmed but knew The County was never known to exaggerate. I had heard more and more about the UN back in Mullingar and how it had been formed in the aftermath of the war in 1946. Now the US and USSR were building up nuclear weapons and some were ominously predicting that 15 years after the end of World War Two, we were due a third World War.

I asked The County what it meant for Ireland and whether we should remain neutral.

'Why don't we just mind our own business and let them fight it out if that's what they wanted?' I asked.

The County then explained that Ireland was too small to take a military role in the Cold War but that it could contribute diplomatically. He then told me about Robert Emmet's speech from the dock when he was sentenced to execution after the Irish nationalist uprising in 1803:

> Only when Ireland can take its place among the world's nations, then and not til then, let my epitaph be written.

'It is now up to countries like Ireland to mediate in world affairs,' The County said 'and to represent neutral countries for our own good and the good of all people.' He moved forward in his seat to emphasise the gravity of the situation: 'colonial imperialism had already caused two world wars and if it was left alone then Cold War imperialism will trigger the next one. Ireland had never benefited from being part of a colonial empire, and indeed partition still existed.'

I always understood politics when The County explained it to me. When I read The Irish Independent and heard the news on the wireless, I began to look out for words like UN', or 'colonialism' and what Ireland's politicians were saying, which was gaining such prominence in global politics.

I learned that Ireland had proposed resolutions to discuss ending the apartheid regime in South Africa which was proposed by an Irish diplomat called Conor Cruise O'Brien. He argued that apartheid was an abuse of human rights and therefore an international issue, which had implications for peace and stability in the region. The 'free world' I read, had vetoed the resolutions because South Africa was an anti-communist ally. As the Irish press questioned the hypocrisy of such a stance it surprised me to read that the Eastern Bloc, where people supposedly weren't 'free', had supported the resolutions to end apartheid.

I was to hear a lot more about Conor Cruise O'Brien over the next few years in many articles and interviews where he argued for what he called 'self determination' for countries still under colonial rule. What I did not know at the time was that our paths would cross so closely and what an impact he would have on my life within just a couple of years.

Even The County appreciated Ireland's approach to foreign relations: 'At the UN we now vote with a conscience for what we see as the right cause,' he explained. 'Neither the east nor west can rely on our vote if their case is unjust, we are known at the UN as "the Bloody Mavericks"'.

The County then did something I thought he would never do, he complimented de Valera and his lieutenants at Fianna Fáil, for giving Ireland a foreign policy that he and the rest of Ireland could be proud of.

'Jaysus' I said, 'you'll be voting for de Valera next time!'

'I will in my hole!' he responded.

That weekend at home was very special for another reason; my oldest sister Mary had moved back home with her husband Paddy, having completed her nursing training in Dublin.

'I have news for you Mickey,' she said excitedly. 'You are going to be an uncle!'

'Jaysus that's great!' I said, 'does that mean its going to be a boy?'

She also had some other good news up her sleeve. She was not only moving back home for a while, she was bringing with her the most sought after electrical product anyone could have in their own house, her own television.

'This is smashing altogether,' I said to her. 'A baby on the way and our very own television!'

We spent more time adjusting the television aerial than we did watching it. Just when we thought we had it tuned in, I'd shout out to The County: 'That's it, perfect!' But by the time he had got off the roof the picture would be gone again. After a few attempts at bending and tuning we just left it alone, occasionally a gust of wind would blow the aerial round to the right position and for another 20 seconds we could see and hear what was going on, but then the picture would blur and eventually vanish into fuzzy horizontal lines. We didn't turn it off though, just the novelty of having a television in the house was great, a luxury that only the rich could afford.

When I returned back to Mullingar, I went to bed as usual at 1 a.m. My room at the Bridge Bar was only big enough to fit a shortened bed, and there was just enough room for a small suitcase under the bed-frame. I had seen on the television, programmes about the typical American household with images of pony-tailed Boston housewives, dressed in neat white blouses and chiffon scarves, using new appliances like refrigerators, electric heaters and even toasters. Luxury conveniences were very rare in Ireland but we heard that those who had emigrated to America and England were buying all sorts of handy electrical devices, some even buying cars and fine houses. My eyes had been opened to the luxurious world of materialism, of comfortable living with mod cons; it was how the other half lived. Despite the economic slowdown, I thought London still had everything: music, film-stars and lots of well-paid work. In Mullingar I had a good enough job, but the money would never have been enough to make it over to London anytime soon.

Unlike Edgeworthstown, in Mullingar I was anonymous, they even called me Michael not Micky, and no-one knew that I was only 14. I had never been asked my age. I wondered if I would be able to tell the army that I was 18 and enlist as a soldier. If I could earn £4 a week I'd be in London in no time.

When the soldiers from the barracks came back in on my fifteenth birthday, I thought I would try it out.

'Good evening lads, what can I get ye?'

'Two pints of Smithwicks please Michael. You seem in good form,' one continued, 'did he give ya a pay rise?'

'No, he didn't,' I said. 'But it's my birthday today!'

'Oh that's grand, how old are ya Michael?

'18,' I said, pretending to be concentrating on pulling their pints of Smithwicks.

'Well happy birthday' they replied and offered to buy me a pint.

'No thanks,' I said. 'I've taken the pledge, but when I get to 21 I'll have a drink with ye.' I was delighted that I had got away with it – they believed I was 18 and even offered to buy me a pint.

The conversation then shifted onto Elvis being drafted into the US army on his eighteenth birthday the previous year, enlisting in Memphis, the home of his recording studio, Sun records.

'He didn't want to join at all,' suggested one of the older drinkers called Padraig 'he just wanted to carry on singing'

'Jaysus, don't we all' responded another, whose own singing career amounted to a version of the Soldier's Song at closing time.

'But they couldn't give him special treatment' concluded Padraig, 'and let all the other fellas do the fighting for him.'

Ireland did not have national military service, just a small professional army, little used because of Ireland's neutrality. One of them joked that Ireland was the only country in the world where the navy makes it home for lunch.

I imagined how I would look dressed in a soldier's uniform after I had seen photos of Elvis in his army shirt and tie, the background lighting making him look like a Hollywood star.

The soldiers continued our conversation:

'So now that yer 18, when are you getting married Michael?' they cajoled.

'Ah not this year anyway,' I joked. 'I'm too busy for all that.'

'Ah yer right Michael; yer best te stay single.'

'What are ye telling him that for!' another interrupted. 'Of course ye have to get married Michael, after all,' he then paused, 'why should you be happy!' and they all laughed and took another mouthful of Smithwicks.

Realising they were on a topic of great amusement they continued.

'No, ye'll have to find yourself a girl Michael,' another butted in, lamenting his own experience:

'Ah, when I was 18 I already had two kids and my wife had left me, but then a terrible thing happened,' he stopped and we all waited in anticipation to hear this terrible outcome. 'She came back!'

I couldn't wait any longer. If I could become a soldier it would mean decent work, great money and good craic. Having just celebrated my birthday and reached the wise-old age of 15, it was time for me to take my first gamble: I would try to bluff my way into the army the following week.

CHAPTER THREE

'Je ne regrette rien!'

Date: October 1961
Location: Jadotville, The Congo
Status: Prisoner of war

Most of us were still shell-shocked from the siege, not that anyone would be brave enough to admit they were suffering from desperate loneliness or trauma as we whiled away the long prison days: a soldier never consciously admits to having frightening memories or mental turmoil. But a battle carries on in a soldier's mind long after the guns fall silent, a struggle that was obvious in all 156 men holed up with me in this makeshift prison. It was in their eyes where I could see the pain; fixated resolutely on the walls that were denying us freedom, the vacant and hopeless grip of a 2,000 yard stare abruptly halted within a few measly feet. The anguish didn't discriminate between soldierly rank and in some ways it was the officers and older soldiers who seemed to suffer most. Just like everyone else they couldn't talk openly about what they prayed for; probably the same as the rest of us: mothers, wives and families: wondering if they were safe, warm or had enough money; 157 of us recounting their other life back home and what in God's name they were doing in an African gaol. The sad faces and mannerisms reflected the sound of a distant tune I could hear being softly whistled in a room above us, that

I recognised as the song I had sung along to as a child: 'Gartan Mother's Lullaby'; that an Irishman's greatest yearning is for his home:

> The curse of the Celt! .....there's no home-sickness in the world like an Irishman's passionate longing for home and kin.
>
> Kenny, by Leona Dalrymple (The Reilly & Britton Co., Chicago, 1917),

It was during the stillness of night that our destructive demons were most apparent; revealed in the yelps and screams of those lucky enough to be able to sleep. It would happen about four or five times each night: bolt-upright awakenings in cold sweats, the piercing shrieks easily audible through flimsy hotel walls against a silent but overbearing Congo darkness. The gist of the torments was always the same: 'Kill him!' 'Bombs!' 'Get yer head down!' 'We're all gonna die!' Then haunting cries of 'Mammy!' and 'Please God!' would ring out loudly, echoing in the shadows before the sound of sobbing, as the ghastly nightmare slowly petered out with a tearful whimper. Perhaps it was the shame of what we might disclose in the frank honesty of dreams that we were all scared of, that others may realise we were in-fact only human. Regardless of the day-time bravado, the ribbing and the jokes, none of us was as tough as we would have liked to be.

My bed was on the bottom shelf in the store-room, the most concealed place I could find. On the shelf above me was Dowler and above him was Pakie Monahan. It didn't really matter where I lay; I was still unable to sleep, so I would stand up to peer out of the store-room window to count the twinkling diamonds in the night sky just as I had when I was a boy. Sometimes I must have totted up over a thousand, more than I ever counted in Ireland, then returned to the shelf to let my mind wander off along a slumbering journey about home, or what The County might be saying to me, only to be yanked back to the frightening realisation that the demons might let slip my age if slumber became too deep. It was an irrational fear, the men in the 35th 'A' Company would never let me down but I still didn't want to be found out. If I was going to die, I wanted to be regarded by those around me as a man, not a boy. The other thing that occupied my thoughts was the ridiculous shame of wetting the bed – again irrational and not that I had ever done such a thing. But it was a risk I would rather not take, perhaps because it was once a licence to 'be walked to the gate' or get kicked out of the army back home. What an irony that was: 'And they turned out to be the lucky feckers that didn't end up here,' I thought to myself as I lay there; awake and cold; wondering what might happen tomorrow.

When I was younger the Picture House had been my refuge and back in Ireland, I could imagine that my brothers and the Dolly Dolan would be heading out that Sunday evening to again be inspired by the heroes of film which would no doubt promote for them fulfilling dreams about some heroic deed that would surely impress everyone in the town. There was no such inspiration or retreats in the reality of The Congo war, something the films had never told us about.

I convinced myself that maybe Pakie Monahan and Dowler were right and we would be freed in the morning, so perhaps I should look forward to a cheery dream about my future, about emigrating to London maybe, but most likely it will be another night of tossing and turning with just occasional interruptions from the ever-present demons. If I'm lucky, I thought, this could be a night when

I will only hear the distracting sounds of a distant fart or a sudden pig-like snore to keep me amused.

The sun rose predictably by Swahili time at 0600 the next morning. First up, as usual was the platoon sergeant John Monahan; inspection would be an hour later. Having spent the last month in the Leopold's storeroom it was now spotless. The floors had been sterilised and every object was rigidly in place, the hallmarks of a military cleaning regime that every soldier has drummed into him during basic training. I didn't appreciate it back then but I appreciated it now, taking care of a tiny bit of space that was still ours, giving us that little bit of pride we all need to keep going.

'It's as clean as Ajax!' as Pakie described it: all inspected three times a day by our officers, keen to maintain some semblance of discipline and morale despite our lowly status as prisoners of war. If our officers found any dirt or even discovered us languishing around we could still be put on a charge, not that it seemed to matter when compared to other outcomes we were facing.

We had no bedding to inspect, just the empty shelves we had laid on during the night, along with our only personal possession, a neatly arranged basic wash-kit. As expected, John Monahan did his inspection promptly at 0630, but this morning he was not embarking on his normal scrutinising routine:

'We have a formal parade at 1100 hours this morning lads,' he announced, with a notable intensity in his commands. 'We have a VIP visitor inspecting us, the head of the Katangan independence movement, Moise Tshombie.'

'Fuckin hell!' Dowler blurted out accidentally as we were all 'standing-to' beside the shelves. Luckily, John Monahan ignored him.

'The inspection will take place outside the front of the prison and we will line up in platoon order,' Monahan continued. 'We'll be ready to take our positions at 1040 hours.'

Moise Tshombie was the self proclaimed president of the breakaway province of Katanga. He was also the leader of the Katangan gendarmerie and mercenary units that were keeping us captive. Although like most politicians he would have denied any involvement, he had the ultimate authority on whether we lived or died and we knew he could have us shot at any time. He had been directly implicated in the execution of The Congo's first elected prime minister Patrice Lumumba just a year beforehand and it was widely believed that he personally gave the order for mercenaries to shoot.

We discussed amongst ourselves what Tshombie's visit could mean. Pakie Monahan still seemed convinced that we would be set free:

'They don't want to keep us here,' he cited, 'and if their big president is coming, he will only want to be associated with good news.'

We knew however that the visit could mean anything; a PR photo opportunity, a chance to send a warning back to the UN or a final chance for us to avoid the firing squad. Either way, this could be the most important day of our lives.

With such weighty possibilities, I took my turn in the bathroom for my morning shave with renewed urgency, a sense of hope that I had not known since becoming a prisoner. If we could make the right impression on Tshombie, let him see that we are good people, then he may decide to release us, I considered.

First in the bathroom were our officers, once so dominant and masterly back in Ireland but now reduced to using the same bathrooms as us. I never had much time for officers during basic training, the way they shouted at people and never said thank you. In the Athlone barracks we used to mimic the way they would march stiffly around the barrack square, with a headmasterly gait and a short wooden cane held up under their arm. Hegarty, my fellow trainee in Athlone, would have commented that 'it wasn't the canes they had under their arms that made officers turn into bastards, it was the canes they had stuck up their own arses!' I laughed as I remembered the way he would impudently walk around with his arse held-in tightly, like someone who has the runs breathlessly hurrying for the nearest bush. Hegarty was also here in Jadotville but being in a different platoon he was in a different room of the hotel, so I had not seen him since we had become prisoners.

But these officers in charge of us in Jadotville were different, and I was glad to let them go in front of me to use the bathroom, they had earned our respect as brave soldiers, fighting in the same trenches and had survived on the same rations during the siege. There were however growing rumours that whilst the officers in Jadotville had behaved with honour, the same could not be said of those that had sent us here in the first place. In the queue for the bathroom some were asking why those back in Elizabethville had ignored the obvious intelligence that the residents of Jadotville were hostile to the UN, and that a single company of men was effectively abandoned in an area of military inferiority given that Jadotville was the base for the pro-Katangan mercenary forces. It was also causing some discontent to some that there were no attempts to re-enforce or re-supply us during the siege. On hearing some of the complaints I had a flashback to being back in the trench and remember being told: 'Elizabethville is sending re-enforcements,' but none arrived; then two days later 'Elizabethville will try again to re-supply us' again none arrived. Then the most morale crushing of all: 'we have repeatedly asked for re-enforcements and supplies but Elizabethville is no longer responding to their radios – we have been abandoned'.

I immediately became concerned, not for what had happened in the past but because of my recollection of how authority tended to work back in Athlone, that officers would typically sweep things under the carpet. Many likened it to the heirarchy of the Catholic Church that disclosed or hid information according to its own needs knowing that the chain of command was its ultimate protection. Like some churchmen, there were some officers back in Athlone who only liked to make themselves look good and play power games that supported their next promotion. If the officers back in Elizabethville were at fault, I knew they would have been busy covering their tracks, hiding any trace of their wrongdoings in Jadotville during the last month whilst we were here in prison. The Irish state had not been involved in any war since the Irish republic gained its independence in 1921 and Jadotville was the first time that the military of the Republic were involved in an armed battle since that time. Having no experience of war, I wondered how they would react. Although many young Irishmen signed up independently with the allies to fight Nazi Germany, the Irish government and its army were officially neutral. But, as we had discussed back in the Athlone barracks, you wouldn't have believed it had you heard some of the officers claims, full of hyperbolic talk about what should be done and how brave they would have been had they been involved. As every soldier knows, there is nothing as destructive as an armchair general and those officers in Elizabethville being implicated in our deployment may prefer that we don't get to tell our story of what really happened.

As I stood in the doorway of the bathroom I watched the officers of 'A' Company in front of me shaving, like a teenager watches his father, careful to mimic the actions of a grown man. It wasn't just us teenagers that could have been the victims of some image conscious major or colonel, after all 'we were but to do or die', but the officers in front of me had also been abandoned. Being in prison had already effectively stripped them of their officer rank but their bare chests also took away any pretext of seniority. Strangely I felt sorry for them. Underneath their officer caps and more important looking uniforms they too had thin pale bodies and probably, like me, none had eaten properly since the start of the siege. Once the officers had finished shaving, they quickly mopped away unruly blobs of shaving lather and dressed themselves, keen to spend as little time as possible in the humbling prison washroom where the pretence of their authority was so noticeable. It reminded me of the old adage I had read back in Athlone: that every military career eventually ends in failure, now that they too had seemingly become victims of some dubious superior authority.

Despite having read so much about military justice, I remained optimistic. I didn't want a military career anyway and I satisfied myself in the knowledge that our government, the Irish state and the Irish people we were representing, would be the final judge when the truth eventually comes out.

I peered into the cracked and rusting mirror to begin my shave. For the first time since becoming a prisoner, it suddenly hit me; I could barely recognise myself. Where I once saw the image of Johnny Cash slicking back his hair, I now saw a gaunt figure with deep, dark-ringed eyes, an angular unnourished face and a sallow complexion the colour of a freshly peeled spud.

The County would have noted that I was like Oscar Wilde's character Dorian Gray; although young on the outside, the image seen in the reflection of the mirror as hideous as the sins that I had witnessed. I imagined what the Dolly would have said had he looked at the same image:

'Jaysus Mickey! Ya look as if ye've seen a ghost!'

I had indeed seen a ghost but I was sure it was the same 'me' I was looking at.

Just like the officers before me, I hurriedly finished up in the bathroom and returned to the old-store-room, where the conversation had been taken over by what the armchair generals may be conspiring. It seemed so ironic that we were about to be paraded before the notorious leader of our enemy and we were more worried about what our own officers back in Elizabethville were plotting. It made Tshombie's visit even more important, we really needed something miraculous to happen to get us out of here.

As we stood to attention outside Leopold's, the motorcade finally arrived like a presidential procession with the prominent red croisettes of the Katangan flag fluttering from each corner of Tshombie's black limousine. Elsewhere in this diverse province of Katanga he could have been loudly applauded and cheered, but in other areas he would have been killed like a rat within a moment. As such, the motorcade was also flanked by heavily armed military vehicles manned almost exclusively by white soldiers, either ex-Belgian paratroopers or hired mercenaries.

We stood motionless as the motorcade pulled alongside as a huddle of journalists and photographers made a final jostle for the best vantage point to capture the right photo for their readers back in Europe. The pictures would make front page stories back on the covers of many popular broadsheets in Brussels, London and Paris where the old colonial supporters would manipulate the scoop to covertly support the principle of continuing white rule in Katanga. The combined power of the mining companies, banks and newspaper editors in reality found all this talk of self-determination tiresome when confronted with the reality of a loss of earnings. Tshombie was regarded as a white man in black skin by most Congolese, a puppet leader with a lavish lifestyle financed by the mining companies. He was known as someone who would continue to allow the colonial conglomerates to carry on exploiting the riches of The Congo under the façade of a symbolically significant black leader.

As the motorcade stopped, the chauffer jumped out to open the limousine door for his president, but Tshombie took a little time to stir from his seat as if to build up the anticipation of a grand ceremony among his subjects and captives. When he did finally emerge, I immediately noticed he was wearing white gloves, the ultimate sign in colonial Africa that a black man had been accepted by the great white hunters but also an indication that he too no longer considered himself black. Some Jadotville locals clapped and cheered his arrival, chanting 'Tshombie,' the colour of his skin clearly no longer an issue for them as it was their interests he was protecting. It was as if they didn't mind accepting one or two native Africans as long as they assisted them in the subjugation of the majority. Tshombie was also trapped in the same ideology. If he did not support this enclave of white colonial power, then without the emperor's clothes, he and his family would be seen for what they were: black African human beings, and in this part of the world that was considered vastly inferior to whites. He had no choice: for his and his family's sake, he needed to carry on pretending to be a white man.

He then proceeded to remove the gloves as one would imagine royalty, slowly loosening each finger with the dexterity of a Paris showgirl, before laying them on the arm of his ingratiating chauffer. This visit was indeed a PR show for the assembled press and we were just useful props.

The inspection from Tshombie amounted to a smiling saunter along the front row, with not a moment of eye contact except with the camera lenses of the assembled press. Behind him however, was the piercing eagle-like eyes and darting stares of the infamous head of the Katangan gendarmerie Colonel Muke, easily identifiable from his nickname – Old Stoneface. This was the man who had reportedly led his police militia army to clear out Baluba villages with a barbarity that is usually the preserve of wild jungle animals. It wasn't just his appearance that gave away his identity, he also wore four strips of gold braid on his shoulders indicating his rank as a colonel and he was one of the few Congolese nationals to be wearing decent military boots, an honour restricted solely to a handful of commissioned black officers.

His face was as severe as his name suggested – pronounced cheekbones and a taut jawline rigidly keeping every feature motionless. His tightly pursed lips and a narrow frown suggested that today he was feeling particularly bitter. It was only later that we found out why.

Tshombie stood up on the makeshift speakers' platform comprising of a few sturdy boxes, smiling as he opened his address in heavily accented English.

> Soldiers representing the United Nations, you are here because your organisation has brought conflict to the town of Jadotville in the independent state of Katanga, which we, its citizens wish to defend ... I will do everything in my power to have you treated well as prisoners and hopefully your leaders will commit to ending their offensive in Katanga and let life here return to normal, else it will end with severe consequences.

We all knew exactly what those consequences could be. Tshombie continued:

> I ask the gentlemen of the news agencies assembled here to join with me to ask the UN authorities to stop their offensive against us, to let our own loyal police service administer justice here in the democracy of Katanga. The armed campaign launched by the UN will only lead to more bloodshed especially if UN soldiers continue to carry out atrocities against our innocent people as has recently taken place in Elizabethville.

'What did he mean by that?' whispered Dowler next to me as Tshombie continued speaking:

> We are taking all steps to secure a peace in Katanga that respects our rights as a new independent state, which refuses to be ruled by communist rebels. We have pledged to treat our prisoners well and ask the UN to do the same. As a gesture of goodwill, I have made arrangements with the Red Cross for

you to send and receive letters from your families back in Ireland.

Prompted by Old Stoneface raising his hands to clap, Tshombie stood waiting for some applause from us for his apparent generosity; though none materialised. This was the same leader who stopped our letters and mail being delivered and we were not about to start thanking him for allowing it through. It was a very typical colonial strategy of stealing people's possessions, then at the same time making them totally reliant on the perpetrators to give them back.

While none of us joined in the clapping, receiving post was the best piece of news we had heard in the last month, definitely worth the wash and shave that morning, I considered. Everything else in Tshombie's speech was only meant as a rallying call for Katangan independence supporters and intended for the newspaper columns of colonial Europe.

The entourage shook hands with some of the mercenary officers, then posed for a few more photos and left as quickly as they arrived, some of the photographers chasing after the limousine with flashing lenses.

Our company sergeant Prendergast then told us to stand down and to return to our accommodation. The journalists too prepared to depart from Jadotville, they had done their job in this war and got their story, they could return home. It all seemed very unfair, we had done our job too but we were heading back to prison and the confines of the old store-room. We knew that we were no longer regarded as free civilians but it almost felt that we were no longer considered human.

In the afternoon, the efficiency of the prison grapevine went into overdrive: as most of Tshombie's speech referred to recent events which we had no idea about. Much of what he said seemed to emotionally inspire his entourage as Tshombie seemed to be pleading for peace. Dowler however wasn't fooled by his performance saying that they were crocodile tears and that 'the lump in his throat wasn't as big as the one the UMHK were putting in his wallet.'

But what did Tshombie mean by the atrocities taking place in Elizabethville? Our answer came from a journalist who had explained what happened to one of our officers while Tshombie was saying his farewells.

An 'incident', he described, had taken place back in Elizabethville involving a unit of UN soldiers from India as Operation *Morthor*, which had sparked the Jadotville siege, continued to cause fighting. We knew the Indian unit in question from conducting joint UN patrols and manning security barriers, and they would often ask us to join them in a game of cricket, although none of us had even held a cricket bat before.

We all commented that you couldn't wish to meet nicer people than the Hindus, as we called them, as we worked with them at the refugee camp in Elizabethville before the siege when we first arrived. But their pleasant characters allegedly changed suddenly when one of their brothers was attacked and killed by members of Muke's Gendarmerie. The story we heard was that the unit sought out the three gendarmes responsible for the murder by asking local villagers, eventually finding them hiding out in a recently burned out Baluba village. Reportedly, the Hindus first of all beat up the accused men, then brought them back to their HQ, the central Post Office building in Elizabethville. As the three gendarmes were dragged through the UN security checkpoint, the Swedish guards apparently commented that they were still being kicked and punched repeatedly, whilst crying and begging for forgiveness. The Swedes knew they could not be helped and if they tried to intervene they would most likely have been killed themselves.

The three gendarmes had become infamous around Elizabethville and known as the butcher, the baker and the candlestick maker for the way in which they hacked, roasted and set light to their victims. Apparently, like me they were only teenagers, caught up in tit-for-tat brutality between their tribes. After being captured, we then heard that the three were taken by the Hindus to the roof of the PO building, which had four floors, where their legs and arms were smashed with the FN rifle butts, the cracking of bones clearly audible back at the Swedish checkpoint. They were then told to clamber off the edge off the roof, like a degraded sailor has to walk the plank, their remaining limbs breaking loudly on impact with the ground. Apparently, it took them three days to die, their faint whimpers eventually giving way to what must have been a happy release of death. Those around the PO building who apparently witnessed the event could clearly hear the dying men and felt they had to intervene so the Swedes begged the Indian commanding officer,

'Can we at least give them some water?' they apparently asked.

But they were told that it was impossible; the Indian officer pointing towards the shut front doors of the PO building, where two Indian UN soldiers stood guard, their guns crossed clearly indicating that no-one was allowed to enter.

'No-one will be allowed to go beyond those doors,' apparently insisted the Indian NCO in charge, intensely mindful of the sensitivities of the brotherhood custom. 'If you want your men to live, please do not stop them.'

The reporter then commented that one of the Swedes he interviewed noted, 'Oh the cries of the poor bastards, as they lay their dying all that time, those cries will always haunt me.'

'Jaysus, was it any wonder Old Stoneface had a face like thunder!' noted Pakie Monahan.

More immediately, as any prisoner of war is acutely aware, if atrocities are committed by one side, even if it is only an allegation and unsubstantiated, they can just as easily be committed by the other side. Whilst we understood that it may have been a part of the Hindus culture of brotherhood to avenge a killing, we were also aware that it was in the culture of The Congo tribes to avenge a tribal death by cannibalism. We even heard that the graves of dead enemies would be dug up by warring tribes as part of the cannibalism ritual to release the spirit of bereavement. Throughout central Africa it was believed that only by eating the bodies of their adversaries was sufficient for revenge allowing the spirit of death to be set free.

Apparently, the journalist had also reported that the conflict back in Elizabethville was confined to a few violent incidents such as what happened with the Hindus but in total 11 UN soldiers including one Irish UN soldier had been killed. His name was Pte Gaffney who some in 'A' Company remembered as a fine fella from back home. As many as 50 members of the Katangan gendarmerie had also been killed in Elizabethville but the battles had been contained within a few hours. The battles in and around Elizabethville were over relatively quickly and did not get drawn out for five days as had happened during the Jadotville offensive. Apparently the last thing the reporter said to our officer was that the Katanga gendarmerie and mercenaries were still disbelieving that they had lost maybe 300 dead in Jadotville whilst all of 'A' Company was still alive. But there was still doubt as to how many of us would survive prison as we were the only POWs held by the Katangan independence army, who were now using their independence claim as a condition of our continued survival.

As Tshombie had promised us; a bag of mail was delivered from the Red Cross and my heart thumped as I was handed four neatly folded envelopes officially addressed to:

Pte Michael Greene 35th 'A' Company UNOC, The Congo,

I knew immediately they were from my mother as soon I saw the three Irish postage stamps on the front. I noted that the letters were written on Maggie Canavan's most expensive paper: a 'Basildon Bond' writing pad, almost as if the better quality paper would have more chance of reaching its intended recipient. The letters had already been opened, we presumed by Tshombie's censors but luckily none of the contents of my letters had been blackened out as some in the store-room were complaining of. 'So perhaps the Basildon Bond had worked!' I joked.

The letters were written about a week apart over the last four weeks. As I deliberately slowly read through them, each sounded more and more desperate which was understandable given what they were being told about our situation. First they had read on the front page of all the newspapers that we had been massacred during the siege by the fouga jet fighter who had strafed our positions:

FIVE IRISH SOLDIERS KILLED

Irish Independent, Friday 15 September

The next day came the even more chilling estimate.

REPORTS OF 57 DEAD UNCONFIRMED

> 'the battle of Jadotville, where the 35th 'A' Company is besieged is still raging on with just a few holding out to the last man with re-enforcements and supplies unable to break through.'
>
> Irish Independent, Saturday 16 September

None of the people at home were told the names of those who had been supposedly killed, each speculating that it must be their son, husband or father. My mother narrated in her letters that she had travelled down to Athlone every day to await news, but none came until a few days after the siege ended when it was announced that a miracle had happened and we had all survived. Apparently the mixup was caused by the fouga jet pilot who had spotted 57 white body bags lined up outside our trenches and presumed they were carrying our dead. They were in-fact pillow cases packed with our kits, which we kept outside the trench to avoid them being saturated on the piss-soaked earth. My mother then explained that she had arranged for a bereavement mass to be said for me and Dag Hammarskjöld at St. Peter's in Edgeworthstown but had written another letter to me anyway in the hope that God in his mercy had been protecting me and that I hadn't been killed.

I read another letter that she must have written just a few days later where she explained the papers had announced that we were presumed alive although they could not establish yet if the wounded would pull through. Any immediate relief for my mother was abruptly ended when she was told that I was a POW, and they had no idea how long we would remain in prison or whether we would be executed. I could sense the roller-coaster of emotions she must have been going through with desperate sentences like: 'Please let us know that you are alive and well Mickey?' 'We are all praying for you every day at mass.' And the simple but most heart-rending of all: 'we are desperately missing you Micky, please God ye'll be home soon. With much love, Mum, Dad and Phillip.'

I knew she would have held the same letter up and given it a kiss, just as she always did when she sent a letter to my sisters in England, so I held up the same Basildon bond paper to my face trying to gain any familiar scent of her motherly warmth that could provide a release from this god-forsaken place. I nosed around each corner of the letters for a faintest hint of soap, or her perfume, or even the smokey odour of burning turf from our open hearth, anything that would provide a sensation of her love or a reminder of home; but there was nothing.

I immediately started to write a return letter on one of the writing pads provided by the Red Cross. I didn't know what to write as I didn't want to worry her with any more talk of war, bombs and killing. We had also been told by the mercenaries that anything we wrote would be censored and not to include any derogatory remarks about our living conditions or negative comments about the Katangan independence movement.

Dear Mam and Dad

> *Hope this letter finds ye all well. All is well here in The Congo although as ye may have heard we got into a little bit of trouble a couple of weeks back here in Jadotville. It's all sorting itself out now*

though and we are all looking forward to being home for Christmas.

But that was it, I could think of nothing else but thankfully my writing block was interrupted by Dowler:

'What are ya doin?' he asked.

'What do ya think I'm doing' I replied, 'I'm writing a letter home,'

'There's no point in doin that,' he quickly retorted 'we'll be home before the letter gets there, and if them Belgian censors get hold of it, they'll cut out more holes than ye get in a piece of cheese, they're like feckin mice. What are ya writing anyway?'

'Ah just the usual old bollocks,' I replied. 'The weather is lovely here', 'looking forward to Christmas with all of ye', 'tell everyone I was asking for them,' that sort of thing.'

'Well, whatever ya do,' Dowler insisted 'don't be feckin tellin them what them Hindus did.'

'I don't think I will ever tell anyone about that Sean.' I replied mournfully.

I finished up the letter with some lines that I knew would give my mother some comfort.

The food here is grand ... and we say mass everyday, we have our own company priest. Good bye and God Bless. Mickey

As I licked the envelope, I thought again about home. I could imagine my brothers and the Dolly Dolan calling me a 'feckin eejit' for volunteering for The Congo. 'Oh yeah,' they would be saying, 'he thought he was the big fella, and him just a young gosson going off to a war in Africa!' 'And the silly fecker barely out of short-trousers!'

The four letters from home were not only my connection back to my family, they were the only thing I could remember about a normal human existence, my only hope and my sanity; so I read them every chance I had: when I got up in the morning, when I came back from the bathroom, after each meal; then once more in the evening, before the sun-light was extinguished by the enveloping darkness of the long Congolese nights. Each time I read the letters it conjured up different images of home and without having any other books available to read, it was also the only stimulation I had. The County used to say to me that 'without books, God is silent, justice dormant, natural science is at a stand, philosophy lame and letters dumb'.* These letters from my mother provided everything I could have hoped for from any novel.

When I was in basic training back in Athlone I used to while away my free-time reading books, journals, diaries and manuscripts about war as the army libraries didn't seem to include any other material. I still treasured the romantic images of the Hollywood films, but the books had taught me more about the real history of warfare. Most of the others recruits went to the nearest Pub or wet-canteen as we called them, but I was always concerned that I would give away my age with some adolescent drunken rambling or just be sick from drinking pints of stout. So instead, I became a bit of an expert about World War One, a war that cost so many Irish lives in the mud and misery of the trenches. It was also the trenches we had built in Jadotville that we belived had saved our lives. Although they were only a few feet deep, 'more like shallow graves,' as Pakie

* Thomas Bartholm, 1672

jokingly described them, they had protected us from the crossfire and bombs overhead which had accounted for so many enemy forces. But the trenches were wretched nonetheless, baking-hot during the day and freezing at night; damp, dirty and filled with a rotten stench, just as I had read about in the Flanders field 40 years earlier.

But the '60s was supposed to be an era of precision warfare, whereby weapons could be directly targeted at enemy forces, it was not supposed to be fought out in trenches with soldiers slugging it out over a few feet of ground like in World War One. Many of the youthful Tommies back then were like me, just young boy soldiers who thought they knew everything about war but in reality knew nothing, cheerfully volunteering alongside their PALS whilst holding out their forged birth certificates.

Just as my mother had been lining up outside the barracks in Athlone for news in October 1961, back in 1915, mothers queued outside the telegram shop – Hughes' in Longford to hear whether their boys had survived. It seemed that the bleak history of WWI had repeated itself.

When I joined the army, I had been so full of youthful enthusiasm and could remember very clearly being so nervous about signing up on my very first day. 'They're bound to find out I'm only 15' I must have said to myself at least five times that morning. I wondered how things might have turned out had I been rejected for being too young, but remembered my pride and relief at being given my own army serial number Pte Greene: 809385. I thought about the months I spent in basic training, the comraderie that you never abandon a fellow soldier and how we had built ourselves up at the prospect of coming out to The Congo becoming intoxicated with those thoughts of duty and honour. It allowed me to grow up very quickly, but, as I reflected on the siege and the battle of Jadotville I knew that there were no films or books I could have read nor any amount of training that could have prepared me for war. Every battle is different and all plans abruptly change once an enemy has been engaged. A soldier has to immediately react to the situation or most likely he will be killed. All of Private Fortescue's procedures, duty rotas and even time itself becomes disorderly. And, as anyone who has been drawn into active combat can testify: the shiny buttons, square bashing and tying your boots up to the right height are all great until the bullets start flying, people are being killed and you're lying down in your own piss and vomit, outnumbered twenty to one.

I lay back on my shelf and took another puff of my cigarette, it was like that idealic life back in Athlone all happened just yesterday: but, 'non, je ne regrette rien' [no, I regret nothing] I muttered to myself.

CHAPTER FOUR

Mammy's little soldier

Date: – April 1959
Age: 15 years and 1 month
Signing up

MY VOICE HAD BROKEN ABOUT eight months before so I was aware that I had to avoid any high pitched intrusions. I was wearing the Sunday best suit I shared with my brothers, The County's Longford GAA tie, and I had bought a new white shirt with my previous week's wages, completing my older man's attire. My parents thought I was just applying for a job as a barman at a hotel and needed to look smart, they had no idea I was trying to join the army. My mother would never have allowed it and I was still young enough for a good clip round the ear. But I reasoned it would be The County who would absorb my mother's wrath and would hopefully have pacified her before I returned home in three months time after I had completed basic training. After that, it would be too late for them to do anything – I would be a regular soldier.

I had nothing to lose, even if the army figured out I had just turned 15, I may have to carry on working in a bar but I could still use the new shirt for mass on a Sunday. With polished shoes and new laces I strode up to the entrance gate of Mullingar barracks.

'I have come to join the army today, will ye tell me where to go?' I questioned in my deepest manly tone.

The guard at the gate seemed unaware of anything too suspicious in my request. He was carrying a gun and dressed in army uniform with 'MP' written on his helmet and on his left arm.

Well it's too late to join today,' he replied 'the offices are closed on a Wednesday afternoon. But if ya head off to that billet over behind the main barracks, ye can sleep there for the night and we'll take ya down to Athlone tomorrow morning to be enrolled in the recruiting company.'

He was polite and didn't seem that much older than me.

I was emboldened: 'just behind this block here?' I affirmed, having already begun walking.

'That's right, there are plenty of beds in the dormitory with blankets and everything ya need down in the store cupboard at the end, the washrooms are just behind them. There will be a bus here at 0830 hours which will take ye to Athlone, they'll let ya know where the offices are when ya get there. There will be a breakfast beyond in the canteen from 0600, tell them you're a new recruit.'

'Tanks a million,' I acknowledged as I headed off for my first night in army accommodation.

In the dormitory, I sat on the bed I had just made up, I didn't know which one to choose as there were 40 beds, so settled for one in the middle, my only criteria being to keep away from doors and windows to avoid draughts. The dorm had been little used since the last British garrisons left Ireland in 1923, the Irish army being far too small to make use of all the buildings they left behind. The facilities had however been kept immaculately, not a cobweb or a speck of dirt in sight and in such a big room I wondered how they cleaned the ceiling which was about 20 foot high. By my calculations you could fit our whole house into it about four times, but there was only me staying here. I had never had so much room to myself, I had shared a room with three brothers growing up and when I moved to Mullingar, my digs had been a small draughty bedroom, with the noise of the pub in the background. This place seemed haunted by space and silence.

I walked through to the washroom, noticing the echo of my every step and like the dormitory it seemed vast and empty with the cold off-white tiles adding to the eerie stillness. I thought it would have been a perfect setting for a Hitchcock thriller, like *Dial M for Murder* when the calculating Tony Windace tries to kill his wife Margot. The haunting atmosphere made me uneasy and I was the only person here. Thank god it would be only for one night.

I was up and ready to catch the bus to Athlone as soon as the sun broke which was at about 0430 the next morning. I hardly slept a wink and was first in the canteen for breakfast at 0600 as the sentry had told me. I had prepared my responses in case anyone asked me: 'I'm a new recruit,' or 'I am just joining the army today,' or 'the sentry told me to stay in the barracks and to wait for the army transport to Athlone'. Luckily no-one asked, in-fact no-one even talked to me, there was no 'good morning,' or 'nice day?' – nothing. Back in Edgeworthstown everyone spoke to each other but here the people, the buildings, everything seemed cold and impersonal.

I arrived into Athlone just before ten and headed straight for the recruiting office. The secretary handed me a form to fill in and a pencil. I started to fill in the spaces: Name: Michael Greene. Age: 18. Date of Birth: 09.03.41. Home Address: Railway crossing house,

Terenare, Edgeworthstown, Co. Longford. I confidently handed back the form and offered her a copy of my birth certificate to which I had made a minor modification; I had changed my date of birth from 1944 to 1941. I watched her every eye movement as she jotted down a few particulars but she made no remarks. She handed back my birth certificate without even a glance at it.

'I don't need to see that' she said. 'You need to go to the sanatorium for a medical and a hair cut, take this form with you, then come back here.'

'I will surely, tanks a million,' I said.

Everyone had to have the same haircut, short back and sides, although they left it a bit longer on top. Up until that point The County had always cut my hair, but he would only trim off a few curls so that I didn't look like Shirley Temple.

Being that this was the first time my hair was going to be cut properly, I imagined how I would look, 'perhaps like Burt Lancaster in *From Here to Eternity* I hoped, or better still like John Wayne in *Sands of Iwo Jima*. My ambitions of looking like a matinee film idol posing in my army uniform for a soft focus photograph were, however, short lived.

'We call it a regulation short back and sides,' said the barber. 'In the barracks they call it a scalping!' He proceeded to start shaving the side of my head.

Within barely a minute, I couldn't believe what was staring back at me in the mirror. My ears looked enormous and my small pale head looked as if it had never seen the sun. My nervous silence could not be held back any longer. 'Feckin hell' I belted out, looking down at the carpet of blonde curls lying on the floor, 'one minute I have a big warm woolly head of hair and the next minute

I look as if I have just came out of the sheep sheering pen, all skinny, cold and pink!'

'It's just a regulation short, back and sides,' repeated the barber impassively.

This is feckin terrible I thought, I won't be able to show my face in Edgeworthstown for months.

'Would you like to buy some Brylcreem?' said the barber, 'It's just water and beeswax and it gives your hair a gloss,' he paused, 'Elvis uses it.'

Those were the three magic words and despite not wanting to have a gloss or shine for my pale pink head, I bought my first tub of Brylcreem.

'I'll be seein ya in a month,' said the barber as I stood down from the stool.

'But sher, a month is that all? They'll be barely bristles by then!' I appealed to the expressionless barber.

'In the recruiting company you arc required to have a haircut every four weeks,' he insisted, 'that's what the rule book says.'

Next came the medical. I was to see Doctor Gohan at 1100. I didn't know it at the time but Dr Gohan was infamous in Athlone barracks as a fiery, belligerent and much feared doctor. Some joked that when he joined the army he applied to be a docker, but they mis-heard him and made him a doctor. Many would later impersonate him when they reported sick:

'Get out of my office, you lazy malingerer! Don't be wasting my fecking time! Get out!'

Most wouldn't even bother to report sick when he was the duty doctor as more often than not they just got a bollocking. The best you could expect, they said, was to get 'MD' (Medicine and Duty), as he would never give what they were looking for, i.e. 'ED' (Excused Duty).

He looked about 45 and had seemingly escaped having the regulation haircut, with a thick mop of red hair, overhanging eye-brows and a suspicious deep-set frown.

'Take your shirt off and stand over there against the wall,' he said firmly, 'I need to measure how tall you are.'

I stood as tall as possible, straining my neck to get the most height.

'You're 5 foot 2½,' he said, '5 foot 2 is the minimum you know, now hold out your tongue.'

As he pushed a flat wooden spoon inside, he said, 'say ahh.'

'Ahhh!'

'No problem there,' he said.

He then reached for his stethoscope and listened to my quickened heart.

He made no comment.

I then stood on the weighing scales, similar to those used in the greengrocers where my mother bought vegetables, only bigger.

'You're 8 stone 4 pounds,' he said. 'Now read those letters on the wall.'

'T, Z, R, P,' I recited, 'is that right?' I asked seeking some re-assurance.

'Right.' he responded, as he began looking inside my newly exposed ears.

Finally, he told me to take my pants down. It was an uncomfortable few moments which seemed like minutes: cold implements, poking around.

'Cough please,' he said. I didn't want to think about it.

'If I can just get through this I will be home and dry, I don't want to sign up for the full pension, just three years, then I'll be off to London.' I contemplated.

'Fine,' he said. 'Get dressed, you're in fine fettle.'

I returned across the parade ground to the recruitment office with a completed medical certificate, with the breeze lapping around my freezing pink head and my ears feeling almost luminous.

I was then shown in to see the company sergeant or C.S. Purcell.

'I see you are from Edgeworthstown, Michael?' he enquired politely, 'I was stationed at the Manor House during the Emergency,' he recalled.

The Manor House was a big stately home that had been built by the Edgeworth family in the 1670s, the family that gave the town its name. It had now been acquired by the Sisters of Mercy and was being used as an old people's home.

'Yes I was stationed there for three years,' he went on, 'and I have a sister-in-law that lives in Ardagh, do you know it?'

'Oh feckin bollocks!' I thought. I knew the place and the family well, it was barely a mile from our house.

'I have heard of it, but don't know it that well,' I answered vaguely. 'I've been living in Mullingar for a while now.'

I was now ashen-faced with unease as I sensed suspicion in everything I was being asked. My mother would have remarked that I was like a hen with an egg, as I shifted my stance uncomfortably from foot to foot.

'I think I knew your father,' he then paused without clarifying.

'Oh Jaysus that's it,' I thought, 'everyone knows The County,' as my heart started to beat faster. 'He's bound to know, or knows someone that knows, that The County does not have an 18 year old son, even my older brother Kevin was only 16.'

'Are you sure you're 18?' he finally asked.

'I am sure, yes sir. I was born on the ninth of March, 1941. I was 18 two weeks ago.' I blurted all the details out as quickly as possible. My heart was now racing. He could easily say that he didn't believe me, in which case I would offer him my amended birth certificate. Or he might tell me that he needed to check my age with people he knew in Edgeworthstown. And besides, I thought, they have to allow me to join now, I've already had my head shaved in the regulation short, back and fecking sides, if I'm sent back to Edgeworthstown, Franco and the Dolly Dolan will piss themselves and I'll have to buy a wig!

'OK Michael,' he said, 'you will be assigned to the ordnance division here in Athlone, you will need to pass basic training which will take 13 weeks. This will start as soon as we have a full training platoon. You report to Corporal Scully in 'A' block after you have picked up your uniform from stores. You will be billeted there until you complete basic training and then you will join the 6th West Battalion here in Athlone. Read this form, it is a three year contract, and sign at the bottom.'

I hardly read the form, just glancing through for long enough so that he wouldn't be able to tell that I just wanted to get the fuck out of there, so I quickly scrawled my signature.

'Welcome to the army, you're now Private Greene,' confirmed CS Purcell, the pleasantries of calling me Michael now done away with, 'your serial number is 809385.'

I strode out of the office, what a relief that was all over. 'Anyway,' I thought, 'now I am all signed up and ready to go.'

The 13 week course was to begin in two days' time, but first I had to get my new uniform. My measurements were all on my medical papers: waist: 26 inches, chest 34 inches, leg 27 ½ inches.

'Here you go,' said the quartermaster, handing me a green bundle of neatly-pressed army attire. The jacket and trousers were made of rough wool, the same material as my Sunday best suit I was wearing, only it was known in the army as bulls-wool.

'That's grand,' I said.

'What size shoe do you take?' questioned the quartermaster.

'Size 5 please,' I answered as he seemed to be taking an interest in my newly shorn head. He returned with the boots and a dark green helmet.

'Try that on,' he said, handing me the helmet.

My head could almost rattle inside this big green bowl they had given me, the peak falling down in front of my eyes.

'It would have fit me an hour ago when I had a load of hair,' I joked.

'Well that's the smallest we've got,' returned the quartermaster sternly, clearly not amused by my humour, 'ye'll have to make do.'

I arrived at A block complete with my uniform, boots and oversized helmet balanced on my arms in front me and was met by corporal Scully. I knew I was in the right place because everyone had bald pink heads after being 'scalped' with a sorrowful look in their eyes, like Victor Mature when he had his hair cut off in Cecile B. DeMille's *Samson and Delilah*.

'Hello, I am Michael Greene,' I announced to corporal Scully, 'here is my paperwork from the recruiting office, CS Purcell told me to report here for duty.'

Scully took the papers and corrected me. 'You are Private Greene 809385 reporting for duty ...Sir!' he emphasised.

'Sorry Sir,' I responded, 'I meant; report here for duty Sir!'

He then showed me to my billet area for the next three months, a single bedstead, with a three inch mattress, five blankets, two sheets and one pillowcase all folded up neatly at the bottom. I also had a tall wooden cupboard next to the metal head rest. Four feet either side of the bed were identical bedsteads, but with made-up beds. Corporal Scully then introduced me to their owners.

'On your left is Private Hegarty.'

'How are ya?' I offered politely. Hegarty said nothing.

'And on your right side,' continued Scully, 'is Private Havistock-Brown' who acknowledged me with a quick glance and a swallowed smile.

'This is Private Greene,' said Scully, and he then turned back to me. 'Basic training starts in two days' time, each morning there is an alarm at 0600 and at 0820 hours we assemble in the yard for PTs (Physical Training). Tomorrow we are going for a run so make sure you eat breakfast early, remembering not to eat too much, and are ready for roll call, a full kit and bed inspection at 0800.'

'Thank you, em Sir!' I remembered to say.

Scully returned down to his space at the end of the billet. As he was the corporal in charge of the billet he had three cupboards neatly arranged so that he had his own private area out of sight of the other beds.

I could sense the eyes of the platoon on me as I put down my bag and began to make up my bed as the others had done.

'It's a nice day?' I said.

'It's OK,' replied Havistock-Brown brusquely.

Hegarty still didn't say anything.

Opposite my bed, on the other side of the billet, was another recruit called Mick Tighe, who had already been given the nick-name of the Tiger. Just like the Dolly Dolan, if he wasn't chatting to someone he would be whistling and if he wasn't whistling he would be singing. The only difference was his repertoire of songs wasn't limited to the old Irish ballads like *Danny Boy.* The Tiger also knew rock'n roll greats like Elvis and Buddy Holly. The fella next to him was called Eddie Lynagh and must have noticed that I was looking around appearing a bit lost and opened a conversation.

'D'yis smoke Michael?' Lynagh asked.

'Aye, I do,' I responded, glad of the interaction: 'I smoke woodbines, they help me guard against throat-scratch,' I remarked remembering a slogan I had seen on a packet of 20 Pall Mall. 'Would ya like one?'

'Aye, that would be ggggrand,' replied Lynagh with a noticeable stammer.

We lit up the woodbines.

'Tanks,' said Lynagh, walking off, which disappointingly signalled the end of that discussion.

On the first morning I stood by my bed ready for the roll-call, yelled out by Scully in alphabetical order:

'Havistock-Brown!'

'Yes Sir!' he roared back.

I braced myself as he neared my name:

'Finlass!'

'Yes Sir!'

'Galvin!'

'Yes Sir!'

'Greene!'

'Yes Sir!' I roared, hoping it was not too loud or too quiet. However, that sort of thing didn't seem to bother Hegarty who was next:

'Hegarty!'

'Yes Sir!' he shouted back almost twice as loud as everyone else.

I could see Scully rolling his eyes as he continued with the roll-call.

Next was the kit inspection; and Scully continued to check everything around the bed and in every cabinet moving things ever-so-slightly to ensure everything was straight. He stopped in front of me and I was told in no uncertain terms that my bed had not been made up right, the buttons on my jacket were not clean and my boots were both filthy and not laced to the right height.

'This will not be tolerated during basic training!' declared Scully.

Having thought I had done everything correctly I asked Havistock-Brown what I was doing wrong. This time he was more communicative, and showed me how to make my buttons and boots shine perfectly.

'Jaysus, I thought they were shiny already' I said.

'Corporal Scully likes to be able to see his face in them,' replied a slightly embittered Havistock-Brown. His upper-class name was not the only thing that was unusual, he also had an English accent so I determined to ask him at some stage whether he had been to London, but right now I kept my attention on my buttons, which gave me the opportunity to keep the conversation going.

'But sher, it's hardly going to make a big difference how shiny me feckin buttons are, is it?' I inquired.

'Don't be saying that in front of Scully!' interrupted Havistock-Brown quickly, in a posh shrill voice, 'or he'll feckin tear the arse off you. And if he has to tell you about your buttons for a second time, he'll be roaring like a stuck pig, and then we will all get lectured on fucking Private Fortescue again.'

'Who's Fortescue?' I asked.

'Private Fortescue was the hero that kept the laces that tied the boots, that belonged to the soldier, who saved the Colonel, that held the fort, that secured the battle, that won the war,' recounted Havistock-Brown obviously having heard the tale of Private Fortescue regularly since he had enlisted a week before. 'If he comes back tomorrow and sees that your bed and buttons are not right again he'll tear a strip off you and tell you how your dirty buttons will lose the war for all of us.' Then he imitated Scully's rant, 'Every war is won or lost before it is ever fought!'

'Aye, he can be a real bbbastard!' interjected Lynagh in a typically short burst.

'This must be what it was like in Stalin's Gulags,' I thought. All of this standing to attention and 'yes Sir!' business also reminded me of my old teacher at school, Master Madden, who used to walk up and down the classroom clicking his heels, whilst talking to himself. This is where the poor old fella must have been trained, I concluded.

The next morning I made no mistakes, my buttons and boots were glistening. Everything was perfect, my mattress was neatly turned up with folded bedclothes and I had even found some spare cloth that I used as padding inside my helmet to stop it from rattling.

Scully did his inspection at 0800, and made no comments, I was delighted with myself.

Before parade, I strolled confidently into the bathroom eyeing myself in the mirror. Although I was only just 15 and 5 foot 2½ at a stretch, the uniform made me feel

Mammy's Little Soldier: Pte Michael Greene, 809385

at least 20 years old and a foot taller. I was no longer Mickey the Bun, I was now Private Michael Greene with an official sounding serial number: 809385. 'Look at me,' I said to myself, 'a grown man, already 15 years old with my own radio and wages that even The County himself would work for.'

As I rubbed some brylcreem onto my scalped head, I thought after all this basic training I'll let my hair grow back, and then I can comb it into a duck's arse and be a rock 'n' roll singer again. My eyes sparkled with mischief as my gamble of joining the army seemed to have paid off; ha, just a few of them Hail Mary's and all my fibs would be forgiven. I smiled and tilted my head down, like I'd seen in the photographs of the rock n roll stars, looked at my mirror image: 'Hello, I'm Johnny Cash,' I imitated in my deepest Arkansas drawl.

Over the next day, I began to speak more to Lynagh. I'm sure he would have been more chatty if he didn't have a stammer but his sentences seemed to end abruptly as he approached hard letters like B, M or G. He was constantly smoking a cigarette, providing a diversion to his evident speech impediment, but his friendly demeanour suggested he was eager to make friends.

The Tiger also joined in our conversation and told me that he had been working in England for Tarmacs on the building of the M1, which would be opening later that year, the first motorway in the UK. Like all work in England it seemed, he had earned great money – £6 a week, but he said he missed Ireland, the craic and wanted to move back home. He said he preferred the easy life, and that 'the hours over in England were long and the foremen were always on yer back'. He swapped stories of what life was like in England with Havistock-Brown. They would talk of the big Irish communities in Camden Town and Kilburn to which I just listened attentively. It surprised me to hear that Havistock-Brown was actually born in Ireland but had moved over to England when he was young, explaining his English accent, but had returned to Ireland a few years before with his parents. His first name was Eric but the other recruits on hearing his posh double barrelled sir-name had immediately given him the nickname of Cromwell. However, I just called him Havistock-Brown as I knew from The County that 'Cromwell' was not a nice thing to call anyone.

As days went by, Hegarty also joined in the conversations, telling us that he was a former boxer from Mullingar. I noted that he was smaller than me and wondered how he got through the medical as Dr. Gohan told me that 5 foot 2 was the minimum height, and he was barely 5 foot. Although he was small, he had big farmer's hands, and a hard mischievous look on his face like Babyface Nelson, the infamous Chicago gangster played by Mickey Rooney, a look that said he couldn't give a fuck what anyone thought.

In total there were 30 recruits in the training company, billeted in two equal groups of 15, in blocks A and B, and each morning we would meet for parade at 0820 before going onto various courses: guns, armoury, gymnastics, boxing, orienteering etc. As I looked around at the other recruits I thought 'surely, they can't be 18,' but as they didn't ask me about my age, I wasn't going to start questioning them. Many had probably joined for the same reason as me; to get money for a fare to England or beyond, apart from the Tiger and Havistock-Brown who for some reason that I couldn't fathom, had returned to Ireland. After the first week even Corporal Scully seemed to calm down and as long as we passed inspection and didn't wake him up at night he was OK.

During the first week of basic training, two young looking lads from B block were called out of the parade and I could see them 'being walked to the gate', the term we used for being kicked out. Their true age, we assumed, had been discovered and they had been discharged, they would have to save by some other means to get the fare to England.

The corporal in charge of B block was however becoming infamous among the recruits. His name was Corporal Haydn and we were told he would insist on checking that your finger nails were clean when he did his inspection. The Corporals took it in turns to conduct the drill so once every two days Haydn would be in command. Back in A block, Scully was strict but he was nothing compared to Haydn. Exercises with Haydn would have you clambering up and down rope ladders, crawling like a lizard on your stomach through muddy fields, and more press-ups than I could count. By the end of it I thought my thin adolescent arms would drop off. To those that couldn't keep up, he would come up with all sorts of petty punishments designed to be demeaning, like carrying your gun over your head while running around the parade ground. All the while he would just be yelping insults at you like a right feckin eejit.

It made me think how unfair the army hierarchy was that officers could order you about like a dog and the only thing you could say was 'yes Sir!' while they walked around, as Hegarty noted, 'with a cane up their arse.' We resented officers and the power they had which in times of war could mean that they could order you to your death. The Irish army followed the same hierarchical structure as all armies: officers were the highest ranking, followed by NCOs like CS Purcell and then the corporals like Haydn. If someone was above you in the pecking order, which in my case was everybody, they didn't ask you to do something they just shouted at you until you did it.

The entire billet including the washroom had to be cleaned every day by the two recruits who had been assigned billet duty which meant once every 15 days each recruit took it in turns to scrub the place spotless. They would then have to report to Corporal Scully that the facilities had all been finished to the required standard .....Sir!

Michael Greene, Danny Hegarty and Eddie Lynagh cleaning floors in the recruitment company. April 1959

I couldn't understand why everything had to be cleaned so meticulously and why there were so many rules we had to adhere to:

'Jaysus all of these orders would sicken ya' I lamented to Hegarty 'and why don't they tell the time like everyone else instead of using that 24 hour clock bollocks?' Hegarty again said nothing.

'And ye could eat yer feckin dinner off this!' I followed up as we scrubbed an already spotless floor.

'Aye, and this disinfectant would make them canned vegetables taste better as well' he finally replied.

Before the army I had never eaten canned vegetables which tasted as if they had been stewed in salt water for a month. The only canned food my mother kept was Golden Circle treacle for baking cakes.

'De ye know, my old dog Nasser even has fresh vegetables with his dinner?' I told Hegarty.

'Well ye wouldn't let yer dog eat them canned vegetables would ye!' he exclaimed, 'ye'd have to be an awful cruel bastard to do that.'

The next morning I went to the canteen as usual around 0600 for breakfast, the best meal of the day, with rashers and sausages, but when I returned to the billet I noticed something had changed: Lynagh's bed opposite mine and his closet were empty.

'Where is Lynagh gone?' I asked Havistock-Brown.

'Oh, he's been walked to the gate,' he replied coolly, 'Scully was taking his bag out when I came back from breakfast, that's the end of it for him.'

'But what did he do?' I asked innocently.

'Dunno, he was probably one of them underrage fellas, and if you're not old enough, the rule book says they will kick you out,' clarified Havistock-Brown in his matter-of-fact English accent.

I gulped nervously: 'That's a bit rough,' I quickly noted hoping to avoid Havistock-Brown's suspicions about my own age, 'after all Lynagh was able to do all the excercises as well as the next fella.'

'Doesnt matter, rules are rules,' Havistock-Brown retorted, 'but I don't know if that was what they got Lynagh for, all I know is the only other ways to get kicked out of here are if you are too old, yer short sighted, have flat feet or you're a white cap.'

'What's a white cap?' I asked.

'It means that you're queer', he said pompously, 'you can't be a soldier in the Irish army if you're a queer. Oh, and you can't be a bed-wetter either.'

'Jaysus I didn't know that,' I asserted, 'seems terrible feckin strict if ye ask me.'

'Well don't worry as they won't ask you, it is what the rule book says,' sighed Havistock-Brown, a phrase he loved repeating and one we had all heard many times, 'and that's why we have to fold up the whole mattress every morning, so they can check under the bed and around the floor.' Then Havistock-Brown reverted to his normal gloomy perspective, 'but there's no other way out of this fucking place except via military prison and believe me that's not a nice place. Actually, I'm not even sure if you can get kicked out if you're a white cap,' he started sarcastically 'the fucking doctors here grab hold of your bollocks in the medical and no-one says anything to them!'

I laughed with embarrassment remembering my own medical a month beforehand. Although he was posh and obviously educated, Havistock-Brown liked to moan and he made it clear to anyone who would listen and who didn't call him Cromwell, that he didn't like the army.

Like me, Lynagh probably just wanted to get through basic training and get a regular army position. I presumed he would now have to return to his family in Galway, with little chance of getting a decent job, probably just helping out on a farm or in a bar.

'I'd rather eat stones,' I mumbled, in the same dismissive manner as The County.

Lynagh had been my smoking buddy, never much conversation but friendly enough and a decent fella. I thought it was unfair that he got kicked out for whatever he did that the rule book didn't allow so later that day after our excercises had been completed I remarked to Hegarty .

'Would ya believe they kick ye out of this place if ye have a piss in yer sleep?'

'Too feckin right,' Hegarty immediately insisted pointing out the practical implications, 'well how would ya like it if yer fast asleep one night and some fecker, happily snoring away like a little piglet in the bunk above ya, pisses down on ye?'

'Aye, I suppose so,' I conceded, 'not a nice thing to wake up to.'

Although I had always smoked with Lynagh, I soon found plenty of other recruits to smoke with in the recruiting company and along with cards seemed to be the constant past time of free time in the army. Most nights we would play either poker or 25*, not with big stakes but enough to keep us interested til lights out. One evening, we were back in the billet playing our usual game and I said to Havistock-Brown and Hegarty:

'Jaysus all this shouting and yes sir business is cat altogether, these feckers just roar for the sake of roaring.'

Havistock-Brown agreed dejectedly, 'Well that's it now for three years, there's no way out now until April 1962. Yes,' he paused, 'three long years – that's what you signed up for in the recruiting office.'

I felt my face dropping with each word Havistock-Brown spoke.

Hegarty wasn't moved and just took another pull on his cigarette, pinched between his thumb and middle finger, and reverted to the poker game we were playing.

'There's yer two shillings and I'll raise ye another two,' he announced confidently as he exhaled smoke simultaneously between words and down through his nose.

I folded. 'Never draw to an inside straight!' I cited, having longed for the opportunity of imitating Tyrone Power in *The Mississippi Gambler*; and I threw my cards away nonchalantly.

---

* 25 is a traditional Irish card game, based on trumps, each player receiving 5 cards with a trump-suite card being turned over from the deck. Each round scores 5-points until the winner reaches 25.

'That, as they say, is the luck of the draw,' replied the victorious Hegarty.

Apart from playing-cards, the only other thing to do during free time in basic training was to read and the barracks had a huge supply of books although every one of them was about war. I read about the British army of the First World War or 'Kitchener's new model army' as it was called after the Secretary of State for War launched an appeal in 1914 for 100,000 volunteers at the start of the European offensive. Although the minimum age to join was 18, or 19 for overseas duty, it was estimated that 250,000 underage soldiers signed up, with the lure of 'new boots, a paid job, regular food and a trip to France'.

Many of the underage soldiers were discharged if the army checked their birth certificates with a notice that they had made 'a mis-statement as to age'. But some, I presumed like myself, had changed the document that could have given them away and they went on to fight at places like the Somme, Ypres or Passchendale, the forgery ultimately costing half of them their lives. The County had told me that back in Edgeworthstown, prominent members of the local community, often responsible for distributing community rations, actively recruited boys of 15 or 16 to fight in the trenches. They became part of a 'Pals Battalion'* whereby the young men of the town signed up 'as-one' to join the war. Unfortunately, as the Pals fought together they also died together which meant that the effect on the communities where the Pals signed up from was overwhelming. The County's own football club of Longford had been devastated during the Great War and of the 40 houses on Chapel Lane

* Groups of men from the same factory, football team, bank, and similar, joining and fighting together.

Longford, 40 men had volunteered, of which 10 were killed and 18 were seriously wounded.* The motivation for the recruiting sergeants was 'sixpence per man' for each recruit they enlisted, and therefore they ignored the minimum age requirement as the money they made would ensure a comfortable income and the best seats in the balcony of the church. Within a day or two the young recruits were dispatched to the front and sometimes it was just a week before the telegrams were received back at Hughes' in Longford that they had been killed on active service. Approximately 314 such telegrams were received over the course of the war in Longford with a notice from the King and Queen of the regret they felt for your family and the Army at the loss of your son. The mothers of the dead volunteers sat outside Hughes' clutching the death notice and wailing in despair. Some of the young girls in the town who had been 'promised' to slain soldiers, would never get married and have their own children and now faced a life as a 'widowed Miss' in a shattered community, although some took on the role of 'Auntie' to war orphans.

I read with pride about the 150,000 Irish volunteers who fought in Flanders field, of which 35,000 remained buried in the trenches, denied the final dignity of a Christian funeral. By the time the Great War was over, Ireland was in the midst of an independence struggle and while those that died were honoured, many that survived the horror of the trenches were treated by some as traitors by those who wanted the British out of Ireland including its leading politicians,† whose public condemnation led

---

* www.irishidentity.com/extras/hidden/stories/armistice.htm. Courtesy of the Longford Leader

† 'A coward if I return, a hero if I fall.' Neil Richardson

to many returning serviceman being ostracised by their communities and treated as cowards. Consequently, life for many in their home country became unbearable and they were forced to emigrate. By the Second World War, Ireland was no longer a British colony, it was a free state of the British empire and officially neutral but over 40,000 young men made the journey over the Irish Sea to volunteer for the allies of which 10,000 were killed. Incredibly nine of the Irish volunteers were awarded a VC but this time, life for the returning soldiers after the war had ended was again made uncomfortable after they were ordered by the Irish government to wear civilian clothes to avoid embarrassing De Valera's neutrality policy. Those who gave their lives to defeat the Nazis were never honoured for their sacrifice by the Irish state and were merely reported in the press as having died 'while working in Britain.' *

As we heard more and more about the reality of the concentration camps, the holocaust and the efforts of many Irishmen to fight against such tyranny, the way the Irish state treated its returning soldiers throughout its modern history seemed almost embarrassing, compounded by reports that De Valera was the only International Head of State to send a letter of condolence to Germany on hearing of Hitler's death. Irish politicians preferred to hark back to the Easter uprising and their anti-British struggles that painted themselves rather than the unfortunate soldiers of the two world wars as the nation's heroes. It wasn't surprising given the Irish state's neutrality that I found few books written about the Second World War in the Army library; but given that many Irish regiments fought in the Great War, there

---

* www.greyfalcon.us/Ireland.htm

were many shelves lined with books about this, although it too started a long way from Ireland's shores. I read that it began in the Baltic States with the assassination of Archduke Ferdinand, the heir to the Austro-Hungarian Empire causing them to wage war on Serbia. But all of a sudden, the build-up of colonial rivalries exploded as pacts and treaties evaporated and countries lined up to wage war on each other, culminating in Britain waging war on Germany to help out 'plucky little Belgium'*. The result was 'the war to end all wars'.† Within just four years 20 million people, including 12 million civilians, had lost their lives.

The more books I read from the army's library, the more I became engrossed reading the accounts of bravery; of the soldiers who would literally walk across no-man's-land towards the German trenches, fearlessly firing their Enfield 303 bolt action rifles until their final breath. The courage of these men just seemed incredible, as the sky rained bullets and bombs amidst what was described as 'the shrieking of dying soldiers in corpse-littered battlefields.' But it also seemed a terrible waste of life just to walk to your death for such a small piece of Belgian land. Now in 1959, many regarded the Great War as needless and had gained nothing for either side. It was now viewed as a war that could have been avoided with diplomacy, but this enlightened rationale came far too late for its many dead victims. The survivors said it was like a turkey shoot where young men were just mown down by a sheltered enemy just picking them off one by one after Sir Douglas Hague and the head of the British army: Field Marshall Sir Henry Hughes Wilson

---

* Source: www.bbc.co.uk/history_wwone_01.shtml

† H. G. Wells, 1914

who was co-incidentally born in Edgeworthstown, had ordered them 'over the top'. I recalled Father Curran's sermon from mass when he read from John's gospel:

> Greater love hath no man than this, to lay down his life for a friend.
>
> John 15:13

Although many Pals Battalions were almost entirely wiped out; they were simply dismissed by their commanders as 'setbacks'. Unbelievably, some of the Generals who had given the fateful orders accused the dead of 'lacking an offensive spirit'*. I shook my head almost dumbfounded and wondered what more could the dead men have given. It seemed to me that a soldier's lot was never rewarded, condemned by their senior officers when in battle or condemned by politicians if they were lucky enough to return. These armchair generals were known within the Irish army as barrack room barristers, willing to hand down judgements on the men engaged in the fighting, from the comfort of a rear position. The thing that shocked me most was when the underage volunteers became shell-shocked and froze from the trauma of constant bombing and gunfire; they were shot at dawn on the orders of their own officers. When the firing squad was unable to give the young recruit an immediate end, the officers themselves would administer the final 'coup de gras'.†

---

* 'A Lack of Offensive Spirit' - Alan MacDonald

† A death blow intended to end the suffering of a wounded creature. The phrase can refer to killing civilians or soldiers, friends or enemies and with or without the consent of the sufferer. In the context of an execution, it means shooting into the cardiac or temporal region of an already shot, but not yet dead person during a military or civilian execution.

There were others who avoided the bullets from both their own officers and the enemy, but just became impaled on enemy wire, the Germans even commenting that the British Tommies were as brave as young lions but being led by donkeys. Apparently nearly 100,000 men from all over the British Empire were killed at the Somme alone.

I read about one private who joined up when he was 17 and had also forged his birth certificate, borrowing his father's bowler hat to look 18. The following year, he went on to be awarded the Victoria Cross (VC), the highest decoration for valour, for attempting to rescue an officer while under intense fire in no-man's land. A VC, as I read in the appendix, is only awarded for the most extraordinary bravery, for the most daring acts of valour or self-sacrifice, or the ultimate devotion to duty in the presence of the enemy. However, it is not medals themselves that are important I read; a soldier just needs to know that their people and their government have not forsaken them, that their lives were worth something. One book commented that a soldier's sacrifice should never be forgotten or as Rudyard Kipling, whose only son was killed in WWI at the battle of Loos, declared: 'lest we forget.'

It also struck me that the families and home life of those who fought and died were never mentioned, what one book called 'the forgotten victims of war'. It was as if everything in the life of the soldier had become just another single entry in the war's casualty statistics. Surely these soldiers had mothers who worried about them and fathers, like The County, whom they were keen to impress. Similar to Hollywood films, most of the stories I read seemed to paint war in an honourable light almost as if fighting was the only thing that soldiers dreamed of and as if their families never existed. Most of the accounts were written by officers, whom Havistock-Brown noted gave fine accounts of their brave deeds and the horrors of the front line, writing from their leather-bound desks seven miles away. But there were very few accounts from the uneducated Joe Private types like me. From basic training I could tell that officers loved guns and shooting things, unlike me who was really only there for the money and just loved films and rock 'n' roll. I understood that in war there maybe no place for compassion or humanity but surely, I considered, there were soldiers whose main concern, like mine, was their family and who didn't really like going round killing someone else's children. Perhaps that's why Lynagh had described officers as 'sons of bbbbitches' I joked to myself.

I then read that the youngest VC ever awarded was to an Irishman called Andrew Fitzgibbon as part of the Indian medical establishment after they stormed a fort during the second China war in 1860. Fitzgibbon was ordered to attend to the injuries of a dhoolie-bearer during the advance, after which he attended another wounded man in open ground under intense fire. At 15 years and 3 months he was only a month or so older than me. Of the 157 Irishmen that had been awarded the VC, this one gave me the most inspiration. I felt reassured about my lack of years; if Fitzgibbon was able to achieve this then I would surely be able to get through this basic training. But the following day I nearly managed to get thrown out for the most ridiculous reason.

We reported for parade as usual at 0830. I had all my buckles and buttons polished and was almost admiring my reflection in my buffed boots. The drill corporal was Haydn, typically authoritarian with his wooden cane held up under his arm, so we knew it would be another

Privates Michael Greene and Daniel Hegarty, June 1959

tough exercise. We would start by square bashing on the barrack square, marching to the orders being bellowed out by Haydn.

'Eyes Front!' shouted Haydn, and 'Right Turn! And … March! Left! Right! Left! Right! It was rigid, everyone marching like clockwork at an exact pace of 120 paces per minute.

Marching in front of me was Hegarty, who had the same smug, couldn't-give-a-shit look on his face that he always had. He would often mutter something under his breath but this morning I heard this huge long fart. It could only have been Hegarty. As we turned to march back towards the barracks he carried on farting. I started to laugh and looked round to see that he had the neck to just stand there with just a fixed grin on his face, his eyes still faced the front almost motionless.

Haydn came up to me. 'Something funny Greene!?'

I stifled my smile, 'no Sir!' I roared back.

We carried on marching, but Hegarty wouldn't stop, he was still farting like a drain with virtually every step. I knew that I shouldn't but the more I tried not to laugh the redder my face went, Hegarty's small little legs, huge boots and even bigger ears making it all the more comical. What was making it funnier was that he was doing it all with a smile on his face, as if he was taking the piss out of the seriousness of Haydn's grand parade like Charlie Chaplin and the Keystone cops.

'Will ye quit farting for feck sake!' I whispered to him as he stood expressionless while I was still going red with laughter.

'Fall in Greene, you are on a charge,' roared Haydn, 'report to the charge office!'

'Yes Sir!' I roared back, and I immediately made my way to the main admin buildings followed by Haydn once he had passed command to another corporal.

The seriousness of the situation did not hit me until I went into the cell-like guard room where I would be kept until I was to go in-front of Colonel Collins, the head of Athlone barracks.

Once inside the charge room, Haydn closed the door behind him.

'You are being charged with insubordination!' roared Haydn, 'do you understand me?' his eyes filled with anger.

'Yes Sir!' I roared back.

'You will remain in the charge office until further notice. You will not speak to anyone until you are brought in-front of Colonel Collins tomorrow morning at 0800 and charged under army regulation 27, is that clear!?'

'Yes Sir!' I roared again, realising that his voice was becoming more and more enraged.

'Did you hear me?!' he repeated. 'I said, is that clear?!' Haydn was now standing only about four inches in front of my face, his eyes staring down threateningly over me. He seemed filled with a hatred that unnerved me.

'Yes Sir!' I roared even louder.

He then stomped out of the guard room, locking the door behind him. I had never been locked in a room before and I knew that I was now really in the shit. What I didn't know was that it was also the last time I would see Corporal Haydn.

As he slammed the door behind him, I blew out my cheeks, relieved that this first encounter was over. Haydn's fury seemed out of proportion, but he was a corporal and I thought could effectively do what he wanted. I looked around the guard room; it was only about 10 foot square with one bed and one bucket positioned in the corner on the concrete floor. There was no other furniture, the windows were barred and the door only had an outside bolt on it. It looked and felt like prison. I thought they were bound to find out now that I was only just 15.

More immediately, I wondered what I would do for something to eat; it was only 0930 or so in the morning and my charge was not being read until 0800 the next day. As I had been ordered not to speak to anyone, I would just have to go without food for a day I considered. Insubordination sounded like a serious charge and I thought about the stories I had heard of the military police or military prison, which everyone said were a lot harsher than their civilian equivalents. One of the soldiers who had come into the Bridge Bar in Mullingar used to quote Groucho Marx saying:

'Military justice is to justice what military music is to music'

I had never been so out of my depth, the best I could hope for, I pondered, was a fine of three days' wages. But it could be a lot worse, I did not want to be thrown out of the army but neither did I want to end up in Arbor Hill, the military prison near Dublin. I sat back on the bed, my head resting against the cold brick wall and contemplated the trouble I was in, especially as I no longer had the security of a civilian legal system. Haydn seemed so angry I feared he was capable of anything.

Only half an hour or so later, I heard the bolt being unlocked. As the door opened I felt relief that I would have some human interaction but after Haydn's threats was fearful as to what I should do and what the next instruction might entail. They could be transferring me to a more secure prison for the night I thought as I sprang up off the bed and stood to attention. Corporal Scully stood in the doorway.

'You're being released, Greene!'

'Yes Sir!' I roared automatically not wishing to say it too quietly for fear of being shouted at again.

I didn't move however, I just stood there waiting for the next order.

'Well go on, get out!' insisted Scully. 'Go back to the billet, Company Sergeant Purcell wants to have a word with you.'

I only began to realise then, that he said I was being released. Without any more delay I marched out of the guard room and over to the billet, but was confused and didn't know whether to smile or be worried about what CS Purcell wanted to speak to me about. The thought kept running through my head that CS Purcell had checked with the people he knew back in Edgeworthstown and had found out about my age.

When I walked into A block, apart from CS Purcell sitting on a chair at the end, the room was empty as the other recruits were still continuing their training.

He called me over.

'So I want you to tell me exactly what happened.' he said, his voice as always stern but rational.

I was still a bit uneasy but explained as instructed.

'We were on parade with Corporate Haydn,' I explained, 'and I started to laugh.'

'And why were you laughing?' interrupted Purcell firmly.

'Well one of the fellas, erm; I don't know which one,' I quickly asserted, 'erm ... farted Sir.'

Purcell began to smile.

'Go on,' he said.

'Corporate Haydn told me to stop laughing, but then I heard another fart, which made me laugh again. Haydn then told me I was being charged with insubordination and that my charge would be read in front of Colonel Collins tomorrow at 0800 Sir!'

'OK' sighed Purcell, and I thought for a moment that he gave me a knowing wink, but I didn't dare smile for fear of ending up even deeper in the shit.

'The charge has been dropped,' he said, 'join up with the rest of the platoon at 1100 for arms training.' His voice sounded unusually relaxed, his normal harshness had for once diminished.

'Yes Sir, I will Sir! Tanks Sir!'

I hadn't been so relieved since Lassie arrived back to the Yorkshire farm to young Roddie MacDowell in *Lassie Come Home*.

Not until the next day did I hear the news about Corporal Haydn.

'Fucking hell Greene!' exclaimed Havistock-Brown in his typically posh but raised voice. 'Did you hear that Haydn has been discharged from the army?!'

'What!' I said, genuinely shocked, 'what for?' I wondered if my being released from the insubordination charge had anything to do with it.

'We don't know, apparently he's been reported for bullying or not taking orders,' speculated Havistock-Brown.

'But did this have anything to do with me being charged yesterday?' I asked 'I didn't feckin report him for bullying.'

The last thing I needed was to be implicated in having a corporal discharged which would surely mean trouble down the line. I also knew Haydn had a brother, who was also an NCO, who could make things very difficult for me.

'No, apparently a couple of fellows in B block had reported him, and they had asked to leave the recruiting company, but at the moment we don't know, no doubt we will find out.'

We never did find out why Haydn had been discharged. Rumours circulated that he had an argument with the commanding officer or he was angry about not being promoted, but none of us knew the real reason. Neither his brother, who remained in the army, nor any other officer ever mentioned what happened or more importantly ever gave me a hard time because of it. However, I had learned my lesson; the army was not a place to laugh. From then on I learned to chew my tongue when I thought I couldn't control myself laughing, and the more I felt like laughing the harder I bit. Little did I know at the time that it would also come in useful to stop myself crying.

In a strange way the episode with Corporal Haydn established me as one of the boys in the training platoon.

It seemed to break the ice and gave us all something to joke about, easing the tension of passing basic training. We joked about the Fortescue effect, 'the fart that Hegarty did whilst tying his laces, that saved Private Greene, that finished the corporal, who saved the Colonel, that won the war!'

Hegarty found it all very amusing and described Haydn as a modern day Moses who had come back from the burning bush with his own ten commandments.

'And the first commandment,' Hegarty noted, 'was "thou shalt not fart!"'

It was our way of making light of the rigid orders and power structure of the army. Some of the trainees in B block told me how relieved they were that Haydn was not with them anymore:

'He was a right feckin bastard!' stated one, 'we were all ready to leave until you and Hegarty managed to get rid of him, we couldn't believe it when you just carried on laughing at him after he told ye to stop!'

The Tiger just took the piss out of me. 'Jaysus, don't be farting in front of Greene,' he would say 'or ye'll get discharged.'

I noticed that when we were not exercising or training, the Tiger would always be lying down, still chatting, singing or whistling, but always horizontal on his bed. I used to ask him if he wanted a smoke or a game of cards but he said he had a pulled muscle in his back, and was uncomfortable leaning or sitting down.

'Well why don't ye go to see Dr Gohan?' I said to him.

'I already did,' he responded, 'he just told me that it was growing pains, not even medicine and duty, just duty for me!' He joked: 'So don't be going farting near my bed, just because ya know I can't get up!'

After the Haydn incident, I also got to know 'Hegarty' quite well, One day when we were both shaving in the washroom he told me that he would only be 18 in six months' time but that he had told the recruiting officer he was already 18 as the work was lousy back in Mullingar and there was no money in boxing. Although he was the most laid back person I had ever met, he insisted that I was not to tell anyone in case an officer found out and he would be walked to the gate.

'You won't feckin believe this,' I happily revealed, 'I've done the same, I won't be 18 til next March!' Although it would be nearly three years til I was 18, being partially honest about being underage felt like a weight had been lifted off my shoulders. I also felt some comfort for not being the only one who had told a white lie about their age when joining up. I elaborated to make my story more believable:

'Aye,' I said, 'I was working for a few years in pubs, but sher with the wages that yer getting in dem places, ye couldn't wipe your arse with, so I decided to join the army nearly a year early.'

'Yer feckin jokin me aren't ya!' said Hegarty, 'but there's you shaving every day, Jaysus I thought you were 19 or 20!'

I was impressed by my deceptive ability. I only shaved every day as I didn't want anyone to suspect anything unusual, I could easily have got away with shaving once a fortnight. My face used to be red raw, with cuts and rashes all under my jaw. The only thing that would cool it down was talcum powder, water it seemed just used to make it burn and my face used to steam on the cool Athlone mornings.

'Oh, I'm just hairy I suppose,' I offered, but now that I knew him better I asked him a question that had always puzzled me, 'how did ya get past the medical with Gohan?' I began asking a bemused looking Hegarty, 'just that he told me that ye have to be a minimum of 5 foot 2 to be allowed in the army.'

'Sher amen't I 5 foot 3!' replied Hegarty immediately and with such confidence that my response was limited to:

'Are ya?' and although I towered over him by two inches I just conceded 'Jaysus, I'm only 5 foot 2 and a half!'

Hegarty said nothing, and just carried on shaving. Perhaps, I thought, he stood on tip-toe when he was being measured but if anyone could get away with it, I thought, Hegarty could.

'Nobody even checked my birth certificate,' Hegarty announced, 'I'm not sure they're that bothered.'

'Aye, nobody checked mine either,' I responded, 'but ye won't be telling anyone that I am also not 18 yet?' I made sure as I finished shaving.

'Of course I won't' said Hegarty. 'Jaysus, if they kick anyone else out, there'll be no-one left to do their cleaning!'

Other recruits were also beginning to share stories about themselves. One fella was the oldest of 14 children who said he 'just joined the army to get away from the clatter of feckin kids everywhere'. There were others whose parents had left them with their grandparents as they went in search of their fortune in America. In some cases, they knew they would never see their parents again, the letters and Christmas cards had stopped many years beforehand, presumably their parents' fortune had never been made. There were stories from all over western Ireland, some were great craic, reminding me of the Dolly Dolan back in Edgeworthstown, whose anecdote about Joe Murray's glass eye on the mantelpiece

I pretended was my own. Many recounted tales of evil schoolmasters who would 'beat the shite out of ye' for writing left handed or with a raised knuckle and how some families had been disrupted by alcoholism and poverty.

What most of the recruits seemed to have in common was a love of music and films, and as the platoon began to feel more relaxed many would tune their wireless into radio Luxembourg, the best station for rock 'n' roll music in Ireland. The quieter recruits preferred Radio Athlone, which was similar to Radio Eirann that my mother played back in Edgeworthstown and just recounted mainly local news stories. One or two read books by Allen Ginsberg, Jack Kerouac and other authors and poets known as the beat authors, who had come to prominence a few years beforehand in America advocating a rejection of western conformity. 'The beatnicks' they told me, 'believed in a relaxed approach to life, men could have long hair and drug use was encouraged to free the mind. They also believed in free love 'with as many girls as ye want' and that women would soon be able to take a 'pill' to stop them getting pregnant. They also rejected doctrinal religions like Christianity in favour of eastern faiths or an inner spirituality. It all sounded like bollocks to me, so far removed from the army but also from normal Irish town life. If I walked around Edgeworthstown smoking pot and dressed in flowery trousers people would just think I was a right eejit, although I liked the sound of having lots of girlfriends and getting away from all this rigid 'yes Sir!' shite.

We also began to discuss politics, a subject where thanks to my conversations with The County, I knew as much as the older recruits. Many were similar to me in that they were socialist but loved to gamble on cards or horses so didn't like the idea of communism, but mainly we spoke about Irish politics and, unlike my family, most supported de Valera. I argued what The County had told me that he had never helped the working man and that he let Michael Collins take the bullet for him, but they seemed adamant that he was a hero of the rebel independence movement of 1916 and if it weren't for him, the Irish would still be waving little Union-Jacks in O'Connell street Dublin.

It was as if the survivors of the Easter uprising and the siege of the GPO could do no wrong even 40 odd years after the event. Nobody spoke about de Valera's current political decisions like their trade policy or social security, just about the wrongful executions of Irish martyrs and holding out against the British in the siege of the GPO building in Dublin for five days.

'No wonder the feckers got re-elected' I considered.

One recruit recited the poem about an 18 year old medical student from Dublin called Kevin Barry who was executed in Mountjoy prison Dublin, having been denied prisoner of war status, during the war of independence in 1920. As he emotively recited the poem, I could see him puff out his chest as if he himself were about to be executed:

> Just before he faced the hangman,
> In his dreary prison cell,
> The Black and Tans tortured Barry,
> Just because he wouldn't tell.
>
> The names of his brave comrades,
> And other things they wished to know.
> 'Turn informer and we'll free you'
> Kevin Barry answered, 'No'.

'Shoot me like a soldier.
Do not hang me like a dog,
For I fought to free old Ireland
On that still September morn.

Lads like Barry are no cowards.
From the foe they will not fly.
Lads like Barry will free Ireland,
For her sake they'll live and die.

When he finished, he quoted Barry's last words to his executioner:

'It is nothing, to give one's life for Ireland. I'm not the first and maybe I won't be the last.'

Nobody said anything for a few moments and as I stood there in my army uniform, I felt an intense surge of Irish nationalism and identity. Each morning on parade we would salute the Irish flag reminding me of the stories of patriotism I had heard from The County and from those in the barracks. I still had an inherited distrust of de Valera, but I was as proud of a free Ireland as anyone.

By the end of basic training, I felt more assured that the discipline and rigour of basic training had made me appear more grown up, although nobody except Hegarty still had the slightest idea I was underage. Within just three months, my life had been totally consumed by the army as I ate, slept and drank a soldier's life. It was as if my civilian identity had been taken away by military discipline and order. Everything I wore during the week was army issue and I had spent all my wages on new clothes for when I was off duty, as the ones I had worn before I enlisted now just seemed like rags in comparison.

I didn't throw the old clothes away however, as there would surely be some use for them at home.

The day we passed out of basic training I felt both pride and relief. I had kept my age a secret and even got a commendation for PTs having come top of the recruitment company in acrobatics and gym work. I wasn't very good with guns, the Lee Enfield I had been issued was too big and cumbersome, coming up to my chest when I stood it on the ground, but I managed to get through the final parade where we had to present arms and hold the rifle in three set positions. My only other weakness noted in my review was my natural tendency to 'tick-tock' when marching. They remarked however that I had largely overcome this during basic training. Marching still didn't come naturally to me but after the first couple of bollockings I made a point of following Havistock-Brown's first movement with his arms to get the correct rhythm.

There was no fancy passing out ceremony, nor were there any guests or family members present, just an ordinary parade followed by CS Purcell announcing the names of those recruits that were being made a 1 star private. Of the 30 recruits that had initially signed up, 26 made it to the passing out parade and we were all called forward one-by-one to shake Purcell's hand and then we stepped back into line.

Then we heard the announcement we all had longed for: 'troop dismissed!' as we knew we had our first long weekend leave for three months. We had five days off after which we were to report to our divisions at our home barracks. Many were being assigned to other barracks in western command, some as far away as Galway or Donegal. Hegarty was going back to Mullingar, but Havistock-Brown, the Tiger and I were staying in

Athlone. We all said our goodbyes as most headed off to the pub to celebrate. I went along for a couple of glasses of Smithwicks but I couldn't wait to get home to Edgeworthstown with my new pressed clothes and to tell them that I had passed out and been promoted to a 1 star private.

I was a little bit nervous about seeing my parents again having joined the army without their permission but a letter from my sister Kitty had told me that The County had convinced my mother that three years in the army would be good for my discipline. I had also sent my second month's wage packet home to placate the wrath I was expecting. As I sheepishly arrived home, I knocked quietly on the door and walked in. Unbelievably, my mother leapt out of her armchair and seemed delighted to see me. Then she remarked how well I was looking.

'Oh Mickey look at ya, yuv gotten so tall, ye'll be a fine man,' my mother said enthusiastically, but then again she always said that. 'And look how smart he's dressed Frank,' she continued, as she proudly grabbed my arm. The County nodded a distant approval.

It was great to be home amongst friendly faces and in familiar surroundings, the bubbling pots in the open hearth and wireless still chattering away in the background. However, all was not as I had dreamed, there was something very noticeably missing. My sister Mary had found a place of her own and that meant that we no longer had our own television, something that I hadn't been able to watch for the previous three months.

'Good job as well' said my mother, 'stuck inside the house watching a little box tied to the roof, which you can barely see! A wireless is much better.'

It was now summertime and it remained light outside until 11 p.m., so we shifted some chairs out next to the railway crossing and listened to the sound of crickets. A couple of farmers went past having been busy all day making hay, the sweet aroma of freshly cut grass filling the air on the cool summer evening. Many said it was the greatest summer they ever had, with all the hay harvested weeks ahead of schedule, the threshers put away for another year. My mother had also collected a pale of blackberries from nearby bushes, which normally wouldn't ripen til August. We turned up the wireless and were even allowed to play music on the wireless again: 'Mise Eire' on Radio Eirann with The County pointing out that it was how traditional Irish music should be played. To him, Irish music was not just about 'jigs, flutes and fiddles'. We even joked about the train smashing through the crossing gates a few years beforehand as my mother emerged from the house with a jug of buttermilk.

'Will ya sit down and rest yourself, mam?' I said to her, although I had never known her to rest when I was growing up.

'Aye, a woman's work is never done,' she replied 'but I suppose it's a special occasion, my boy being promoted and sitting there in his army uniform.'

I was eager to speak to The County about all the Irish political thinking I had learned whilst I was away, with poems like Kevin Barry and I also wanted to discuss the latest international news since most of the recruits just spoke about Irish politics.

The County seemed buoyed both by Ireland's increasing international role in world politics and the chance to explain his perspective. He told me about the independence movements in Africa that were now being supported by the UN's policy of self-determination so that African people could govern themselves, a policy which Ireland's diplomats had formulated for the former African colonies.

He also told me that at the UN, Conor Cruise O'Brien had proposed that all countries outside NATO and the Eastern bloc should agree to stop developing nuclear weapons since there was already enough to blow up the world 20 times over on the condition that the UN protects a non-aligned country's sovereignty in case of aggression.

'Well that makes sense' I said 'what's the point of spending millions on weapons that we won't use, especially as we are supposed to be neutral?'

'Yer right son,' replied The County 'but O'Brien is not making himself any European friends over at the UN headquarters in New York.'

My mother interrupted, 'will ye quit filling the boys head with all this shite about war and bombs; Jaysus, his first long weekend away from the army, and there's you telling him all sorts of nonsense.'

The County went quiet; we didn't have much else in common and I could tell that politics was the only thing he really enjoyed discussing with me.

My mother optimistically opened another conversation to break the obvious silence:

'So what are the other boys like Micky?' she questioned, like most mothers ask their child after a first day at school.

'Ah they're grand,' I replied, 'aye, good craic.'

With that conversation exhausted, I was eager to re-open the discussion of politics with The County and took my opportunity when my mother returned inside the house. Naïvely I asked him:

'But why should countries like Britain and France simply give up their African colonies, just to let the Americans or Russians take them over?'

'Because they signed the Atlantic charter in 1941,' replied The County eagerly, 'this guaranteed that if America helped them to win the war, then in return the colonial powers had to agree to allow colonial states to have self-determined governments. Just after the war,' he went on 'Churchill said that the charter took on a life of its own and now the European powers have no choice but to withdraw, Africa has a right to self-determination, but the colonialists will try to hold onto the money.'

Then he continued with his train of thought before my mother had interrupted him:

'Conor Cruise O'Brien is leading the campaign to end colonialism, so they'll all have to get out of Africa. This is the end of colonial empires, which they thought would last a thousand years!' He seemed full-of-himself that his 1956 prediction after Suez was being proved correct.

'De Gaulle thinks that the UN is just interfering and that O'Brien and the head of the UN, Dag Hammarskjöld, are trying to undermine everything that France have achieved over centuries,' The County noted with a hint of sarcasm.

I had seen Dag Hammarskjöld, the UN secretary general on the television in the Bridge Bar. He was in his mid 50s and had one of those plump, well-fed faces that looked like he shouldn't have a care in the world. But his eyes looked heavy and almost sad, like my mother's when she was worried. He too looked over-burdened by the strain of his work with countless and mounting world crises landing on his desk.

By then my mother re-appeared in the doorway, having watered her two Star of Bethlehem plants we had in the window. She was carrying tea and currant bread and The County realised it would be in his best interests to keep quiet although he leant over and gave me his copy of the Irish Independent:

'There ye go son,' he offered. 'There's a few good articles in there for ya to read.'

When I was back home in Edgeworthstown everything was peaceful, we chatted away until it got dark and turned off the wireless. My mother did not like to leave the light on above the door as it attracted night insects so we returned inside.

I had arranged to meet my brother Franco and the Dolly Dolan the next day while they were at work as yard boys on Barney Farrel's farm, and had already prepared myself for the inevitable piss-taking.

'Will ya feckin look at you!' bellowed the Dolly as soon as he saw me 'Jaysus, you look like an advert for Connaught cleaners! And will ye look at the head of it! What happened to all yer blonde curls Mickey?'

'Aye, I had to have it all shaved off,' I answered defensively but then I realised that I had better join in the craic or they would be laughing at me for weeks, 'so I says to this feckin barber, I want ya to make me look like Elvis. OK says the barber. But then I looked in the mirror only to see this bald pink head looking back at me, and a big pair of ears that I never knew I had!'

'Elvis my arse!' roared the Dolly, 'did the feckin barber used to work in one them concentration camps?!' As we all laughed, I felt self-conscious that I was dressed too smartly, so had to tell them some stories about how terrible it was in the army, which I was sure would cheer them up.

'They are all feckin gob-shites!' I recounted, 'ye have to say "yes Sir!" every time someone opens their mouth to ya, and have yer buttons and boots shining so they can admire themselves in them. It's no craic at all, I even got charged for laughing when someone farted!'

'Jaysus' interrupted Franco, 'sounds like the Yakety Yak song,' which had become famous as the rebellious kids' anthem of the '50s. Both he and the Dolly then chanted in unison:

'Yakety Yak!' then putting on their deepest voices, chanted: 'Don't talk back!'

'Aye, yer feckin right!' I replied, nodding my head deliberately. Moaning about taking orders had, however done the trick; I had complained almost as much as Havistock-Brown which had reassured them that my job was as miserable as theirs. 'So has there been any craic here?' I asked them.

'Ah plenty of craic Micky!' replied the Dolly. 'Franco and I were working here a couple of weeks ago with Barney himself. Franco was holding the ladder for him. Then,' pointing at Franco, 'he noticed that Barney was wearing a pair of tights under his trousers, so he says to him, "Barney, ye have a ladder in yer stockings!" So de ya know what Barney says to him: "well, climb up that ladder and kiss me feckin arse!" Oh Jaysus Micky, it was gas! Ya should have been here!' The Dolly was already laughing raucously at his own joke, an infectious humour that could make any ordinary story seem hilarious.

Like most of the Dolly's stories, I wished I had been around to enjoy them, but at the same time I was so proud that I had got through basic training, although I didn't dare tell them I had been promoted and was now a 1 star private. However, I wasn't able to hide my new army discipline completely:

'So I hear we are goin to a dance this evening out by the Ardagh crossroads?' I asked.

'Aye, it's celeidh and old time,' replied Franco, 'lots of reels and jigs, there should be a big crowd.'

'Ok,' I said, 'I'll see yuz there at 1945,' and as soon as I said it, my eyelids dropped in anguish at the imminent onslaught.

'Will ye listen to that bollocks! Nineteen-Forty-Five,' the Dolly deliberately recounted, as he and Franco laughed loudly at my army timekeeping, 'ahh… mammy's little soldier wants to meet promptly at Nineteen-Forty-Five!' he again imitated with exaggerated pompousness in an accent not dissimilar to Havistock-Brown's, 'just come along when ya want Mickey, we'll feckin see ya when we see ya!'

I turned up at the crossroads at five to eight, intentionally ten minutes later than the time I had suggested. Only a couple of others had arrived, one with a violin and the other like me just ready to dance. It was not long however until we had a full ceileidh band: three violins, two piano accordions and an assortment of cymbals, triangles, flutes and tin whistles.

About 40 people in all, turning up in ones and twos and some just passing through, or having just finished working on the farms for the day, stopped and clapped as we danced along to all the ceiliedh tunes like the walls of Limerick and the Siege of Ennis which my sisters had taught me. They also played 'old time' waltzes and foxtrots as the makeshift band tapped their feet and swayed to the rhythm of the music. The Dolly was as lively as ever, dancing a step quicker than everyone else, almost trying to cram in as much fun as he could. When one of the reels finished he was standing in between two farmers' daughters, so he quickly escaped to the sidelines where I was standing:

'Feckin hell Micky that was close,' he said still panting, 'I was nearly caught for a dance between them two heffers!' Then recalling a similar situation that Groucho Marx found himself in, he imitated:

'So I says to her, I could dance with you till the cows come home,' he began laughing to build up his punch line, 'but on second thoughts, I'd rather dance with the cows till ye come home!'

It had only been a couple of days since I passed out, but the army seemed a million miles away, everyone just enjoying themselves, laughing, singing and dancing on the long summer evening. People here were not talking about guns, parades or uniforms, instead they just had the craic, or how great the weather had been and about the new dance halls that were springing up all over Ireland. The Temperance Hall in Longford and The Cloudlands in Rooskey were getting huge crowds, and even Edgeworthstown had The Auburn which would have an evening of 'Ceileidh and Old Time' once a month. In the dance halls there was no alcohol, just mineral bars, so just a quick glass of lemonade and they'd be off dancing again. As the weather had been so good, people recounted their stories of how they used to travel for hours for a night at the dance halls, most hitching lifts with passing farmers and often sleeping in fields or on the side of the road. Then almost as quietly as everyone had arrived, they all gradually dispersed, talking and joking as the sun set.

It was back to the army the following Tuesday and I was to meet my new mess mates in Athlone barracks. Most of the people I knew from basic training were assigned to other barracks but there would be a few familiar faces.

I was detailed to the ordnance division whose job it was to supply everything the army required: guns, bullets, tents, uniforms, toilets, everything. The biggest part of the job was escorting the supplies to where they were needed, as we had to account for every item taken from the main quartermaster until it reached its final destination. I was shown around the stores by another private called Sean Dowler who had joined the army about six months before me and was also in my new barracks. He showed me where all the bulls-wool uniforms were kept:

'Regular soldiers only get one change of uniform every year, so give them a couple of sizes too large in case they get too fat at Christmas,' Dowler explained, 'it gives them a bit of room to grow into it. Some fellas eat so much in the winter they'd be walking around the barracks like sows wearing a vest.' Then he lowered his voice and confided, 'it's one of the advantages of being in ordnance, we can change our uniforms as often as we want and no-one will know, but don't be tellin anyone now Michael.'

I liked the way he called me Michael, it was unusual not to be called Greene as I had been known in the recruitment company so I thought I would respond by calling him Sean:

'What about my helmet Sean?' I asked him. 'I was given this during basic training and ye could fit an ass and cart into it. I have to pad it out with paper to stop it rattling around my head. They told me it was the smallest they had.'

'Aye, we always say that; it saves us having to go back and get another. We'd end up running round like flies round a cow's arse if we didn't,' Dowler laughed. 'It was probably me who gave it te ya!'

'Aye, I think it was Sean!' I responded.

'Just go and switch your old helmet for a new one when no-one is around. Always remember Michael, the Lord only helps those who help themselves!' he laughed, 'and ye'll probably want to pick yourself a new bum-freezer as well while yer at it, the one ya have on is big enough for a bullock.'

A bum-freezer was the short fitting jacket which was supposed to stop at the waist but mine easily covered my arse and down over my hands.

'Ya must have thought I would be doing a lot of eating Sean!'

'Aye, ye look like ye could be a fat fecker!' he hollered.

'Feck off,' I responded, knowing that he was only having the craic.

Then he asked something I was not expecting:

'What did yiz do to Private Havistock-Brown, Michael?'

'I didn't do anything to him Sean' I replied, 'why?'

'Because he didn't report for duty' he explained 'and when the family were contacted, they said he had gone back to England. He's gone AWOL'

'Feckin hell!' I said, 'I know he got a bit of stick from some of the boys calling him Cromwell, and he used to moan a bit, but I didn't think he would do that!'

Well that's it for him,' sighed Dowler. 'He won't even be able to come back to Ireland, or the MPs will sling him in Arbour Hill til he's served his time.'

If I had wanted to leave the army that badly, I thought, I could have just pissed in the bed, or pretended to be short sighted. It may have been a bit humiliating being walked to the gate but it sounded a lot easier than Arbour Hill Military Prison. Initially I was surprised to hear that Havistock-Brown had gone AWOL, but, just like with what happenend to Lynagh it made me realise that the army could change so quickly, one minute someone is there, next they are gone. Then everything just carries on just like before and within a day or two no-one ever mentions it again.

'I can't understand it,' Dowler continued, 'he [Havistock-Brown] did all the hard work getting through basic training, and he then goes AWOL, the feckin eejit.'

I couldn't understand it either but then again I could never understand why he had wanted to come back to Ireland in the first place.

'Well I'm sure he'll be having good old craic over in London,' I suggested.

Dowler was from Legan, only a couple of miles from Edgeworthstown. He was what The County would call 'a decent sort of fella'. He was similar to Havistock-Brown in that he didn't like all the army discipline but was a lot happier, no doubt helped by the fact he didn't have a posh name and an English accent. He also seemed much smarter, always one step ahead of authority, and I could tell already that he had a shrewd eye for a smart deal and an easy job.

I told him I was from Edgeworthstown, not far from Legan.

'Oh I know it well!' he responded 'I'll be able to give you a lift home some weekends.'

'A lift!' I said, 'in a car?!'

'No, a piggy back,' Dowler retorted, 'ye feckin eejit ya, of course in a car!'

Nobody I knew in Edgeworthstown had a car, a couple of old rich families who needed to go to Dublin on business had one, but they were still rare enough for us to stare at enviously when they went past. A new car would cost over £400 and our wages were only £4 per week.

'Jaysus, how were ya able to afford a car?' I asked him.

But Dowler just tapped his nose and gave a wry smile as if he had a valuable secret he could not share.

It wouldn't have bothered me if he had stolen the car off the Pope himself, I was just happy that he would be able to give me lift home, a journey of about an hour, which on the bus would have taken me at least two and a half hours.

He had a black Morris Minor 1000, which he kept immaculately, washing and cleaning it every other day. The inside had hard leather seats and a wooden dashboard. Dowler not only had a car he had all the luxuries.

'Ah but the petrol is very expensive ya know,' he happened to mention as I headed back to barracks; he wasn't going to forget to tell me that.

I had seen big American cars like Buicks and Cadillacs watching American films at the Picture House, many with open top roofs, and some were even bright blue or pink. The new Minis had just been launched over in England but the only cars I had seen in Ireland at the time were the Morris Minor range, nearly always black but occasionally grey, but I still couldn't believe that Dowler at only 18, owned one. My favourite car, that I had only seen in adverts, was the French Citroen DS, which compared to any other car I had seen was a goddess. It seemed curvy and stylish and in the advert shown at the Picture House, it was displayed outside a Burlesque theatre complete with a statue of a can-can girl lit up in alternating red and green neon lights. As a pouting madame sat stroking its front wing she described it as 'very avant garde' in a soft French accent making it just the sexiest thing on the road. Having four wheels was rare enough in Ireland, but four wheels AND sexy were an impossible dream.

Pictures of sexy French ladies were kept by many regular soldiers stuck to the inside of their lockers in the barracks, often with suggestive French captions like 'ooh la la!' or more provocatively 'se soir?' ['tonight?']. During basic training we would never have been allowed to keep evocative pictures of glamorous ladies unless we wanted to hear another account of Private Fortescue who kept the laces, and tied the boots of the feckin Brigadier. The regular barracks in Athlone were however much more comfortable than the billets, there was a large communal area complete with fabric sofas, and importantly a television, but the most notable change was the amount of room between the beds, about three times as much room as we had in the billet.

Next to me in the barracks was another private called Patrick Monahan who was known as Pakie and was also from Edgeworthstown. I vaguely knew his family from mass but fortunately he went to the Glenn School whereas I went to the Boys' National School, so importantly he wouldn't know I was underage. Monahan had the uncanny ability of making a joke about anything and everything, his face always full of mischief. The first thing he said to me was:

'De ya see the 'derriere' [arse] on that lovely Brigitte Bardot Michael?' he asked pointing at a poster from Bardot's 1956 classic *Et Dieu Crea la Femme* [*And God Created Woman*].

'I do of course Pakie,' I responded 'Jaysus it would be difficult not to notice an arse like that!'

'Well ya see Michael, if I spent the night with her, I'd teach her how to fly.'

'Why's that Pakie?' I asked, expecting a Peter-Pan type of story.

'Because Michael,' he explained 'I'd have to give her arse a bite so hard, she would fly out of the window!'

We both laughed still adoringly looking into the come-to-bed eyes of the liberated young French actress bunching up her peroxide blond hair. The stereotypical dumb blondes of the fifties now had their own fantasies in this new era of sexual revolution, but none of them ever seemed to live in Ireland.

It was great to be next to someone as cheerful as Monahan after being in the recruitment company in-between Havistock-Brown, who was always miserable, and Hegarty who only laughed when he wanted to. In their own ways though, I knew they had both helped me through basic training but now they had both left Athlone, Hegarty back to Mullingar and Havistock-Brown to the ignominy of going AWOL. However, there were others from the recruitment company who had been stationed in Athlone including the Tiger, still singing the latest ballads and whistling but always complaining about the pulled muscle in his back. But with the three of them; Dowler, Monahan and the Tiger, I knew it was going to be good craic as a regular soldier. Dowler was the best piss-taker I had ever met while Monahan's humour would lift spirits and, just like the Dolly Dolan back in Edgeworthstown, he laughed even louder at his own jokes.

Having a television in the barracks also made a big difference and unlike the trainees in the recruiting company, the regular soldiers including Dowler and Monahan were much more informed about world events. Sometimes a discussion would break out about 'white rule' in African states which was likened to the discrimination against Catholics in Ireland from the time of Cromwell until independence in 1921. As a result there was much support for what we heard was called pan-Africanism. The leader of the pan African Congress (PAC) movement was Kwame Nkrumah of Ghana who was becoming famous as the leader of an independent and free Africa who believed that through African unity they could transform downtrodden colonised society into prosperity and opportunity for all. He advocated that the enormous wealth in African states should not only be plundered by avaricious Europeans but must also provide for African people. To the poor and homeless Ghanaians he was a hero, he would provide for basic welfare and had achieved something they had longed for, the end of colonialism and a self determined government. I read that Ghana or the Gold Coast as it was previously known before March 1957, gained independence through non violence or Satyagraha (soul force) employing the same philosophy as Mahatma Ghandi in India 12 years earlier. It was held up as a model of how other African states could govern themselves and overcome their colonial past.

> Seek ye first the political Kingdom and all
> else will follow.
>
> Kwame Nkrumah

Although I was only 15, I was now reading the Irish Independent every week. If I did not return home at the weekend, The County just put his copy away and gave it to me on my next visit, complete with circles, ticks and crosses, clearly indicating where his sympathies lay.

One week there was an article, which The County had put a big red circle around, about the Secretary General of the UN, Dag Hammarskjöld of whom it said 'had the most impossible job on earth' and that 'from

Suez in 1956, to Castro's communist revolution in Cuba, he was continually finding a balance between the competing world powers amid the threat of nuclear war.' 'Hammarskjöld's approach' the article went on: 'is one of preventative diplomacy, carried out through endless rounds of mediation, compromises and concessions.'

From what I could see the UN itself had nothing to gain, it did not seek a victory for any particular side just a solution by peaceful means. The same article pointed out that Hammarskjöld was often being derided when policies did not tie-in with a major power's foreign ambitions. In America, the McCarthyists* said that the UN had become infiltrated by communists but conversely it also quoted Khrushchev, accusing him of being an agent of western imperialism. However, in the Irish press it was different; Hammarskjöld was regarded as one of the few world leaders with any integrity, and probably the only one with a genuine interest in humanity and peace.

In terms of political turmoil, Africa was now continually in the news, and I could almost feel the tension rising as the reporters voices became more urgent. In one broadcast the Irish correspondent explained that colonial white rulers of Africa continued to resist democracy, and as a result more militant movements are springing up all over the continent including the Mai Mai in Kenya, the FLN in Algeria and the more moderate ANC in both South Africa and Rhodesia. In The Congo, we were told that the Belgian government would only grant full independence over a transitional period of 30 years, which

---

* Named after the US Senator J. R. McCarthy, the term McCarthyist was used to define someone who made accusatory claims, often unproven, against pro-communists, undermining the victim's credibility and suppressing opposition.

initiated the 'Independence Now!' movement led by a young activist called Patrice Lumumba.

The previous weekend I had seen my first epic movie, 'in glorious technicolor' back home at the Picture House in Edgeworthstown and I likened the stories I had heard about Lumumba to Ben Hur played by Charlton Heston. Given that we were all working, the four of us: me, the Dolly, Kevin and Franco were now sat in the middle seats with the velvet cushions and having enough money, we had more woodbines and sweets than we could ever finish in three hours. Just as the dramatic music sent a pulse through all four of us, the screen beamed out:

BEN HUR

A TALE OF THE CHRIST

A METRO GOLDWYN MAYER PRODUCTION

From the very first scene of *Ben Hur* our mouths were gaping in anticipation, we barely remembered to even light-up our woodbines. At one point, whilst chained in the galleys, Ben Hur gets whipped by the Roman consul Quintus Arrius who torments him by saying:

> Your eyes are full of hate, Forty-One. That's good.
> Hate keeps a man alive. It gives him strength
>
> Quintus Arrius: *Ben Hur* 1959

Ben Hur was the best film we had ever seen and The Dolly said that if they showed films like that at mass on Sunday, there wouldn't be any spare seats in the church and everyone would believe in miracles.

That evening at the Picture House, two words entered our vocabulary: 'epic' and 'biblical', both representing something magnificent. From that moment, the Dolly now called a warm sunny day in Edgeworthstown 'feckin biblical', and he no longer told 'stories', he told 'epics'.

Ben Hur had been the hero of his people and now, when I watched the news coverage of The Congo, just as the audience in the colosseum had roared their approval for their champion, crowds cheered Lumumba wherever he went. It was like he was their favourite gladiator. Lumumba was also reported as being tormented at the treatment of his family and fellow citizens and had resisted efforts by the Belgians to become a puppet leader for them which would condemn The Congolese to a life of servitude choosing instead to seek independence for The Congolese. He was not however, only up against the Belgian colonial empire, but also against the other white colonists, the French, British and Portuguese who all coveted their African colonies and did not want to set a precedent by granting freedom and independence to native Africans. We were told that the vast mineral wealth within the continent was too valuable for them to forego and the African people provided a ready supply of cheap labour. The European rulers were not going to let an ideological young African [Lumumba] just take it away from them.

Even if there wasn't a great film being shown at the Picture House, when I was not on duty I still preferred to go home to Edgeworthstown with Dowler at weekends, as neither of us wanted to hang around the barracks or the Athlone pubs which were known in the barracks as wet canteens. The journey itself was enjoyable in his beloved Morris Minor and I goaded him that it was like the film *Genevieve* about the aristocratic London to Brighton vintage car rally in the early fifties, only this journey was mostly along narrow grassy lanes between

Edgeworthstown and Athlone. The area we drove through was known as 'Goldsmith's country', which had become famous in the writings of Oliver Goldsmith, the famous Irish writer and poet. Goldsmith wrote about the state of the Irish countryside which in the eighteenth century was going through huge depopulation due to poverty and a society that was becoming more concerned about money 'where wealth accumulates and men decay', he wrote. One particular day we were returning back to Athlone and the weather was unusually 'biblical' as we followed our normal route from Legan, through Carrickboy, then onto Ballymahon, winding through Glasson – the village of the roses, before finally arriving in Athlone.

Dowler told me that he didn't like going to the wet canteen because he was a member of the 'Pioneer Total Abstinence Association of the Sacred Heart' or just 'The Pioneers' as they were known, who required abstinence from alcohol and would identify themselves by a label pin with an image of the scared heart on their collar. A few years beforehand, like most Irish 12 year-olds, I had taken 'the pledge' at my confirmation which meant I couldn't drink until I was 21, but I often had a glass of Smithwicks with the other soldiers to avoid suspicion that I was underage. My mother too was a pioneer which had taken over from the temperance movement in Ireland advocating a teetotal way of life for Catholics. As Dowler showed me his label pin on the reverse side of his jacket collar I told him that he must be 'a goody two shoes', a character in one of Goldsmith's most famous novels *The History of Goody Two Shoes*.

He told me to feck off but just as we passed the statue erected in the memory of Oliver Goldsmith in Ballymahon his attention was drawn to something far more immediate: his car had began to splutter eventually coming to a stop. He had run out of petrol. It was still half an hour by car to the nearest garage in Athlone, an 'epic' journey of 12 miles.

'Are ya sure you've run out of petrol Sean?' I asked.

'Of course I'm feckin sure,' insisted Dowler, 'ye'll have to get out and push Michael.'

'Push, my arse', I protested, 'I can't push this old banger for 12 miles!'

'Well how the feck do ye think we'll get to Athlone?' he requested, aware that he had already given me the only plausible answer.

'Well I don't know about you Sean but I am gonna thumb a lift.'

'Just push the fecking car,' Dowler ranted, 'we'll be there in half an hour!'

Knowing that I would never have got another lift had I abandoned him, I got out and pushed the car all the way to Athlone and into the nearest petrol garage. It took us three hours.

As I was pushing, I looked around at the deserted villages that Goldsmith had spoken about in the eighteenth century and wondered whether now in 1959 if we were going through another period in Irish history when everybody seemed to be emigrating. Many houses we went past had been abandoned and become dilapidated. Of those that had stayed, large families like mine were growing up with few opportunities unless they moved abroad.

When we reached the petrol station in Athlone, Dowler put in 5*s*. of fuel which about half-filled the tank.

He then asked me, 'Anyway, have ya got any petrol money for me Michael?'

'Ye cheeky bastard!' I roared back, 'ye should be paying me for carrying you and your feckin car all the way here!'

Dowler laughed, 'I had the engine turned off anyway Michael, I knew you wouldn't give me any petrol money so I thought I would give the engine a day off and let ya push!'

'All the money that yer getting and you wouldn't even give the car a drop of petrol,' I replied, 'that's why ye don't go into wet canteens, incase ye'd have to buy a drink!... ...Aye, pioneer my arse!'

It was actually good craic pushing the car to Athlone, it not only gave me the opportunity of taking the piss out of Dowler but it also allowed me to dream about my own journey to London after I left the army.

Back at the barracks, Pakie Monahan said to Dowler that he would be far better off with 'an owld ass' as they never ran out of petrol and that 'although they could be a bit stubborn you don't have to push an ass 12 miles!'

'Jaysus my car doesn't need petrol either Pakie,' Dowler responded. 'I know well they can be a bit stubborn, but I just get some old ass to push me 12 miles while I sit at the wheel!'

It was an argument I knew I couldn't win, so I changed the subject and asked Pakie:

'Where's the Tiger gone, he's usually lying down on his bed when he is not on duty?'

'Oh Jaysus, I nearly forgot te tell yiz,' Monahan replied, 'ye know he was always complaining about the pulled muscle in his back, well it turns out it was broken. He's in feckin hospital.'

'A broken back?!' I responded, 'he's been talking about having that pulled muscle for months, we thought he was just coddin us along, even Dr Gohan told him he only had growing pains.'

'But sher Gohan would only give ye ED if ye came to him in a coffin,' Dowler interrupted, 'we'll have to go to see him.'

Sure enough when the three of us walked into the medical unit, there was the Tiger in bed at the end of the ward, surprisingly sitting up but covered from his neck to his waist in plaster; his arms thrust rigidly forward as if waiting to be hugged. Immediately I thought he looked like Lon Chaney Jr. in *The Mummy's Curse*, and had to try not to laugh.

His face lit up when he saw us:

'About feckin time yiz came to visit me' he said, having strained his neck around as much as the plaster-cast would allow. He was peering at us out of the corner of his eyes whilst talking straight ahead. 'Everyone else gets lots of visitors,' he began to rant 'while ye just sit there playing cards and scratching yer arses back in the barracks!'

'But ye only have a pulled muscle, Tiger,' I joked, 'them other people are genuinely sick.'

'Aye, ye've been talking to Gohan,' responded the Tiger, 'good job he wasn't on duty when I had the x-ray or I'd still be walking round with a broken back.'

Before we carried on taking the piss out of him, The Tiger asked Monahan:

'Pakie, d'ye see that wooden ruler over there on the table?'

'Aye,' replied Monahan.

'Will ye push that between me and this plaster-cast and scratch my back,' the Tiger was clearly in some discomfort, 'I am so feckin itchy,' he revealed, 'its like being tickled by 1000 naked women, each holding a pint of Guinness and none of them would offer me a drop.'

'Well, ye should tell them girls to dress themselves, Tiger!' exclaimed Monahan, laughing at the irony of such a predicament. 'Some girls have no manners!'

As we carried on taking the piss out of the Tiger, we took it in turns to scratch him with the ruler; which limited his complaints to 'No, just over there a bit!' or 'Jaysus, not so feckin hard!'

Apart from his obvious discomfort with itching, we were all a little bit jealous, he had got ED for a whole month; previously unheard of from the doctors in Athlone.

Having now been a regular soldier for nearly eight months I returned home again to Edgeworthstown for Christmas; the last one of the decade. I had lots of money in my pocket, and I was determined to make it the best Christmas ever. I bought bottles of lemonade, cakes, sweets and my mother a new coat. She was delighted, it was her first new coat in 20 years and she was laughing like I had never seen before. She was so happy she even let us play pop music in the house again which seemed to make everything brighter.

Two of my brothers, Kevin and Franco, said that when I came home, it was like the return of the Prodigal Son and that if we had a fatted calf it would surely have been sacrificed as well. Times felt good, having enough money made my mother happy, we had no dogs tied up in town and there was more food in the house than we could eat. Music was emanating out of the wireless with the powerful voice of Brenda Lee, or as she was more commonly called Little Miss Dynamite singing *Rockin around the Christmas Tree*. It was great, the army had provided me with smart clothes, money and a happier family.

On Christmas Eve, The County asked me:

'Are ya coming for a pint?'

Jaysus, I thought, a pint with The County himself!

I was not much of a drinker, just halves of Smithwicks if all the soldiers were going out, but I would never drink all of it, preferring minerals like lemonade or club orange. However, I knew if I went out with my father, I would have to drink pints. Nothing less would be expected from a son of The County.

'I will, surely!' I responded enthusiastically.

'Good, now don't tell yer mother, we'll have a drink in the Mostrim Arms tonight,' he whispered not wanting my mother attending to the fire, to overhear.

As we went through the door to his favourite pub, a few of the regulars welcomed The County.

'Good evening Frank, can I get ya a drink?' They asked. Thanks to being a football legend, The County was never short of being offered a drink but he said,

'No thanks, I have to buy this man a pint,' and he turned to me and asked, 'what are ya drinking Micky?'

'I'll have a pint of Smithwicks please,' remembering the words of respected bar veterans from Doyle's and the Bridge Bar. I stood there in my crisply pressed trousers and shirt and as conversation elsewhere in the pub returned to farming, I remained chatting with The County at the counter. We spoke about everything, about the Tiger's broken back and life in the army to how Manchester United were having a great season again after the Munich air disaster the previous year. He told me how he had enjoyed becoming a grandfather and the new trains they were getting on the railways. It was great, I was speaking to The County 'man-to-man'. I lit up a woodbine and sipped my Smithwicks and thought, 'I am definitely a man now.'

The next morning was Christmas day and I was sick from all the Smithwicks and woodbines, not to mention all the lemonade, cakes and sweets I had eaten, but my mouth was anything but sweet; it tasted more like I'd been licking the floor of Barney Farrell's hen-coup. My head was pounding and I was in no shape to listen to my parents having an argument about me.

'What are ye trying to do to the young fella?' my mother quizzed The County, 'he's barely old enough to wipe his arse, and there's you making him drink pints in the pub! And he's broken his pledge, ye'll have to go to confession Micky.'

I suddenly felt very much like a 15 year old boy again.

'Ah, will ya leave the lad alone,' replied The County. 'A few pints never hurt anyone, he'll be fine after a while, he's just a bit hung over. De ya fancy a hair o' the dog Micky?'

Just the thought of another Smithwicks brought back the sickly aroma of fermented beer and I dashed out of the house holding my mouth just long enough to avoid being sick over an unsuspecting Nasser.

The County laughed as if it was some kind of initiation ceremony.

'Would ya like some rashers and eggs Micky?'

'Quit, will ye!' interrupted my mother, 'he'll be lucky if he's right for his Christmas dinner.'

'I'll never drink again,' I said to myself, wondering how I was feeling so bad whilst The County looked as if he'd been drinking holy water all night.

It took me two days to recover but with the new decade of the '60s approaching, there seemed to be a great deal of energy about the place. From now on I would stick to lemonade but young people everywhere seemed emboldened with vitality at the heart of which was a burgeoning music scene. As the new-year celebrations began there was real excitement and a feeling of freedom. The social shackles of the conforming '50s seemed to be disappearing. In the dancehalls they were now playing Jerry Lee Lewis and his pumping piano belting out *Whole Lotta Shakin Goin On* followed by his very controversial *Great Balls of Fire*.

My favourite song of 1959 was the Isley Brothers' *Shout* and the frenzied lyrics then boomed out from wireless all over Ireland:

> And a little bit louder now…
> And a little bit louder now…
> Everybody shout now!

At home on our stone floor, I would imitate Kelly Isley who did the splits on stage. My PT training meant I could easily do the splits but my speciality was springing back to my feet and up on my toes then re-joining the chorus,

> Everybody shout now
> Everybody shout-shout…shout-shout-
> shout…shout
> Shout…shout…shout-shout-shout…shout

The Isley Brothers represented something that was growing in popularity from the music that was coming from the US; they had black skin, which in African and Southern American political and social circles may have been undesirable but over the radio in Ireland they sounded great and everyone was invisible. The Big Band rocking jazz and the doo-wop, honky-tonk beat of the '50s was being joined by the rebellious sound of rock 'n' roll and the distinctive pulse of rhythm and blues. There was also a new type of music, which like 'the blues', they claimed was sung in the cotton-fields of America. This was soul music. The record label MOTOWN from the MOtor TOWN of Detroit was recording black artists that were becoming more and more popular. Not only did Motown have the Isley Brothers, they also had the Temptations and Marvin Gaye.

Most evenings, the mix of music could be heard throughout the barracks as off duty soldiers dialled their tuning needles into evening music shows. My favourite was Radio Luxembourg broadcasting on 208 metres medium wave. Despite the fading signal which seemed to have a background whistle, 208 became the bandwidth of choice for young people everywhere. '208' sourced their records directly from the recording studios and purported not to play music that would favour any individual artist or political opinion. Elvis had become popular with both the white and black communities across America, the first 'crossover' performer who they said had transcended social and political barriers by breaking down segregation in the music industry, which in turn allowed black artists to become popular in white communities. Crossover music became the trend and Chubby Checker singing *The Twist* began causing a revolution in the kitchens and dance halls throughout Ireland.

When we were off duty during the day, with Radio Luxembourg playing in the background, I would try anything to look both older and trendier as the new fashions of rebellious music, counter cultures and non-conformity had even managed to influence Irish culture. I started smoking 'push to open' cartons of Sweet Afton cigarettes, made by Carroll's of Dundalk and named after a poem by Robert Burns. They were considered to be Ireland's only contribution to a lifestyle of bohemian creativity after Jean Paul Sartre had been pictured smoking a pack on the left bank or 'Rive Gauche' of the Seine in Paris. The French language, the lifestyle, and probably most importantly, their provocative actresses made Paris even cooler than Hollywood. The most enjoyable thing when not on duty was lying down and smoking on my bunk, while Radio Luxembourg played it's most popular song "Non, je ne regrette rien" by Edith Piaf. Ahh... Sweet Afton.

Flow gently, sweet Afton! among thy green braes,
Flow gently, I'll sing thee a song in thy praise;
My Mary's asleep by thy murmuring stream-
Flow gently, sweet Afton, disturb not her dream.

Robert Burns, 1791

When Radio Luxembourg wasn't broadcasting, we listened to Radio Athlone, and it was noticeable how the colour of skin was being featured more and more in the international news segment. In February 1960 we were told that four black students had launched a sit-down protest at a Woolworth's lunch counter in Greensboro, North Carolina where seating was reserved for whites only. The protests, they said, spread to larger American cities like Charlotte, Raleigh and Nashville. A civil rights movement was gaining momentum in the US led by Martin Luther King, arguing that although black people had the right to vote in national elections, they were denied the right in local elections resulting in continued segregation in public services e.g. education and public transport. A more militant black consciousness was also emerging that rejected the non-violence approach of the civil rights movement and advocated self defence by whatever means necessary. Its most vocal leader was Malcolm X who changed what he called his slave name, from 'Little' to 'X', which, he said, symbolised the African name that had been seized from his ancestors on an

African slave-ship. He described white people as a race of devils who were inferior to blacks. Fearful whites in the southern States we were told, demanded a continuation of segregation or the 'southern way' to protect themselves and, in their defence, quoted 'the greatest American president of them all', Abraham Lincoln.

> I will say then that I am not nor ever have been in favour of bringing about in any way the social and political equality of the white and black races … Although there is no reason in the world why the negro is not entitled to all the natural rights enumerated in the declaration of independence, the right to life, liberty and the pursuit of happiness… I am not, nor ever have been in favour of making voters or jurors of negroes, nor of qualifying them to hold office, or intermarry with white people; and I will say that in addition to this that there is a physical difference between the white and black races which I believe will forever forbid the two races living together on terms of social and political equality.

Abraham Lincoln 1858 debate with Stephen Douglas

The same month as the Greensboro protest, Harold MacMillan gave a speech in Cape Town, where similar racial segregation policies were being implemented by South Africa's pro white National party. Macmillan spoke of the 'winds of change blowing through Africa' and that 'whether we like it or not, this growth in national consciousness is a political fact.'

Whilst he was addressing a white south African audience, we were hearing on the wireless that black people in Africa were demonstrating for an end to the apartheid policies that stopped them getting work or living in certain areas under the auspices of the 'pass laws'. Immediately I thought of the Nazi era where the Jews were made to wear a yellow Star-of-David and have their passports identified with a 'J'. The South African propaganda machine of the ruling white government led by Henrik Voerward told reporters that they advocated an American doctrine of 'separate but equal' and that apartheid was 'a policy of good neighbourliness.'*

As I had discussed with The County, Ireland's politicians were still leading the campaign against apartheid and supported African states' drive to end white colonial rule. Although the white population in South Africa was said to be too powerful, the democracy movements of other African states were demanding change immediately. In a decision that had significant implications for the Irish army, the Irish government announced that they would commit Irish troops to defend the authority of the UN in non-aligned African countries that requested their assistance.

The Irish government insisted that its soldiers would only be used as peacekeepers in defence of the ideals of the UN, but suddenly the prospect of Ireland becoming involved in a conflict beyond its own borders for the first time in its history was becoming real. This heightened the interest in the barracks as the images of war we had seen in the movies stirred up memories of heroic battles, and people began to use grand military words like 'courage' and 'honour', all adding to the anticipation of defending the cause of Ireland abroad.

* Tomaselli, Keyan (1990) *Culture, Communication and Media Studies – Freedom Square – Back to the Future.*

Just one month after MacMillan's speech, the headline now was that 69 black Africans had been killed when South African police opened fire on demonstrators in Sharpeville, in the Transvaal region, later becoming known as the Sharpeville Massacre. The South African government, we were told on the news, 'publicly justified their actions by saying that the demonstrations sought to undermine the state's policies as set out in the suppression of communism act and the group areas act.' As Verwoerd's National Party in Pretoria knew only too well, any policy that claimed to be against communism would be supported by the US and the rest of the so-called 'free world'. However, in the non-aligned and neutral countries like Ireland, there was complete shock. To many Irish, with their own history of colonial tyranny and oppression, revolution and independence seemed the only answer for many African states.

Even to young naïve soldiers like myself, Dowler, Monahan and the Tiger, we knew this commitment by the government to send troops would be complicated by deep-seated prejudices and disputes in Africa, but at the same time we were angered by such obvious unfairness. The new decade of the 1960s may have been lifted by music and a growing social enlightenment but old style colonialism and the hostile atmosphere of the Cold War seemed to consolidate entrenched attitudes towards native people, race, religion and power. Underlying all of the motives, the vast untapped mineral resources meant Africa had something that all of the opposing sides wanted – money.

The broadcaster on Radio Eirann noted that in other parts of Africa, independence movements had succeeded, but now there was increasing coverage of more dangerous independence struggles like The Congo and French Algeria. I knew from The County that Conor Cruise O'Brien had advocated talks between France's President de Gaulle and the Algerian independence movement: the Front Nationale Liberation or FLN a couple of years beforehand. De Gaule finally conceded that democracy in Algeria was inevitable by uttering the words 'self determination' in a speech. The white colons of Algeria felt betrayed and we watched the television reports showing barricades in Algiers adorned with the slogan 'Vive Massu' [Long live Massu]. Massu was the leader of the French colons known as the Pied-Noir [the black feet] and the civil disobedience campaign became known as 'La semaine des barricades' [barricades week].

The Pied-Noir were determined to carry on with European colonial rule and were against any democratic vote as they only comprised ten per cent of the Algerian population, effectively signalling their demise. Now in 1960, ceding power of an African colony represented an intention to all white Europeans that their mother countries were prepared to abandon them because of international pressure and in the case of Algeria, the surrender by France to the FLN.

In contrast to the stories we heard from Irish reporters, the British news coverage we saw alleged that the FLN were savages and were responsible for acts of terrorism including murder and torture against innocent whites who had only brought commerce and prosperity to the colonies. The reporter, mindful of British interests in Rhodesia, Kenya and Uganda where independence struggles were also taking place, was firmly on the side of the native French colonials who he argued were being targeted by terrorists. 'Their lives are being torn apart,' he stated, 'the whites have a right to protect their livelihoods'.

The County had often said to me that the first casualty of war is truth, as journalists write what their paymasters want. He often spoke to me about the Beaverbrook press in the UK which represented the PR agenda of the UK establishment, including banks and mining firms, which had so much to lose from losing its colonial territories. Clearly the colonial powers had an interest in winning the PR war and retaining the status quo that supported their mother countries. But on the Irish news the perspective on Algeria could not have been more different. The main terrorist organisation, it said, was now a group of disenfranchised Pied-Noir or Ultras known as the Organisation de l'Armee Secrete or OAS. They had bombed French institutions and killed Algerian civilians in response to their betrayal by de Gaulle. Many were former members of the French Foreign Legion known as Legionnaires, who, we were told, were largely made up of thieves and cut-throats but were considered the hardest army in the world. As some of the native French fled back to France, many Pied-noir businesses became unviable, and the OAS members needed money. The white Europeans of the colonial empires were gradually loosening their grip on power and the retiring Legionnaires no longer had a place called home. As many parts of Africa descended into anarchy, many OAS operatives sought out lucrative work as soldiers of fortune or mercenaries in a vastly rich but increasingly unstable continent.

Monahan and Dowler would often joke that if they did anything wrong they could always run away to join the French Foreign Legion as we had heard that they would overlook previous wrongdoings, even murder, and provide an escape to a new life with a new identity. The price of this escape was a minimum five year commitment to the Legionnaire brotherhood, cut off from family and friends.

I had seen the Abbot and Costello film where they ended up accidentally enlisting as Legionnaires complete with white kepis and red rolled blankets, looking like right eejits clambering up huge sand dunes in Algeria, searching for a camel.

'They'll take any old mad bastard,' insisted Dowler, 'thieves, murderers, misfits, rapists, even fellas from Edgeworthstown!' clearly a swipe at me and Monahan.

'Ah but they wouldn't take you Sean,' affirmed Monahan who knew exactly how to deal with Dowler's humour, 'ya'd never do anything wrong, ya don't drink, smoke or curse, and yer still hangin onto yer communion money, they'd never take a mean old bastard like you!'

The Legionnaires had achieved almost mythical status amongst soldiers because of the renegades that joined and because the training would make ours look like a holiday camp. We heard they had to pull themselves on ropes without a safety harness across 300 foot ravines and learn to jump from low-flying planes. Even the present day members lived under the code of 'no surrender' an honour dating back to the Battle of Cameron in 1863 where the three last survivors of an original 62 Legionnaires refused to surrender against 2000 Mexicans. They were also noted amongst soldiers for leisurely marching at only 88 paces per minute, 32 less than our regular parade marching whilst singing repetitive songs about how they detested the Belgians:

> Well there's sausage, there's sausage,
> there's sausage,
> For the Alsatians, the Swiss and the Lorrainers;

There's none left for the Belgians,
there's none left for the Belgians,
They are malingerers;
There's none left for the Belgians,
there's none left for the Belgians;
They are malingerers!

Whilst the code of the Foreign Legion was to serve France with honour and fidelity and to never surrender arms, de Gaulle's apparent U-turn had meant that Algeria, the Legion's spiritual home for 130 years had been surrendered – and therefore the thing they held most dear; their honour, was being devalued.

Algeria's independence had also given inspiration to other native African freedom movements. In the barracks, we watched riots taking place in Kinshasa in The Congo, the colony of the Foreign Legion's fabled enemy: Belgium. The 'Independence Now!' movement was now causing civil unrest against what The Congolese saw as a protracted 30 year plan for independence. Only weeks after MacMillan's 'winds of change' speech, we suddenly heard that Belgium had lost control of The Congo and would immediately grant full independence. Elections were scheduled to take place as early as June 1960, with Patrice Lumumba expected to win.

It wasn't just politics that was dominating world news, the music from the States was what young people everywhere were talking about. In the Spring, Elvis Presley had completed his military service and signalled his arrival back on the world stage with the album: *Elvis is Back*, which included such greats as *It's Now or Never*.

Now, when Monahan opened the door of his bedside cabinet he would burst into a verse of 'Are you lonesome tonight, will you kiss me tonight?' staring longingly at his latest magazine photograph of Brigitte Bardot, his idolised French sweetheart pictured in army attire, promoting her latest film *Babbette Goes to War*.

The Tiger, Dowler and I, all fans of rock 'n' roll ourselves, teased him that Elvis only sang Devil music, a phrase we heard was used in the US on Gerry Falwell's show, 'Old-Time Gospel Hour', and that he should instead be singing songs from Elvis' first gospel album, *His Hand in Mine*.

'Yer talking bollocks!' responded Monahan as he turned his cabinet round to show us the collage of pictures of his busty French heroine.

Like Elvis I just wanted to complete my military commitment and then leave the army. The hierarchical system seemed to be out of step with the mood of the new decade as we heard more about student movements, civil rights and freedom campaigns and nowhere more so than in Africa.

Whilst we couldn't have a freedom campaign in the army, similar to young people everywhere we were wary of authority and in the army this authority was delivered by the officers. I was guarding a delivery of tents and toilets one day with the Tiger, Dowler and Monahan when an officer came up to me and asked me what I was doing. I happily explained to him in detail that we were on our way to the Curragh to deliver tents and toilets, where exactly they would be dropped off, how long the journey would take and when we expected to get back to Athlone. When the officer had gone, Dowler looked at me with complete dismay:

'What are ya doing, explaining everything to them, ya feckin eejit ya?' he asked, 'tell them nothing. Hey Pakie, de ya hear what he's been telling the officers?'

Before Monahan could respond I jumped in, 'But I had to Sean, he asked me what I was doing.'

'Had to my arse!' Dowler explained. 'One officer once told me, "we learn as much as we can off ye, and then, when we know it all, we can tell ye what to do."'

I didn't know what to say, so Dowler carried on ranting at me:

'Just tell them as little as possible and just keep calling them 'Sir' – they like that. But in future if they ask ya what yer doing, just tell them yer packing the van ....Sir! Then they'll ask ye what for, so tell them to make a delivery..... Sir! Where to: the Curragh .....Sir! But never tell them exactly how long it will take and what time ye expect to get back. If ye have to, make up some bollocks about getting authorisations.... so it's difficult to tell.... Sir! Now we'll be tearing around like feckin hares to be back in time. We wanted to stop off in Moate for our dinner and a game of cards.'

I had managed to stop the Tiger from whistling his latest tune and even Monahan didn't make a joke. This time I knew I had messed up.

Dowler was right as usual. If I was to have an easier time in this new era of freedom and civil rights movements I had to be smarter dealing with authority.

At the end of June 1960, I remember that it was another unusually biblical day of sunshine in Athlone and we were playing cards in the barracks with the television on in the background. I had been reading a letter from home that my sister Mary had her second child, a daughter that would be named after my mother – Katleen. She was overjoyed and told me in great detail of all the features and tiny characteristics of my new God-daughter. 'She has eyes like you,' she said, 'and her mother's nose'. Unlike football or politics, nothing delighted my mother more than babies, it was like they gave her a new lease of life. My attention was suddenly distracted to other babies being hoisted above their mothers' heads over in another newscast from The Congo. On the TV, crowds of young people were celebrating in the capital; Leopoldville singing their new national anthem 'Debout Congolaise' [Arise Congolese]. Even on the fuzzy black and white television I could tell that everyone had worn their brightest most colourful clothes which were probably The Congo's version of Sunday best and carrying flags of the MNC, the political party of Patrice Lumumba. They were holding up the babies as a sign of a better future because something momentous had taken place: they had elected their first government in their first ever democratic elections. The Congo had officially become an independent country, bringing to an end nearly 80 years of colonial rule.

Lumumba's MNC party had won the election and he was to be installed as the new democracy's Prime Minister, marking him out as a hero and now the most prominent African leader in the media. His dream was to return The Congo to a place where all tribes and cultures were respected, where the community of Congolese people could flourish together. He was a slim man, intelligent looking with small round glasses and a distinctive goat-like beard. The crowd sang along to the beating of drums and the people were ecstatic as King Baudouin I of Belgium and his entourage of Belgian officials looked on from the balcony of the Palais de la Nation. The newscaster translated from French as the King rose to announce the independence of the largest country in central Africa. Alongside Lumumba, Joseph Kasa-Vubu was appointed the country's non-executive President. Belgium had capitulated in the face of such a strong independence movement and fearing an Algerian style colonial war, granted the people of The Congo what they had yearned for – a self-determined government. Whilst the crowd waited in anticipation for the words 'independence' and 'freedom', King Baudouin spoke of the bravery and courage of his ancestor King Leopold II, whom the city of Leopoldville was named after, who he said had achieved so much when he owned The Congo between 1885 and 1908. He went on to speak of the supreme efforts of the Belgian officials who had worked tirelessly to bring civilisation to The Congolese people. This was a proud Belgian achievement he said, and The Congo was a monument to Belgium's skill and ingenuity in Africa.

The crowd was stunned into silence. They hated being a Belgian colony and regarded their independence as a release from tyranny. Then unexpectedly their new elected leader, Lumumba rose to address them. Suddenly the music re-started and they burst again into singing and dancing, then hushed as he was about to speak:

> Victorious fighters for independence, today victorious, I greet you in the name of The Congolese Government... I ask you to make this June 30, 1960, an illustrious date that you will keep indelibly engraved in your hearts, a date of significance of which you will teach to your children.

The rhetoric then changed from one of electoral victor to one of bitter enemy.

> This was our fate for eighty years of a colonial regime; our wounds are too fresh and too painful still for us to drive them from our memory.

> We have known ironies, insults, blows that we endured morning, noon, and evening, because we are just niggers. Who will forget that to a black one said 'tu', certainly not as to a friend, but because the more honourable 'vous' was reserved for whites alone?
>
> I ask you unconditionally to respect the life and the property of your fellow citizens and of foreigners living in our country. If the conduct of these foreigners leaves something to be desired, our justice will be prompt in expelling them from the territory of the Republic.'

Lumumba was then later reported to turn to his former Belgian rulers, leaving them in no doubt about the resentment felt by The Congolese people.

> Nous ne sommes plus vos singes. [We are no longer your monkeys.]

The crowd erupted, the babies now bobbing up and down as the crowd danced and sang to the rhythm of tribal music. Lumumba was their 'Liberator'; they chanted his name and cheered as the Belgian officials slipped away off the stage, enraged that a black man had dared speak to them in such a demeaning way. While the crowd cheered, the indignant officials, seething from their apparent humiliation, began plotting against these promises of fairness and equality. They had a very different vision for the future of The Congo, which certainly did not fit with Lumumba's idealism. On such a momentous day, the news correspondent seemed very gloomy about the prospects for the new democracy.

In the barracks we were told that volunteers were now being sought for peacekeeping duties 'should the need arise' as the Irish government's commitment to the United Nations as a non-aligned country would require them to provide assistance in the event of hostilities in central Africa. Athlone was the largest barracks in western command and we were told it was likely that we would be called on to provide troops along with Dublin, the Curragh and Cork. The volunteer peacekeepers would be drawn from the infantry divisions who had already been trained for peacekeeping duties including riot control and public disorder. Even though myself, Monahan and Dowler were in the ordnance division, and therefore unable to volunteer immediately, The Congo became the big topic of conversation and we watched and read every report.

Within days, Lumumba had made his first populist move: he would grant a pay rise for all public departments. He had made one exception however; there would be no pay rise for The Congolese national army, the Force Publique. The reporter described it as a significant event, although Monahan pointed out wryly that it would be even more significant if we ever had a pay rise. The Force Publique was established during King Leopold's rule with a structure where only whites became officers and blacks were limited to being foot soldiers. These same soldiers watched in envy as all the other government departments received pay rises and promotions but their status remained the same. Lumumba made just one change to the Force Publique hierarchy, he appointed his assistant Joseph Mobutu as the head of the army, but that there would be no change to the structure of the army, that white officers would remain in command and that there would be no advancement for black regulars. Lumumba then demanded absolute loyalty and obedience. Not surprisingly, the army mutinied and they rampaged through Congolese towns still draped in MNC election colours, targeting Belgian owned shops and government buildings, pillaging, raping and sometimes killing everything that got in their way.

As we stood around watching the disorder on the television, the Tiger took the opportunity of pointing out the clear dissatisfaction of the Force Publique soldiers to Dowler:

'It's no surprise that the army mutinied,' he claimed, 'when they see all them other fellas being promoted and driving round in new Citroens and Minis, whilst they are left driving them owld Morris Minors like yours Sean. Aye, that would be a terrible insult to any soldier!'

Dowler typically didn't bother to respond, and just smiled as everyone laughed. As usual he would find a better time to return the jibe about his beloved car.

Just days after the independence celebrations it seemed to us that The Congo was in turmoil as the country began to collapse into anarchy. Belgium despatched troops against Lumumba's orders, to protect, they claimed, the innocent white Belgian population. When the paratroopers arrived they immediately took control of areas of economic interest along with key installations, e.g. airports and communications buildings, which were all located in The Congo's southern province of Katanga. It did not seem a co-incidence that the day after the arrival of Belgian troops, that Katanga itself became the focus of news reports as its leader Moise Tshombe claimed its own independence or what it called 'succession', claiming that it needed 'to protect itself'. Katanga was also the province where the country's mines and mineral wealth were located, holding the keys to the fledgling country's wealth. If the succession of Katanga succeeded, the other five provinces of The Congo were effectively bankrupt. Tshombe, we heard, was covertly backed by the Belgian government back in Brussels seeking to retain power for their ex-pat companies, the largest of which was the Union Miniere du Haute Katanga (UMHK), the massive mining conglomerate that had made a staggering 30 billion Belgian Francs' profit in 1959 from its Katangan mines, with all the taxes being paid to Brussels.

Although the Belgian government was much criticised by foreign governments for their Congolese policy, the taxes paid by Congolese ex-pat companies to the Belgian state had provided significant funding for infrastructure, schools and hospitals back in post war Belgium. Any loss of this revenue would mean economic hardship for The Congo's former colonial master and political suicide for its leaders.

As the virtuous circle that the colonial powers throughout Africa enjoyed was being threatened, the Belgian government and corporations undertook a policy of providing certain black politicians and businessmen with a lavish lifestyle if they maintained policies that would continue to fill the coffers of the Brussels Chancellery. Moise Tshombe was one of those politicians being handsomely rewarded for being the voice of the succession. At the UN and in public policy statements, Belgium and the other colonial powers were careful not to formally recognise Katanga as an independent state, as they would be in breach of the Atlantic charter and therefore incur the wrath of the Americans. It seemed clear that what the Belgians said publicly was not what they were manipulating privately. Monahan sarcastically pointed out; 'they say publicly they want to help The Congo from drowning but they won't take their feckin foot off its head.'

Lumumba, hesitant of contacting the apartheid-supporting Americans, threatened to contact the Russians to stop both the Katanga succession and the rampaging Force Publique. Both had the potential to break-up his fledgling democracy. Although America was seeking an end to colonialism, and therefore opposed to the succession, it was still preferable to the spread of communism, and they would not tolerate Lumumba calling in the Russians. If Lumumba carried out his threat, a Cold War showdown was looking like a real possibility.

To avoid all out civil war in The Congo and a possible nuclear confrontation, the UN was called in. Irish troops recruited from infantry divisions were dispatched immediately. In the Irish army nothing ever happened quickly but the call up of the Irish infantry for UN duty happened within days. Unbelievably, I was on my first ever holiday in the Sligo coastal town of Mulloughmore when the request for the first volunteers soldiers was made. As I strolled along the beach and admired the Ballygawley hills, apparently Athlone barracks became a hive of activity. When I got back to Athlone, Dowler told me that the lads in the infantry divisions were desperate to get over to The Congo, despite the reports of turmoil, and that the quota of volunteers was filled within hours.

'The Tiger,' he told me, 'volunteered immediately, he couldn't get on the plane quick enough.'

It seemed that the chance of being where the danger was, made it like an exciting adventure that nobody wanted to miss although our briefings by senior officers told us that the duties would only be similar to that of the Guarda Siochana, or police work. The Irish government re-stated its intention that it would play its role along with the other non-aligned countries but only commit to peacekeeping duties.

Then Lumumba demanded that the UN be used to expel the Belgian troops by force or again he would call in the Russians. Lumumba had now managed to cause outrage amongst all the non-aligned countries including the Irish government, who insisted that the UN stick to the original mandate, and that the UN troops remain non-combatants. When Belgian paratroopers did not leave The Congo, Lumumba made his 'fateful mistake', as it was described in the Irish press: he carried out his threat and called in the Russians.

President Kasa-Vubu immediately dismissed Lumumba as Prime Minister after only 67 days in office but Lumumba responded by dismissing Kasa-Vubu. Constitutionally the country was in disarray, so the new head of the military Colonel Mobutu announced a suspension of government for three months to allow the situation to be resolved, placing his new Prime Minister Lumumba under house arrest.

In the midst of the crisis, we were told that Kasa-Vubu had returned to his bed and had not been seen for three days.

'Perhaps he has a bad back just like the Tiger,' quipped Dowler.

'Aye, it's a good job the Tiger isn't around,' I said, 'or he'd be telling ya to feck off!'

But Dowler found it all very amusing and continued teasingly, 'or maybe Kasa-Vubu just has them growing pains in his back, like Dr. Gohan diagnosed.'

Events in The Congo then took a dramatic turn. Lumumba 'escaped' from house arrest but had been re-arrested en route to his stronghold city of Stanleyville in the north of The Congo. The once loyal aid of Lumumba, Colonel Mobutu, now had him imprisoned under the military law he had imposed. Although it was very much against the wishes of the electorate, this was clearly a popular move with Western governments. Mobutu then did something that would make him very popular with the US: he announced that all Russian and Eastern bloc soldiers were to be expelled from the country. It didn't take much to figure out that, just as the Belgians were rewarding Tshombe, the Americans via the CIA were rewarding Mobutu.

With the dispatch of Irish troops now stationed in The Congo, the first troops ever sent by an Irish government to an overseas conflict, the heart of Africa remained in the headlines. It seemed that the world's attention was gripped by the political turmoil and the threat of a broader and potentially devastating conflict, which was both scary and exciting.

Our excitement suddenly turned to outright revulsion one autumn afternoon in 1960. It was reported that nine peacekeepers from Dublin had been killed in Niemba in the troublesome southern province of Katanga. But most scary of all, they had been eaten.

'Feckin hell! They've eaten the poor feckers,' shrieked Dowler as the rest of us stood around wondering if this could be true.

In all of the horrendous stories we had read about war; from the trenches of the Great War to the concentration camps, of mutilations, torture and murder, we had never heard of cannibalism.

'What kind of police duty is that?' Dowler went on, 'and where the fuck was their support?'

As the story unfolded we were told that the Irish UN troops were on a routine patrol when they were mistaken for Belgian soldiers by members of the Baluba tribe, who were armed only with bows and poisonous arrows. The patrol, comprised of eleven peacekeepers, fired back but were easily outnumbered and only two managed to escape.

'It was a mistake,' said one of our officers at the morning briefing, 'they were mistaken for Belgians'.

'So is it alright to eat Belgians?' Dowler whispered next to me.

Two weeks later the nine victims of Niemba had their funeral in Dublin which we watched in the barracks back in Athlone. It was the biggest funeral seen in Ireland since those of Charles Stuart Parnell and Michael Collins with hundreds of thousands of mourners coming out to honour the funeral cortege. The word 'Baluba' entered the Dublin vernacular as the worst sort of human animal. We were told in the barracks that what was not known by those that attended the funeral was that the coffins were empty and had just been weighed down with stones.

We all knew that Niemba was a military disaster. If the officers had looked at intelligence reports they would have known that the area was unstable between the rival tribes, and anyone with white skin would be a particular target. They were also cut off from any kind of support, effectively leaving them open to ambush and in a helpless situation if they were outnumbered. One of the first things we learned in military training was never to get cut off, to keep supply lines open and to observe intelligence reports. We all suspected an army cover-up but the press coverage of Niemba meant this was not an easy incident for the army to hide. Questions were being asked by the media about military incompetence and all of Athlone seemed to be talking about it. The Irish army continued to insist calmly that it was simply a case of mistaken identity.

I knew something else from my basic training, from when Cpl Haydn and Lynagh were discharged, that the army hierarchy liked to move things along when something controversial happened. Usually there was no explanation and no questions would be asked but with Niemba it was different; the people of Ireland wanted answers.

To abate their appetite the army issued a report that one of the soldiers killed at Niemba, Private Browne had given up his life to save the life of one of the two survivors: Private Kenny. Browne became the hero the army needed, and everyone's attention was diverted from the horror of Niemba, as they began talking about his selfless heroism that saved Pte Kenny. The explanation was that Pte Browne was single and was willing to lay down his life for Pte Kenny who had a young family back home with Browne apparently providing cover that enabled Kenny to escape. It was an emotive story of an Irish hero and the army posthumously commended Browne with a coveted medal of honour for giving up his life to save a fellow soldier. The Irish people's quest for answers was partially abated.

However, some journalists still questioned the army's incompetence in the massacre and regarded the hero story as a distraction from the open questions regarding support and supply lines. More questions were raised in the barracks when rumours reached us that the 'hero' story might have been a deliberate distraction. Apparently the truth of what happened was that the group was indeed cut off and as they had been ambushed by the Baluba, it was every man for himself, each soldier firing desperately to survive. Pte Browne did what he could to fend off the Baluba as did all eleven of the soldiers that were surrounded, but Kenny only survived because of his survival skills and most importantly he was very lucky. It was a nice tribute to Browne, one of eleven heroes that had effectively been abandoned but we reasoned amongst ourselves but if the story of him selflessly saving Pte Kenny's wasn't accurate, it was a terrible guilt to be placed onto Pte Kenny; that another gave up their life for him.

The Irish soldiers were not the only victims of the Baluba tribe. Not long after, 13 Italian airmen were captured, cut up and distributed to eat amongst cheering bystanders. Cannibalism was a war trophy in this jungle offensive, symbolising victory to the warring tribes and especially valued if the prize was the one the natives feared most: the white man. The horror of the stories we were hearing raised tensions in the barracks further but in a strange way, as the danger rose, so did the excitement levels. The Congo now represented a real war and not just doing police work. As all of Ireland tried to absorb what had happened at Niemba, it seemed ironic that now nearly every soldier in Athlone wanted to get involved.

'It's what we joined the army for,' said Dowler. 'What's the point of signing up if you don't volunteer when the war comes along?'

In the First World War I had read that it was socially unacceptable if a soldier became a conscientious objector because they had taken the 'King's shilling' during the non-war years. It made me think that when I first joined the army my only aim was to get the fare to London. But now that I had enlisted and had read the stories of brave and honourable soldiers in campaigns like the Great War, I felt something very different. Just like Elvis, I still didn't like guns or fighting but I still had the images from Hollywood lodged in my mind and naïvely believed that war was romantic and that the good guys always won in the end.

As the furore over Niemba ebbed away, something very different gripped the entire nation of Ireland: the election of a new president. But this wasn't just any election fought between garrulous old men, out-bragging each other about holding up the GPO in Dublin 44 years ago, this was Ireland's finest son, John F. Kennedy, standing for president of the most powerful nation in the world: the United States of America. It was also the first presidential election that we were able to watch on the television and we were inspired by the bootlegger's son from County Cork attempting to become the first Irish catholic descendent ever to hold the office. He would also be the youngest president at only 43. One of the features of his campaign that made him more popular in Ireland was that he was a keen supporter of the civil rights movement in the American south.

We did not hear the result until two days after the elections but when we did it was incredible; Kennedy had won, beating the poker-player Richard Nixon or Tricky Dicky as he had been labelled in the campaign. All of Ireland celebrated. Shops sold colour pictures of Kennedy posing statesmanlike and peering triumphantly into the distance against the backdrop of an American flag. People were holding presidential parties and his fore-fathers' home town of Cork held a victory parade. Pubs all over Ireland celebrated with Irish and American flags hoisted from every post. Although Ireland remained officially neutral in the Cold War, the Irish people were firmly pro-American now that an Irishman was president.

Kennedy was to be inaugurated as the 35th President of the United States at noon on 20 January 1961 which left Eisenhower the outgoing president in charge, the press calling him a lame duck president.

If I were to go to The Congo I would have to transfer to the infantry division, albeit temporarily, which I discussed with Dowler and Pakie Monahan. We all agreed to attend the next volunteer presentation to be held in Athlone barracks the following week.

The presentation was held in the gym of Athlone barracks and we were told that a battalion of volunteer troops was required from Ireland's Western command for a tour of duty in 12 weeks' time.

'The tour of duty is to the Belgian Congo for a term of six months,' the officer announced. 'This is not a conflict situation, we are peacekeepers but we are on 'active service' under the authority of the United Nations Overseas Command (UNOC). That means we are there to maintain peace and are not allowed to use force except in self defence. You are not allowed to fire unless fired upon.'

'Suits me' I thought, 'I don't even like guns.'

Given the increasing tensions and what happened at Niemba, Dowler's more astute mind could see the flaw in this command, and he put up his hand to ask a question.

'So do we have to wait until we've been shot, before we're allowed to shoot back?' he asked.

'Not exactly,' came the reply in an authoritative manner but seemingly aware of the irony implied in Dowler's question, 'you are not authorised to shoot first, only to defend yourself, but you are on active service.'

Whilst this still didn't make sense, these were the instructions that had been agreed at the UN in New York by the world's heads of State. The presentation was just passing on the official instructions to the UN army which were obviously impractical. However, nobody wanted to be the one to undermine an officer with a follow up question.

At the end of the presentation there was some other 'grave news he had to tell us ... that could make the situation in The Congo more volatile. Patrice Lumumba, the country's new president had been executed.' Then he cut off the possibility of any follow-up questions by saying, 'I have no further details at this time.' A gasp ran around the hall.

The rumour was that the CIA had been instructed to assassinate Lumumba after he had sought aid from the Russians. The secret service of the free world that advocated openness and democracy planned to poison The Congo's democratically elected leader with a lethal injection. American officials publically dismissed any such conspiracy. The other rumour was that the CIA was beaten to Lumumba's assassination by the Belgians who, ever since his 'we are no longer your monkeys' speech, had plotted to remove Lumumba by whatever means as he was a threat to their economic welfare. To us, it seemed that both the US and Belgians publicly supported democracy, but that the people of The Congo had not elected the candidate they wanted so one of them had Lumumba executed. As the rumours were denied and unsubstantiated it seemed little wonder that we were not provided any further details, the truth was almost inconceivable.

The furore over Lumumba's murder caused uproar and many in Ireland likened it to the execution of the leaders of the Irish independence movement. Eerily similar to the last words of the Irish patriot, Kevin Barry 40 years beforehand, prior to his death Lumumba apparently uttered, 'Freedom is the ideal for which throughout history... throughout centuries, men have fought and died.'

The Russians were also in uproar and threatened to intervene in The Congo. They spoke of a western conspiracy implicating Britain, France, Belgium, the US and the southern African states of Rhodesia and

South Africa. Even in sleepy Athlone, we thought that this conspiracy could tip the Russians into a nuclear confrontation. Hammarskjöld convened an emergency UN meeting attended by all the world leaders including Khrushchev, Eisenhower, MacMillan, Tito, Castro, Nehru and many others, to pass a resolution allowing UN soldiers to use force in The Congo if necessary. Hammarskjöld pleaded to the leaders at the UN,

> There should be no hesitation because we are at a turn in the road where our attitude will be of decisive significance, I believe not only for the future of this organisation but also the future of Africa, and Africa may well in present circumstances mean the world.

The main difference in the resolution being proposed by Hammarskjöld was that this allowed the UN to use force to keep the warring sides apart and not just in self defence. However, UN soldiers were still only allowed to fire if they were being fired on. After much debate and objections mainly by the Eastern bloc, the UN resolution was not passed as it was argued that more debate was needed. Back in the mess we all discussed The Congo and whether we were going to sign up. Dowler was still talking to us about his point about having to be shot before being allowed to shoot back that he asked in the briefing.

'Apparently, the UN is looking to authorise us to take all appropriate measures,' he stated, reading methodically the UN proposal from the front page of the Irish Independent, 'to prevent the occurrence of civil war in The Congo, including arrangements for ceasefires, the halting of military operations, the prevention of clashes and the use of force if necessary in the last resort. But,' he continued, 'it remains clear that we are not allowed to fire unless fired upon. This is what they are trying to pass under some UN resolution?' he pointed out incredulously.

'Well back in Edgeworthstown we say that's about as much use as tits on a bull!' I interjected as we all knew that the wording of the resolution was fine for politicians but useless if you were a soldier.

'Aye,' clarified Monahan, 'that means when we tell the cannibals to quit causing trouble, they stand there gaping at us, salivating and licking their lips at the lovely rump steaks who will only fire their guns after the barbecue!'

I had to laugh, Monahan had a way of making the most dire situation sound amusing. But this was no joke, the reports from The Congo were that hundreds of people were being killed daily, as Belgian whites fled back to Europe and tribal conflicts spilled over. The peacekeepers would be flying in just as everyone else it seemed, were desperately trying to get out.

As the day of Kennedy's Presidential inauguration finally came, we all gathered expectantly to watch his speech on television. The actual event had taken place about four days before but the newsreels from America always took some time to reach Ireland. We were told that there had been heavy snow in Boston which affected the quality of the recording but that didn't bother us, as Monahan pointed out that it always snowed on television in Ireland.

When Kennedy spoke I could genuinely feel the hair on the back of my neck stand up:

> Together let us explore the stars, conquer the deserts, eradicate disease, tap the ocean depths, and encourage the arts and commerce.

The way he commanded the audience was mesmeric. Even in Athlone as we watched him speaking on the television, we watched in total silence, almost hypnotised by his promises of a new beginning. This was what the freedom of the '60s could achieve and Kennedy had the necessary vision and the right policies. He was a ground-breaker who made us believe that anything was possible and despite his relative youth he was a veteran of war having been awarded medals for bravery in World War II and was a champion of social equality.

In his speech he hit all the right chords with a generation that yearned for peace, fairness and equality amid the heightened rhetoric of the Cold War. He called this 'the new frontier' having said that both soviet and western imperialism was the biggest threat to human freedom, just like The County had told me. It was like the fiction of Aldous Huxley's 'Brave New World', where everyone lives a plentiful and peaceful existence in a unified world state, could in part be becoming a reality. When Kennedy was denounced as being too youthful, he conceded that he was the first US president to have been born in the twentieth century but that it was his generation that had done the dying in World War Two and not the leading. He'd seen first hand how terrible war was and he wanted a new future of world justice:

> Let both sides join in creating a new endeavour, not a new balance of power, but a new world of law, where the strong are just and the weak secure and the peace preserved.
>
> J. F. Kennedy

After the rumours we had heard about the CIA's involvement in Lumumba's death, directly implicating

Eisenhower, Kennedy seemed like a leader with a level head who would surely look to treat Africans fairly. He then finished by calling on all nations to fight against the 'common enemies of man: tyranny, poverty, disease, and war itself.'

Suddenly it wasn't just Sweet Afton cigarettes that made being Irish cool. We were the voice of the decent countries at the UN and we were respected as a fair and independent minded nation. And now America was going through a new beginning, led by an Irishman.

That day John Fitzgerald Kennedy became a saint in Ireland.

Back home in Edgeworthstown people were still talking about Kennedy weeks after his inauguration. Even Maggie Canavan's was selling photographs of the new saintly looking president surrounded by little American and Irish flags. I had to buy one, which I would place on my bedside cabinet back in the barracks. These were the days when smoking was good for you so I also bought 60 throat-scratching Sweet Aftons, far too many for most films at the Picture House, but that night we were going to see another biblical epic, *Spartacus*.

Having seen *Ben Hur* the previous year, the 'epics' were now the most eagerly anticipated films at the Picture House. Better still, along with my two brothers and the Dolly Dolan I was able to afford the velvet cushioned seats with arm rests; we had finally made it to the best seats at the back of the Picture House.

I sensed the Dolly fidgeting with excitement, clearly eager to stand up and claim to the Romans that he was Spartacus, when the Romans ask the hero to identify himself amongst the crowd, so I held his arm, preventing him from making an eejit of himself.

'Will ye let go of my feckin arm!' he said to me, 'yer not in the feckin army now!'

We then all gulped when we heard the ultimatum given by the emperor Mark Anthony, as Tony Curtis and Kirk Douglas sit pensively facing each other, knowing they had to fight to the death, the victor being crucified the next day.

I found out afterwards that Spartacus had been the hero of Karl Marx and that its screenwriter, Dalton Trumbo, had been blacklisted by the Hollywood studios in the McCarthy witch-hunts labelling him a communist sympathiser, which effectively ruled him out of winning an Oscar that year. Many spoke about about how under communism the individual is always subordinated to the state, where freedom of thought was considered a thoughtcrime as totalitarianism had been defined in George Orwell's *Nineteen Eighty-Four*.

The Cold War was being played out in many different arenas but apart from what I had heard was taking place in The Congo, it was not a war I could relate to, there were no guns, tanks or trenches and the leaders were small old men who meddled in politics rather than noble warriors like Spartacus or Ben Hur.

On my way home, inspired by *Spartacus* I wondered what noble cause I could fight for. With The Congo conflict still in the headlines I considered whether I could make a difference for the good side in Africa. Could this be my chance to become a hero and to be held in the same esteem as The County back in Edgeworthstown?

When I returned home one weekend, I knew The County would be up-to-date on the events being reported in The Congo. It was a conflict that still was so confusing, with all of the various influences and changes taking place. The County however understood exactly what was going on.

He explained to me that the conflict in The Congo was a three way war. First President Kasa-vubu, and the Head of defence Joseph Mobutu in Leopoldville were supported by the Americans. Secondly, the socialists now called the Lumumbaists and led by Antoine Gizenga in Stanleyville were supported by the Russians, Czechs and Chinese; and third the Katangans led by Moise Tshombe were backed by the Belgians and supporters of white-rule in Africa including covertly, Britain and France.

The County then summarised: 'The Congo's future is being determined by America, Russia and the colonial powers, most notably Belgium. They are all paying The Congolese politicians to implement policies that further their own interests, while the people of The Congo continue to live in poverty.'

'But does it make any difference if The Congo becomes communist?' I asked innocently, 'when it happened in Cuba I know the people weren't allowed to gamble anymore but if that's what the people have 'self-determined', then why not let it happen?'

'The Americans want the Belgians out because the people are dying in poverty. Poverty means hunger and hunger means they'll become communists,' noted The County 'but they can't let the Russians take control of the resources in The Congo as all the money would be diverted from a NATO supporting country (Belgium) to fund the spread of communism,' he described. 'And if the Russians get hold of the mines then they also have control of the west's most valuable Cold War commodity.'

I was confused, 'de ya mean diamonds or copper?' I asked, knowing that The Congo had the largest known reserves in the world.

'No,' he said 'there is one commodity that the West sources from The Congo that could tip the balance in a nuclear conflict, which was used in the Little Boy bomb on Hiroshima, and they cannot let the Russians get control of it.'

I still did not understand what he was saying, so he mouthed it slowly. 'URANIUM.'

The vital component of the Little Boy bomb had been sourced from the Shinkolobwe mine in Katanga, which with a single detonation had devastated the southern Japanese city and forced Imperial Japan to surrender to the Allies, ending the Second World War.

'The country's future is now being bought with brown envelopes,' The County described 'stuffed with money and paid to politicians so that they can live in luxury, whilst the big money and power is retained by external governments.'

I knew that Belgium had petitioned against UN policy, wanting their paratroopers to be expelled. The Belgian government however maintained that its presence in The Congo was only to protect their civilians arguing that if they withdrew their forces, native Belgians would be massacred.

The following month on 15 February, the Russians increased their criticism of the regime in The Congo, and demanded answers off the US about their involvement in Lumumba's death. It was JFK's first major diplomatic confrontation as US president and he responded by denying any involvement in the execution and ordered the Russians not to intervene in the pacification process taking place in The Congo. The US ambassador to the UN, Clare Timberlake, maintained that using the UN was the best way of furthering the interests of democracy and the will of The Congolese people, but they would feel compelled to act if the Russians attempted to take over the country.

Khrushchev was however not happy with the UN's efforts and continued to demand that Belgium's troops be forcibly withdrawn by UN soldiers. He then switched his focus towards the head of the UN, Hammarskjöld saying that he should be replaced as the Secretary General by a 'troika' of UN leaders so that East and West could be properly represented.

With the UN under increasing pressure, the council of members in New York finally ratified the proposal for UN troops to use force if necessary.

The press commented that the heightened rhetoric was reminiscent of the period of appeasement in the run up to World War Two, which eventually gave way and resulted in Britain and France declaring war on Germany. This time however the stakes were that much higher with both sides possessing nuclear weapons.

We all knew that regardless of the political upheaval and terrible stories, this was an adventure to an exotic country that would be too good to miss. I quoted a line from *The Man from Laramie* starring Jimmy Stewart, when the sheriff says to him, 'It's your neck Lockhart, if you want a Christian funeral, you better leave some money with the undertaker.'

Similar to the UN, the man from Laramie was seeking to overcome a wrongdoing far from home. Although we wouldn't be wearing buck-skinned jackets I noted that in our briefings we were told we would be on active service which sounded like we would be on the front line fighting, but stories I had heard in the barracks and from the Tiger who had recently returned from his first tour, meant that this could mean anything from cooking and cleaning to directing traffic as most soldiers, even in times of war, never got near the front line. The stories I had read about World War One were that the chances of reaching the trenches was only 1 in 8. By the 1950s and the wars in Korea and Guatemala, technology had advanced so much that only about 1 in every 20 soldiers would ever become engaged in actual armed combat. Being that we would only be going primarily to keep the peace, I calculated, the chances of me getting to see an actual conflict zone were disappointingly unlikely. Whilst the odds of witnessing the war were generous, The Congo still provided the opportunity of a great holiday and the excitement of being a little part of history.

When I was a boy back in Edgeworthstown, I had seen *The Wizard of Oz* for three weekends running at the Picture House, as the film reels were only changed once a month. I remembered the vibrantly colourful world of Oz, similar to the imagined world of The Congo, with its gold mines and lush green forests, but as I looked out on this February day in Athlone, it was raining just as it had been for the previous month it seemed. I dwelled on how emigration was draining Ireland of its youth and vitality just as I had read about in Goldsmith's poem. At the age of 16, Ireland seemed dull, wet and empty, and life seemed to be flourishing in the big world outside. I looked at the posters pinned in my bedside cabinet; Paris was buzzing with intellectuals, the arts and their sexy avant-garde ladies. London was swinging and twisting the night away and America was still going crazy for Elvis and rock 'n' roll. Even some smaller towns like Liverpool and Hamburg had an emerging music scene with bands like Jerry and the Pacemakers and the Beatles; famous people from humble backgrounds who were changing the world.

However, at the back of my mind was the ever-present risk of my true age being discovered. It was made worse by the thought that if I volunteered for The Congo we were meant to be 19 for overseas service. I wondered if they would re-check my birth certificate or ask me somehow to prove my age to be allowed overseas. But the excitement of a tour of duty in The Congo was like a reward for all the monotony of life in Athlone. I envisioned myself sailing up the mighty Congo or Zambezi rivers aboard *The African Queen* talking to Humphrey Bogart and Audrey Hepburn. The sunshine was glistening through the lush vegetation and I could almost hear the sound of Tarzan in the background as I stood prepared to defend the most noble of causes: Ireland, the defenders of world peace. My mind just concentrated on the heroic role I could play, the spectacular scenery, the strange black-skinned people, the jungle and the wild animals. The County once told me that George Bernard Shaw had famously said that 'an Irishman's heart is nothing, but his imagination'. My imagination had gone into overdrive, this was my adventure and although I had to do some police work, I became intoxicated with the temptation of volunteering for The Congo.

I went home to Edgeworthstown again the following weekend and told my mother that I was going to volunteer for a tour of duty. She didn't like it, her eyes narrowed as they always did when she was worried.

'I don't want ya to go Micky,' she pleaded, 'yer not even old enough to be in the army; and The Congo is a terrible place, look what happened to those poor fellas from Dublin who got surrounded in Niemba a few months ago.'

'That was a mistake mam,' I said, recounting the version of events given to us in the barracks, 'they were not supposed to be there and the Balubas mistook them for Belgians, not UN soldiers.'

'And how will they know that yer Irish?' questioned my mother almost desperately, 'what's the difference between you and them? Ye look as Belgium as they do!'

It was the same point that Dowler had made but I had prepared my response:

'Because we wear the blue helmets of the UN mam,' I said, trying to sound soothing, 'I am not going to fight with anyone, we are 'non-combatants', we're only there as peacekeepers like police officers, you know, stopping people without lights on their bikes, and telling them all to calm down. And they will be paying me eight pounds a week, that's double my current wages, along with all my board and lodgings out there. When I come back, I'll have lots of money and we can all go to London.'

My boyish optimism was lost on my mother. Her eyes remained downcast as if helpless in the knowledge that her son was now old enough to make his own decisions.

I turned to The County for re-assurance, if anyone would understand the need for UN soldiers to help end colonialism and stop the Cold War it would surely be him, but he said nothing. I hoped at the very least, he would be impressed with the wages. 'Isn't that right dad,' I asked assuredly, 'it's great money for doing police work?'

'It's great money,' he offered, but sensing the opposition of my mother he quickly distanced himself from anything that would sound supportive. 'But we still don't want ya to go, yer mother's right, yer too young even to be in the army, and The Congo is a dangerous place.' He paused, perhaps realising how idealistic and determined young men can be: 'But its up to you now, we know we can't stop ya,' he offered, which to me was the tiny shred of encouragement I was looking for.

As I left, I noticed on our mantelpiece that the pictures of the sacred heart and Michael Collins had been joined by a portrait of John F. Kennedy, similar to the one I had bought a month beforehand from Maggie Canavan's. Ringing in my ears was Kennedy's plea to active citizens, 'Ask not what your country can do for you; ask what you can do for your country.'

I returned to Athlone, my head full of fantasy and ambition. My mother did not know that Billy the Kid and Davie Crocket were also only teenagers when they became heroes. I'd seen John Wayne play the king of the wild frontier a few months before and I remembered the inspiration I felt as he launched himself into his fight against the Santa Anna's at the Alamo. Apparently Crocket was of Irish descent, and at the Alomo they said he was surrounded for 11 days. When he had run out of ammunition he walked to his certain death, clicking his empty revolvers whilst being peppered by enemy bullets.

'Remember the Alamo!' I said to myself, 'and I bet Davie Crocket didn't do everything his mammy told him.'

This was the young nation of Ireland's first involvement in an overseas conflict, and I thought that it was what the rebel and freedom movements were all about. I remembered all the stories The County had read to me when I was a boy by famous Irish authors and the mythological heroes he would tell me about before bed-time, like Finn MacCool, the legendary hunter warrior and leader of the Fianna. I may not have had a bag of magical weapons but I set off for Athlone with an added spring in my step and again felt the pride of being a soldier in uniform. I told myself that I should be honoured to be in Ireland's army and to be called on to serve on a UN tour of duty.

> Go, traveller, and imitate, if you can, one who strived with all his strength to champion liberty.
>
> Jonathan Swift

The alternative just seemed dreary in comparison. I remembered the British WWI poster where the young boy is seen asking his conscientious objector father, 'What did you do in the great war, daddy?' Now, two generations later, it was our turn and Ireland was looking for its volunteers. My answer was not going to be that I delivered feckin tents and shithouses back in miserable Athlone.

I signed up for a six month tour of duty to The Congo the next day.

CHAPTER FIVE

A glimmer of hope

Date: November, 1961
Location: Jadotville, The Congo
Status: Prisoner of war

TSHOMBIE'S VISIT TO US IN PRISON prompted something we had not expected: we would finally be allowed to leave Leopold's in Jadotville as early as the following day, but unfortunately this didn't mean we were being released, only moved to a more secure detention base about 100 miles up the road at the Katangan army base of Kolwesi. Apparently, we were told that Leopold's had only been a short term solution. With negotiations having reached a deadlock with the UN, Tshombie felt that we should be moved somewhere more long-term and less exposed to a possible rescue bid. He reportedly discussed this with Old Stoneface when they were inspecting us. They had agreed that Leopold's hotel did not have the appropriate prison security with locks and bars that would keep us confined as he wanted; and that a more secure facility would extinguish any hopes of escape we may still have.

Leopold's certainly wasn't Colditz or Alcatraz, but the chances of escape from Jadotville were virtually non-existent although it is in every imprisoned soldier's military ethic to attempt a break-out. Escape was certainly not a game that any of us took lightly but even the most laid back soldier once captured by their enemy feels that its part of his military duty to consider escape routes to somehow become involved in the good struggle again and to salvage the feeling of lost soldierly identity.

In the films at the Picture House they always portrayed escape as another compelling contest, a nail-biting game where the prisoner is always the good guy against the villains that locked them away. But here in The Congo at least, the idea of escape was an almost ludicrous proposition. If we managed to get past the armed guards and around the barbed wire surrounding us, there were at least 80 miles of incredible dangers back to Elizabethville, along a single track heavily armed road. Had we attempted to escape, we would have been lucky to be recaptured by mercenaries or even Muke's Force Publique and sent back to prison. But more likely we would have been captured by the local Lumba tribes-people and roasted alive in front of a salivating crowd. Escaping into The Congolese jungle would have meant making our way through dense forests and living off the land which would have been near impossible, becoming disorientated within hours from blinding sunlight and no fresh water. Additionally there were more poisonous berries, insects, snakes, frogs and deadly jungle animals here than anywhere else in Africa. As precarious as it was, prison could keep us relatively safe, although we didn't know how long for.

'Congratulations Michael!' announced Pakie Monahan triumphantly as we made our way out of Leopold's towards the bus that would take us to Kolwesi. 'Now, didn't I tell ya we would be let out today? Aye, I had a good feeling about today alright.' He seemed oblivious to the crowds that were gathering and were still shouting abuse at us as we boarded.

'Youz bastards!' cried out a young woman surrounded by three naked children, with another clearly expected soon.

I quietly took my seat on the bus, our limited sense of freedom from Leopold's overshadowed by a stirring of guilt at our own culpability in their distress.

'Those children will never understand,' I thought to myself, 'why they had to grow up without a father, or why another generation of white men had taken away their main source of food. We would never get the chance to explain to those young Congolese orphans that it was we who were attacked and that we had only been defending ourselves; that our mission had been to help civilians in their country.'

It would probably be the case that the same children would grow up only hearing the propoganda of the Katangan independence movement, nothing about the broader conflict, the atrocities being committed or the sins of the modern day mercenaries. They may never hear about the legacy of brutality and exploitation inflicted by Europeans that the Katangan Independence movement supported by the Belgian state was striving to continue. Or that The Congo was a place where Irishmen had only been trying to help, just like many other Irishmen had tried since Belgians took control of the region in 1885. Each time however, the efforts to stop the persecution of black people had been in vain, and the colonial white bwanas always managed to re-emerge and re-establish their absolute power. On my journey out to The Congo I had learned of the role of Roger Casement – the famous Irish rebel, and The Congo Reform Agency – the CRA. Their efforts 60 years beforehand around the turn of the century had been somewhat successful, bringing about the end of one era of exploitation and atrocity.

Unfortunately, it was only replaced with another era of colonial white rule, again at the expense of the native peoples. It was the CRA that petitioned for an end to torture of political prisoners and we heard in Leopold's prison that Amnesty International, its successor movement, had been lobbying for our protection, its first major project since it was formed in May 1961, a few months before the Jadotville siege. We were told that Amnesty had been very busy behind the scenes convincing Tshombie's forces that proper treatment for us as political prisoners was essential to any future recognition of their credibility. Although our treatment and existence in Jadotville had been meagre, we were probably the best looked after prisoners in The Congo's history. Were it not for Amnesty, we would surely have been tortured.

As we departed on our long bumpy journey to Kolwesi, our spirits were lifted on hearing the news that there were at least negotiations underway to secure our release although they hadn't been successful yet. The Tiger too was buoyed enough to start singing one of his favourite songs:

> It's a long way to Tipperary,
> It's a long way to go.
> It's a long way to Tipperary,
> To the sweetest girl I know!
> Goodbye, Piccadilly,
> Farewell, Leicester Square!
> It's a long, long way to Tipperary,
> But my heart's right there.

It was my favourite song as it allowed me to dream again of emigrating to London, if and when we were eventually released. I thought about the huge advertising hoardings I had seen in photos of Piccadilly Circus with Bovril, Coca-Cola, Schweppes Tonic and the huge 'Guinness Time' clock overlooking the busy atmosphere and crowds of people, with the distinctive black taxis and red London buses. Then, I took a final look over my shoulder at Jadotville as the sight of Leopold's Hotel vanished into the haze of red dust.

Pakie Monahan too had been inspired by our departure and had a joke to tell us:

'Did yiz hear that Tshombie died and went up to the Pearly gates to ask St Peter if he could be allowed into heaven?' he began. 'So he calls up to the gates and says: "Good morning St Peter, ye promised that if I answered the prayers of them innocent Irish fellas and let them out of Jadotville, ye would allow me into heaven, to enjoy the company of them lovely young angel girls." The reply came back from the Pearly gates,' Monahan continued, ' "Well, yer not getting in here today!"

"But St Peter!" Tshombie pleaded, "I had to kiss many white Bwana arses to let those men leave Jadotville, look at my tongue!" ' Pakie comically stretched out his tongue as if he himself was pleading to St Peter. Then he carried on: ' "and the innocent Irish soldiers are now on their way to Kolwesi as promised." ' Monahan paused momentarily before continuing:

'But the reply came back again from behind the Pearly Gates "Well, yer still not getting in here, is that clear!" "But St Peter, why?" pleaded Tshombie, "we had a deal!"

"Because that deal was made with St Peter and he is off sick today; and I'm St Patrick, and I'm telling ya to fuck off!" '

Pakie was one of the few people I knew who could tell a joke just like the Dolly Dolan back home in Ireland and everyone on the bus, about 30 in all, was laughing. Apart from the parade for Tshombie the day before, it was the first time we had seen most of the other members of 'A' Company for the last month as we had been confined to our own rooms in Leopold's.

There were also two Scandinavian UN soldiers, one from Sweden, one from Norway, on the bus who had landed a helicopter trying to re-supply us in the middle of the siege. Their names were Eric Thors and Bjorne Hovden. They both spoke fluent English, emphasizing every consonant, and were both also laughing loudly at Pakie's joke, Eric following it up with:

'Yes, and when St Brigitte is standing in for St Peter she will also tell Tshombie to fuck off!' raising another round of laughter.

If there hadn't been a thousand other acts of bravery during the siege, the landing of that helicopter by the two Scandinavians would have been the bravest thing I had ever seen. It happened on the second day, during the most intense gun-fight which hadn't stopped for the previous seven hours. The Fouga jet had also just strafed us twice and was presumably heading off to re-fuel before returning to continue the bombardment, leaving us totally beleaguered and unable to peek above the safety of the trench.

Then suddenly we heard the tractor like sound of helicopter blades in the distance and, as it got closer, we could see the letters 'UN' in bold black letters on the side. I remember Dowler shouting out:

'Look the cavalry is coming!' I looked up just as a hail of enemy gun fire let loose on the helicopter. We could hear the bullets 'pinging' loudly off the helicopter's fuselage but the pilots Eric and Bjorne carried on flying through the danger, either undeterred or completely mad. They then began to lower the helicopter amid a maelstrom of bullets and winds being whipped up by the chucking propellers.

I could see a couple of men from our company running crouched down, holding their blue UN helmets, towards the helicopter as it landed behind the Purfina garage out of sight from our trench. Our machine gunners provided cover fire for them as the helicopter landed in open ground in view of the enemy but we presumed that anyone in the helicopter would have been at least injured during the approach and probably killed.

Word then reached us in the trench that both pilots were both miraculously unscathed; despite the helicopter being peppered with bullets and rendered 'non-operational'. So, they were stuck with us under siege in Jadotville, but worse still, the supplies they had brought with them, four jerry cans of water, had become contaminated from its previous load of fuel oil and was undrinkable. Their attempts to re-supply us with water may have been in vain but their efforts made them heroes. They hardly even knew who we were, save for the odd polite acknowledgement when we were on joint UN patrols. They could just as easily have returned to Elizabethville on hearing the sound of gun-fire but they were determined to try to get help to us, and for that, all of us were eternally grateful.

Eric and Bjorne were then quizzed by others on the bus as to why the Irish UN commanders back in Elizabethville did not send re-enforcements or try to re-supply us. Apparently, we learned, there was an attempt made by the Irish UN battalion to provide re-enforcements but the convoys were ordered back when it came under fire at the Lufira bridge, the main crossing point of the Lulua river. We were told that the convoy was called 'Force-Kane' which if it had broken through and held the bridge would have provided enough arms to repel the mercenary and tribal attack on us and would have allowed us to consolidate our position or provided a breakout escape route. Some on the bus were quite bitter that the convoy turned back so easily, effectively leaving us abandoned, but despite my youth, I was more circumspect about the situation the convoy may have found themselves in at the Lufira bridge. I remembered how I felt when we were first attacked in Jadotville, suddenly hearing guns being fired in our direction and diving for cover. I had no idea what to do and in some ways, I just followed the example of those men and officers around me – their unquestionable hardness that made me similarly grit my teeth and try to act brave. As the siege continued, we all grew more battle hardened and became accustomed to the dizzying sound of gun-fire and mortars, but I could not forget that the initial fear was truly unimaginable. So I tried to reason with others on the bus that it was probably the shock of coming under fire that caused Force Kane to turn back.

What I couldn't understand however were the other stories that were being widely talked about in prison that the Irish UN commanders back in Elizabethville had launched an operation called *Morthor* on the morning of 13 September, a couple of hours before the start of the siege in Jadotville. Operation *Morthor* was intended to forcibly confront the mercenary forces to end Katanga's succession. The order was given by the head of the UN authority in Katanga, Conor Cruise O'Brien who had decided that ending Katanga's independence by force was the only way forward, which must have been planned with the UN military leaders well in advance. Whilst the orders had been given to Irish UN commanders in Elizabthville, they had not passed on the information to our officers on the ground in Jadotville even though we had reported that we were trapped and under siege three days beforehand. We had also reported that we were surrounded by a large mercenary army and civilian militia in Jadotville, leaving us exposed and cut off in the event of hostilities. It was operation *Morthor* that instigated the mercenaries to launch their attack on us whilst most of 'A' Company stood unsuspecting at mass just a couple of hours later.

When we were stationed in Elizabethville prior to our transfer to Jadotville we had sensed antagonism towards 'A' Company's officers from the other Irish UN officers in charge of them but to launch an attack on the Katangan forces whilst not telling us seemed deceitful. Given our cut off position, it seemed to us like we had been left out for the wolves. The last thing that was beyond explanation was that the Irish UN officers in charge in Elizabethville also refused to answer their radios during the battle as our code operators desperately called for assistance and re-enforcements.

The Swedes had no answers for us, they had done everything they could and had risked their lives to help us but they too were left abandoned in the same precarious situation as us in Jadotville, with no re-enforcements or supplies.

'Well there's nothing we can do about it now!' noted Pakie Monahan, 'or we'll be sitting round again with faces like the Stations of the Cross, wondering what might have been. And maybe,' Pakie's face sparked into life, 'St. Patrick will again be manning the Pearly gates when them Elizabethville officers get to their judgement day!' Again the mood on the bus was lifted as we bumped along en-route to our 'more secure long-term' confinement in Kolwesi.

I looked out of the window at the burned-out villages, which had become the trade-mark of this ongoing war in The Congo. Large circles of blackened grass, where once stood native huts and a deathly stench of soot were often all that was left. Some piles of burning wood were still smouldering, the embers giving off whisps of smoke that evaporated quickly into the surrounding shrubs and bushes.

Further on up the road, the jungle on either side was as green as the hedgerows of Ireland, occasionally opening up into an expanse of rolling grassland. All it needed, I dreamt, was a little babbling stream and an old stone bridge and I could have been just like John Wayne in *The Quiet Man*, skimming pebbles and whistling away the tune *The Isle of Innisfree* on the Uilleann pipes; the ideal image of Ireland I had lodged in my mind from the Picture House. It had been the thought of doing our duty for our old homeland, a country that had emerged with such pride after its own history of famine, tyranny and repression that had inspired most of us to volunteer for this tour of duty and to fight for our fellow countrymen during the siege.

We didn't know it in prison, but the Irish government back in Dublin had been insisting on our safe release. Tshombie was trying to extract a heavy price by demanding recognition of the Katangan state, something that the UN and international community could not provide.

The press barons back in Europe, being handsomely rewarded by the banks and mining companies, were, however, continuing to covertly support Katangan independence. Whilst they were careful to avoid any direct criticism of international policy they had undermined the UN by tarnishing the image of its leaders. With Dag Hammarskjöld killed and no longer available to criticise, they had switched their attention back to the head of the

UN in Katanga, Connor Cruise O'Brien, who had initiated Operation *Morthor*. Whilst O'Brien was popular in non-aligned countries because of his unwavering position in criticising apartheid regimes, he was equally unpopular in colonial countries because of his support for self-determination and independence struggles ever since the Suez crisis five years beforehand in 1956.

As a result, the press accused him of starting a war in The Congo, a country where former colonial people deserved more protection and that the armed confrontation against the Katangan succession had no basis in the UN remit or international law. They even implied that the death of the UN secretary general Dag Hammarskjöld was a result of O'Brien's policy which, in tactics typical of a PR war, they omitted to mention that it was the Katangan mercenary forces that had shot down Hammarskjöld's plane. They also omitted from their accounts any mention of atrocities by the Katangan independence movement who were ethnically cleansing villages that didn't support their succession and that a refugee camp on the outskirts of Elizabethville of over 100,000 Congolese civilians now only had the protection of the UN to avert a human catastrophe.

The US and non-aligned countries' governments remained generally supportive of the UN but the formidable combined powers of the western press, banks and mining companies were determined to establish a new era of some sort of continuing white power. As a result of the PR strategy of the western press, the Katangans were able to justify our continued imprisonment and as the image of the UN plummeted, it became more difficult for the Irish politicians back in Dublin to remain on the right side of public opinion. They didn't want to be seen defending, as the press had portrayed, a maverick and immoral Irish envoy and what were being portrayed as 'trigger happy', Irish UN troops in Jadotville. Even though we didn't know it when we were in prison, public opinion even back home in dear old Ireland had began to shift against us.

In the back of every soldier's mind when they are sent away to a war is the thought that they are being supported by the people at home. The single thing a soldier fears most is if they no longer have public support. If opinion at home was influenced with misinformation then so too would our integrity be questioned, but if public opinion was lost completely then we may no longer be even welcome back home in Ireland.

It was all very different when we first signed up for The Congo some six months beforehand. We had been given a farewell parade in Athlone with grand speeches and flag waving. I marched proudly, upright with my head held high, almost carried along by the support and cheers of a proud nation. It had been the destiny I had always dreamed of as a young boy as, I presumed, it must have been how The County had felt when he led out Longford at Croke Park. The politicians were very eager back then to be snapped, smiling alongside us talking of Ireland's great contribution to world peace. But a politician makes a fickle friend and will adjust his feet with the shifting sands of political fortune. I paid little attention back then to fortune tellers and during that parade I was concentrating on trying not to tick-tock when I marched past the main stand saluting enthusiastic dignitaries. I never even knew nor cared what a propoganda war was, the only important thing for me was that no-one knew I was underage. I was about to embark on my own epic adventure, with all those vivid images of films from the Picture House and celebrities to inspire me.

CHAPTER SIX

The white man cometh

Date: May 1961
Location: Journey to The Congo

WHEN I VOLUNTEERED, it was the spring of 1961 and given the mood of the new decade, Hollywood needed to re-create a different breed of legend to satisfy the more sophisticated and permissive generation of the '60s. The likes of Paul Newman and Audrey Hepburn were appealing to rebellious adolescents all over the western world with their defiant and non-conformist style. By now, TVs had become commonplace in pubs throughout Ireland, and the new gimmick was the green baize of the pool table encouraged by images of 'Fast Eddie' Felson, the pool shark played by Newman in *The Hustler*. To the dismay of priests everywhere, living to excess was the reason why God created champagne, the tipple of choice for the likes of Frank Sinatra, Dean Martin and Sammy Davis Jr, high-profile members of the notorious Rat Pack. They wore distinctive dark tapered suits that defined the new 'mod' era, with pencil slim ties and pronounced winklepickers. The brown woollen jackets and off-white shirts of the 1950s had been discarded, in favour of dark linen smartness and sunlight soap whitened collars. This was aimed at a youth culture that had grown up out of earshot of world wars but amidst the social and sexual revolutions of the new decade. The Rat Pack possessed all the combined attributes for a '60s blockbuster: singing, drinking, laughing and womanising.

It all represented 'progressive thinking', it said on the glossy magazine covers next to a picture of Marilyn Monroe attending the glitzy film premiere of her latest movie *Misfits*. She had a split in her white dress that ran all the way up her thigh and a smile that understood the mayhem she was creating in the minds of lustful young men like me. When I looked back at the magazines of the '50s, they seemed to be austere and straight-laced in comparison. Women were wearing neck high collars whilst smiling sweetly, their legs concealed by more practical long gowns. Perhaps, I considered, I would never have seen films like *Gentlemen Prefer Blondes* and *The Seven Year Itch* had Norma Jean Baker not discarded her Georgia Tech sweatshirt to become the 'Talk of Hollywood' by appearing in Playboy magazine and becoming known thereafter by her stage name of Marilyn Monroe. Films had also changed and unlike the 'name in lights' we had become familiar with in the 1950s that seemed to focus on a single star, they now included a number of audacious heroes, with titles like *Oceans Eleven*, with all of the actors now sharing a starring role in the great heist.

Even Kevin, Franco and the Dolly Dolan back in Edgeworthstown had abandoned their racoon tailed hats in favour of brylantine slick-backed hair and drain-pipe trousers. As their quiffs now required regular maintenance they would pluck a comb from their rear trouser pocket for a quick preen. Although being a cowboy in the wild-west had become as old fashioned as our disused gramophone player, we still had nostalgia for the good old days of westerns shown on Sunday evenings at the Picture House with the inevitable gunfight. But even in the Wild West they now focused on a group of gunslingers like Yul Brynner, Eli Wallach and Steve McQueen in *The Magnificent Seven,* all equally heroic in their defence against the banditos.

On the poster outside the Picture House in Edgeworthstown, they displayed an arrow-shaped group of seven cowboys riding into the dusty Mexican town, their eyes squinting in the hazy sunshine. The banner claimed:

THEY WERE SEVEN
THEY FOUGHT LIKE SEVEN HUNDRED!

Enough to inspire any thrill seeker that the golden days of the Western were still with us.

Back in Athlone, we were also being assigned into our own set number of men for the tour of duty to The Congo. I looked eagerly for my name on the notice board, an alphabetical list of the men selected to serve in the UN's 35th Battalion and sure enough I was on the list under the title 'A' Company.

I ran my finger over the entry to make sure:

Pte Michael Greene, Longford: Year of Birth: 1941.

'Ha,' I thought, 'I had got away with it again! They'll never know that I was born in 1944.'

I then immediately looked for other familiar names: Dowler, Monahan and Tighe as we had all volunteered at the same time and sure enough they too were listed in the same 'A' Company. There were also a number of names I recognised from my time in the recruitment company: Finlas, Battles, Galvin: and then the biggest surprise of all, Pte Daniel Hegarty, who I hadn't seen since he was posted to Mullingar when we passed out of basic training.

The 35th Battalion comprised of three Companies ('A', 'B' and 'C') and support divisions, in all totalling about

600 men. In 'A' Company there were 145 men split into four platoons of which ten were officers, including a doctor and a priest. Monahan was quick to point out:

'The doctor might save yer life but the priest will save yer soul.'

I was unconvinced of the need for a priest and quipped back what John Wayne had said to the Reverend Clayton in *The Searchers* as they are about to be attacked:

'There's no more time for praying! AMEN!'

But a priest was mandatory for every division in the Irish army and we were told that a mass would be held every day while we were in The Congo.

Of the remaining personnel in 'A' Company there were 28 corporals, 11 sergeants, 2 quartermasters and 1 company sergeant. The remainder were orderlies and privates, many from Athlone or other barracks in Western command like Mullingar and Galway. Most of the names on the list were unfamiliar but I was just delighted to have found my name among them. Commandant Patrick Quinlan was the officer in command of us but all of the officers assigned to 'A' Company were well regarded amongst the rank and file soldiers, with Monahan noting:

'We have luckily avoided all the real bastards anyway!'

In the rigid hierarchy of the Irish army, officers generally never spoke to privates like me, with orders being passed down through the company sergeant (known as a CS) and the platoon sergeant. Our CS in charge of 'A' Company was called Jack Prendergast, who had a notable air of invincibility and without doubt the toughest man I would ever meet. I was assigned to the support platoon of 'A' Company, in the anti tank gun unit with Dowler and another young private called John Conway.

I was the lowest rank of the three of us in the unit and was responsible for carrying shells to the anti-tank gun, Conway for loading them and Dowler for firing. Our Platoon Sergeant was called Sgt John Monahan who was no relation of Pakie's but who was as tough as Prendergast. Unusually for an officer, he told us to call him John – a level of familiarity that most officers would never offer as most liked the hierarchy of authority. We regarded Prendergast and John Monahan as perfect soldiers, impeccably turned out, disciplined and uncompromisingly hard. I knew both would not bother to question me about being underage as long as I was able to do the job and besides I had become used to pretending to be three years older than I was.

I had my final trip back to Edgworthstown that weekend and fresh from watching *The Magnificent Seven* down at The Picture House the week before, I proclaimed,

'For our six month tour of duty to the unfamiliar and mysterious province of Katanga in The Congo, there are exactly 600 of us!'

The Dolly and my brothers Kevin and Franco were intrigued about Africa and I elaborated on some of the stories I had heard back in Athlone:

'Aye,' I noted, 'the women carry these huge pots around on their heads doing all the work while the men just sit around having the craic.'

'I thought the men leapt from tree to tree like Tarzan,' questioned the Dolly, 'and when there's a spot of bother, he yelps out like a proper eejit and all the elephants and tigers run out to help him!'

I laughed at the thought, but the Dolly wasn't finished:

'So Micky, ye'll know now what to do if ye run into them Baluba fellas, tell them yer Tarzan and start roaring,' and he started roaring like a sick cat.

Unbeknown to me at the time, it was the last time we would all go the Picture House together. Typically it was

Sunday evening and we all set off into town, stopping at Maggie Canavan's to fully arm ourselves with packets of Sweet Aftons and fizzballs before taking our seats proudly at the back of the theatre. I had hoped it would be a cowboy western as it would be the last film I would see before I set off for The Congo, but instead it was *The Great Impostor* with Tony Curtis playing the character of Ferdinand Demara, who posed as an officer, a dentist and a Buddhist monk amongst other characters. Apparently, it was based on a true story with Demara lying and conning his way through various tight situations whilst deceiving everyone around him. It made me feel a little cocky about my own deceit of my age as; after I volunteered, nobody asked any questions or checked my birth certificate. When I passed the final medical complete with jabs for malaria I had no doubt that I too was a great imposter and no-one was going to catch me out.

Apart from the malaria and small-pox jab, the 600 men of the 35th Battalion came armed with Ireland's most reliable cures in the form of the old wives tale, which covered numerous diseases from gout to the scour. They were, almost always natural remedies using various plants or herbs, sometimes sweetened with fruits and honey or warmed up with a drop of Irish whiskey. With almost every cure in Ireland at our disposal we would surely be invincible against every jungle disease. As we packed up our bags back in the Athlone barracks, some had packed gorse and heather cuttings, which were supposed to repel parasites like mosquitoes. For the diseases that the jabs or old wives tale didn't cover, including sleeping sickness, dysentery and beriberi, we just carried our rosary beads as having faith, many Priests and mothers claimed, was the best defence of all.

We went to a briefing the day before we left Athlone, and I heard a voice from a few seats behind:

'Feckin hell it's Michael Greene! – here remember Michael – Thou Shalt Not Fart!' It was the unmistakable voice of Danny Hegarty.

'Jaysus, how are ya Danny?' I asked stretching my neck round.

'Ah grand,' replied Hegarty. 'Just looking forward to my holidays in Africa!'

'Aye,' I replied, 'too good to miss! I need to work on my rat-pack sun tan.'

We then spoke about what he had been doing back in Mullingar, 'ah lots of singing, dancing and owld quare ones taking advantage of me Michael!' he told me with some enthusiasm.

I faced forward again as the briefing began. We were told that biting insects including mosquitoes would make nests in your hair using the warmth to reproduce. Like everyone else in the audience I began to develop an itch and, as soon as the briefing had finished, headed straight over to the barber embracing the idea of a refreshing hair-cut. The barber said he had never been as busy, with nearly everyone in the 35th Battalion now wanting the closest scalping possible. After an Irish winter we were all as white as ghosts, with newly shorn heads, normally an indication of a new recruit, uncovering a previously shaded almost virginal white skin. The embarrassment of having 'big ears' again seemed a small price to pay but the only alternative was to arrive in the tropical heat of The Congo having the discomfort of creepy-crawlies 'biting the livin Jaysus out of ye'.

After the scalping, Pakie Monahan joked to us that we could all take 'the cure' when our tour of duty finished in six months' time.

'What cure is that?' I asked, wondering which old wives tale we would be hearing.

'The cure for baldness of course,' replied Monahan, 'they reckon that if ye crush up some goose eggs, then rub it into yer scalp with pig's manure and fresh nettles, then let a cow lick it, that ye would have a full head of hair by the following Christmas.'

We all laughed. 'Aye, that's what the owld farmers say back in Edgeworthstown,' I countered, 'and all they get for Christmas is fleas!'

The Tiger had also brought some heather cuttings with him from his home town of Elfin in Roscommon, which a neighbour had told him would protect him from midges. He had been out on the first tour to The Congo eight months beforehand and didn't catch any diseases although he was required to have another medical after the problems he had with his back a year before:

'So I says to the doctor,' he explained, 'I'm fitter than any man in this barracks except maybe Prendergast, and that's only because he eats bullets with his breakfast. But Jaysus Christ,' he continued, 'it would have been terrible scourge seeing all of ye heading off on yer holidays and leaving me behind in Athlone.'

'Ah, we wouldn't leave ya behind Tiger' joked Dowler, 'ya have that bit of briar from Roscommon, them feckin balubas wont stand a chance if yer with us.'

The Tiger then recounted some stories from his first tour, telling us that the Balubas were in many cases 'the innocent fellas' and didn't cause any bother to him when he was there, re-iterating that the Niemba massacre had been a case of mistaken identity. He also told us about all the wild animals he had seen: rhino, giraffe, zebra; all adding to the anticipation of what we were about to embark on.

Not only was The Tiger the only one of the four of us to have been to The Congo he was the only one who had ever been out of Ireland, as Dowler, Pakie Monahan and I had only ever dreamt of being on a plane. According to The Tiger, flying was much better than travelling on a ship. He told us the story of when he went over to England, he travelled from Dublin to Liverpool aboard the *Princess Maude*, a cattle boat that had provided transport to many emigrating Irish during the '50s. I had heard countless pub stories from those that came home for Christmas, as to how the *Princess Maude* had the same design as the ships used in the D-day landings in 1944, with a flat bottomed hull that bounced rather than sailed over the water. It always made me laugh hearing the stories of the journeys on the *Princess Maude*, surrounded by cattle 'with feckin cows, pigs, hens and shite everywhere!' But in just two weeks' time, we too would be travelling by aeroplane to The Congo, how the upper classes travelled, not something that working people and privates like me could normally aspire to.

Before that, we had to attend two weeks of peacekeeping training at the Curragh camp which would include crowd control, riot duties etc., before we set off for Africa. We boarded our transport vehicles for the two hour road journey from Athlone to the Curragh, packed in along the sides on benches, bumping and swaying along the country lanes. The Tiger started us all singing *The Boys of The County Armagh*.

> There's one fair county in Ireland,
> With memories so glorious and grand.
> Where nature has lavished its bounty,
> On the orchard of Erin's green land.

Three Longford boys: Michael Greene, Sean Dowler, Patrick Monahan. Athlone barracks prior to departure – May 1961

No matter where I wander,
Through cities near and far,
My heart's at home in old Ireland,
In The County of Roscommon!

Typically the Tiger would replace key words with his own even if they didn't rhyme, in this case Armagh being replaced with his home County, Roscommon. More often he would just make up a whole new verse in the tune of the original, with Longford, the home County of me, Dowler and Monahan, often the butt of his jokes:

It never stops raining in Longford
On top of the eejits below,
But when it rains in Roscommon
Then Longford is covered in snow!

The day we were leaving for The Congo, the newspapers were reminding the nation that it was the fiftieth anniversary of the launch of the Titanic from the Belfast shipyard before it set out on its fateful voyage. As it had done most of the winter, it was raining, but being the spring of 1961, the rain at least felt a little warmer. The tension in the Cold War between East and West was also getting notably more heated and I was carrying with me the latest edition of the Irish Independent and read an article about the rising antagonism between the two superpowers.

In the preceding weeks, the pressures had increased after the US backed a failed invasion to overthrow the communist regime in Cuba at the Bay of Pigs on the island's west coast, with Castro calling his victory the first defeat of Yankee imperialism. It was just three months into the great JFK's first term as president and was called a humiliation for the US, consolidating Castro's power. The defeat, we heard, culminated in further restrictions on Cuban people with the catholic religion being outlawed, church property nationalised, and clergy and bishops exiled. Like Ireland, Cuba was once a staunch catholic country but was now officially designated as atheist. Irish society was appalled and after outlawing gambling, it was the final nail in the coffin for the image of Castro's Marxist regime and communist policy. The Bay of Pigs also represented a line being crossed in the sand, as the Soviets and Americans were now prepared to use armed physical confrontation instead of aggressive rhetoric. More directly affecting us, we heard that after the Cuban victory at the Bay of Pigs, Che Guevara, the iconic Marxist who had inspired Castro's revolution in 1959, was planning a Marxist uprising in Eastern Congo, which were looking to invade the province of Katanga, where we were headed on our peace-keeping mission.

'Jaysus, that's all we feckin need,' commented Dowler, 'every mad owld bastard is already in The Congo fighting one another and now the feckin Cubans are flying in.'

'They'll not stop me from going to mass!' joked Monahan.

'Or me from poker!' I included.

'Or me from drinking!' finished the pioneer Dowler.

Whilst we tried to make light of it, we knew the weapons that the superpowers had at their disposal in 1961 placed the world in a very dangerous situation, which they referred to threateningly in The Irish Independent with the headline 'The Edge of a Nuclear Abyss'. The County had drawn a big red circle around a story that both sides in the Cold War now had enough bombs and missiles to cause more damage than was achieved in the whole of the Second World War, a conflict that cost more than 20 million lives, with just one ship-load of munitions. It was a policy known to most young people by the ominous three letter abbreviation – MAD (Mutually Assured Destruction), after the American magazine of the same name which parodied the stupidity of war, bomb shelters and killing people. Human endeavour it seemed had surpassed itself; it was now able to completely destroy itself just at the press of a button.

The names of the armaments we heard about just compounded the threat of war as weapons were labelled with coded abbreviations to shroud their potential threat. Even Dowler who always seemed to know everything about weapons couldn't keep up with the technology although typically he knew the names of everything. 'Cuba's army', he told us, 'has Soviet-made T-34 and IS-2 tanks, backed up by SU-100 tank-destroyers.' 'Their air force has MIG 17s,' he told us, 'also supplied by Russia, while the US has Lockheed T-33 jet fighters and B-26 Invaders.'

It all sounded like a different language to me and I had no idea what all the letters stood for as Dowler went on explaining that the US also had at its disposal TSR2s, and rockets which he claimed could carry nuclear tipped ballistic missiles faster than the speed of sound.

It was as if the weapons were from some kind of futuristic psychological thriller like *Invasion of the Body Snatchers* with each side using ever more menacing rhetoric. I mimicked the ominous warning they issued at the end of the film to the 'fair-minded citizens of America':

'We must be vigilant because they (i.e. the communists) are among us, and if we come across them we should call the FBI.'

Whilst a new vocabulary was being created for the Cold War , travelling in front of us in the army transports were our armaments for The Congo, only our technology was that mainly used in the First World War, like Vickers machine guns. Our Lee Enfield bolt action rifles had been updated and replaced with Belgian Fabrique Nationale (FN) rifles, which were known by their Cold War title: 'the right arm of the free world'. However, there was no need to make up threatening abbreviations for any of our weapons, as there was nothing secret about them: just reliable mainly hand-held armaments which were hopelessly out-dated amongst all this nuclear talk. Ironically though, compared to some of the warring tribes in The Congo like the Baluba we were well-armed. They still used bows and arrows, just like the American Indians in the westerns.

The world was by now very aware of the crisis in the heart of central Africa served by daily news reports of murders, mutilations, rapes and genocide. Prior to the crisis erupting ten months before, most Irish people hadn't even heard of The Congo. Some remembered that it was a country in central Africa that had been discovered by Henry Morton Stanley, the famous British explorer. As kids we used Stanley's famous expression: 'Erm...Dr Livingstone I presume?' because he had 'by chance' bumped into the revered Doctor Livingstone near Lake Tanganyika, hundreds of miles from either coast of Africa. The implausible encounter between Stanley and Livingstone seemed to us about as likely as bumping into Fred Astaire and Ginger Rogers dancing through Edgeworthstown.

Whilst Dr Livingstone died in Africa, never recounting his version, Stanley mapped out the kingdom of The Congo by following The Congo and Zambezi rivers and crossing the interior of the African continent, something never previously achieved by a European. Although this was the place described as the cradle of civilisation for humanity where primates or Homo Erectus first came down from the trees and learned to walk 1.8 million years beforehand, Stanley was credited with discovering Africa in the mid-nineteenth century.

As a result, the intrepid Stanley became a hero in 1870s London and it was his map of the continent that was submitted to the National Geographic, the same maps that we had been given when we volunteered. Aside from the map, Stanley provided descriptions of the native people who, he noted, had a propensity not to wear any clothes, walking around 'stark naked,' although he spoke of elaborate headdresses worn by some of the native cultures.

Along with the maps we had been given some other basic literature on The Congo and were encouraged to read up about its history. The only book I had on The Congo was an old children's manual called 'TinTin in The Congo' about the intrepid young Belgian adventurer donned out in his khaki hunting gear and bush hat travelling to The Congo with the black-bearded Captain Haddock wearing his trademark fisherman's jumper and his loyal pet dog Snowy whose life had become 'terribly boring' back in Belgium. So, they decide 'to do a bit of lion-hunting', and end up blowing up rhinos and fighting crocodiles. The book depicted The Congolese with big drooping eyelids and round white-sausage thick lips, an image that stuck in my mind as I had never seen a black person in real life except through the snowy black and white television film-reels. As TinTin was a children's comic, I didn't show anyone else in case it showed up my age but many of the others in 'A' Company had read other books and stories about Africa's fabled heart of darkness.

Dowler said that he now knew more about The Congo's history than about Irish history while Pakie Monahan said he hadn't read as many books since he was at school.

'Jaysus, I never knew ya went to school Pakie!' mocked the Tiger.

'And at my school they taught us to read, not just feckin sing and whistle!' responded Monahan.

'Aye,' smiled the Tiger smugly, 'no textbook would have been able to teach ye to sing like me.'

Monahan and the Tiger continued to goad each other but now that we had set off from Athlone to the Curragh en-route to Stanley's African discovery, not all of the stories that were circulated in the back of the truck were suitable for children or - adults for that matter. The Niemba massacre had created many embellished tales which circulated through 'A' Company about cannibalism and particularly the Baluba tribe, the perpetrators of Niemba, who comprised the largest tribe in Katanga. I wasn't sure if the stories were true but they were terrifying. The Tiger told us that in order to cut through human flesh more efficiently the Baluba would file down their teeth into Dracula-like points.

'They preferred to capture their enemies alive,' he told us, 'then tie them up and carry them back to the village for a ritual sacrifice.' It seemed inconceivable but he continued describing in great detail: 'though still alive they would then have their beating heart, eyes and genitals cut out.' We all cringed as the Tiger explained that these were considered the delicacies and reserved for the tribal leaders or witch-doctor. 'The remainder of the human carcass,' he went on, 'was then barbecued on an open fire and distributed amongst the tribe.'

'The Baluba, and many of the native Congolese tribes,' the Tiger continued telling us, 'believed that eating other humans would provide great strength for future battles. Young children, from babies to teenagers often from opposing tribes were coveted but the greatest fortitude and courage would be gained by eating the delicacies of one the Baluba feared most: the white man.' We all gulped. 'But the Baluba's intense fear of Europeans; who they called 'the great white hunter', was claimed the Tiger, 'well-founded and justified given their brutal history.'

Apparently, no country had ever suffered as much from the slave trade as The Congo, which I remember The County had described to me as 'the greatest crime in human history.' Like many of his stories he had told me as a boy, I wasn't old enough to understand the true impact of slavery on African people as we had become accustomed in school and mass to hearing about poor black babies and hardship in Africa. What I didn't know was that an estimated 30 million Congolese people were captured and transported to plantations in the new world, which the history books described more academically as the largest forced migration in history. 30 million people was over twice The Congo's entire population in 1961. The County had told me that the slave trade had also existed in Ireland and along with the partition of the six counties in the North was the reason why there remained such long-standing resentment towards the British Colonial Empire. He told me the descendents of the Irish slaves were still known, even now in 1961 as 'The Black Irish' or 'Red Legs' in the West Indian islands of Barbados and Jamaica, with many distinctly Irish names like McGrath and Shaughnessy still surviving in the Caribbean 100 years after slavery's abolition. McGrath was my mother's maiden name and I often wondered what might have happened to my distant relatives or their descendants, but my mother would never speak of such topics telling me to 'take the world as it is not as it ought to be.'

The Irish and African slave trades were major colonial industries forcing about half a million Irish into servitude in the cotton and coffee industries under Cromwell's decree that Catholics be banished 'to hell or to Connaught', when the British and other colonialists triumphed in their imperial empires.

I remember The County telling me that those Irish who were condemned to the hell of hereditary slavery had no rights whatsoever. There was no legal difference between an African slave or an Irish slave as neither were 'freemen' meaning that they were not provided birth or death certificates and were just regarded as possessions. However, a story that The County told me stuck in my mind that an African slave was worth about four or five times that of the Irish, as their minds weren't affected by Catholicism, the planters and slave-owners preferring what they termed 'anything but a papist', which they believed made them prone to rebellion and uprisings. Irish slave women were bred with African slave males to make the offspring slaves more suited to the hotter climate. Ironically these became the most valuable slaves called mestees, as the lighter complexions, particularly with the young girls, proved popular with the gratification-seeking plantation owners and supervisors, who preferred these to the darker skinned mullattoes or sambos. The County also told me stories of the slave ships where both Africans and Irish slaves were kept, chained up in dire living conditions and worked to the point of death. To ensure the ship owners redeemed the insurance loss, dead or seriously ill slaves were routinely tossed overboard and recorded as 'lost at sea' as there would be no payout if a slave starved to death whilst shackled in the galleys of a ship. Apparently, none of the Irish slaves ever returned from their 'hell' in the plantations. The lucky ones and their descendents that survived were eventually set free after the American civil war, but none ever made the voyage back to Ireland.

The slave trade made fortunes for so called gallant British aristocrats operating the slave-ships like Sir Frances Drake and Sir Walter Raleigh until slavery was finally outlawed in the British Empire by William Wilberforce in 1833, although the US continued with the slave trade until the end of their civil war in 1865. I had read about the abolition of slavery, and the great battles between the confederate and union forces at Shilo and Gettysburg culminating in victory for the union. The County too, had read many books about the civil war and about what had happened to the Irish slaves. He had explained to me that Abraham Lincoln didn't originally legislate to free the slaves until three years into the war, and after the Southern states had blockaded cotton supplies to Europe in an attempt to gain their colonial support. Even then, Lincoln's legislation only sought to free slaves owned in the confederate states and not those owned by the union supporting legislators. Leading abolitionists including Wendell Phillips heavily criticised Lincoln's policies saying that he was not doing enough to end slavery. Many began to question what would become of the freed slaves once the Emancipation Proclamation and 13th Amendment (to end slavery) had been enacted. Lincoln considered setting up colonies in the slaves' original homelands of Africa and South America to deal with the huge number of displaced people. The African colonies were to be set up in The Congo and other West African nations not yet owned or colonised by European empires. A hopeful future was what was envisaged by Lincoln but there was no policy of a colony or homeland envisaged for freed Irish slaves as the Irish state remained under control of the British colonial empire. The Red Legs, The County told me, were destined to remain stateless, huddling into small outcrop communities and living a meagre existence.

Just as I had looked forward to watching cowboy westerns, The County said that when he was a boy he would look forward to watching films about the American civil war down at the Picture House in Edgeworthstown. He said that the films of the master and slave society was portrayed as an honourable way of life and that even in the music halls, the blackened face minstrels with chalky white lips mimicked the former slaves harking back to the good ol' days of plantations singing 'I wish I was in Dixie.'

'But the reality for the slaves was nothing like that,' The County told me. He then went on to explain with some consternation that he had to stop taking my mother down to the Picture House because 'the place became overrun with kids yelping like eejits and flinging things around in the dark,' which made me laugh with embarrassment.

With the defeat of the Confederates and slavery being abolished, it became illegal in the US to use any human being as a possession with no rights of their own. But many people in the Southern states no longer wanted their former slaves occupying the same land. Defeated confederate leaders and politicians argued that all areas south of the Dixie line remained the legal jurisdiction of whites only as they owned the land and there was no place now for their black and Irish former slaves. Some of the same confederate leaders became wizards or leaders of the emerging anti-black vigilante groups like the Ku Klux Klan (KKK), who dressed in body length, white cassocks and pointed conical hats. The KKK may have hidden their identities behind a white hood but claimed a membership of over half a million men. The popular idea of white supremacy also led to the formation of paramilitary white groups like the White league and Red Shirts who defined themselves as the military wing of the national US democratic party, whose mainstream leaders in congress and the Senate argued that there was no way that people of different skin colour (and from different religions) could live together. If the master and slave were allowed to be equal, they argued, the consequences would be disastrous, ending in the humiliation of white civilisation by the inevitable assimilation of cultures through marital union.

With such widely held community and political support, motions were proposed in the US senate to keep the southern states as white homelands by senators like Benjamin Tillman of South Carolina who sought to legalise the lynching of negroes.

> We have never believed him (the negro) to be the equal of the white man, and we will not submit to his gratifying his lust on our wives and daughters without lynching him.
>
> Herbert, Bob, *The Blight That Is Still With Us*

It was estimated that 1500 lynchings took place without a trial, judge or jury, between 1865 and 1870. The lynchings were led by groups like the Klu Klux Klan but covertly supported by political leaders who argued that the crimes were understandable and almost justifiable as the possible punishment was not as great as they would suffer from the greatest indignity of all: having their virginal white daughters threatened by barbarous and uncivilised former slaves.

> The snows will fall from heaven in sooty blackness, sooner than the white women of the United States will consent to the maternity of negro families.
>
> John Tyler Morgan in *Imagery of Lynching: Black Men, White Women, and the Mob,* Dora Apel, 2004 Rutgers University Press

Brandishing burning crucifixes, the KKK and white paramilitary groups spread terror across the Southern states, protecting their white communities by setting fire to their ex-slaves at ritual bonfires and lynching any young blacks, catholics and jews that had ignored their 'don't go out after dark' curfews. Senior US politicians acknowledged that the civil war left a problem of displaced people, so Lincoln remained supportive of a plan to set up slave colonies. The policy to send the slaves back to Africa began to gain momentum as it was again discussed in the US congress to appease the growing consensus, especially amongst southern whites, that areas should be segregated and the resultant displaced people should be allowed to return to their homelands.

Segregation laws in the southern US were eventually passed and formalised under the 'Jim Crow laws' which came into law in the mid 1870s. The old 'Dixieland' states then became known as the 'Jim Crow South' and were characterised by being vehemently anti-black.

Pakie Monahan joked that in the Jim Crow South, the Irish red-legs were also regarded as black men with white skin, or 'the white niggers of Europe', and subject to the same discrimination and recriminations as other slaves.

But 100 years later in 1961, as we swapped stories about The Congo's history, it seemed inconceivable to us that the attitudes of previous generations could still have such an impact. The best selling novel of the previous year – 1960, was *To Kill a Mockingbird* by Harper Lee which told a story of a black man called Tom who was falsely accused of raping a white woman in one of the affected areas in the racially divided deep south of America. Most of us on the bus had read the book, where the white lawyer, Atticus Finch, defends Tom, but is labelled a 'nigger-lover' by the white community. The principles of Atticus Finch were being much talked about even before we left for The Congo with Finch becoming regarded as an honest and principled white person after he even manages to convince the town bigots to imagine life from the perspective of the downtrodden or to envisage life in another's skin. The book was a 'de rigueur' read for any aspiring teenager like me who preferred to be associated with such honourable behaviour, but as the conversation on the bus developed, it was clear that there were important legacies from slavery, its abolition and resultant political decisions made in the US and Europe, that had a major impact on African states – and in particular, The Congo.

Racial segregation in all public facilities and banning interracial marriages was still very much a belief of southern Africa and southern American states despite the civil rights legislation of the late 1950s. In Africa, the politial leaders made no effort to change the status quo but in the US, The Jim Crow laws were finally overturned which formally outlawed segregation on interstate buses and trains. To test the laws robustness in the US, groups of young black men would intentionally board these buses and trains in white stronghold areas, risking beatings and possible lynchings if they were outnumbered by white supremacists. Apparently, we heard that JFK had been forced to commit federal troops the week before to ensure the safety of freedom riders in states like Alabama and Georgia. The central tenant of segregation was based on the 'separate but equal' ideology that we were hearing so much on the news in both The Congo and in Henrik Vorwoerd's implementation of apartheid in South Africa. Whilst the original Jim Crow laws were continuing to be challenged at the time by peaceful protest in the US by Martin Luther King's civil rights movement, the American administration was in no position to lecture colonial Africa on racial fairness with segregation still a major part of US life. More importantly, American policy in the late nineteenth century had such a major part to play in the darkest part of The Congo's history, as the legacy of the 'Jim Crow south' and the homelands policy created a vacuum that was to establish the environment for the worst human catastrophe the world has ever known.

Although most former slaves were born in America, after abolition opportunities for them were very limited. With life so intolerable, many began to yearn for a return to the land of their forefathers, many having originated from The Congo, believing that a black homeland would be free from discrimination and where they would be allowed to prosper. However, the reality for many in the decades following abolition was that their ancestral homes in Africa had become the target for the spread of European imperialism, far-flung colonies seized from natives and where white men were becoming very expert at exploiting indigenous people.

One place that hadn't been colonised by the 1870s was central Africa, a fact that had not gone unnoticed by the King of Belgium, Leopold II, who was also aware of past US presidents' support to return displaced former slaves to their African homelands. Just a decade or so after the civil war, Leopold set up a committee to conduct studies of The Congo region. In 1879 the same committee appointed the noble explorer Henry Morton Stanley, giving him the mandate to map out a perimeter to The Congo kingdom. Stanley had detailed the vast rubber and gum forests where wild rubber and herbs grew on vines to such an extent that its supply could equal or even surpass that of Amazonia. Leopold viewed this vast swathe of land in central Africa as holding the raw material that would provide the vast riches he yearned for after Charles Goodyear and Thomas Hancock and invented 'vulcanisation' of rubber some 25 years earlier. The process of mixing sulphur with heated rubber had made The Congo's most abundant resource weatherproof and the world's most valuable and versatile plastic, known as elastic metal.

With Stanley's map and a catalogue of fingerprint signatures from tribal chiefs throughout The Congo region, Leopold lobbied the sympathetic US congress and senate for recognition of the state as a protectorate of the King of Belgium under the auspices of his charity; the International Association of The Congo, which could demonstrate that the land already legally belonged to him because of the signatories. The documents were obtained during Stanley's expedition and while the tribal chiefs may not have understood the language or meaning of such a legal document, they had 'signed' the documents with which Leopold then used to claim the territory. To further his case to US lawmakers sympathetic to displaced former slaves, Leopold provided a compelling account of his charity and philanthropy that he envisioned for this native black, African homeland. He claimed that through his Royal charity and patronage he would provide humanitarian and evangelical redemption. He also declared that under his guidance he would bring civilisation to the savage hordes who, without his benevolence, would continue to practice barbaric rituals including human sacrifice, bestiality and polygamy. Lastly, he gave the former African slaves the idyllic aspiration that their new potential homeland would be a 'free state' and that his first priority would be to abolish the Arab slave trade, just as had been achieved in the recently enlightened and emancipated United States and British Empire.

With racial and social policies remaining at the forefront of American politics since the end of the civil war, Leopold knew his emotive claims would appeal to both abolitionists and white supremacists, both keen to establish such a spiritual black homeland as a protectorate for displaced and disillusioned African Americans.

In the truck en-route to Dublin, and not yet knowing the history of what happened under Leopold, I was also convinced of the honourable intentions of Leopold which sounded as if all sides would have something to gain from such a protectorate and an evangelical education to which I joked,

'So just like Irish kids, all The Congolese young fellas had to go to mass on Sundays from then on?' I asked mischievously, 'I wonder if they all had to share the same Sunday best suit like me and my brothers.'

'Aye,' replied Pakie Monahan curtly, a response that suggested I hadn't quite twigged the gravity of the story he was telling me.

'But,' Monahan explained, 'The Congo had not been colonised by anybody until 1884 when the US, in return for a commitment to send former slaves back to their homeland, became the first country to recognise The Congo Free State as a protectorate of the King of Belgium's charity.'

With such strong support and recognition from the US legislature I was keen to find out what happened next in The Congo's history, and what could have caused it to end up in the mess it was only 80 years later with peacekeepers needed to avert a civil war and a possible nuclear conflict.

'So what happened next?' I eagerly asked expecting perhaps a force of nature or some kind of unforeseen accident to be the only things that would have prevented the King of Belgium's noble and well intentioned charity from succeeding.

Both Monahan and Dowler then began to explain that back in Europe, the 'scramble for Africa' was well under way and each of the European powers wanted to control Africa's natural resources. With such wealth at stake, the European heads of State gathered in Berlin in 1885 to discuss dividing up Africa between the 'civilised' countries of Europe, all now acknowledging that slavery had indeed been a great crime. The major colonial empires now re-drew the map of Africa, mostly in geometrically straight lines and assumed control of most of the continent, forming 50 new angular shaped countries.

Dowler held up his map of Africa against the canvas sides of the truck, pointing out the rigidly straight boundaries of countries that he was referring to, taking time to explain:

'Within the space of just 20 years, most of Africa was ruled by European powers, overriding thousands of years of native and tribal cultures.' He then pointed down to Southern Africa and continued with his explanation:

'Britain was granted colonies from down here in the Cape,' then he rolled his finger up through the centre of the map 'to all the way up here to Cairo which includes all of this area,' as he circled the areas around northern and southern Rhodesia. He continued his explanation using his map to help his definition:

'Much of West Africa over here in this area was given to France,' he outlined, 'while Germany's chancellor Bismarck claimed South West and East Africa including Cameroon, Rwanda, Burundi and Tanzania. So that left this big gaping hole,' he pointed out, 'in the middle called The Congo that hadn't been claimed by anyone.'

'But I thought it had been given to King Leopold and his charity?' I asked.

'Only by the US,' Dowler answered 'but having already gained the recognition of the United States, the

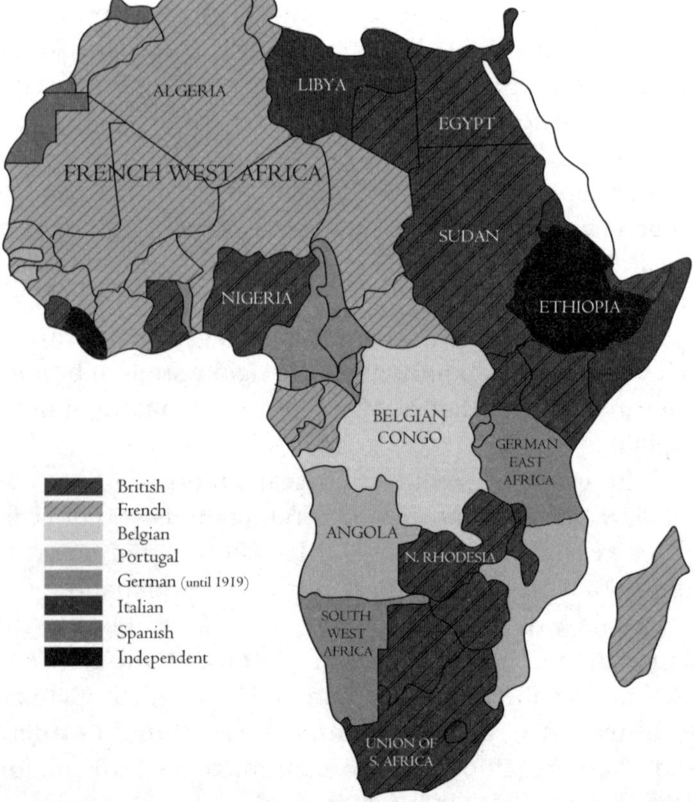

European Colonial Division of Africa 1885

major European powers of Britain, France and Germany told Leopold he could have it as long as he allowed free trade through it. Basically none of them wanted the other major powers to control central Africa and they did not regard little old Belgium's King Leopold II as a threat. Besides,' he continued, 'they; just like ye, ya eejit, believed all that bollocks about his charity and promises of churches and civilisation, the same yarn about leading

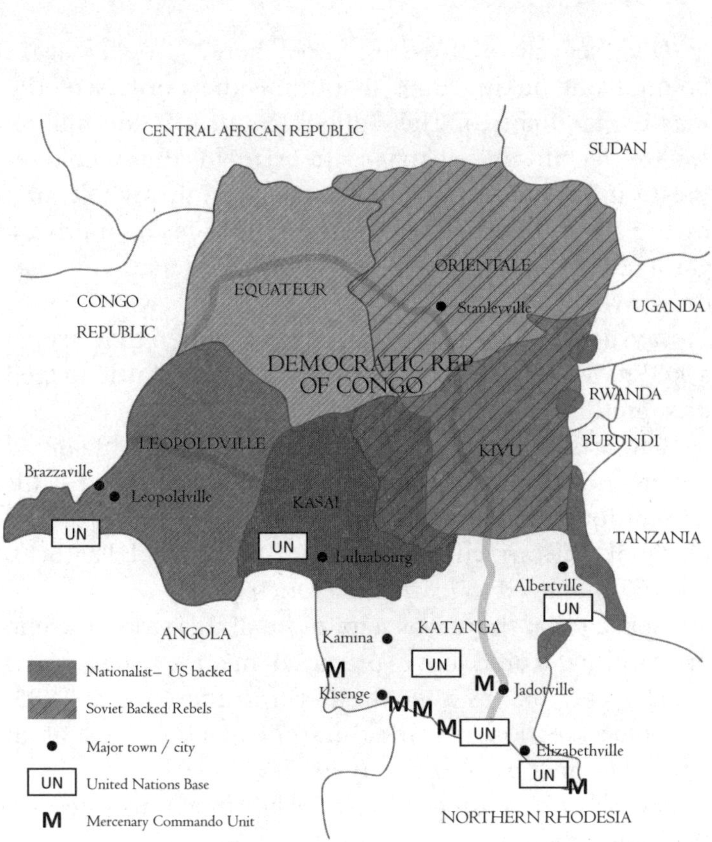

The Democratic Republic of Congo 1961

them to the promised land of sunlight and European civilisation as he had told the Americans.'

I was still none the wiser as to how The Congo degenerated from a place that had seemingly everything going for it, the proud possession of the King of Belgium under the auspices of his noble charity, with the recognition and support of all the major powers, to become what I had heard of being called the Heart of Darkness.

'D'ya see all of this huge area here?' Dowler again pointed out, taking time to outline the borders of the massive landmass of The Congo, 'it's nearly one million square feckin miles, that's the size of the whole of Western Europe. And Leopold was given this whole area by the US and European governments as his own private garden, D'yiz know, that is the largest garden anyone has ever owned?'

'Jaysus what would ye want with a garden that size?' I asked naïvely, 'unless he has a fierce load of cattle to feed or something.'

'The really stupid thing is,' Dowler answered, 'Leopold never set foot in his grand garden or as he called it his 'Magnifique Gateau Africain! That means his splendid piece of African currant-cake to all of ye fellas who haven't managed to learn yer French yet.'

I sensed that there was a lot more of this story to come but nothing could have prepared me for what I was about to be told, as after the Berlin conference in 1885, Leopold's kingdom became the scene of a holocaust or an annihilation of a race of people.

The account started with a fairly innocuous question from Monahan.

'What d'yiz think the currency of The Congo became when Leopold took over?' He asked probingly.

'Erm Belgian francs, I suppose,' I answered.

'Wrong!' Monahan replied, without offering what the correct response was.

'French francs then?' I guessed again.

'Nope,' quipped Monahan similarly dismissively.

'Oh for feck sake, I don't feckin know, how about punts?' I suggested lightheartedly.

'Wrong again!' he quickly answered, 'the answer would ye believe is human hands.'

'Ahh feck off!' I roared, knowing that Monahan had the uncanny knack of turning even the most horrendous story into a joke.

'I'm feckin serious,' he stated, 'the unit of currency when Leopold took over The Congo became human hands.'

'Is he being a feckin eejit or does he think I'm a feckin eejit?' I asked Dowler as if it were all some big wind up.

'He's being serious Michael,' Dowler responded almost unbelievably, 'they used to cut off human hands to balance their books.'

'But they'd have surely died if they had their hands cut off?' I suggested, still in a state of disbelief.

'Well most of them did die,' replied Monahan, 'millions of them; and if ye think hands are bad,' he continued, 'they only settled on human hands after trying out other body parts including ears, noses, feet and even penises.'

I visibly squirmed at the mere suggestion but noticed that Dowler's face wasn't smiling and was again nodding in recognition that Monahan was telling us the truth.

Immediately the atmosphere in the army transport truck changed; the jolly light-heartedness of a group of teenagers heading out on an exotic holiday had first been quietened by the details of the slave trade but the gruesome story of accounting in human body parts culminating in a holocaust caused a deafening silence.

Without doubt the Holocaust of the Jews had been the scariest story I had known as a boy, with films like *The Search* and *The Stranger* that I had watched down at the Picture House, showing graphic images of concentration camps and emaciated victims. The horror of the war years was being relived in the days before we left Athlone with the publicity surrounding the trial of Adolf Eichmann after he was captured by Israeli agents in Argentina, and who had been given the sinister title of: 'The Architect of the Final Solution.' But the Holocaust of The Congolese had never been mentioned in our accounts of history, perhaps I thought because it didn't take place in 'civilised' Europe or maybe, more suspiciously, because the colonial powers and their rulers had too much blood on their hands. It seemed to me that the history books, western politicians and even the film industry had completely turned their backs on the biggest human tragedy of the last 60 years.

Pakie Monahan was holding an old looking book tightly in his hands and he told us that it concluded that by the end of Leopold's reign in 1908 the population of The Congo had fallen from 30 to 10 million, an estimated ten million of which having been murdered; the young, sick and elderly being systematically wiped out. The mass killing of ten million people was staggering enough, even surpassing the Nazi era but The Congo's population was further reduced by ten million as people died from disease, malnutrition and a plummeting birth rate. This wasn't a war, just an industry of death.

Monahan continued to talk us through what he had been reading: 'First, Leopold's agents, including the venerable Henry Morton Stanley, constructed the railroad that would cut the journey time for rubber and other commodities being transported from the heart of The Congo's rainforests to the main port, from six weeks to one day. The young Congolese fellas,' Monahan described, 'who were physically strong enough to work were initially forced to labour on the railroad and the ivory industry, in a system known as porterage. The porters,' he explained, 'were chained together and worked to death, working round the clock, hammering through rocks and clearing the jungle.' I knew from the details that Monahan was providing that he was still telling me the truth although it was scarcely believable. He carried on describing what he had read. 'Yer man Stanley became known as "Bula Matari" or "The Breaker of Rocks" as he relentlessly carved a route through the mountains of central Africa for his railroad. And if the porters did not work hard enough they could be shot or whipped with a chicotte, "the white man's weapon of choice,"' noted Monahan menacingly, 'the chicotte being a long whip made of dried hippopotamus hide that caused blood to spurt for ten feet when whipped against bare human skin.'

'For fuck sake,' I interrupted, 'how were they allowed to do this when they had become part of Belgium's empire?' But Monahan already knew the answer:

'Under Belgian law, the flogging with a chicotte could only be legally carried out on black Africans,' he told us expertly. 'Under Leopold's system, native Belgian people retained access to the country's legal system, which made it illegal to flog a white man.'

'But the law did not apply to black people,' Monahan explained, 'and would ye believe it if I told the laws to legally flog black people in Belgian colonies was not abolished until the 1940s during World War Two, when they needed the same fellas to fight against Hitler – that's less than 20 feckin years ago ya know,' summarised Monahan.

'Them feckers are worse than the feckin Nazis if ye ask me,' I noted, 'but who did all of this flogging and murdering? Because I didn't see any 'wanted' posters on the news and none of them have been arrested like Adolf Eichmann.'

'As the railroad tracks were laid,' answered Monahan, 'Leopold began hiring commissioners from across Europe to enforce his business policies and to manage the outposts of his new business venture. It was these commissioners and their henchmen who carried out the atrocities.'

'And did any of them ever get tried in court when Leopold found out what was going on?' I asked.

'Did they fuck,' Monahan replied brusquely, 'it was Leopold himself that was directing the business through his so-called grand charity. He didn't feckin care how he got the rubber and ivory he needed to fund all of his plush palaces and his lavish lifestyle. And what's more,' Monahan continued, 'not one of the slaves from America was ever returned to their ancestral homeland of The Congo; Leopold had just been lying to get the recognition from the US.'

'What, none of the former Congo slaves ever made it back home either?' I checked.

'Not a sinner!' confirmed Monahan.

Dowler then took over the story:

'Aye and when, oh what's-his-name, erm Paddy Dunlop from up there in Downpatrick invented the inflatable rubber tyre, yer man Leopold was about to get himself very rich indeed as every fecker with a few bob tucked under their pillow suddenly wanted a motor car instead of an owld horse.'

'Does that include the tyres on yer goddess of all motor cars, Sean?' I asked Dowler cheekily, trying to lighten the conversation.

'No, but it does include that Juicy Fruity gum from their gum trees that yer chewing on,' he quickly retorted. 'Anyway my tyres didn't come from The Congo, but when tyres were first invented the forests of The Congo comprised of over half a million square miles of rubber trees, enough rubber to transform Leopold's private little garden into the most profitable "charity" ever!' Dowler emphasized the word with understandable irony.

He paused for a moment, 'and enough chewing gum to keep ye chawing like a cow for a few more years as well Michael!'

'But where did all the money go to?' I asked removing the gum from my mouth to avoid any further retribution, 'because every penny we ever gave to charity as kids always seemed to go to the poor black babies of Africa?'

'Oh Leopold was a really generous fecker alright,' noted Dowler, 'if ye liked looking at his big palaces or walking around his lovely lush botanical gardens in Brussels admiring his lovely carved statues, then he was a great fella altogether. But none of the money ever returned to The Congo. Aye, all of that shite he told everyone about European enlightenment was just bollocks.'

'So while all the Irish back in the last century sent their charity money to The Congo,' I enquired, 'Leopold was taking it straight back to Belgium?'

'Aye, it seems that way alright,' replied Dowler.

'But why did he want to kill all the poor Congolese fellas? I continued pressing 'or at least hack off their hands?'

'Leopold governed a slave labour system to make himself lots of money,' Dowler began explaining, 'whereby the native Congolese were forced to gather more and more quotas of rubber to satisfy world demand. The native men and young fellas were rounded up and sent out into the forests to gather the rubber whilst their families were held, bound and chained together by the neck and hands in owld shacks. If the quotas were not met then Leopold's agents would demand a severed hand from a family member for each unit of the rubber quota that wasn't filled, the dismembered hands being accounted for to balance the books. Most of the victims were killed this way.' Dowler noted, shaking his head.

'But even if the quota was achieved there would be no pay for the rubber gatherers, and their families were retained as hostages until the next quota was fulfilled, and then the next quota. A minimum of waste food was supplied to keep the hostages barely alive in the shacks. Though many of them were starving, the Congolese refused to eat any processed meat products given to them by their captors as it was rumoured to contain the severed body parts, known thereafter to The Congolese as "Mzungu Yangu" or "white man's meat."'

I had never heard such an appalling story in my life, the sheer inhumanity of it all making me retch at the thought of white man's meat and what The Congolese had endured under Leopold's reign.

'Well, I'll tell ye all now,' I insisted, 'I won't be eating any Mzunga Yangu or any other shite when we get to The Congo.'

'Aye, nor I,' replied both Monahan and Dowler at the same time.

'Ye will when ye get to see the vegetables they give ye in the rations,' laughed the Tiger, 'once ye've had a few tins of bully beef and dog biscuits, ye'll be so sick of them, yer mouths will be watering when ye see one of their fine boars trotting past.'

'I had no idea that the place was like this at all,' I noted, 'are ye sure yer not all just codding me?'

'Well read it there for yerself,' replied Monahan, 'here ya go.' And he handed his slightly damaged hardback book that he had been referring from.

The book was written by Mark Twain and was called *King Leopold's Soliloquy,* which Monahan outlined was all about the sins of the Belgian monarch, Leopold, during the time of his rule. It told of the cruelty inflicted on The Congolese people, implying that Leopold's henchmen believed they deserved to be treated callously because they were black.

'And it's still a bit like that over there in The Congo,' the Tiger claimed, recalling his experience from his first tour of duty, 'ye'll see it all for yerselves, the black fellas have a terrible rough time of it, better than it was during Leopold's time because they're not being murdered anymore but a desperate existence all the same.'

'But surely they have figured out a way of beating the white fellas at their own game?' I asked, 'after all, there are still a lot more of them.'

'No, its not as easy as that,' replied the Tiger, 'Leopold's system caused huge internal conflict between the native Congolese tribes as the desperate rubber gatherers would kill each other and raid neighbouring villages to steal enough rubber to fill their quotas, enough to keep their imprisoned family members alive. So there was already deep seated bitterness between the tribes after Leopold but when the Belgian government took back control, they continued to favour one tribe over another. It was another case of colonial "divide and rule" policy which favoured the smaller ethnic tribes at the expense of the larger ones which were then used for cheap labour. And ye know what that meant?' he paused for a moment, 'it meant even bigger profits for first Leopold, and then the Belgian companies that came after him to exploit the native Congolese. Aye, more palaces and feckin botanical gardens,' scoffed The Tiger.

'And now,' he continued, 'ever since they won their independence last year, the larger tribes have been taking it out on the smaller ethnic groups who caused them so much trouble in the Leopold and colonial era. That's the biggest problem the UN are faced with on on these tours of duty, the tribes are still killing one another.'

It seemed that the legacy of the Leopold and colonial wrongdoing was only now becoming apparent as the Tiger continued recounting his experience from his first tour:

'Back in the time of Leopold, many of the young Congolese orphans, some as young as six, were trained and recruited into Leopold's army, which he called the Force Publique. They were then taught, when they were just kids themselves, to administer savage beatings with the chicotte on behalf of their commissioners.'

'And did ye see any of these kids when ye were over on yer first tour?' I asked.

'No, but we heard all the stories about how brutal they could be if they raided a village,' replied the Tiger. 'The kids are given special prizes of food rations and alcohol when they do a raid, which fuels their minds to commit atrocities, including chopping off opposing tribes' hands exactly the same as it was in the Leopold era. And I'll tell ye now,' he noted ominously, 'when we get over there ye'll see that some of the children are the most dangerous of anyone and are still used by the Force Publique for all sorts of appalling crimes.'

'Jaysus,' I observed, 'and all for a bit of owld rubber, so that fellas like Sean can drive smoothly around in nice motor cars.'

'Ah it wasn't just about rubber Michael,' retorted Dowler, who also had become expert reading about this era of Congolese history, 'it started with rubber but then they found out that the country had more deposits of copper, gold, diamonds, tin, gum and palm oil than anywhere on earth.'

'And uranium,' I interrupted remembering my conversation with The County, 'the most valuable commodity in the Cold War at the moment.'

'Aye, and uranium,' confirmed Dowler. 'Apparently, although he was in his 70s by the early 1900s, owld King Leopold went skipping around his botanical gardens when he was told the news back in Brussels that his fine piece of African currant-cake had more riches than even he had ever dreamt of. Furthermore, the slave-labour system he had already introduced for rubber meant he could pilfer all The Congo's booty effectively for free.'

'For more plush palaces back in Brussels?' I suggested.

'Aye,' confirmed both Dowler and Monahan as the Tiger continued explaining:

'By the turn of the century, even owld Leopold's claim that The Congo was overseen by a registered charity had gone, all the money now going straight into Leopold's personal bank account. Factories opened all over The Congo kingdom supplying raw materials to the rest of the world. Then, the commissioners placed baskets of hands, or any other human thing they could cut off, next to the factories' gates, to "encourage" the slave-workers. As demand for The Congo's resources soared so did the quotas for raw materials but the resultant loss of life was unimaginable.'

As Dowler, The Tiger and Monahan recounted the stories to us nobody said anything, all realising what The Congo people had suffered was worse than anything we had imagined. The country where we were heading had such a brutal past, the legacy of which would have taken centuries to put right. All I could think about when I heard the stories of the baskets of human body parts, were the unsightly baskets of fish-heads I had seen when I was on holiday in the fishing village of Mulloughmore, but Leopold's baskets were filled with hacked-up human beings, and as many as ten million of them. If slavery had been the greatest crime in human history as I had previously been told, then colonialism, I considered, was surely the second worst.

Just as the Allies had finally managed to stop the Nazis, I was glad to hear Dowler and Monahan tell me that a couple of Irishmen had helped bring about the end of The Congo holocaust. Roger Casement and Henry Guinness (a grandson of Arthur), along with a British/French journalist named Edward Morel, formed The Congo Reform Agency, or CRA in 1904 at the height of Leopold's regime. Firstly Morel wrote *Red Rubber*, chronicling the accounts of witnesses, telling the world about the brutalisation taking place within The Congo's rubber industry. As an accountant he recorded the witness statements and matched them to the financial records from the rubber industry that estimated the number of possible victims of The Congolese genocide to be approximately ten million.

The figures were supported by Casement's research into the brutal annihilation of tribal peoples and the CRA immediately petitioned European heads of state for an end to what was described by Casement as the 'systematic exploitation and genocide of The Congolese people.'

Casement had been sent to The Congo to investigate reports of atrocities as an emissary of the British King Edward VII and in a letter sent to all European heads of state in 1907 described the colonial system of trading The Congo's rubber and other commodities as 'a façade masking naked exploitation on a continental scale.'

'It was from Casement's report,' Monahan recounted, 'where I first read about the baskets of hands placed outside the factories. I couldn't believe it at all at first, about the brutalisation of all The Congo people which had been caused by the civilised white men of Europe. According to Casement,' Monahan finished, 'just the sight of a Victorian steamer spewing black smoke through its big owld chimney would make The Congolese 'fly into the bush' such was their fear of the great white hunter.'

'The Belgians denied it all of course,' noted the Tiger, 'and still do to this day, although they did eventually take The Congo back off Leopold in 1908 because all the other countries told them they had to.'

'How could they deny it?' I asked, 'given they had witnesses telling them about it, and accountants looking at the books?'

'Ah, it's like yer man Eichmann and the rest of them Nazis,' replied the Tiger, 'they killed six million Jewish fellas and not one Nazi admits to it.'

'Apparently,' intervened Monahan, 'not only did Leopold's agents deny any wrongdoing, they said they had all the time been helping The Congolese people; that they had generously provided missionaries and delivered civilisation through the will of God and an eternal life to those that could see the light.'

'But what about all the human hands they cut off?' I insisted, 'how's that the will of any God?'

'Oh no, they had an even better excuse for that,' replied Monahan, 'they said that was all part of Leopold's humanitarian philanthropy of providing hospitals that had created surgical procedures to remove infected and gangrenous limbs.'

'What a load of owld bollocks!' I muttered, 'this feckin idea that religion and so-called civilised or superior white people have a right to commit and cover up these human slaughter-houses was just like or even worse than the Nazis.' It seemed that the cover up of the genocide of The Congolese was a propaganda campaign like no other.

Monahan then went on to explain that because of Casement's report and the work of the CRA, the

Belgian government did put an end to Leopold's abuses when they annexed control of The Congo to the State in 1908.

'And as for Leopold himself,' he announced with some satisfaction, 'he died in 1909, a rich man, but a real miserable owld bastard. But we all know the story of Casement,' Monahan continued, 'after he helped stop The Congolese holocaust, he returned to London and became an anti-colonialist and a leading voice in Ireland's own demand to end British rule here in Ireland.'

I knew some stories about Roger Casement from what The County had told me but none about his links to The Congo. Apparently, Monahan and Dowler told me, Casement said that The Congo enabled him to look back and understand more fully the tyranny that was taking place under colonial rule in Ireland, culminating with him becoming a signatory to the proclamation of Irish independence in 1916. Casement was the son of a prominent Ulster protestant shipping merchant from Belfast, and had worked for the British crown in both The Congo and Peru but as a signatory to the proclamation he was sentenced to death at the command of his former employer. He was hanged in His Majesty's Pentonville prison on 3 August 1916. The next day, the Times reported that Casement was executed because he was found guilty of being 'a willing agent of Germany' and was a 'promiscuous homosexual', both sure headlines to win the propoganda war in a socially conservative wartime Britain. Details from Casement's 'black diaries' were also published, supposedly justifying both accusations. His CRA colleague Edward Morel was also imprisoned in Pentonville because he was a pacifist, regarded at the time as an imprisonable offence as it was deemed to be in alliance with the German enemy.

'And after World War One was over,' noted Monahan, 'they went and gave the German colonies of Rwanda, Burundi and East Africa to the Belgians as well.'

'Jaysus,' I noted, 'I read when I was back in the recruitment company that World War One cost 35,000 Irish lives, including half the fellas in Edgeworthstown. They should've given East Africa back to the African people as Casement had told them, not feckin Belgium, but they had already hanged the poor fecker for being anti-colonial.'

Back in 1959 when I was working back at the Bridge Bar in Mullingar, Casement became one of the best known martyrs of the Irish independence movements when his diaries were handed over by the British public records office, the first time the country was given the full picture behind his trial and execution. The publication had caused such dismay throughout Ireland at the duplicity of the British government of the time and the press. The County had often quoted Casement's speeches to me particularly from his trial as he conducted his own defence. In the light of what I had been hearing about Leopold and Belgium's abuse of power, the quotes now seemed as relevant to The Congo as it did back then for Ireland:

> Ireland that has wronged no man, that has injured no land, that has sought no dominion over others. Ireland is treated today among other nations of the world as if she was a convicted criminal. If it be treason to fight against such an unnatural fate as this, then I

> am proud to be a rebel and shall cling to my rebellion with the last drop of my blood.
>
> Roger Casement.

The battle to give justice to the native Congolese was, however, not finished, even after Casement had been instrumental in forcing Leopold to hand over control and some commentators continued criticising the Belgian state up until the outbreak of World War One in 1914 as it was reported that while the killings and mutilations slowed, the slave labour system still existed. The cause of the CRA was assumed by other famous writers whose works caused more outrage and embarrassment back in Belgium, now implicating the Belgian state directly in the deaths of Congolese by disease and malnutrition in what some observers claimed was a state regime that had been superficially re-structured to continue the profitable exploitation of the Leopold era.

As well as Twain's book, Dowler had been reading a book written by Arthur Conan Doyle, the author of the renowned Sherlock Holmes detective books. Dowler told me it was titled *The Crime of The Congo*. In it he described a town, first discovered by Henry Morton Stanley back in 1878, where the population had dropped to just one eighth of when it was discovered and where the previous tribal way of life had been all but wiped out. Even after Leopold's rule had ended and the Belgian government was in power Conan Doyle wrote:

> Her colony is a scandal before the whole world..... the country is (now) sunk into a state of cowed and hopeless slavery.
>
> *The Crime of The Congo*, Arthur Conan Doyle, London, Hutchinson & Co., 1909, Fourth Edition.

I had seen *The Hound of the Baskervilles* with Peter Cushing and Christopher Lee at the Picture House, adapted from another of Conan Doyle's famous books. After everything I had read and heard about The Congo, from slavery to Leopold's colonialism, could be summed up with Sherlock Holmes' simple realisation:

> 'It's murder, my dear Watson – refined, cold-blooded murder.'
>
> *The Hound of the Baskervilles*,
> Arthur Conan Doyle, 1901

'It didn't take a detective like Sherlock Holmes to figure out why the Congolese people had such a deep-seated fear of the great white hunter,' I pondered to myself, as Prendergast interrupted my thoughts and our conversation by announcing to us that after our training in the Curragh Camp near Dublin we would be flying to The Congo where we would be flying over Belgium, and close to its capital city of Brussels. In *The Heart of Darkness* Joseph Conrad had called it the 'sepulchral city', which I reasoned, had good reason to appear morbid and had a great deal to answer for.

Casement's work for the CRA, we had heard on the news just the week before, also became a focus of global attention as we were about to fly out, when a man called Peter Benenson founded Amnesty International in response to reports of continuing torture and human rights abuses. Although Amnesty now had a global remit, much of its initial work would be carried out at its birth-place in The Congo where reports of abuses were still rife some 50 years after the Leopold era. The CRA was described as the 'predecessor movement' to Amnesty which had no political agenda, just a humane one. I was pleased to hear that Casement had effectively been exonerated with the publication of his trial details and that Amnesty International would continue the work that he pioneered but, little did I know at the time, that we would be one of Amnesty International's first assignments.

The old Baldonnel airfield near Dublin, from where we were embarking for The Congo, had been re-named Casement/Baldonnel military base in memory of the executed Irish hero. With our training at the Curragh complete we arrived at the airfield and quite a crowd had gathered, including family members who had come to say their good-byes, many of whom had travelled over from the west of Ireland. My mother too had travelled over that morning with my youngest brother Philip from Edgeworthstown and I went over to them in the crowd. I immediately noticed the worried look in her eyes which always troubled me. She gave me a hug and a kiss on the cheek. I was so embarrassed, in front of all my mess mates and me mammy gives me a big kiss.

She handed me a letter postmarked from London which she had only received that morning from my sister Kitty.

'There's a letter from Kitty for ya,' she said, as she started sobbing along with a few of the other mothers. I was now a couple of inches taller than her and the strong robust woman that had worked 18 hour days whilst raising eight children now seemed vulnerable. Her face appeared small and genteel, her voice timid and her eyes full of fear and worry. For the first time, I considered the impact of what my decision to volunteer would have on others and that perhaps there were dangers in The Congo that I was too young to appreciate.

I tried to comfort her again. 'Mam, I'm just going to do police work, I'm a peacekeeper, I'm not going to fight.' My words however were of little use.

'Please be careful Micky and look after yourself, we'll light a candle for ya, remember to say yer prayers and don't forget to write'.

Lighting a candle had become the symbol of lost youth in Ireland during the great famine as many generations of Irish families held a candle in their front window when their sons and daughters emigrated to England, America or Australia. During the 1950s there had been the biggest emigration of Irish people for 100 years and the image of a lit candle was again being used to symbolise young people leaving the family home. After being lit at the leaving celebrations, the candle was supposed to provide hope of a swift return, but the hope was nearly always short-lived. The family would mourn the departed after the last flicker of candle-light had been extinguished. Just as Kennedy's ancestors had boarded a Cork steamer back in the 1840s, many people I knew back in Edgeworthstown had joined the masses of people in 1959 and 1960 looking for better opportunities in foreign lands, including three of my four sisters who had moved to London. The CIE national strike of 1960 had meant that my family had fallen behind on bills and we again found ourselves with dogs tied outside various shopkeepers around the town. Ireland had been made a 'free-state' in 1922 and only became fully independent from British rule in 1951. So effectively being born under British rule, we would have no problem with work permits in England. With three of my sisters emigrating, The County had wanted the rest of the family to move to London but my mother told me that they would not go until I had returned safely from The Congo.

It was time to board the plane. I gave my mother a hug and to avoid causing further embarrassment I diverted my eyes away immediately to shake young Philip's hand. He was still only 11, just delighted to have been on a train to Dublin and oblivious to any of my mother's fears.

'Ye'll be a good boy and look after yer mother?' I said to him, imitating The County's voice.

'I will surely!' he replied, delighted to be so entrusted.

I re-joined the troop and CS Prendergast gave the order to stand to attention and march towards the Globemaster jet that was to be our transport to Africa.

'I see your mammy gave ye a big kiss Michael,' Dowler happily pointed out as I returned into line, murmuring the Shirley Bassey 1959 hit, *Kiss Me, Honey Honey, Kiss Me*.

'Ah, feck off!' I replied.

'Oh it was so sad, I nearly cried myself!' he continued, mocking a sniffle and padding his eyes, obviously enjoying my embarrassment.

'Quit will ya!' I snapped back, 'nobody will be sorry to see ye leavin! And besides,' I maintained, 'RTE or the BBC have their cameras on ya, and all of Ireland will be looking at ya whingeing like a baby.'

The Niemba massacre had captured the attention of the nation and the radio stations and television cameras were there to report on our mission by recording our departure from Casement/Baldonnel. We thought they would just be taking a few pictures and wishing us well but we were told later that the reporter dramatically built up the tension in his newscast. Pointing at us as we marched onto the plane he stated:

> These volunteer soldiers, some as young as 19, are among the first to be sent by the Irish republic to its first conflict overseas. But this group of soldiers are

no longer just peace-keepers, no they are not. They have been given the remit by the United Nations to use force if necessary to prevent an all-out civil war in Africa's Heart of Darkness: The Congo, a place of terror where many UN soldiers have been killed and where nine of our soldiers became the victims of Baluba cannibalism just a few months ago. Why, we may ask are we sending our sons to a country far from home, a country so mistreated and exploited by colonial Belgium, to solve a conflict of Belgium's making? These soldiers are not fighting for any victory but may pay the ultimate price in this brutal land. We may ask the question again: why?

Whilst we did not know what the reporter was saying, we were all aware of the television crew filming us as we headed towards the plane. I was on the outside of the parade marching right past the huge rolling lenses and I smiled shyly as my moment of television fame had come. All I could think of was the pubs in Ireland showing the news, places like Doyle's back in Edgeworthstown and The Bridge Bar in Mullingar with people pointing up at the snowy screen just as I had done when watching Pope Pius. I thought I had better look as natural as possible just in case the Dolly, Kevin and Franco would be watching and saying things like,

'Will ye look at Micky, he looks as if he has a stick up his arse!'

'Aye, and smiling like a proper eejit!' and everyone in the pub would be falling about laughing at me.

In reality, TV news coverage of The Congo conflict was never amusing and most people watched out of fear of hearing more bad news. Politicians opposed to Ireland's role as peacekeepers in The Congo described it as a war we couldn't win and that our official role as non-combatants would mean nothing to uneducated tribes who feared everything European after centuries of the slave trade and Belgian colonial rule. Furthermore our new mandate of being allowed to fire our guns if we were fired on could mean, some argued, that we could become embroiled in a civil war based on guerrilla tactics.

The Congo was now commonly referred to as the 'Heart of Darkness' as portrayed in Joseph Conrad's book written some 60 years beforehand which a few of us had read while we were training in the Curragh. The book featured a couple of erstwhile British merchants sailing on a steamboat up swamp-like rivers surrounded by native cannibals and living the lowest form of human existence. The book's main character was Mr Kurtz, characterized as one of The Congo's commissioners enforcing Leopold's regime, who had fenced off his property with illuminated human skulls mounted on posts. I had assumed that it must be a fictional story like Frankenstein with the image of the skulls similar to how we would carve-out a swede and place a candle inside on Halloween. It didn't seem possible that the book could have been based on a true story, but the stories told by Monahan, Dowler and the Tiger had convinced me that it probably was. Kurtz eventually dies screaming, 'Oh the horror, the horror!' as he reflects on the life he has led and inflicted on others.

I was thinking about The Congo's history as I strode towards the Globemaster Transport Jet that had been supplied by the US military and which was to be our transport to Africa, but my mind was taken over by the thought that I would actually be flying in a plane. As a boy I used to look into the sky when I heard a plane flying overhead and marvel at how they could stay in the air, soaring like a huge bird into the vast, blue sky.

'Jaysus, will ye look at the size of them wheels?' I noted, pointing at the Globemaster's massive tyres which were over six feet high, way above my head. The plane too was enormous, easily big enough to carry all the men of 'A' Company and quite a few more of 35th Battalion, along with armoured cars, guns, ammunition, boxes of medicine, piles of ration packs and tinned food. 'There's enough here to feed a feckin army,' Pakie Monahan pointed out sarcastically, 'these Globemasters were the planes that had kept West Berlin supplied during the airlift in 1948, supposedly where all this Cold War business started.'

We sat along the sides of the plane with porthole windows above our heads, in a hammock-like seat made of interwoven green straps. The battalion of Irish peacekeepers that had been sent to The Congo the previous year in July 1960 were issued with heavy bull's wool uniforms which was greatly criticised as the wrong equipment for the scorching hot Congolese days. The ordnance division that myself and Dowler belonged to got the blame for the useless uniforms but as I pointed out:

'Sher, we only distribute the equipment that we've been given.'

In the previous couple of months however we had received stocks of light combat uniforms suitable for the hot humid days we were expecting. Our back-packs were on the floor of the plane in front of us, up against the supplies and rations which would act as a foot stool for when we wanted a nap…ahh the luxury of it all.

I felt nervous but exhilarated, smartly dressed in my army uniform, just like Phileas Fogg setting out on my own epic journey to undiscovered continents. No-one I knew from my home town of Edgeworthstown had ever made it to Africa but this was not a film at the Picture House; I would now get to see them huge elephants and giraffes in real life.

'Chocks away!' yelped Monahan in his best RAF 'Battle of Britain' accent as the plane started and began to move towards the runway.

Then I remembered the Munich air disaster of a few years beforehand and the news reports I had heard back in Doyle's pub, that some of the Manchester United players including Duncan Edwards, Tommy Taylor and Liam Whelan didn't like flying, and had moved to the back of the plane believing it to be safer. Apparently Whelan was heard saying 'this may be the death of me, but I'm ready' as he took his seat before take-off.

My heart was thumping as the Globemaster's engines emerged from their slumbering motions and roared into life, the vibrations juddering through my whole body. Within moments the Globemaster had taken off. It seemed to stagger and surge during the first few minutes and then Dowler asked a question we were all wondering:

'How the feck is this thing going to make it all the way to Africa?'

The smell of diesel and the sound of spluttering pistons reminded me of Barney Farrell's old transport van back in Edgeworthstown except thankfully the Globemaster had four jet engines. The look on Dowler and Pakie Monahan's faces was one of terror and I wondered whether I should concede that I was absolutely shitting myself as well, but I didn't flicker and they said nothing either.

To distract my attention I opened the letter from my sister Kitty that my mother had given to me back at Casement/Baldonnel:

Dear Mam and Dad

I hope this letter finds you well. We are all well too and have arrived in England safely. The crossing was a bit rough, surely a bit of a rollercoaster, but we are here now anyway…

I knew that Kitty would not want my mother to worry; so when she described it as 'a bit of a rollercoaster' then it was probably a lot worse than the 'thrills and spills' of Disney's Matterhorn Bobsled Ride, the new roller coaster we heard had opened in California.

… We have already found our own flat to rent not far from the twins, which is close to the city of London so it will be good to find work. Our new address is Flat 2, 26 Gloucester Road, Peckham, London, England. We have already seen Big Ben and travelled on the tube, and there are many red buses running close to our new flat.

It must be great I thought, being able to catch a tube train and living in the centre of the great city of London. I was smiling to myself when I was abruptly returned to the reality of my situation reading in the next line:

Tell Micky that we are all thinking about him and we will write to him every month. The Congo is in the news here every day, talking about atrocities against the 'innocent whites'. They are saying over here in the newspapers that it is all the UN's fault, but we know that the Belgians are just trying to keep hold of the money. We are very worried about him though, please tell him to look after himself.

Please write soon. Good bye and God bless.

Love Kitty

As I put the letter back in my pocket I noticed the surging and spluttering of the Globemaster seemed to settle down, or perhaps I just got used to it. I stretched up and peered out the window and could see the coast of Ireland disappearing as the Irish Sea spun out below us.

Monahan had also stood up next to me:

'Fecking hell this is high,' he said and then quoted Yuri Gagarin's widely reported remark when he first entered space only six weeks previously, 'I see earth, it is so beautiful!'

The first man in space had been the biggest news story of the year when the Russians had put Gagarin, 'the Columbus of the cosmos' into space aboard Vostock1, but this wasn't a bright eyed Jack Russell, this was the first human in space. After firing off in a rocket, we were told that Gagarin orbited earth at a speed of over 17,000 miles per hour, what they called 'hypersonic' speed before eventually landing in the Saratov region in Siberia only 108 minutes later. The stories we had heard as children about the man on the moon, now seemed like a real possibility.

Importantly, Gagarin's voyage occurred within days of the Bay of Pigs disaster, and was regarded as another momentous victory for the Russians in the Cold War. Russia's triumph reaffirmed many African nations' belief that a socialist government could offer them prosperous security and technological advancement. Although NASA had also put their own astronaut into space just one month later, it was too late as they had been beaten to it by the Russians. Just as Nkrumah had set out in Ghana, African leaders again used this victory for Russia and re-iterated the ideal of communism compared to the capitalist system of 'wage slavery', which was based on the achievements of the individual versus the achievements of the country and its people as a whole. Capitalism, they protested, was what the Europeans had imposed on Africa, which they claimed had never provided anything for the overwhelming majority of people.

As the propaganda from Gagarin's achievements heated up we discussed our voyage to The Congo which would take three days, travelling at what Dowler called 'Guinness speed' with stops in Malta, Tripoli and Kano in Nigeria before finally arriving in Elizabethville in the south of The Congo. Some, including myself, were amazed that we were now flying above the clouds and many remarked at how delighted they were they had 'made it out' of Ireland almost as if it was one of the leper colonies they showed in the Ben Hur movie.

But now we were on our way to Africa, I wanted to discuss everything African, including films.

'In Hollywood they say that the Boer War saved the film industry,' I pointed out, recounting a magazine article I had read. We then spoke about the 1955 film *Untamed* with Tyrone Power and Susan Hayward in what the Dolly had read somewhere was called 'Africa's version of Rawhide', only it was Zulus rather than Indians who attack the wagon train. When I first saw the film some three years beforehand, I remember being slightly disappointed that a so-called 'epic' began in County Kildare during the potato famine, hardly an epic backdrop I remembered thinking. But the rest of *Untamed* didn't disappoint as the heroes joined up with the Dutch pioneers of Africa, the Voortrekkers, fighting their way through Africa's jungles, mountains and vast savannhas. It helped us to visualise what our home for the next six months would look like but now that I was sitting on a plane en route to this beautiful continent, a place teeming with such wild animals, incredible birds and reptiles, I again wondered how it could have become so blighted by conflict, with all this shite about colonialism and Cold-War.

I had read many books about the 'Great War' back in Athlone, about the terrible conditions in the trenches and about the young Tommies going over the top. African conflicts were equally brutal. The way these wars were captured in the movies, however, portrayed a class struggle of colonial gentlemen versus native savages, with very little sympathy for the latter. One of the most famous African films had been *The Four Feathers* with Ralph Richardson and John Clements who plays the British officer Harry Faversham. After he is accused of cowardice, signified by the four white feathers, he embarks on a mission to the Sudan in the 1880s to overcome the infamous Fuzzy Wuzzies: the black, wild-haired dervish warriors who had captured the city of Khartoum. In the comfort of the Picture House, I breathed a sigh of relief when Faversham re-establishes his brave credentials with a famous victory over this devil-like enemy. It only occurred to me after hearing all about The Congo's colonial history and remembering Kipling's poems that I had read in Athlone that perhaps it was colonialism itself that was wrong:

> Then 'ere's to you, Fuzzy-Wuzzy, an' the missis and the kid:
> Our orders was to break you, an' of course we went an' did.
> We sloshed you with Martinis, an' it wasn't 'ardly fair;
> But for all the odds agin' you, Fuzzy-Wuz, you broke the square.
>
> Fuzzy Wuzzy – Rudyard Kipling

The savage image of the African warrior was pitted against the invincible British as they formed in defensive squares of 1000 men, fending off attacks from all sides with superior firearms. Just as the nuclear age made our Vickers machine guns obsolete, the British army used the Martini-Henry rifle which they haughtily claimed had 'some guts behind it', the weapon advantage proving decisive in their ultimate victory.

Whilst the British would be dressed in smart red jackets, black trousers and elaborate white helmets the natives would be dressed only in loin cloths with a necklace of big-cat teeth clanging loosely around their necks. The most famous colonial battle I read about took place during the Ango-Zulu war at Rorke's drift where 150 men of the British infantry and Natal irregulars defended a supply station against 4000 Zulu warriors. 11 British soldiers were awarded the VC, the most ever awarded for a single battle. Before the battle, I read the Zulus would advance slowly swaying to the rhythm of war drums, thumping their leopard skin shields, and forming in their famous cow-horn formation around the British flanks. Apparently the noise of nature was the only thing that African armies feared so they would reproduce the intense sound prior to battle. The banging thud of war drums gained intensity as the attack became more imminent. It made my heart beat a little faster just at the thought of it and I remember thinking that the British soldiers must have been petrified but instead they were described as calmly checking and polishing their bayonets in the morning sun as the Zulus advanced. The battle lasted all day and all night until the surrounded garrison's supplies were nearly exhausted. Suddenly, the incessant clamour of drums stopped and the Zulus halted their advance, finally acknowledging that the British were fellow warriors and would be respected. Amazingly only 17 British soldiers lost their lives against a loss of 400 Zulus in what was described as the greatest defence in the history of the British empire.

Before I joined the army I would enjoy, as much as anyone, watching a film about the mighty strength of the British army at the Picture House – defending the might of the empire, the so called 'greatest achievement in human history'. As we watched the inevitable victory, me, my brothers and the Dolly would cheer on the gallant British soldiers but were unaware of the utter catastrophe wreaked on their victims. Apparently many people even in Britain became 'pro-Boer' after watching the film *Ohm Kruger* who led the Boer army in their defeat to the British in 1900. When the film was made in 1942 dear old Uncle Kruger had become a harmless old man; blind and living in exile in Switzerland. He narrated the account of how the British, an empire determined to control the lucrative gold fields of southern Africa and dominate the world, waged war on the South African republic, by seeking to capture the Orange Free State and the Transvaal. But Uncle Kruger's account included the details of rape and murder of the Boers including members of his own family. His emotive version was recounted to an audience unsuspecting that it had been manipulated by the Nazi propaganda machine. I had seen so many films about the aristocratic British overcoming an evil enemy, but never with them portrayed in such a negative light.

To govern well, you need good propaganda.

Joseph Goebbels.

As pictured in the final scene of *Ohm Kruger*, we heard that it was in fact the British who had set up the first concentration camps during the Boer war. In one camp, 80 per cent of the inmates died including an estimated 27,000 women and children. I wondered to myself: had I really sat there at the Picture House willing the same army, nobly dressed in their smart red tunics, to such a devastating outcome?

> History will be kind to me, for I intend to write it.
>
> Winston Churchill.

When we would arrive in The Congo, we were told we didn't have any enemies as such, we were there only to keep the peace. The Katangan forces under the leadership of Moise Tshombie however, regarded the UN as their opponents because we didn't support them with their succession and we were therefore allied with The Congolese nationalists. We were also considered an enemy by the foreign 'soldiers of fortune' or mercenaries, many fresh from the Algerian conflict. Most had been hired to fight with Tshombie by Western mining firms in a conflict they regarded as 'white versus black Africa'. Belgian troops also considered us 'adversarial' and regarded our presence as an obstacle. If we were not there however, they would surely be attacked by the central government forces [aided by the CIA] and the Lumumbaists [aided by the Russians] already massing on Katanga's borders. It seemed ironic to me that we were actually protecting the Katangans from their 'real' enemies who would overrun them if we were not there.

Additionally, disparate tribes were being agitated to wage war on Katanga by the Russians or Cubans, both with their own agenda of overcoming the Americans. The Balubas were at war with the Lumba and the Hutus were at war with the Tutsis after 'the winds of destruction' attack by the Hutus in 1959 resulted in a massacre of Tutsis.

There seemed to be so many countries' flags and tribal cultures competing for victory in this particular conflict. They were being kept apart by a UN force with its hands tied behind its back. If they ever made a film out of this war I reasoned, every side could depict the innocent Congolese civilians and us, the UN as the baddies.

Whilst the position of the UN was precarious, throughout history it seemed, whichever way the cards fell it always seemed that the native Congolese were on the losing side. Having suffered for the last 80 years from colonial domination and exploitation, in June 1961, one year after being granted independence, it was no different.

Lumumba had indeed tried to be the saviour of the downtrodden when he won them independence, and wanted a return to a traditional native hierarchy. This however was too much for the colonial powers and just like Roger Casement and Kevin Barry, the colonial powers needed Lumumba dead.

The truth about Lumumba's execution was beginning to emerge just as we were flying out to The Congo. He was apparently killed by agents of Moise Tshombe, the same President of Katanga, where we were heading. Lumumba was imprisoned and flown down to Katanga from Leopoldville, savagely beaten and summarily executed with help from Belgian paratroopers and mercenaries. The CIA it was rumoured, had also planned to remove Lumumba but were beaten to it by Tshombie and the Belgians. Both rumours were of course strenuously denied.

It made me think again of what I had read in Kitty's letter; that the newspapers in London were saying that the trouble was all being caused by the UN so I said to Dowler and Monahan.

'De ye know they're saying in England that this Congo problem is all being caused by us, the UN?'

'Aye! sighed Monahan, 'we are only allowed to break up fights, and yet they say it's us that has started it all.'

'It's only because the UN in New York has just voted to impose sanctions on Belgium because they're refusing to leave The Congo,' interrupted Dowler, 'and the British and French bankers don't like it as they are losing money, so yer big newspaper men in London are being given a big handful of money from the mining companies and are getting their papers to print all sorts of shite.'

I was reassured, and remembered that The County told me that truth was the first casualty of war. Although I now had no way back for six months, I wanted to know that it was the noble side I would be on when I arrived for my holiday in The Congo.

Along with a visit to the shrine of Our Lady of Knock, the only holiday I had been on before was to the seaside at Mullaghmore in County Sligo the previous year, a popular seaside resort with the soldiers in Athlone. We joked about the great waves that you could jump into from the beach if you could bear the freezing water.

'Sher ye might as well be castrated by the time ye come out' noted Monahan.

'Aye, not even Brigitte Bardot could help ya there!' I responded.

Monahan's eyes seemed to light up at the mention of his French sweetheart but we were distracted by the announcement from Prendergast that we were coming in to land for re-fuelling in Malta.

I had often seen the Mediterranean Sea on films at the Picture House, always calm, blue and inviting. An image had stuck in my mind of one of the big box-office films of 1957 called *Boy on a Dolphin* with Alan Ladd that showed Sophia Loren playing Phaedra walking out of the Mediterranean in a one piece orange swimsuit dripping from the surf and bathed in sunshine. She was undoubtedly the most gorgeous woman me or the Dolly had ever seen. To me, Sophia Loren was perfect; tall, dark haired and beautiful. Cliff Richard we assumed, must have been talking about her when he sung about his 'Living Doll' but she was also the kind of girl that you could take home to your mother as she played intelligent women and was a good Italian catholic. And probably more importantly when talking about bringing a girl home to meet your mother, unlike Monahan's idol, Brigitte Bardot, Sophia Loren's arse wasn't hanging out in every magazine picture.

After what seemed like ages on the plane as we came down the steps to Maltese soil, we all began running towards the Mediterranean having already removed our boots and were busily rolling up our trousers ready for our plunge into the warm Mediterranean Sea, gently lapping Malta's beach.

Monahan and the Tiger had run ahead of me excitedly singing the Bryan Hyland song, Itsy Bitsy, Teeny Weeny, before reaching the water, splashing wildly as they sprinted in. I was not far behind, but was barely into my fourth splash when I heard:

'This water is feckin freezing!' It was Monahan shrieking, and almost as quickly as we ran in, we were all running out again like little penguins.

'Jaysus, it's never like it appears in the films!' I noted disappointedly, 'it feckin colder than Mulloughmore!'

It was even too chilly to paddle for long, so we put our boots back on and arranged a game of football on the sandy ground not that far from where the Globemaster was re-fuelling. It was skins versus shirts, and I was happy to be a skin in this beautiful sunshine.

We had about nine on each side. There were a few lads I didn't know from Galway, some others from Mullingar, with me, Monahan and the Tiger making up the numbers from Athlone. Dowler didn't play, preferring to delay work on his 'rat pack' sun-tan and take a nap under a bush. Some of the NCOs also joined in, but the commissioned officers kept to themselves gathering round a makeshift table with their orderlies fetching them glasses of water. Monahan joked that they were sipping afternoon tea and were more like old women gathering to say a decade of the rosary.

'Aye,' I replied, 'a family that prays together, stays together!'

Football was also a great way to get to know the other soldiers who would be with us for the next six months. On our right wing we had Kieron Lynch from Athlone, our striker was Corporal McManus from Sligo and in goal we had Jimmy Tahenny, possibly the smallest man in 'A' Company who liked to over-exaggerate every save he made calling himself the Manchester United goalkeeper Harry Gregg. We also had on our side Jimmy McArdle, another Longford boy. For the first time I noticed that I wasn't the youngest looking soldier so should relax my constant agitation that I was underage or perhaps, I thought, I wasn't the only imposter who had managed to bluff my way to The Congo. The other side had two strikers who both thought they were Bobby Charlton, so

I played the Johnny Giles role and was defending against PJ Sweeney from Leitrim and Tommy McDonagh from Galway. Every time one would get the ball, they would immediately mimic the squeaky and excitable voice of the legendary football and horse-racing commentator Michael O'Hehir:

'And he's passed it to Sweeney, who breaks through the Athlone back line, with their defenders falling down all around him like flies! He swings it into the mighty McDonagh at full forward, who shoots and scores the most beautiful goal Galway has ever seen! All of Ireland will wish they were here to see that goal!'

'If there is anyone out there listening in, give us just five minutes more!'

It wasn't quite the same as listening to the All-Ireland back at home with The County but it was great craic.

After about half an hour the pace of the game slowed as sunshine and energy sapping sand had made football too much like hard work. The commentary continued even as the game finished: 'a victory for Leitrim!' yelped Sweeney, 'lovely Leitrim! The pride of the west! ... have won the All-Ireland in the blazing sunshine!' We headed for the shade and a bit of a breather, as Monahan called it, in the form of a Sweet Afton cigarette. I put my shirt back on as I was beginning to go a little red from sunburn.

Being in the army, people inevitably knew a famous war story about Malta and it emerged that during the Second World War, the tiny Mediterranean island endured 156 days of continuous bombing in 1941 with only three light aircraft versus the mighty Luftwaffe and Italian Air-Force. In order to keep Malta supplied, Britain launched Operation Pedestal but only 5 of the original 14 supply ships made it through the minefields and U-boats. Even 20 years later, we were told, the Maltese locals still celebrated the 'Santa Maria Convoy' because it arrived on the Feast of Assumption, the day the Holy Mary ascended to Heaven which, I noted, was also the name given to our parish church back in Edgeworthstown. The convoy had arrived just as their provisions were exhausted, bringing them food, water, medicine and ammunition undoubtedly saving their lives.

Looking out over the sandy beaches and opal blue sea it was difficult to imagine that this was once the most bombed place on earth, but after only a couple of hours in this Mediterranean paradise it was time to board the plane again. Next stop was Tripoli in Libya, about two hours' flight from our home for the night; the Wheelus American air-force base.

The game of football had really broken the ice and within a few minutes the plane was buzzing with conversations about The Congo, evil King Leopold, the Balubas, the Belgians and of course home – Ireland. Anyone who wasn't becoming very aware of The Congo's brutal past would have needed to be asleep but there was too much excitement on board for that. I began talking to one of the lads I played football with; 'PJ' Sweeney, who told me he had recently completed an armourers course in Dublin. He joked with me that he had wanted to join the engineers division so had kept quiet when they looked for volunteers for the armoury division.

'But I was sent to the armoury division anyway for 18 months!' he said.

'Well they always like ya to volunteer first!' I replied.

'Aye, a volunteer is worth ten pressed men!' laughed PJ, 'so anyway, I never did make it to the engineers.'

Just like many of the privates, PJ told me he had grown up helping out on the farm and had an education interrupted by menial jobs but he had seen the same advert for the army as I had in the pioneers magazine with the headline: 'Join the Army, Protect Your Future!'

'I was glad to volunteer for this trip though,' PJ continued, 'having the chance to be a policeman in Africa and to see places like Malta would have been too good to miss.'

As the conversation unfolded he went on to tell me he was from near Kiltyclogher in County Leitrim, which he proudly stated 'was the birthplace of Sean MacDiarmada,' who along with James Connolly was the last of the signatories of the proclamation to be executed in 1916.

'It was MacDiarmada,' PJ recounted, 'who had read out Padraig Pearse's letter of surrender in the siege of the G.P.O.'

PJ continued to explain: 'Aye, just like when Lumumba told the Belgians, "we are no longer yer monkeys", MacDiarmada made the similarly famous declaration, "damn your concessions England, we want our country."'*

'Aye, history seems to be repeating itself,' I responded as it seemed that everyone who knew anything about Irish history could relate to the plight of The Congolese and their opposition to colonialism.

It was the threat of a broader conflict, however, that was causing the most concern at the UN. This had forced Dag Hammarskjöld to insist that forceful intervention by the neutral UN was the only way of averting a wider catastrophe. Angola, Tanzania, Northern Rhodesia and Uganda had already been drawn into the conflict but ominously the Russians were building up their forces from their stronghold in the north and now controlled a third of The Congo. The situation was so acute we were

* Seán MacDiarmada

told that half of the entire US armed forces was placed on a fifteen minute warning, as many believed the situation in Africa could spark World War Three.

'We were told after World War Two that this must never happen again,' PJ continued, 'but it seems that politicians and governments never learn their lesson.'

JFK had pledged logistical support to the UN by way of transport planes like the Globemaster and accommodation at US military bases like Wheelus. At that moment, I didn't care about who was funding us, but was just delighted to be getting off the Globemaster for a night's sleep in a comfortable bed in Tripoli. It had been a long journey flying from Dublin but more pressingly, my head, back and shoulders were now bright red from sunburn in Malta. It was a very sobering moment when I also noticed I had 'red legs'.

'If ye rub some vinegar into yer back,' claimed Dowler, 'ye'll be brown by tomorrow morning.' It sounded more plausible than rubbing pig-shit and nettles into your head but I remained sceptical.

'Is that another feckin old wives' tale Sean?' I asked.

'No, but it might as well be, as we have no vinegar anyway!' Dowler laughed, 'ya should have followed me into the shade rather than running round like an eejit playing football.'

As usual, Dowler had been one step ahead of the rest of us who like me were all by now shining red from sunburn. On the plus side, we no longer had pale white patches but we all walked off the plane in Tripoli with our shoulders held high and our arms out in front of us in case anything, including our own bodies, would come into contact with the tender reddened skin.

Although sun cream had been around since the US Pacific campaign after the Japanese bombed Pearl

Harbour, there had never been much demand for it in the Irish army. My first night on African soil would be uncomfortable to say the least.

The next morning we went to the canteen at the Wheelus military base, known as 'Little America' because everything; the people, the planes, the food, literally everything, had been flown in from America. As usual, the officers of 'A' Company sat at their own table in the canteen having given their breakfast requests to a couple of their orderlies. When the orderlies approached the buffet style counter, an American General noticed they had more than one plate:

'They're for the officers sitting over there,' explained one of the orderlies.

'Put the plates down,' ordered the General with a commanding voice that echoed his status as the highest ranking military person I had ever seen, and promptly walked over to the officers' table.

'Everyone serves themselves in this canteen, gentlemen; one plate only. You queue up over there just like me, them and everyone else,' commanded the General.

'We all stood motionless with plates in hand, as we watched our officers humbly getting out of their seats and joining us in the queue.'

'He's right,' Commandant Quinlan announced, 'from now on, we'll serve ourselves.'

The Irish army had retained many of the traditions of the Victorian British establishment where officers were waited on and orderlies attended to their every whim, from cleaning boots to fetching meals. No-one before had ever dared to challenge the age-old custom of officers being brought their meals to a separate dining table and served with silver cutlery and table-cloths. Even for the '60s, this was ground-breaking stuff.

Not only did the officers join the queue just like the rest of us, they even sat down at the same tables. A couple of the younger officers were overheard saying, 'no bloody discipline, these Americans,' but Quinlan had set the example and whilst he was in command of 'A' Company the old outdated rules were no longer observed. I smiled: the new-found equality of the '60s had finally reached the Irish army.

It was now my turn to be served at the food counter.

'What would you like for breakfast sir?' asked the American canteen steward in his neat white overalls and a distinctive southern American accent. He was the first black man I had ever spoken to, but I wasn't hungry after having spent most of the night lying on my front.

'Have ye any vinegar?' I asked.

'Sure we have some vinegar!' replied the slightly surprised steward, 'what would you like with your vinegar, some potato chips?'

'No tanks, just some vinegar please,' I confirmed.

'Well, there you go,' and he passed me a bottle, 'well, enjoy your vinegar!' he remarked, clearly thinking that Irishmen with their bright red faces must be proper eejits.

'Tanks a million,' I said as I gladly headed straight for the washrooms, as the Americans called them. I took off my shirt and started to apply the vinegar to my sunburnt shoulders. The vinegar was freezing against my burning skin and so acidic it felt like being stung by a swarm of bees.

'That feckin Dowler!' I roared.

Needless to say, the vinegar hadn't worked and when we re-boarded the plane en-route for Kano in Nigeria, I was as red and sore as ever.

'How's yer sun-burn?' asked the Tiger.

'Ah, no problem,' I replied gritting my teeth, 'how's yours?'

'Just a bit itchy,' he said, notably upright and not daring to sit back.

With Prendergast as the CS, it was always best not to acknowledge pain of any kind; and with Dowler in the same platoon it was definitely not worth admitting to have been taken in by one of his hoaxes.

The discomfort of sun-burn would be keenly felt on what we were told would be a five hour flight to Kano, 'flying south-south-west over Libya and Niger before arriving in Northern Nigeria that evening.'

I had thought over Africa I would immediately see vast savannhas or jungles teeming with lions, leopards, elephants and giraffes just like I had seen in the Tarzan films but apparently we would be flying over the Sahara, and all I could see when I reached up to peer out of the porthole were oceans of sand. 'Africa's great desert' was almost three and half million square miles and 1200 miles from top to bottom; the largest desert in the world. It was the size of the United States with a population not much more than Athlone, just wave after wave of golden dust; no trees, no vegetation, no people, nothing, just endless and featureless sand. One book commented that Africa was a continent dominated by deserts, from the Sahara in the north to the Kalahari and Namib deserts of the south, which together made up a quarter of the continent.

When we reached Kano, Dowler with his typical resourcefulness had managed to get hold of a more detailed map of The Congo, showing the location of Elizabethville. It was the first time I appreciated the size of the country as Stanley's old map didn't have the location of the major cities that had emerged in the last 60 years. I also looked at other countries that I would likely never get the chance to visit in Africa. Now that we were flying over Nigeria, I noted to the west of us was the Ivory Coast and Ghana where Nkrumah was still advocating his dream of a socialist United States of Africa, while out to the East was Uganda and the Sudan. My eyes were then drawn down to The Congo, the northern part of which was on the equator. Back in Tripoli we were told by the Americans that it would be a bit stormy over the equator as there was usually a build up of 'precipitation', better known back in Ireland as 'pissin rain'. Our destination: the city of Elizabethville in the south of The Congo, bordering Angola to the west and Northern Rhodesia and Tanzania to the south and east.

The whole plane was now a hive of conversations, pointing down at maps and telling each other their own stories, how they ended up volunteering for The Congo and what they were expecting when they arrived. We were all in the same boat, decent fellas who were a bit shy at first, and so proud to be representing Ireland on such a high profile international peace mission. The Tiger too had been relatively quiet during the first couple of flights but as we took off from Kano en route for Katanga, like the rest of us he had become familiar with everyone and joined in the buzz of getting to know everyone in 'A' Company. Inspired by the journey, and when he wasn't chatting, he would return to his repartee of songs like Ricky Nelson's *Travellin' Man*, followed by Sam Cooke's *Wonderful World.*

I didn't know much about geography or biology either but as I again stood up to peer out of the port-hole window, I was amazed. Yesterday's featureless views of the Sahara had today given way to the lush green tropical forests of central Africa. Although we were still two hours from Elizabethville, we were now flying above The Congo, the place we had all been discussing so much for the last couple of days. All I could see was greenery, thick with trees, plants and shrubs which looked from our vantage point like endless fields of broccoli, cabbage and brussel-sprouts. I knew this must be the vast empire of rubber trees that had so compelled Leopold to carry out his genocide, but as I looked down it looked like nature had restored its mighty power, running riot as far as the eye could see.

The County used to tell me in the words of Oscar Wilde:

> One should absorb the colour of life, but one should never remember its details. Details are always vulgar.
>
> Oscar Wilde, *The Picture of Dorian Gray*

Despite its past, The Congo was the most complex and diverse living system on earth, with over half the earth's known species of animals, birds and insects. 200,000 elephants, buffalo, black rhinos, antelope and hyenas roamed below us through Africa's mightiest forest living alongside the world's largest collection of gorillas, baboons, apes, monkeys and chimpanzees, our closest living evolutionary ancestor. This was what they called a miombo forest, a diverse subtropical jungle like no other, but most captivating of all in this fantasy world of mythical creatures lived the legendary black maned lions, the peerless King of the jungle and the largest in all of Africa, which could only be found below us in Katanga.

Amidst the never-ending greenery were clearances where we could see the jungle watering holes known as 'Byes' where I could begin to make out the distant shapes of some of The Congo's wildlife, including passing elephant herds and wild boars. Byes were the stop-off point where all the jungle characters would call by for a drink and where all seemed welcome although they remained wary of The Congo's two most prolific predators, the leopard and more ominously, humans. Similar to the black maned lions of Katanga, many of the species we were told could be found nowhere else on earth like the red river hogs and the Bongo antelope with its thin white stripe down its side.

It was just as Father Curran had described the Garden of Eden at mass and, I concluded, with half of all the animals on earth, Noah's ark must surely have stopped off here.

The beauty was everywhere but danger was never far away. As we got closer to our destination CS Prendergast gave us our final briefing telling us first about our billeting arrangements when we landed at Elizabethville. He then went on to say,

'Now lads, I want ye all to listen. Many people are hostile to us, the UN, but ye should always wear yer blue helmets and never get involved in arguments with other soldiers or local people. Never go to an area without support or without having considered the intelligence ye will have been provided – if ye stray into the wrong village, expect to be roasted alive so don't go wandering as I don't want another Niemba while I'm yer CS. Also, wherever ye are, always keep yer radios on. The Congo is a very dangerous place. Disturb a wild animal or reptile and they'll crush ye in their jaws before ye've had the chance to scream. The rhinos and hippos will just stampede over ye, leaving ye as breakfast for the hyenas and vultures. Tread on the wrong snake, frog or plant and their fangs and spines will inject a lethal venom through your veins quicker than any needle, even eating what may appear like simple berries and mushrooms could leave ye dead within minutes.'

I gulped. The danger and the beauty – this was Tarzan's Africa that I remembered so vividly from the Picture House with Johnny Weissmuller opposite Maureen O'Sullivan [Jane] who was apparently Ireland's first big movie star. In the adverts for Tarzan they would always show a crocodile sliding on its belly into a swamp, the huge African elephant barking like a giant dog just as Tarzan himself would roar, 'ahhh.ah a.ahh a ahh ah!' the calling sign that danger was coming. The biggest danger though, was always the white bounty hunters.

> There had been black men, always. Big black warriors with spears and arrows, little black warriors, swart Arabs with crude muskets and white men with powerful express rifles and elephant guns. The white men bad been the last to come and were the worst.
>
> It was those days that Tarzan regretted, for when the white man comes peace and happiness depart.
>
> 'Men are strange beasts,' said Tarzan.
>
> Tarzan, Lord of the Jungle. Edgar Rice Burroughs, *Tarzan and the Forbidden City* (1938)

The sun was setting like a giant shimmering orange as we began our descent towards Elizabethville, the capital of Katanga. The Congolese were a native people that must have regretted ever setting eyes on a white man, and although Europeans now arrived in aeroplanes instead of chimneyed steamers, the trail of destruction left a terrible legacy and a brutalised people. I looked down at my 'red legs' and wondered whether they would take me in as one of their own, a descendant of a country that too had been a victim of slavery, of famine and colonialism, but my bright blue eyes and freckled fair skin would, I was sure, mean that I was regarded as just another crazy white man, or as they said in Swahili, 'Mzungu Mjinga', and therefore would be treated with the same suspicion as all Europeans.

I may have been wary of some of The Congo's apparent dangers, especially after all I had learnt about their cruel history, but I couldn't wait to begin exploring.

CHAPTER SEVEN

A long time to be a prisoner

Date: November, 1961
Location: Jadotville, The Congo
Status: Prisoner of war

IT WAS NOVEMBER, MORE THAN five weeks since we had become prisoners, which was a long time to reflect on the siege of Jadotville. Our confinement for the last week had been at Kolwesi, the military base 100 miles further away from our base in Elizabethville, where conditions were considerably better than those back at Leopold's hotel.

We had been provided with blankets and camp beds, and many of us remarked that it was probably our most comfortable billet since we arrived in The Congo five months beforehand. The Red Cross was also ensuring that we were being fed three meals a day although only two meals for me as I still preferred to avoid the chicken stew as the thought of 'white man's meat' made all meat meals and especially poultry completely unpalatable.

Pakie Monahan said the stew 'had great eating and drinking in it,' as most of 'A' Company devoured every morsel of the stew, their appetites fully restored after the starvation and thirst of the trenches during the battle of Jadotville. Many thought I must be mad not to eat my ration given our POW status and Dowler joked that he noticed a couple of blue-bottles making a run for it with the sirloin steaks they had especially ordered for me.

The most notable difference with this new prison at Kolwesi was the absence of the vengeful taunts of the Lumba tribe who had bayed for our blood so menacingly from behind the barbed wire outside Leopold's. Members of the newly formed Amnesty International had also visited us in prison and were arguing that we were political prisoners and should be looked after humanely which all provided us with some reassurance. However, the biggest boost to morale was the increasing speculation that we had heard from members of the Red Cross that the UN were getting closer to negotiating a deal for our release with Tshombie's succession government, although each day seemed to bring a new and more improbable demand for our freedom. Yesterday, we heard that Tshombie, in return for letting us go, had demanded that all Katangan independence prisoners be set free, for the UN to surrender control of all government buildings including radio stations and post offices and that the Katangan Force Publique (including ever increasing numbers of mercenaries) be allowed to restore law and order. The UN of course could never allow such demands as it would implicitly sanction the slaughter of tens of thousands of native Congolese and exacerbate the 'Africa problem', as it was becoming known in the rest of the world.

Any concession that appeared too accepting of an independent Katangan state would lead to an invasion by the Lumumbaist and nationalists forces, supported by the Russians and US respectively. The apartheid-supporting government of Northern Rhodesia led by Sir Roy Wellensky had also massed its troops on Katanga's

Southern border in a show of support and had repeatedly threatened to invade should the Katangan succession movement be threatened, making the situation even more precarious and seemingly leading to an even greater human catastrophe. The ultimate threat however was that central Africa could become the battleground of the Cold War and a nuclear confrontation.

Most of what we were being told was hearsay and the last official news we had heard was six weeks ago before the Jadotville siege started. With our radios having been confiscated we had no way of finding out what was really going on in the outside world. Not long before Jadotville the world seemed in a particularly precarious situation as back in Europe the Berlin Wall appeared overnight, splicing the world into two polar military powers.

Despite the wider threat of a nuclear showdown, the main topic of conversation amongst us was the claims we were hearing from Elizabethville. UN observers had been allowed to check on our conditions and general health when we arrived at Kolwesi and had reported to our officers on discussions taking place at UN HQ amongst the Irish senior officers. Although everyone in 'A' Company generally assumed we had been abandoned in Jadotville, the armchair generals as we called them back at UN headquarters had apparently been claiming that they had done everything they could to re-enforce or re-supply us during the siege, and that they believed that no men should be risked to secure our release from prison as we had surrendered.

Throughout our confinement, we had been discussing what the Irish commanders back in Elizabethville may be saying to justify their actions and decisions during the siege. Their apparent explanation was that they were unable to reach us in time as Jadotville was 80 miles away from them and that our capitulation had placed the UN in a weaker negotiating position. This allegation that it was we who surrendered too quickly was more crushing for many in 'A' Company than even prison itself and the subsequent fury that this caused was especially prevalent amongst our officers. Just like us, whilst in prison they had no way of explaining the truth of what happened and would therefore be judged on the words of complicit UN officers, whom we blamed for our current position.

Being that the UN officers in question were Irish I wondered how the Irish government back in Dublin would react on hearing these accounts. It seemed to us that like many unsavoury incidents that happen in the military and indeed Irish society, it was possible our plight could be conveniently re-written with false accounts.

The war in The Congo had taught me many things, but always it seemed where there is power or money at stake, all semblances of humanity and moral behaviour are abandoned. We didn't know what or who to believe anymore, east or west, Tshombie or O'Brien but most concerning of all we didn't know whether we could believe our own senior officers back in Elizabethville or our politicians back in Dublin.

So the long Swahili nights in prison remained disturbed and sleepless, as our demons kept reminding us that we remained captured prisoners under the possible penalty of death. Like everyone else, I wondered what was going on in the outside world, the current state of the war in The Congo and how our imprisonment was being reported back home. Since our arrival in The Congo our experience of the European-owned press was that it only reported the news from a white colonial perspective, so we knew it was very likely that the UN was being blamed for the Jadotville siege, all part of the propaganda war that blighted any attempt to contain the conflict and secure peace.

'D'ya think we will we ever get out of this feckin prison Sean?' I asked Dowler.

'We will surely Michael,' he replied.

'It wasn't like this when we first arrived Sean,' I observed, 'but every day since then something worse seems to happen.'

CHAPTER EIGHT

Arriving in The Congo

Date: May 1961
Location: Elizabethville, The Congo
Status: Peacekeeper

WHEN WE FIRST ARRIVED at Elizabethville airport back in May, after the arduous three day journey from Ireland, we were full of enthusiasm for what we might encounter. Prendergast again spoke to us before we got off the plane saying that we would be remaining within our Irish army company units for the first week after which we would be joining up with troops from other countries for UN operations. They would be from many different parts of the world including India, Ghana, Sweden, Italy, Chad and Nigeria but the overall officer in charge was an Irish commander who Quinlan, the Cmdt of 'A' Company, reported to. Prendergast went on to tell us that we were now members of a UNOC force which he defined with notable difficulty as *'les Opération des Nations Unies au Congo'* pronouncing each letter with a distinctively un-French accent.

I nudged Pakie Monahan during the briefing and whispered: 'I wonder if Brigitte Bardot had tried to say the same sentence, whether she would have made it sound very different?'

'Aye!' smiled Monahan

Whilst remaining seated on the Globemaster, we were issued with our UN helmets, or 'casques bleus' as they were called in the French speaking Congo; the same shape as those used in World War One to protect the Tommies from shrapnel. These were made of flimsy blue plastic, almost like the ones you could buy in Maggie Canavan's when we were kids. They were inscribed with 'UN' in large black letters on the front, our only real symbol of neutrality. We were also provided with other small UN paraphernalia including a laminated card with the following thoughtful inscription:

Of one essence is the human race
This has creation put the base
One limb impacted is sufficient
For all the others to feel the mace
The unconcern'd with others plight
Are but brutes with human face

Saadi (Persian Poet) Motto on the entrance
of the United Nations building NYC

The UN did not directly supply us with any practical army supplies, as our FN rifles and combat materials were all provided with funds from member UN nations, the largest of which was the US administration. It was immediately clear that due to the external nations supplying the weapons to the various adversaries in this heart of darkness, the old colonial battle ground was now a Cold War zone. The US had recently told Dag Hammarskjöld in New York that it would continue to supply anything the UN needed to prevent pro-communist forces from taking over the country. The US was also arming the nationalist forces based in Leopoldville under President Kasa-Vubu. The Soviets and Eastern Europeans, however, were likewise supplying the Lumumbaist forces under the control of Antoine Gizenga based in Stanleyville with similar quantities of automatic weapons. Lastly, the Belgian mining/banking conglomerates, notably Societe Generale and The Union Miniere, were funding the supplies used by the mercenary led Katangan independence army.

The three opposing armies and the UN were therefore fairly evenly matched in terms of small arms although many of the local tribes-people preferred to use their traditional weapons like spears and bow and arrows. The arrows they used were barbed, making them almost impossible to pull out of a wound but their real danger was their arrow-tips which were coated with the secretion of a local Congolese flowering plant called 'curare' found only in the forest canopies of The Congo jungle and which would cause a convulsive death within minutes.

Prendergast told us quite frankly that if we were hit with one of these curare arrow tips, there would be no point trying to save us, and that the rest of the unit should not attempt to save the victim. I gulped again as I stood up to get off the plane.

In the terminal building at Elizabethville airport there were a few small groups of white Belgian colonials, queuing up for their tickets back to the safety of Europe. Across from the queues were the newspaper stands with Flemish and French titles splashed with headlines of 'Guerre Froide Aviver!' – 'Cold War Intensifies', above a photograph of President Kennedy and Chairman Khrushchev chatting in armchairs at a conference in Vienna with an urgent agenda of Berlin, IndoChina and The Congo. We heard that the meeting generated threat and counter threat when Khrushchev threatened to prevent the West from accessing Berlin during a tank stand off at checkpoint Charlie.

The caption below the photograph in English quoted Khrushchev as saying,

'Force will be met by force. If the US wants war, that's its problem. It's up to the US to decide whether there will be war or peace.'

To which Kennedy replied unequivocally: 'Then, Mr. Chairman, there will be a war. It will be a cold, long winter.'

It was clear to us that the possibility of nuclear weapons being used was becoming more likely almost every day, but Dag Hammarskjöld had decided that the situation in Berlin was not as dangerous as it was in The Congo. He defended his decision not to send UN troops to Germany by saying:

> We need to cut the suit to the body… It is much better to have the cloth and go into action as a good tailor quickly when the need arises.
>
> Dag Hammarskjöld 1961
> (Urquhart 1972, p. 230).

The need for UN troops was very urgent in The Congo, Hammarskjöld insisted, and he told the UN General Assembly that it was only the presence of the UN that prevented the Soviet-backed Lumumbaists from rampaging towards us in Katanga and igniting a global conflict. He said that if we could solve the problem in The Congo's southern province then the immediate threat of a wider conflict would be diminished. But the Soviets' patience was also running out with the UN; either the UN expel all Belgians forces immediately and allow the people of The Congo to run their own affairs, they demanded, or they would risk nuclear war with the US by taking over the country.

Within The Congo itself, all of the factional leaders were being covertly encouraged by external nations to defy the ONUC force. With the army and police allied to different Congolese politicians depending on where they were located, ONUC represented the only independent law and order force in the country. But without any backing from the country's most powerful leaders, ONUC didn't have a meaningful mandate. The US government was the only one of the adversaries that was providing aid to the local people, in the form of food and medicine as it tried to avert a famine. This too however was regarded cynically by the colonial supporting press as being politically motivated, and they quoted the Karl Marx philosophy as the true motive of US authorities: that a scarce and primitive existence means hunger, and hunger inevitably means communism.

The same photograph of JFK and Khrushchev would also no doubt adorn the front pages of newspapers back home in Ireland, including The Irish Independent, so I wondered what The County would be making of it all. He would most probably be on Kennedy's side because he was Irish but also because there was very little coverage of the communist perspective given Ireland's reliance on the UK and the US for its international news.

I imagined The County sitting in his armchair reading about the turmoil in The Congo and probably forming the view, just like most of us, that it was the Belgian colonials who were largely to blame. Just before we left Ireland in May 1961, the UN voted for sanctions against Belgium due to their continued use of the Belgian army in The Congo territory, causing the Brussels government to make a symbolic withdrawal. As they withdrew their official forces, the Belgian politicians came under heavy criticism from their electorate at home for abandoning their ex-pat citizens. They decided to covertly back a large deployment of mercenaries to protect the white population. The County would have read that the Belgian banks and mining companies were a key part of the conspiracy since the mercenaries were being paid from their funds. I imagined him laughing at the duplicity of prominent Belgian politicians who were claiming that they only wanted to protect their ex-pats from the atrocities taking place, not mentioning the 30 billion Belgian francs they were receiving in revenue from Belgian companies based in their former colony.

Prendergast had told us that we could identify the mercenaries from their attire: khaki shorts, a matching shirt or safari jacket, long socks, bush hats and light ankle-length rawhide boots with rubber soles that suited the hot African climate, known as *veldskoens*. Even more noticeable, he explained, was their unprofessional appearance.

'We should not expect them to have the swagger of Clark Gable in *Mogambo*,' Prendergast remarked, 'rather they are usually unshaven, loud mouth feckers, out of their boxes on porter and whisky.'

Prendergast explained that within the local Congolese communities the mercenaries were most often called 'les affreux' or the dreadful ones, characterised by a life of drunkenness, decadence, money, danger and in some cases just a love of bloodshed – all of which could be found in abundance in Katanga.

'Ye should be very wary of mercenaries,' Prendergast continued 'and should ye come across them in bars or restaurants in Elizabethville they will often try to start a brawl if they're not already fighting amongst themselves. Don't get involved, just feckin leave them to it!'

Seemingly every gunslinger in the west was seeking work as a mercenary in Katanga with infamous and disparate backgrounds. Some were hardened Pied Noir, fresh from the Algerian conflict, others were old Nazis from the Second World War or French collaborationist members of La Cagoule, the violent French fascist movement that had sought refuge after siding with the defeated Nazis. There were also some that were just young adventure seekers trying to make their fortune, often recruited directly from the Belgian army or from other parts of white Africa including Rhodesia and South Africa.

Seemingly, they all had a common belief that the demise of colonialism conspired against the honourable white man, robbing them of their birthright, homelands and a civilized way-of-life but in reality they were not fighting for a peaceful family existence. Instead they were largely just opportunist thugs, nostalgic for the days of imperial exploitation, an old world order in which they were able to freely plunder from native people with irreproachable violence and brutality.

Some of the mercenaries had achieved almost legendary reputations for their cruelty towards their fellow man; names like Bob Denard, Jean 'Jack' Schramme and Mike Hoare had emerged as revered icons of this most inhuman profession. In our briefing sessions we were told that these three leaders were the officers in charge of commando units, each comprised of up to 500 men, of which there were believed to be at least ten units on active service in Katanga. The units would also recruit from local whites and corrupt Congolese tribes to swell their numbers still further. They would deliberately hire boy soldiers, some as young as nine, because they were easier to brainwash into carrying out particularly brutal deeds. The orders given to the mercenary units, we were told, were simply to wipe out any political opposition to Katangan independence.

Denard was fresh from the Algerian conflict, Schramme was a former colonel in the Belgian army and Mike Hoare had been a captain in the British army in World War Two, although he was actually born and spent his early life in Dublin. We were told that Hoare was leading a particularly ferocious group called '4 Commando' or the 'Wild Geese' who had been especially drafted in by Moise Tshombie, the head of the Katangan independence movement.

Some of the older men in 'A' Company immediately recognised the term 'Wild Geese' from Irish history as the name given to exiled Irishmen after the Jacobite armies lost out to William of Orange in 1691, a history which Hoare must have recalled when bestowing the name on his troop. The defeated King James army were given the ultimatum at the Treaty of Limerick 300 years ago, to enlist with the English army, be executed or be banished from Ireland's shores. Of the 14,000 Irish soldiers that were captured; 3,000 chose to enlist and 10,000 chose to march on into battle and certain death. The remaining 1,000 decided to flee Ireland and were recruited by Louis XIV of France in a legend that became known in Ireland as 'The Flight of the Wild Geese'. These Irish Battalions went on to fight throughout Europe as hired hands for any army willing to pay them but mostly for the advancement or protection of French and Spanish colonial interests. Having had their own freedom destroyed, these original Wild Geese set about devastating the lives of others by becoming the first mercenaries or soldiers of fortune to advance the cause of European colonialism.

To the white population of Katanga, Hoare and the modern mercenaries were treated as revered heroes almost as if they were the liberators of Africa. The papers clearly wanted to create an aura of chivalry about these dogs of war, who had even created their own distinctive rallying call:

> Vive la Mort, vive la guerre et vive le sacre mercenaire!
>
> (Long live death, long live war and long live the cursed mercenary!)

The Belgian white friendly newspapers had printed magnificent stories of fearless mercenaries storming through pro-Lumumbaist Congolese towns and releasing imprisoned whites. In reality, the mercenaries simply killed everyone who stood in their way; but the papers in Katanga were only reporting that it was the communist and nationalist forces that were guilty of genocide and committing atrocities like murdering white missionaries and raping nuns in towns near Stanleyville in the North Eastern province of Kasai. The papers also reported on the ongoing war between the Baluba and Lumba tribes in Katanga and implied that it was only the presence of mercenaries that prevented the bloodshed reaching the white community. But outside of Katanga, we learned Hoare had become known as Mad Mike or The Mad Bloodhound Mike Hoare as he was labelled on pro-communist broadcasts whose troop of Wild Geese, they stated, were prepared to eat, drink and shed human blood in return for money. Although we hadn't long arrived in The Congo, it was clear that whosever side the newspapers were on, an atmosphere of fear was being spread by the media.

The official UN intelligence specifically about Hoare's 4 Commando seemed far less grotesque but very thorough. In our briefings we were told that they were predominantly comprised of Foreign Legion troops as Hoare believed them to be hard but more disciplined. He had also drafted exiled Cubans and some white southern Africans. We were also told their exact meeting points for recruitment back in the cities of Paris, Brussels and Salisbury before they were covertly flown into Katanga on Belgian army transport planes. Dowler commented that we would be queuing up ourselves outside the Cathédrale Notre Dame in Paris should we fancy becoming mercenaries when our tour of duty was over. We were amazed at how much they were getting paid, the regular mercenaries receiving £80 per week, nearly ten times the amount we were being paid. The 'real money' however was earned when they became involved in 'active service' as their wages would be doubled as an incentive. Many of them would agitate for conflict in the hope of receiving the higher bounty. Whilst all was quiet in the safe enclave of the airport, with so many different groups stirring up trouble, our new home in The Congo sounded like a very dangerous place.

Ironically, my biggest fear wasn't the mercenaries, nor the prospect of tribal or nuclear war. I knew that was all beyond my control if hostilities sparked off. My biggest fear remained that my age would be discovered, although I reasoned that even if the officers in charge found out now, they could hardly walk me to the gate, as it was now thousands of miles away. It would also be at least two weeks before the next flight back to Ireland. So being this was to be my home for the next six months or so, I just thought,

'Well sher, I might as well make the best of it.'

The next day Dowler too was full of beans as he emerged out of the airport barracks into the fresh Congolese sunrise:

'Ah, it's grand to have a little bit of sun on yer face,' He noted while stretching his arms up towards the blazing sunshine, 'and surrounded by all these lovely trees and bushes. That's God's way of stopping all of ye eejits getting yerselves sunburnt again!'

'He's a right clever fecker,' I remarked to Pakie Monahan.

I was still a bit sunburnt from the football match in Malta although the redness was now fading. Instead of going brown I was just returning to my natural colour; a bluey shade of white. But I was now careful to avoid the burning sunlight so remained within the walls of the airport barracks.

I noticed Hegarty was lying on his bunk in his typical nonchalant style.

'How are ya Danny?' I asked.

'Bored!' came the abrupt reply.

'Are ya missing the rain already?' I asked him.

'No, just bored of all this moving around, it's like we have been on the move for feckin weeks, and now we are heading off again to the other side of Elizabethville. But don't worry,' he noted sitting up on his bunk, 'I won't be shooting off my toe or anything like that.'

He was referring to a story that had circulated on the Globemaster about one of the privates from the last Irish UN battalion's tour of duty, who shot off his toe because he was homesick. Apparently he thought it was a good 'blighty' wound when he witnessed some of the conditions of the native Congolese and the constant harassment being directed at the UN. Instead of being sent home immediately, the young Private's toe became infected. He was unable to fly back until six weeks after the rest of the battalion.

I presumed Hegarty was just tired from the journey so I left him alone, but the Tiger and Monahan had already reverted to their former selves, the Tiger whistling one of his favourite tunes while Monahan was again looking for any opportunity to make a joke.

'What time is it Michael?' he asked me.

'Not long after six in the morning,' I replied, remembering to add the extra hour ahead.

'Jaysus,' he said, 'I've been asking the time constantly since we got here and each time I get a different answer!'

In The Congo, the locals used Swahili time which was guided by the position of the sun, the most dominant feature in this tropical climate, which rose at 0600 hours and set at 1800 hours all year round as it was close to the equator. At 0700 or 'saa mbili asubuhi' as it was pronounced in Swahili, (translated as 'hour-two morning') we were told we would be setting off in our UN army transports to our permanent base just outside Elizabethville.

As we convoyed in trucks down the high street of Elizabethville, it struck me how modern the town was, and nothing like I had imagined. Wide boulevard streets lined with jacaranda trees in full lilac-bloom, modern designer boutiques and coffee shops nestled amongst glass-panelled offices reflecting the soft blue sky and beaming sunshine. I had imagined African towns to be wooden shacks with traditional goat herders directing their flock through bushy and dusty side-streets, but this was more like how I imagined Cary Grant and Deborah Kerr to live on 5th Avenue in New York. Alongside us on the boulevards were swanky American and European cars, with smiling businessmen busily going about their trade. It all looked peaceful and orderly amongst the white population of Elizabethville as they strolled down the leafy pavements in their impractical European suits.

Some of the major European banks and mining companies had their African 'bureaus' in three or four storey office blocks and they had engraved their company titles onto small polished brass nameplates which adorned each office doorway. Thomas Cook's Travel and the Belgian airline Sabena also spruced up their smart shop-fronts with posters of smiling pilots encouraging travellers to fly away on holiday, something almost unheard of back in Ireland. The airlines were said to be very busy ferrying former Belgian colonials back to the safety of Brussels, but any danger seemed a long way off as our noses were filled with the spring freshness of blooming jasmine and wild flowers, neatly arranged around shop entrances. To the north and east of the town were the ex-pat residential areas, whitewashed mansions with large verandahs and manicured lawns, flanked by masses of rubbery green plants and lit up by neatly arranged pale pink African tulips, and flame red dahlias. There was not a stinging nettle or a briar in sight and not since the Dolly Dolan bought a kaleidoscope from Maggie Canavan's had I seen such a vivid array of colours. These were the homes restricted for the white, mainly Belgian ex-pat community, interspersed between some fine hotels and consulate buildings.

Following the main boulevard to the south of the town, away from the centre, the houses became gradually shoddier, soon degenerating into splintering wooden structures with some boarded up shops and mechanic workshops for the Greek, Italian and Portuguese communities. Further towards the outskirts of town the glass panelling and whitewashed walls had been completely replaced with a shabby line of makeshift bars and brothels known as bordellos. Small red light shades flittered against billowing linen sheet walls as the prostitutes or shakiras stood provocatively outside in their ill-fitting stilettoes and short flowery dresses.

The truck was ignited into life as the shakiras started waving at us, provocatively indicating to us that we should come back in our free time to see what treasures lay behind the sheeted bordello walls.

'We'll have to buy them young girls a pint sometime,' Dowler joked, 'here Michael, ye'll have to ask them "d'yis come here often?"'

I was embarrassed at the very suggestion but as I didn't have a girlfriend at the time, I was an obvious target for Dowler's jokes. Then he continued in an exaggerated high pitched African accent:

'Greetings Big Bwana!' he suddenly blared out, 'why has this big white Irishman called 'Michael Greene Sir come to visit us at our home, would he like to dance "cheek to cheek?". After all, why else is Obi-Gabi here? If not, he should be in his own country tending his own cattle!'

Half the bus was laughing at me as Dowler recounted his jibes mimicking the lurid mannerisms of the big buttocked shakiras, his voice encouraged by the amused response of the other soldiers and becoming more like the exaggerated African accents we recognised in the Tarzan films back home. I didn't say anything but luckily Pakie Monahan diverted attention away from me by doing a Ray Charles impression as he had bought a pair of sunglasses at the airport and told Dowler he was just doing the 'mess around', and when he noticed his impression of the shakiras he told him that he should just 'shake that thing!'

The whole truck was by now laughing as the road became more bumpy but within barely half a mile an overbearing silence abruptly muted the humour as we began to drive past the Elizabethville refugee camp.

The Jacaranda trees and dazzling plants that lined the smooth concrete boulevards of Elizabethville had completely vanished, now replaced by a narrow dusty pot-holed road that smothered us in a reddish mist whipped up by the truck wheels as they negotiated their way through the mogul like bends ahead of us. My eyes squinted to distinguish the sudden change in landscape and through the clouds of stirred-up dust we were able to see how the other half of Elizabethville's citizens lived. Naked, young children stood on the road-side desperately thin but staring intensely at the massive UN transport trucks speeding past their oversized ghostly eyes. It appeared for a moment that some were smiling, but these weren't the grins of well fed western children, rather the malnutrition that had wrenched a thin layer of unfed skin tautly over their protruding skulls, exposing a jawbone of stripped teeth. Older tribesmen stood paternally by, their shoulders hunched in seeming help-lessness at their situation whereas probably a century or so beforehand they would have stood proudly upright carrying spears and adorning big-cat headdresses. But they too were now naked, except for a little box on a string hanging loosely around their gaunt necks. These were the boxes they had all been given on their inde-pendence day just a year earlier, when Lumumba had given them such hope for the future. The boxes had once contained a small amount of money for seeds to home-stead their first crop, which Lumumba proclaimed was for their 'uhuru' or liberty. They were of course long emptied and Lumumba was dead but neither had been forgotten, as the little boxes remained a symbol of the cherished freedom that Lumumba had promised them. The refugees all had another thing in common, they were all members of the Baluba tribe and victims of an ongoing tribal war, forced to abandon their homes and other possessions when the mercenaries and renegade Lumba forces burnt out their villages.

It was the first time we had seen Balubas in real life. Prior to this we had only known Balubas as almost human animals having been so demonised in the Irish press after the Niemba ambush. But these people didn't seem like the ghastly cannibals who filed down their teeth to cut through human flesh. We learned that there were an estimated three million Baluba people, divided into small and disparate communities living in Katanga spread over an area the size of France. The Baluba community specifically responsible for Niemba had once formed a settlement of about 1,000 people in the north of Katanga but had been almost wiped out by Belgian and mercenary led clear-outs. The last surviving 20 or so Baluba males of that community wanted revenge against the white man and didn't distinguish between Irishmen and Belgians just as our newspapers could not distinguish between disparate Baluba communities.

The refugee camp, we later learned, was absorbing hundreds of new displaced villagers every week although it was already desperately overcrowded. One woman sat by the roadside with 5 children huddled next to her. She held out her hands towards our truck begging for some money for food to give to her starving children, two of which already having the deceptive paunch of a rounded belly which here in The Congo meant that severe malnutrition had already taken hold. The mother then gestured a feeding movement with her smallest child saying in her native Kingwana, or copperbelt Swahili language, 'mkoto – baby', and then looking up forlornly towards the heavens as if it would not be long before her youngest loved-one would be claimed back by God.

Behind the refugees on the roadside were their shelters, a patchwork jumble of whatever they could get their hands on, old rags, cardboard, tin-cans, branches and scraps of metal held together by threads of string and probably what little optimism that had left. The lucky residents of these makeshift dwellings had a piece of corrugated iron, which would be very valuable in the rainy season that would surely wash away the other stick-and-paper shacks. Even the feral cats that prowled for food around the refugees and amongst the piles of litter were skeletal with starvation. All I could see in front of me was human misery like I had never seen before and only one thing was certain about the future of these refugees: they couldn't live long like this. The shelters already looked on the verge of collapse, with branches precariously tied to one another but the most striking thing was an overwhelming pungent stench of rotting litter and human waste.

The self proclaimed president of Katanga, Moise Tshombie, had recently been released from prison on the understanding that he re-unite Katanga with the rest of The Congo. He had originally been held for criticising The Congolese president Joseph Kasa-Vubu, but the promises he made whilst in prison were little more than hollow pledges now that he was released, as he continued to pull the strings that would bring about an independent Katanga. He was an expert at propaganda and referred to the refugee camps as bidonvilles, a term used throughout Africa for sub-standard shanty town housing and said that the independent Katangan government would continue to hunt down the rebel Baluba tribes people who were responsible for the tribal war but would continue to help the civilians by constructing more relief accommodation. We all knew, however, that it was his troops who were behind the slaughter and the village clearances, the major cause behind the influx of refugees.

The men in the truck around me had been silenced, we had been going too fast along the road to give the young mother any money for food but we were stifled by a tremendous feeling of guilt at not being able to do more. All of the hopeful progress of the new decade of the '60s in the western world: enlightenment, peace movements and civil rights meant nothing here, as people lived hour by hour by whatever means they could. Our joviality and novelty of being in such a distant foreign country suddenly vanished and we all now sat hushed in the truck embarrassed by our health and happiness against the reality of the refugees situation.

I pondered about all the stories I had heard at mass when I was a child about giving a penny for the poor black African babies and wished I had given more, rather than stuffing my face with Hennessy Balls and broken biscuits on Sunday evenings at the Picture House. But even the pennies I had donated had surely not reached any of these starving victims.

Within half an hour we had arrived at our billeted accommodation on the other side of the refugee camp which was a disused farm outbuilding that we called the Barn. There were no home comforts in the barn, but the refugee camp had taught us all how lucky we were, and none of us dared to complain against the backdrop of the stark and very real hardship of the native Congolese.

Whilst we were accepting of our billet accommodation, we heard that our officers had complained to more senior Irish UN commanders about the poor facilities we had been given. They apparently asked them why the Italians, Swedish, Nigerian UN troops and indeed 'B' and 'C' Companies of the 35th Battalion were being billeted in proper hotels and guest houses while we were provided an old farm out-building, with no facilities and an unstable roof that leaked when it rained. As a result, the officers of 'A' Company were moved to more comfortable guest houses but we remained in the barn although we heard that there were ongoing tensions and arguments between the officers about our continued accommodation which developed into broader disagreements about equipment and how the whole UN operation in The Congo was being handled.

None of the disputes between the officers in charge bothered us and we just made ourselves as comfortable as possible on the barn floor. We had one thin mattress called a hawket and were issued with five blankets. The nights were bitterly cold in stark contrast to the scorching hot days but unlike the refugees just a couple of miles or so up the road, we had food and clothing to keep us warm. One evening, Dowler told us that he had been speaking to some of the Swedish UN troops whose government had paid for excursions to the Victoria Falls in Northern Rhodesia on light-plane flights. They told him about the journey down to the falls following the Zambezi River to the border of Northern and Southern Rhodesia where a curtain of water a mile wide suddenly collapses over the cliffs providing huge plumes of water and permanent rainbows. Just the image I had pictured in my mind was sufficient for me to enjoy such a scene. There was so much beauty in Africa that I could only have dreamed of back in Ireland.

After our training exercises, we would generally stay in the barn where we were able to listen to radios that some, including myself, had bought back in Tripoli. We were able to receive the faint broadcast of the BBC World Service but we preferred the clearer music stations with English commentary from radio transmitters in southern Africa, notably Salisbury and Johannesburg. They played similar music to Radio Luxembourg and '208' back home, although the biggest star over here wasn't Elvis or Johnny Cash but instead was the lesser known Nashville sound of Gentleman Jim Reeves singing his latest hits *Four Walls* and *She'll Have a Go*. Reeves had made himself even more popular with the white community of southern Africa when he recorded some of his hits in Africaans. As a result, his face could be seen smiling on posters around Elizabethville, sharing alternate telegraph poles with the iconic leader of Katanga, Moise Tshombe.

Our first role as peacekeepers was taken up with guard duty down at the refugee camp, which involved protecting the makeshift entry gates to the shanty dwellings and securing the wire perimeters. We also rolled up our sleeves and took off our shirts to help the refugees clear up areas of ground or to tie branches together to make their shelters more secure. To avoid sunburn we would rub dirt over exposed skin, an effective insect repellent as well as sun-protection.

When we weren't down at the refugee camp we were continuing with training exercises, which had been widened to include close combat routines. Having already been assigned to the anti tank gun unit I also had to practice carrying the shells to Conway who in turn was practicing loading the gun for Dowler to launch.

'Ye should be good at carrying them shells,' mocked Dowler, 'I suppose all that practice ye had from working in the bar carryng beer barrels before ya joined the army is coming in useful now.'

It was all fairly jovial operating the anti-tank gun but as soon as Prendergast or our platoon sergeant John Monahan were close by, the joking immediately stopped, and all the exercises were completed silently and efficiently.

The workload of guard duty and military exercises kept us active way beyond standard Swahili time, as we started at about 0430 hours in the morning and worked through til about 2100 at night. Hegarty claimed he was exhausted and that he hadn't worked so hard since cleaning and washing duties back in the Athlone recruitment company. It may have been tiring but at the same time it was exhilarating, particularly being able to help the Congolese civilians trying to survive after the turmoil that had overtaken their lives. As soon as I lay down at night I would be asleep and I would often dream about the work in the refugee camp.

The native people always accepted our instructions without question by calling us 'Sir' or 'Bwana' which made me uneasy since it reminded me of the deferential relationship between master and slave society of Dixieland states that I had heard so much about in the preceding weeks.

'We are red legs ourselves,' I would say, pointing down at my reddened sunburnt legs. But they clearly didn't understand either my English or the link to slavery that Ireland had.

At the end of the day the refugees would be so grateful for our help that they shook and kissed our hands saying, 'merci bwana, merci merci!' as they bowed their heads and backed away from us with the reverence of a royal court serf.

'That's our pleasure,' we would say, vigorously shaking their hands and trying to pat them on the back just as we would have done had we helped someone back in Ireland. 'It's no problem at all.' But they cowered away from us as we tried to engage them in conversation, either because they couldn't understand our English or, more likely, they were too scared to talk freely to anyone who reminded them of the great white hunter.

The Baluba people did however have more confidence around other African nations' troops like those from Nigeria, Chad and Ghana, who were also keen to help their fellow Africans, with their skin colour being far more trustworthy than ours. Strangely, the UN troops from India were also treated with suspicion by the Baluba and we were told that like us, they too were considered to be 'bad ju-ju' as they were beyond the influence of the revered African medicine men.

Witch doctors or Mganga in Swahili used ju-ju spells or black magic as a medicine and a punishment to manage and influence local African people. We were shocked to hear how much belief the local people had in the power of ju-ju. At first I likened it to the stories back in Ireland of the gypsy curse or even the mythical tales of Leprechauns, fairies and the little people, which many seanchais recounted, but no-one believed. However, here in The Congo every tribal member believed absolutely in the power of ju-ju.

Pakie Monahan remarked that the boogie man and his ju-ju medicine are as respected in Africa as any medical doctor back home in Ireland and the only thing the Congolese fear more then the ju-ju man is loud noise. 'They don't even fear falling from heights,' Pakie noted, 'as all of us white fellas do.'

But many of these mysterious men of ju-ju magic now stood in front of us with seemingly nothing, having abandoned all their possessions to escape their burning villages.

The Tiger was obviously dreaming of life back home and commented that the black magic of the ju-ju man was very different to that old black magic called love that Frank Sinatra had just recorded for his latest album *Come Swing With Me,* the album that was the 'talk of Ireland' before we came out to The Congo. The black magic we were gradually learning more about down at the refugee camp was instead sinister, mind bending magic that held the people of a village hostage to anything that the ju-ju man or Mganga said, effectively hypnotising them to control their behaviour. Some used natural herb plants like curare or marijuana as a medicine or a drug. If a member of a village broke a community rule, the Mganga would cast them under one of their mysterious spells that could result in the wrongdoer developing body aches, fever, vomiting and choking. If the offence was serious enough, the ju-ju curse would not be lifted and they could go on to die from excruciating pain. The Baluba believed that non-Africans including the European and Indian UN troops were immune from the power of ju-ju, making them all powerful.

Like us, the Indian UN troops were thankful to be immune from black magic, such was its perceived influence in Africa but remained curious as to why they were distrusted by the Baluba when they were helping them in the refugee camp. We got on very well with the Indians, they understood the 'craic' and had grown up with the same British colonial influences and watching the same films. Their culture also seemed reverential, bowing their heads and greeting us with the salutation, 'Namaste' which was meant to summon the inner peace in those they welcomed. It was how I imagined Mahatma Ghandi acted towards others, except these soldiers didn't wear saris and sandals. After just a few days, it was as if we had known the Indians for years, Monahan making up jokes with them, and the Tiger asking them about their favourite Indian music and singers. Surprisingly they said that they liked Bob Dylan, who had been discovered just a year or so earlier as Robert Zimmerman singing in the hippy streets of Greenwich Village in New York. We had all heard his music on the radios and he had released an album, which Dowler likened to a whining cat that had been smoking too much pot. 'Civil rights' and 'flower power' were all the talk amongst the young people back in their native India and was becoming more popular with almost all of the young UN troops.

The Indian units had been drawn from regiments all over India. Some were very dark skinned, others much lighter; some wore turbans others even wore a crucifix. Despite their diversity we called them collectively 'the Hindus' but they called each other 'brother' as if they were all related. Their accents had rhythm and their happy faces shook in agreement in seeming contradiction of their intention whilst maintaining welcoming smiles and graciousness.

Apart from Ireland, there were also three other countries from Europe that supplied troops for the UN; Sweden, Norway and Italy. Sweden had probably supplied the most peacekeepers given their prominent position within the UN hierarchy most notably with Dag Hammarskjöld being Secretary General. They were also the best equipped of the overseas troops, not only in terms of uniforms and boots but also with useful hand tools like pen-knives, which they put to very good use helping to construct shelters in the camp.

The only troops who didn't join in with helping the refugees were those from Italy, who preferred to keep themselves to themselves, also choosing not to take part in the impromptu games of football or cricket with the Hindus. Instead, the standard Italian guard duty consisted of languishing around holding their tanned faces up to the warming sunshine; their eyes sleepily closed allowing them to remain oblivious to the miserable suffering of the new Baluba refugee arrivals. When the Italians did stir themselves it was only to light up a cigarette to take a laboured puff, then spitting out a jet of saliva onto the baking hot clay soil almost like they were living *La Dolce Vita* (The Sweet Life) sitting outside the Trevi Fountain in Rome, just as Federico Fellini himself would have directed. When they did roll up their sleeves or trousers it was only to cool themselves from the hot Congolese sunshine, revealing impractical soft leather ankle boots and gold identity bracelets.

Within the UN, it was an incredible mix of cultures and nationalities, young men thrown together and most trying to help the native people to survive. We were all frustrated that we couldn't stop the flow of refugees as the mercenary led tribal attacks continued unchallenged in the villages around us. Pakie Monahan described it as the work of the Salvation Army rather than a military army, but our UN mandate was only to protect the people and although we knew where the mercenary commando units were located we were not allowed to actively engage against any side by the UN General Assembly directives. Similarly, the mercenaries were deliberately carrying out their operations in areas that were not under UN protection, targeting villages that we were not able to defend. Additionally, our limited numbers could not stretch beyond protecting the major towns of Katanga, which could be hundreds of miles apart leaving most Baluba villages exposed and potential victims of the ongoing conflict. With the knowledge of such violence taking place in nearby villages many of us felt that the UN should launch some kind of military offensive although we knew this would drag the UN itself into the conflict. Our commanders repeatedly relayed information back through diplomatic circles that more resources were needed to avert a growing catastrophe, but the bureaucratic wheels of the UN general assembly would be too slow to help many of the refugees pouring into the camps who were already in imminent danger.

Many of us stored up our food rations to give to starving mothers and waiflike children down at the camp but after a while this too proved impossible as we would be surrounded by a huge begging crowd as soon as we entered the gates. Within a short time, all UN soldiers were banned from bringing their own rations to the refugees as the risk of a stampede became too high. Instead we were told to protect the food being supplied by the Red Cross, a daily delivery of just three milk churns to feed an ever growing mass of starving people. The food queues were sometimes up to a mile long, with each refugee receiving about three or four spoonfuls of maize per day.

The Red Cross told us that the best help we could give the local people was to spend our pay or 'per-diem' allowances in the local economy. A small flea market had formed on the edge of the camp where hawkers would lay out anything they could sell on a piece of old cardboard. I wanted to get some souvenirs for my mam, and saw two wood carved lions, which I presumed must be the famous black mained lions of Katanga that I had read so much about. I also picked up some salad spoons with intricate handles in the shape of elephants. We were advised when we first arrived that to get the best price we should barter with hawkers as they often doubled the asking price prior to the sale. I gestured to the desperately thin hawker pointing at the lions and salad spoons, mouthing 'how much?' The hawker indicated back to me, 'Five centimes' with an open palm – the price of just one packet of woodbines in Maggie Canavan's. I immediately paid without any further negotiation.

Once a week we were given a night's leave and often these would co-incide with the other different UN nationalities represented in The Congo. We would gather along with the Swedes, Indians and Nigerians around the shanty bars of southern Elizabethville, the main discussion being the terrible plight of the native people and how helpless we felt that the UN could not do more to stop the mercenary led village raids. There was also anger felt by many of the soldiers towards the white population of Elizabethville who were doing nothing to help and were in many ways complicit with the growing crisis. They were supportive of the mercenaries even though the refugee camp continued to grow and the stories of inhumanity and brutality during village raids were becoming more regular and frightening.

We stood outside the bars balancing our drinks on old oil drums, drinking Simba [lion] beer, named after the Northern Congolese tribe, which would arrive in wine-like bottles with long necks. The Italians, who were probably more accustomed to drinking fine Piedmont vintages, would order one bottle of beer between four of them, then sip the beer from water glasses. It wasn't that they didn't have enough money but seemingly they would prefer to spend their allowance on clothes or other pleasures, and were often seen looking to negotiate the lowest possible price with the passing shakiras, then surreptitiously slipping away behind the wafting sheets of the nearby bordellos. Like all the other nationalities representing the UN, the Italians had been issued with condoms from their ordnance divisions but the

Irish, we joked, had only been issued with 'the guilt' which prevented any negotiation with the shakiras for us. However, it didn't stop Monahan from mischievously giving them the wink to approach our table, then directing them to chat with one of us.

'Ahh, Father Curran wouldn't approve of that sort of thing,' was my only excuse as my face went nearly as red as the Hennessy-Ball red lipstick that the young ladies had smudged over their aubergine like lips. Despite all of our reluctance they became more persistent and obvious in their suggestions,

'Vous fucky moi?' they suggested with evocative eyes gazing intently at us, whilst rubbing their hands ever further up our legs.

In the end, we would give them a small amount of money just to leave us alone which seemed to keep them happy, before they moved off in search of more willing customers.

'For fuck sake!' Dowler said almost exasperated to Monahan, 'will ya quit telling them floozie-girls to come over to us, I thought they would never leave us alone, they're worse than my owld dog at home the way they wont stop going after yer bollocks.'

'Well we were told to spend our money in the local community Sean,' I reminded him sarcastically whilst enjoying his discomfort, 'and yer not spending it on beer!'

'Well I'm saving up for a new pair of winklepickers then!' he retorted, 'or I'll give some money to that fella whose selling a few eejits an old pair of wooden lions; just as long as them floozies leave me alone.'

'You just wait and see Sean,' I responded, 'one day them wooden carved lions from Katanga will be worth something.'

'Aye, they'll be worth feck all, or they'll just sit on yer mantelpiece getting woodworm' noted Dowler as he began to relax again after the shakiras were out of sight. By the end of the night, the atmosphere was back to normal, the Tiger would have us all singing again, even encouraging the Swedes and the Indians to sing along with his version of *The Old Bog Road*.

Despite the harrowing and endless work of helping more and more refugees, we had achieved much in our first few weeks in The Congo. Being in 'A' Company, we had also been extensively drilled in combat techniques and defensive strategies and it felt good to get up early in the morning for inspection with the African sun breaking through the trees while listening to the chorus of chatter from the forest animals and birds that made their homes around the Barn. After three weeks in The Congo I wrote a letter home.

Dear Mam and Dad

I hope this letter finds you well. I am well too and everything is grand here in The Congo. It can get a bit hot during the day, tell Kevin and Franco that the weather is biblical and I am getting a great sun-tan. When I come home, ye'll all think I am one of them fellas in the rat-pack!

It's mostly quiet here apart from the birds singing in the trees and we say mass every day.

I knew that my mother would be worried if she thought I wasn't saying my prayers.

I was doing some police duty a few days ago, patrolling near the jungle and I saw a toucon bird, with it's long golden beak and colourful neck. It looked exactly like the one in the Guinness advert saying: 'Lovely Day For A Guinness!'

The sun is always shining here but I often have to stand underneath a tree or next to a bush or else I go as red as a tomato, like I did when we had a game of football in Malta. All the fellas in the battalion are good craic, we watch lots of films at the outdoor cinemoi surrounded by all the bushes and with only the sky as cover. At night, it's as dark as the Picture House in Edgeworthstown with just the stars shining down on us, so every film seems like an epic.

We also listen to the Southern African music channels which are in English and we are able to tune into the Gaelic football commentary from some Irish fella who operates a transmitter in Brazzaville, just over the border. It looks as if it will be between Offaly and Kerry for the football, they seem to have the best teams; so we will all be cheering on Offaly in the All-Ireland later this year.

The white people here have huge houses and many have cars including Citroen DS's and Cadillacs. The money they make must be incredible. However, the black people have very little, sometimes not even enough food even athough they do all the work – it reminds me of my old job back in Edgeworthstown! We're hoping the Belgians will leave them alone soon, so their lives can get back to normal.

Thank you for your letter which I received a few days ago and please thank Kitty for hers also.

Say hello to all from me here in the sunny Congo

Good bye and god bless

Micky

My letters home were deliberately upbeat especially as I knew that my mother and The County would certainly have been reading about the atrocities taking place. I wanted my mother to think I was having a great time and enjoying myself to prevent her worrying, so I deliberately avoided any details of the conditions in the refugee camp and I understated the gulf in lifestyles between the white Belgians and the black natives. She would have been very troubled to read that the colour of skin was such a major determinant of whether a person lived well or died hungry in The Congo.

It was known amongst us as the 'colour bar' and everywhere we went in Katanga it was the defining feature determining the level of health, education, social class, standard of living and human value. If you were white in The Congo, you were born in a hospital, were well educated and were probably rewarded with a good job. But if you were black, you never went into a hospital, were provided nothing in the way of formal education and had little or no job prospects. Even the cemeteries were segregated by the colour bar, with rows of neatly maintained gravestones kept solely for the memory of the white community, the overgrown plots assigned to the blacks kept behind railings on the other side of the Christian mission.

All of colonial Africa was characterised by this gulf in human worth and many areas had imposed segregation of the races as a way to keep the 'black species' from 'spoiling' the lives of whites. All of the European colonialists, the British, French, Dutch and Portuguese used skin colour as an assessment of human worth and regarded the role of the black man as subservient and therefore inferior to whites. 'It was God's will,' many colonialists claimed on radio talk shows we tuned into that were transmitted from Salisbury in Northern Rhodesia, 'to separate the species, just as in nature the jungle herds of wild animals kept to the same species.'

Those of mixed race in The Congo were still labelled with their slave designations as mestees or mullattoes, as the cross-bred Irish red-legs had been called. There were reportedly about 12,000 such people of mixed race in The Congo who were grouped by colour, under the colonial classification system, to be from neither the black nor the white community, so would not be welcomed into the tribal cultures and barred from being part of white Africa.

It was this legacy of the slave trade and the racial classification systems so reminiscent of Nazi Germany that the world community, led by the non-aligned countries, was seeking to redress.

To avoid further criticism at the UN, Belgium claimed that they didn't have formal apartheid policies in The Congo and hypocritically spoke out against South Africa. But everywhere we went the 'colour bar' was very apparent and it didn't seem a co-incidence that all the houses, cars, businesses and indeed anything of any value were owned by the whites. Belgium's policies towards the native Congolese prior to independence had prevented any non-white from their own pursuit of happiness, and most whites it seemed wanted the racial policy to continue, albeit discreetly.

As a result, a year after independence the Belgium government in Brussels was still trying to pull the strings of power in The Congo for the benefit of the Belgian people, their mining companies and the prosperity of their ex-pat white community by supporting the annexation of Katanga. This would keep the institutions and restrictions of the old colonial regime in place. The colonial administrators argued that they had introduced 'civil merit cards' in the '50s to reward certain blacks who would then be granted the same civil rights as whites. These were normally awarded in return for loyalty and assistance to the mining industry, although in practice very few cards were ever awarded. The ones that did get awarded such a card were treated as black men in white skin, a few promoted to senior positions to maintain the infrastructure of white Africa which at the same time enabled Belgium to claim that blacks had the same rights as whites. As a result, the tax revenue would continue to flood into the Brussels chancellery coffers. It was clear to us that it was surely just another re-hashed version of Leopolds's exploitation imposed on the native Congolese, the only difference being that this was being imposed militarily by mercenary led commando units.

One day Dowler, the Tiger, Monahan and I took a walk around central Elizabethville and we remarked on how the only black people we saw mingling amongst the white community were dogsbody shop-assistants or servants. We passed a Kafee Huisje (coffee shop) called Henri's with a cartoon-like picture of le chef, a portly moustachioed cook, complete with floppy white hat, obviously a Belgian ex-pat business whose proprietor, Henri, must have been Flemish.

Back in Belgium we were told that all signs had to display the two national languages, Flemish and French reflecting the antagonism of the two major cultures, the Flemings and Walloons. The directive had been continued in The Congo. As I looked at the 'SnaakKart' [menu] I couldn't make out either French or Flemish menu options, but especially the Flemish, with all the 'J's and 'K's making the words almost impossible to pronounce.

In the end we all chose the only thing that sounded vaguely familiar 'Kase and Tomaatjes op bruin brood' which we hoped was a cheese and tomato sandwich.

Behind the till, I noticed an old photograph of a young man wearing safari clothes standing proudly with one leg resting victoriously upon a slain rhino, holding aloft his prize of a bleeding tusk while his rifle hung loosely by his side from a shoulder strap. I joked first of all that it must be a picture of TinTin in The Congo although it was obvious that it was a picture of the proprietor Henri, showing his customers what a fine big-game hunter he had been in his youth, just as The County back home liked to show us photos from his great footballing days.

Above the photograph of Henri was however something far more sinister, a neatly folded whip, that looked rugged and sharpened. I knew immediately that this was a chicotte, the dreaded weapon of Leopold's era used to inflict terrible suffering during what, I learned, the Congolese called the 'lokali', [the overwhelming]. 50 years after Leopold's rule officially ended, the chicotte remained the most potent symbol of white resistance to self determination and continued white domination. I immediately looked around the café, and sure enough there was not a black customer in sight. More worrying for us however, there was a table of mercenaries who were eyeing us suspiciously, dressed in their typical attire of safari clothes and voeldskins not dissimilar to those worn by Henri in the photograph.

As the cheese and tomato sandwiches were delivered from the kitchen, Dowler left a few centimes on the counter, and we sat down at another of the cafe tables. I could tell the atmosphere was threatening just by the bolting stares being aimed at us from the mercenaries on the other side of the room.

'We'll just eat our sandwiches and leave quietly,' noted Dowler as he too became aware that we had chosen the wrong restaurant.

The mercenaries all had weathered dark ruddy skin and deep-set wrinkles from overexposure to Africa's burning sun, their hungover-bloodshot eyes twitching with resentment. I thought for a moment that one caught me looking at him so I quickly averted my gaze back down to my sandwich.

For a minute or so they continued to talk amongst themselves, gesturing over at our table, the corners of their mouths curling up in agitated anticipation of a possible confrontation. Then one of them started humming a song. I didn't recognise it at the time but it was the Belgian national anthem, *Le Brabançonne*:

> Ô Belgique, ô mère chérie,
> À toi nos cœurs, à toi nos bras,
> À toi notre sang, ô Patrie !
> Nous le jurons tous, tu vivras !

Then all four mercenaries joined in the final three lines chanting and thumping their beers down on the table:

> Le Roi! la Loi! la Liberté ! [The King! The Law! The Liberty!]
> Le Roi! la Loi! la Liberté !
> Le Roi! la Loi! la Liberté !

The rest of the restaurant went silent, as a fight seemed imminent.

'Hey you,' one of them started to beckon towards our table in a stumbling European accent, 'ist you UNOC?'

Although I was the closest, I said nothing, pretending I didn't hear him.

'Yes ONUC,' answered Dowler after a pause.

'And Irlandais?' continued the mercenary.

'Oui, yes Ireland,' Dowler confirmed, clearly keeping his answers short and not engaging their conversation.

The other people in the restaurant remained hushed, except to inch their bags further under their own tables.

'C'mon lads, let's go,' said Dowler calmly, 'these broods taste funny.'

We all stood up firmly from our chairs, which must have made the mercs think we were readying for trouble and they too immediately stood up pulling their chairs out of the way.

'Just walk out lads' instructed Dowler, 'we might land a couple of slaps but they'll be nothing like the thumps we'll get from Prendergast if he finds out we've been brawling with these drunken eejits.'

We then headed for the café exit although the route out unavoidably took us past the mercenaries' table. As I walked within a couple of feet of the puffed out chests of the four mercenaries I noticed the pungent smell of body sweat mixed with stale beer. The four mercenaries could well have been drinking all night for all I knew as none of them had shaved or seemingly washed in days, and their eyes looked more reddened and glazed the closer we were. But they were all huge men, at least a foot taller than me, with club like fists already clenched in anticipation of a brawl.

For four long seconds until we reached the door there was not a sound in the restaurant but as soon as we emerged outside Henri's, the Tiger noted sarcastically:

'Lads, I think they only wanted us to join them in a sing-song.' But we were in no doubt that we nor anyone in the UN, were welcome amongst the mercenaries or indeed amongst the white Belgian community of Elizabethville. It was clear that we too were part of the segregation policy of colonial Africa because the UN was perceived to be defending the interests of black people.

Given the incident at Henri's we were quite happy to be considered alongside the black community as victims of segregation and we felt more comfortable remaining in the shabbier shops and bars in the south of Elizabethville which the teetotal Dowler wryly remarked 'sold better beer anyway.'

Even before we came out to The Congo, we were familiar with stories about the segregation of black and white people in southern Africa and the southern states of America, but it was the first time we had witnessed segregation in practice. The civil rights movement led by Martin Luther King was gaining momentum all over the world but when we listened to the radio during the evenings back in the barn, the headline at the top of every news hour was always about Southern Africa's anti-apartheid demonstrations which they said, were inspired by communists.

'Were better off dead than red!' many broadcasts claimed, using the 1950s McCarthyist propaganda to inspire the white population to rise up to protect their livelihoods. If that meant apartheid then so be it but communism had to be stopped at all costs. The demonstrations by blacks had resulted in violence in Rhodesia and South Africa and we heard reports about a mass strike that had taken place in South Africa organised by the illegal ANC party, a sister party to the ANC parties of The Congo and Rhodesia. The strike was supported by all of the ANC bodies, but this was a civil action that threatened the whole South African economy. In response, pro-white journalists continued to claim that the ANC freedom charter that had been distributed in South Africa, Rhodesia and The Congo was a communist document and that the government would take urgent action to stop communists from taking power.

With immediate effect, we heard that Vorwoerd's government demanded the arrest of the leader of the South African ANC, a 44 year old lawyer by the name of Nelson Rolihlahla Mandela, who we were told had gone on the run. On the radio, he became known as the black pimpernel, the name conjuring up in my mind images of the 1930s classic movie *The Scarlett Pimpernel* with Leslie Howard dressing up in various disguises to avoid capture whilst roaming the back-alleys of Paris during the French revolution. The journalist reporting from Johannesburg even used quotes from the film like 'one to command, and nineteen to obey' as if Mandela were manipulating the people with anti-white communist dogma.

However, the propaganda of the ruling whites was widely distributed around southern Africa including The Congo claiming that it was their white forefathers who had established profitable businesses and trade with Europe and America; and that the present white population should be allowed to inherit such businesses from their ancestors. The native people of central and southern Africa were broadcast as lazy, incompetent and corrupt, and the ANC's Freedom charter they argued, was just the African asking for too much, especially as they had already offered them free black homelands or Bantustans.

Rhodesia's ANC political party was lead by Joshua Nkomo, which had similarly been banned two years earlier in 1959 having declared that they wanted to reclaim half a million homes that had been confiscated and designated as white areas in the last 30 years. Their only policy was to give back houses and property to their rightful black owners. Northern Rhodesia was governed as a protectorate of Britain, and its leader Sir Roy Wellensky also dismissed the ANC's demands.

Compounding the likelihood of a military confrontation, Wellensky supported the annexation of Katanga and sent Rhodesian troops to the border offering military support to Katanga's independence leaders, thus thwarting The Congolese ANC's attempt to restore African rule.

Because the governments of Southern Africa didn't want people to 'misinterpret' the policies, the ANC's Freedom Charter was outlawed, no-one was allowed to print or even read it. But on Radio Brazzaville they were free to read and broadcast whatever they liked and we were told that the ANC in The Congo and in Southern Africa had chartered that all citizens should have the right to vote, to hold office and to be equal before the law. This all seemed perfectly fair to us and indeed sounded very much like Ireland's own proclamation of Independence. After Cuba, I had been led to assume that communist policy was about nationalising churches and outlawing gambling, but this made us think again that perhaps we were not being given the full picture from western governments and bias press coverage. At the time however, it was easy to become implicated in the Cold War rhetoric of witch-hunts and traitors and we were constantly hearing about the enemy i.e. Russian backed insurgent communists [i.e. ANC Lumumbaists] massing on Katanga's northern border. So like everyone else I said nothing, after all we were just supposed to be non-alligned, peace-keeping soldiers and none of us wanted to be labelled a communist sympathiser.

However, the same Irish journalist who transmitted the Gaelic football from the pirate radio station in Brazzaville had no such inhibitions after he had been given a copy of the ANC Freedom charter and had summarised its beliefs in his evening segment. He said that if the document's core demands were communist, of 'men and women of all races shall receive equal pay for equal work, receive living wages and shorter hours' and 'the right to speak, organise, meet together, publish, preach, worship and educate their children freely irrespective of colour, race or nationality'* then he too would be moving to Moscow on the next flight out of Africa.

Certainly, anyone who had seen the suffering we had witnessed in the refugee camp would have been inclined to believe that the west was just a propaganda machine and that communism was the fairest answer for The Congolese. The western press, it seemed, were acting like Orwell's ministry of truth controlling people's mind with falsehoods that would allow the west to perpetuate the gross injustice of white power and native servitude.

But this wasn't a war that was solely concerned with differing political ideals, with politicians, like they did back in Ireland, making grand speeches about education and health policy. The only policy that seemed to matter here in The Congo was who would own the country's vast mineral wealth.

The next national election date for The Congo was set for the beginning of August, in just one month's time and it was clear from posters and radio interviews that Leopold's exploitation of the country's assets had only scratched the surface of its potential treasures. Not only did its geological scandal of riches provide a limitless supply of diamonds, copper, gold and uranium, but there were also topographical riches that were greater than anywhere else in the world.

The most talked about capital investment was the future of the Inga project, a hydroelectric resource that harnessed the power of The Congo River at the

---

* Adopted at the Congress of the People, Kliptown, on 26 June 1955.

coastal port of Matadi, which could potentially provide enough electricity to power all of Europe. To bolster his own ambitions, Tshombie claimed that that the project depended on the success of the Katanga succession movement with him as its president. Ominously he threatened that should the pro-communists gain control over Katanga, then his forces would need to blow up the dam and sabotage the infrastructure of the mines, leaving only a scorched earth for the Marxists to take over. This was the only way he claimed that he could protect the people of Katanga from the ravages of communism.

Within Ireland there had also been a general election, and Sean Lemass remained the Taoiseach, keeping his key lieutenants Sean MacEntee and Frank Aiken within the cabinet. We were told that they re-iterated the strongest support for the Irish troops in The Congo adding that they were encouraged by the positive developments towards peace that had recently been witnessed. To us, these comments seemed completely out of touch with reality, the situation in The Congo was clearly deteriorating, with more and more mercenaries flooding into the country and the rhetoric from all sides escalating with threats of an all out war.

With elections looming and many Congolese cities facing intimidation from political enforcers, tensions began to rise throughout The Congo and our duties became more urgent. It was as if every day brought a new crisis; more refugees, a more brutal village clearing, killings, rapes or burnings all whipped up from the baying pro-white media both within The Congo and back in Europe. We could also see the turmoil for ourselves as we helped carry innocent children, often just orphaned, to any spare space in the refugee camp. More worryingly the violence was beginning to gain a brutality that had previously been the preserve of the Leopold era, with dismembered body parts being piled up on village borders demarking areas where one tribe had slaughtered another. The refugee camp had become such a sprawl, and it was becoming impossible to guard its entire perimeter, which resulted in small gangs of armed men making raids on the camp itself. The most notorious was a gang of three boy soldiers known as the butcher, the baker and the candlestick maker who had become infamous in village clearances for their torture techniques which included hacking and burning off body parts, then setting light to their victims using paraffin oil. The same gang was now conducting night time raids around the periphery of the refugee camp. They wielded axes, knives and bicycle chains indiscriminately, slaughtering anyone, including babies, who stood in their way. The first thing we would know about it would be from the bellowing cries that spread through the camp like a set of dominoes but with the resonance of a banshee-like shriek. By the time we arrived at the scene, the butcher, baker and candlestick maker had made their getaway, leaving behind them a massacre of hacked and burned bodies. The ruinous raid may have only taken a minute or so to complete, but picking up the body parts and burying the dead took us hours: a foot, a baby's hand or the shocked stare of a dead young girl probably wondering what she had done to deserve this with her last breath. The memory of such an atrocious scene would take a lifetime to forget. Although we didn't know it at the time, it was the same butcher, baker and candlestick maker gang that met such a grisly end, down at the Elizabethville PO building when we were imprisioned.

Rape was also being used as a weapon of this war with local village women held and raped repeatedly until they became pregnant by enemy tribesmen, then sent back to their men-folk. Any women already pregnant had their stomachs cut open and their wombs shot out, which for any survivors would mean they would be incapable of reproduction in the future. It was physical and mental torture that was intended to destroy communities.

People in the white community of Elizabethville were determined that their lives would not be affected by the overflowing refugee camp and the stories of atrocities taking place, so they constructed barricades on the main boulevard to the south of the town. It was just like I had seen on the television during the Algerian 'barricades week' with white civilians and mercenaries manning the cordon, armed with rifles and chicottes. Their objective was simple: no-one from the UN or with black skin was to be allowed into the town.

As a result, the UN immediately formed an offensive to take control of the Post Office and other communication buildings in Elizabethville and a siege mentality soon overtook the town. We called this the beginning of the 'phoney war' or, as Monahan translated it for us into French, 'le drolle de Guerre' with no shots actually being exchanged but the rhetoric being used, a sure sign that trouble lay ahead.

With the escalating crisis developing in Katanga, Dag Hammarskjöld dispatched his own special envoy to oversee the increased peace-keeping operations. It was none other than Connor Cruise O'Brien, about whom The County had told me so much in the preceding years as a representative of Irish foreign policy. Immediately on hearing about his appointment we discussed amongst ourselves that this would be a great help for the people in the refugee camp, but would likely antagonise 'white Africa' given that O'Brien was such a prominent proponent of self determination and ending apartheid. He was also viewed with suspicion by the US as his other notable policy was to support China's admission to the UN at a time when Washington was gripped by the McCarthyist anti-communist witch-hunts.

The UNOC force was immediately shaken up on O'Brien's arrival, although we continued to hear about disagreements amongst our senior officers. The 'A' Company that I was part of had been assigned together on training and operations since we arrived in The Congo but would now be split up to cover different deployments. Myself, Dowler, The Tiger, Conway and Monahan were all being sent to Leopoldville to guard the main election locations, with most of the rest of 'A' Company including Hegarty and Sweeney being re-assigned to different roles around Elizabethville. The officers in charge of 'A' Company were understandably furious that their company was being split up and we viewed it as another deliberate put-down for 'A' Company by Irish UNOC commanders.

We began to regard the Irish UN command structure in Elizabethville as more akin to something we had read in *Lord of the Flies* by William Golding; of an isolated community where malevolent human characteristics become very apparent. The officers in charge in Elizabethville may have been wearing UN uniforms rather than Choirboy outfits, but it was clear that they did not get on with the officers in charge of 'A' Company. Monahan even mimicked an angry debate in the officer's mess saying 'I ought to be chief because I'm chorister and head boy. I can sing C sharp."

Unusually however, all the men in 'A' Company supported the officers directly in charge of us as they treated us like professional soldiers rather than their servants and they were prepared to train as hard as us rather than just bellowing out orders. Our drills and excercises were harder than those completed by 'B' and 'C' companies but they gradually became easier and we regarded them as fair and professional. Additionally there were no petty power struggles so prevalent back in Athlone, especially when we were in the recruitment company. Hegarty even took the drills seriously, marching in line and most notably, no deliberate farting.

So when Prendergast told us we were flying to Leopoldville the next day, 1 August 1960, for a four day assignment until the election was over, we immediately packed our kit-bags without complaint. Unlike Elizabethville, Leopoldville seemed calm although everyone was very aware of the trouble that was unfolding back in Katanga. We were not required for guard duty as we had expected, instead we were required for cooking and cleaning around the university, which would no doubt incense the officers of 'A' Company still further. The university was the venue of the parliamentary election that sought to bring the rulers of The Congo's six provinces together to support a federal leader. Two of the three main adversaries: Moise Tshombie from Katanga and Antoine Gizenga, the pro-communist leader from Kasai, did not attend which many claimed made the election result worthless. It was another election that was lost even before the first vote was cast, carved up and gerrymandered among the demarcations of its colonial predecessor. It would mean nothing to the native tribes except that they could expect to be subjugated by a new set of rulers. As Monahan pointed out:

'It is the same trough that they feed from, only different pigs.'

The ballot papers were even written in Flemish and French, way beyond the comprehension of 80 per cent of the native inhabitants. Just like the agreements signed in fingerprints 80 years beforehand by the original tribal leaders when approached by Henry Morton Stanley, the documents only meant something to avaricious Europeans intent on retaining money and power.

Nevertheless, a new prime minister for The Congo, Cyrille Adoula was elected with the hope of bringing stability to the central government in Leopoldville. He was immediately undermined by Tshombie and Gizenga, however, who publically announced that they didn't accept the result, with Tshombie continuing to threaten a scorched earth policy if his Katanga independence party were not given more power.

The sabre rattling was however not confined to the Congolese politicians as the Cold War adversaries sensed something very significant to be at stake. With Tshombie refusing to accept the election result, the Russian foreign minister: Kusnetsov, suddenly compounded the tension by attacking the intentions of Belgium and accusing the UN of being a cover for the continued presence of Belgian forces. He then demanded that the UN be withdrawn if they were not prepared to use force to bring about the end of the Katanga succession.

We returned to Elizabethville a day early amid the growing furore and were assigned to guard Connor Cruise O'Brien's villa given the increased scrutiny he was under. It seemed to us that he and the UN were being placed in an impossible position, some wanted military intervention, but others didn't want the UN to interfere in the rule of law. But one thing was certain; everyone was using and blaming the UN for personal gain.

O'Brien's villa was called 'Les Roches' and was situated in the affluent north of Elizabethville. It was the largest and grandest house in the area, nestled amongst the whitewashed walls and wrought iron balconies of the town's white community. It was more like something out of The Great Gatsby and all the more astonishing given that it was just a few miles from the horror of the refugee camp. Les Roches was a cocoon of tranquillity in the middle of a war zone and I walked around the villa imagining the fine ladies and gentlemen sitting out on the cool shaded verandah sipping afternoon tea from a swinging garden chair. The whole villa was immaculate; a dining room with 14 place settings, four poster beds with velvet curtains and fine candelabra adorning every room. Eight UN soldiers were assigned to guard the UN special envoy and each morning there was a press briefing held in the dining room with restless journalists eager to hear the latest scoop from O'Brien himself.

In the briefings, I stood guard at the doorway, smiling to myself that little me: the Great Imposter himself had now managed to work in the same room as world statesmen and journalists from all over the world. I would hear first hand about the stories that would only be circulated around the world the next day and I thought about The County reading about these very same reports in the Irish Independent the following morning.

Amid the dazzle of flashing camera lenses, I heard O'Brien describe the complexity of the situation, explaining that Belgium had to relinquish control of Katanga and not try to form a state within a state. He was not the cool, calm politician I had expected, rather he sounded almost desperate for the press to report accurately as the dangers of The Congo were so acute. He pleaded with the assembled journalists to report that the other colonial powers had to stop covertly supporting the principal of white power for their own financial gain and that the UN could only maintain peace if there was co-operation from neighbouring countries. He also openly criticised Sir Roy Wellensky of Northern Rhodesia for exacerbating the problem by offering military assistance, which in turn was causing increasing antagonism in the Cold War.

But O'Brien's explanations were fruitless, the press preferring to report on the inconvenience being caused to innocent white ex-pat Belgians and the UN not doing enough to support them. When the briefing was over, I discussed with Dowler and Sweeney how the journalists' faces looked utterly shocked when they were told about a crime involving white civilians but only showed polite contrition when the murders of black refugees was described to them, simply jotting down a few bullet points through feigned sad-looking eyes. The reality of the way the media treated tragedies that affected the local Congolese was, as I described it to Dowler and Pakie Monahan that lunchtime, appalling.

'They really just couldn't give a shit about the lives of black fellas,' I noted, 'but if a white fella's car is stolen, they want to call in the army.'

Both Monahan and Dowler nodded in agreement.

In the afternoons, O'Brien would attend meetings in and around Elizabethville with opposing politicians and UN commanders as the situation continued to worsen. When he was away, we would guard the villa throughout the day as the UN was concerned that the mercenaries or the local white population may seek retribution on the special envoy. Sweeney and I guarded the front door, while Dowler and Monahan guarded the rear with the remainder of the UN patrol assigned around

Sean Dowler and P. J. Sweeney, by the swimming pool at Les Roches villa. Picture courtesy of Phillip Sweeney

the perimeter wall of the Les Roches grounds. It was boiling hot and a million miles away from the turmoil of war, refugee camps and atrocities and I was speaking to Sweeney about the brutality in the refugee camp, greedy corporations like the UMHK and racial segregation.

Suddenly our attention was distracted:

'C'mon PJ! C'mon Michael,' came a roar from the rear patio, 'it's time for a swim!'

'What!' I exclaimed to Sweeney, 'feckin hell, ya won't believe they're going for a swim in his pool!' There was nobody else at home except for a cook and two garden boys who wouldn't have said anything but suddenly all I could see was the bare white arses of Dowler and Monahan scampering towards the pool before a splash; they had dived in.

'Oh Jaysus,' I said to Sweeney. 'We'll surely end up in the shit for this.'

'Well if we're gonna end up in the shit,' he replied, 'we might as well enjoy it!'

The next moment, both Sweeny and I were running towards the pool trying to take off our boots at the same time, before our bare arses had joined the others, mine by diving and Sweeney by hunching his knees to his chest and bombing.

'Yee hah!' I roared as I propelled myself into the air like a rodeo cowboy who had just tamed the bucking bronco before crashing down into the cool water.

We splashed around like puppies in a bath just like when I was a kid with Kevin, Franco and the Dolly, swimming in the river Shannon up near Roosky in Co. Roscommon.

Although I had read so much about war back in Athlone, and knew that each one was different, this one surely had to be the most bizarre. One minute we were encountering unimaginable scenes of brutality, the next we were living the high life as security guards in a grand colonial swimming pool.

Our enjoyment was, however, short lived as our platoon sergeant John Monahan arrived unexpectedly back at the villa. He was fuming.

'It was hot sir,' Dowler answered in his typically minimalist manner, as four of us stood there holding a bundle of clothes out in front of us.

'What kind of feckin excuse is that?!' demanded Monahan,'what has feckin 'hot' got to do with it?!'

'We're not used to the strong sun and we felt faint sir.' Dowler again responded with the only plausible answer we had.

I knew from our duties back in Athlone that it was best for me to say nothing and that Dowler was a master at limited but effective answers.

'Well why didn't yiz have a drink?' quizzed an increasingly irate Monahan.

'There were no drinks available sir!' Dowler immediately replied with his head held high.

We all knew that we could have had water at any time but this was no time to start elaborating on Dowler's replies which seemed to be working.

'Well next time yer on guard duty, make sure ye have enough water with ye!' ordered Monahan, 'O'Brien will now want his feckin pool cleaned, he'll think one of yiz will have pissed in it or something! Yiz feckin didn't piss in his pool did yiz?'

'No Sir,' said Dowler commandingly, 'just needed to cool down Sir.'

'OK, get back to your posts,' finished Monahan. 'But don't feckin do it again, d'yiz hear?'

'Yes Sir!' we all responded together and headed straight back to our guard duties.

As expected, O'Brien did demand that his pool was cleaned, but he made no more fuss about it probably because he had much greater things on his mind. Not only was the situation becoming more unstable around Elizabethville but he was about to be targeted personally by the anti-UN press.

Whilst we were guarding Les Roches, we noticed that O'Brien also had an assistant who took minutes at his press briefings whose name was Maire McEntee. She was the daughter of the high profile Irish Finance Minister Sean McEntee. We assumed that she was just part of the foreign diplomatic service as she spoke to O'Brien in Gaelic and was in Katanga only to assist a UN special representative, but it turned out there was more to the relationship. O'Brien was a married man, but the following day he was reported in the press as having an affair with Miss McEntee. For the eager journalists who had been reluctant to report on the atrocities being carried out by local whites and mercenaries they now had the diversion they were looking for: a salacious sex scandal. They took their opportunity with gusto, a scapegoat revelation that would be welcomed by their editors back in Europe, conveniently diverting attention away from complicit European politicians and corporations.

It was the biggest scandal since Eddie Fisher ran off with Liz Taylor the previous year, subsequently divorcing America's sweetheart Debbie Reynolds. This coverage of the UN special representative had a more sinister intention. If the newspapers managed to damage O'Brien's image, then the entire UNOC force would be undermined. We spoke about the similarities to what happened to Roger Casement when he set about ending the atrocities of the Leopold era. The newspapers eventually found a reason to challenge his authority, in Casement's case the government releasing extracts of his black diaries that listed his homosexual tendencies convincing the public of his moral wrongdoings. Given that Miss McEntee had such a high profile father, the papers now focused on the immorality within Irish political and diplomatic circles which meant that the unfolding humanitarian crisis in the province of Katanga was no longer creating the headlines.

Immediately O'Brien stated that he intended to marry Miss MacEntee, which he announced to the gathered press at Les Roches the following morning. As I again stood guarding the doorway of the press room, I heard him plead with the journalists to report on the effect that the former colonial governments' actions, including those of Britain, France and Begium, were having, saying that their covert support of Katangan independence was having a disastrous impact on the lives of ordinary and innocent Congolese.

'This is very important for ye to report this now,' O'Brien pleaded with the assembled journalists. 'If the attacks from the mercenary led commando units do not end, and Katanga refuse to give up their succession then he would have no choice but to recommend a military intervention by the UN.' It was clearly an important statement from a diplomat under pressure from all sides in the conflict. He explained that the mercenary forces had to leave Katanga immediately or the UN would be forced to expel them, although he conceded that the UN would only intervene as a last resort as there would be undoubted military resistance from the Katangan gendarmerie, civilian white militia and collaborating tribes. But he continued to explain very clearly:

'If the UN continued to resist intervention then the risk of Nationalists or Communists invasion was too high.'

The following day we could hardly believe it when we read the colonial backed newspapers. They portrayed a situation that O'Brien, in the midst of his marital difficulties caused by his own adultery, was preparing to use unauthorised force to expel mercenaries and stop Katanga's independence putting the lives of innocent whites at risk. The lives of black people meant nothing to the journalists and although 200 people had been massacred the previous day,* as reported in the Irish Independent, the British, French and Belgian press didn't mention it. Even the outright slaughter of native people was treated more as an inconvenience rather than something newsworthy of their white readership.

The press was completely managing to counter any decisions made by O'Brien and as a result of his

---

* Headline in the Irish Independent, 2 August 1961: '200 massacred in Congo'

diminished authority, had managed to undermine the whole UN operation in The Congo. Securing peace was a secondary consideration as a political sex scandal was bound to sell more newspapers than the reality of tyranny and white rule. From that moment on we knew we had lost the propoganda war and even back home in dear old Ireland, doubts were beginning to emerge.

The French and British governments in particular questioned O'Brien's role as they sought to protect their dependent African territories from the UN policy of self-determination and the unravelling of their empires. We assumed that they were still humiliated by the Suez crisis of 1956 as Harold MacMillan launched a verbal attack on O'Brien. In response to his own question: 'who is Conor Cruise O'Brien?' MacMillan answered that he was 'an unimportant, expendable man.'

The American administration was supportive of the UN, however, as long as the ANC parties and communism did not gain a foothold in the country, but they stopped short of criticising the white rule policies of southern Africa given that they still had their own difficulties with civil rights movements back home and because white Africa was allied to the 'free world'.

The only vocal support that O'Brien and the UN received was from other African states who had achieved their own self determined governments. Kwame Nkrumah was the most high profile advocate of O'Brien when he issued his 'I speak of freedom' speech. The 'showboy' Nkrumah lambasted the constant criticism emanating from the world's major governments when he was famously quoted as saying about the UN's position in Katanga, 'quibbling about constitutional niceties while the [Congo] Republic is tottering into anarchy, are evidence of the callous disregard for African independence by the Great Powers'.

Nkrumah did not have the vehicle of the western press with which his views could gain any visibility. Even we viewed O'Brien's position as untenable given that the western journalists were not willing to print anything critical of their paymasters who were all clearly part of the same virtuous circle of financial, mining and media conglomerates. But over the next few days, O'Brien managed to withstand the most heavy criticism from the British and French press, insisting that his role was solely to secure peace and to avoid an escalating crisis.

The Russians, however, were continuing to insist that the UN act militarily. On 8 August they affirmed their right to intervene if they were asked for help from the government of The Congo, who they took to be Antoine Gizenga's free communist government based in Stanleyville. The Soviets then issued a statement through their state news-agency 'Pravda' that Dag Hammarskjöld was merely a puppet of the west and a traitor to African Nationalism for not challenging the dictator Tshombie. The threat from the Soviets was given more credibility only a couple of days later when it was reported in newspapers around the world, including the Irish Independent, that they had tested a nuclear bomb:

> Red Horror Bomb Has Power of 100 Megatons
>
> The Irish Independent 10 August 1961

The Cold War showdown that had been threatening so much in recent months now seemed imminent; a war from what we could see would have been caused as much by press misinformation as by political disagreements. Just four days later, the showdown occurred but unexpectedly for us the world's attention was shifted back to Berlin as the iron curtain finally descended and divided the world into East and West. Back at the barn we tuned into the BBC World service to hear that during the night of the 12 August, Berlin was suddenly divided, with roads, bridges and parks in the city all been dug up and barricaded with concrete and barbed wire. It was described by the East Germans as an 'antifaschistischer Schutzwall' or 'anti-fascist protective rampart' with soldiers given orders to shoot anyone trying to cross the barriers. We heard that some houses literally had a wall built through the middle of them while their windows were bricked up. In the space of one night families and loved ones were separated for life. Anyone caught on the east side of the city would not be able to escape to the west, leaving them trapped and forcing them to live under communist rule.

At first, we thought the Berlin Wall may be just another barricade that would be taken down after a week but the diplomatic language from both sides that was dominating radio and newspaper headlines suggested that this wall was permanent and that the world was now clearly divided between East and West. On radio Brazzaville, we heard that Walter Ulbricht, the chairman of the East German communist party, said that the wall was intended to dissuade western aggression and to protect East Germans from being contaminated by fascist capitalism. Just as the camera crews of the world's media attended West Berlin's international film festival just a few miles away, Khrushchev was quoted as saying that he now had the testicles of the west in his iron grip, which with one good squeeze would make the West scream.

The speed with which the Berlin wall was erected was the thing that shocked us most, and was called a 'crime against mankind'* by Western politicians, but we knew the same could happen in The Congo if the communist forces in the North launched an invasion of Katanga. Monahan noted that it began to feel as if the testicles of the UN were also been squeezed, not only by the communists in the north but also by the western European colonial governments and from bias press coverage.

Just eight months beforehand many remembered that JFK's inaugural address had given everyone such hope that a nuclear confrontation could be avoided, although he had forewarned that

> man holds in his mortal hands the power to abolish all forms of human poverty and all forms of human life.
>
> JFK Inaugural Address January 1961

No-where in the world was this power more relevant than in The Congo as the refugee camp was by now absorbing thousands of new Congolese every day and many were dying from disease, hunger and nightly raids by the boy-soldier gangs intent on brutality. We assumed the raids were mostly the work of the butcher, the baker and the candlestick maker as each massacre we were called to attend had their trademark viciousness of hacked off limbs and burned bodies, but then we heard that the raids were now being carried out by uniformed Katangan gendarmerie. The incidents' legitimacy was supported with the resignation of a French officer called Lasimone from the Katangan gendarmerie as he was

* The Irish Independent 15 August 1961

so appalled at the ghastly orders he was being given from his commander, an ex Belgian officer called Cmdt Falques. O'Brien again reported this incident to the press in his morning briefing and even offered Lasimone to tell them the story directly but again the press found a way to argue that O'Brien and the UN were manipulating the truth, and Lasimone's testimony went unreported.

The Hindus who had been guarding the refugee camp during the raids also reported to their media and to UN high command that it was now uniformed gendarmerie and local white civilians who were burning out villages whilst massacring and mutilating the inhabitants. However, this was termed a 'pacification process' on Katangan radio to subdue the Baluba uprising. To divert attention the media then blamed the Hindus for carrying out the reported atrocities, including rapes and beatings in parts of white Elizabethville.

The Belgian ambassador Robert de Rothschild publicly paid lip service to support UN policy, but at the same time spoke about the need to protect white citizens and more menacingly warning of guerrilla warfare against the UN and a scorched earth policy that would result if the UN continued to act so aggressively.

The duties of 'A' Company were again re-organised and, much to our officers' relief, we were operating as a single military unit rather than being divided up and dispatched to non-military roles. However, we began to dread our peacekeeping duties as they invariably involved cleaning up severed limbs and dead bodies, with wailing families clamouring for a last touch of their loved one's stiffening corpses before we carried them away. It was also very apparent to us that whatever we did, the press would only blame the UN, whilst turning a blind eye to atrocities committed against Congolese civilians or against us.

We were required to re-enforce the patrols and defences around the barn as the UN intelligence suspected white civilian militia groups, backed by mercenaries, of preparing to take their vengeance out on UN installations. In our morning briefings, Prendergast told us that were now authorised to give warnings to disarm those we suspected of carrying out brutality and that should they resist, then we should not hesitate to shoot.

'Jaysus them Italian UN troops won't like this,' Monahan whispered jokingly in my ear, 'they won't be able to laze around with their eyes closed now.' But then the seriousness of the situation became very apparent.

'The situation is now kill or be killed.' Prendergast said in his typical matter of fact manner, as he began describing the various threats that faced us. Katanga was fast descending into a tinderbox of armed adversaries. All our leave was cancelled and we were no longer allowed to make trips into town unless we were on official patrols so our time-off was spent busily tuning into any radio news to hear the latest reports of increasing world tensions and killings in The Congo.

'The people at home will just not understand this type of thing,' remarked Dowler. 'If we have to shoot someone then the press will only say it was our fault, nothing about what or who we were trying to protect.'

'Aye, them feckin journalists will see to that.' I replied, knowing how Connor Cruise O'Brien was being miscommunicated in the morning briefings, 'as long as they get their scoop, that's all they're interested in.'

I may have still been an underage adventure seeker who had innocently bluffed his way through this far, but the ravages of war and a deliberate misinformation policy can make a young mind grow up very fast.

It was clear to all of us that O'Brien was doing everything he could to avoid the war flaring up but it seemed that anyone associated with the UN was responsible if anything went wrong. Up until then, the UN had resisted taking military action in The Congo, but the situation was unsustainable and soon O'Brien would have no choice but to intervene.

On the morning of 26 August we were assembled for our normal morning briefing and Prendergast explained that the following night we would be carrying out a military operation to disarm the Katangan gendarmerie and expel all mercenary forces.

'The operation is code-named *Rumpunch,*' he said.

The barn was completely silent as Prendergast then explained the operational details.

'The objective of the exercise is firstly to arrest the leader of the Katangan succession force: Moise Tshombie, from his home is Elizabethville, and to take control of communications facilities in the town where all the Katangan Gendarmerie will be told to hand over their weapons or they will be arrested. Our duties as 'A' Company will be to arrest all mercenary forces supportive of the succession, most of which are located up here north of Elizabethville,' noted Prendergast pointing to a red cross on a map. He then continued: 'We will surround the base in question tomorrow morning at 0400 hours at which time we expect most of the mercenaries to be sleeping. The mercenaries are all armed and some may take it on themselves to discharge their weapons in which case we will engage them in live-fire until they surrender their arms. The mercenaries will then be escorted to waiting planes that will take them out of Katanga and out of this war.'

It all sounded straightforward as Prendergast assigned each unit specific tasks and at 0100 we set off from the barn to begin Operation *Rumpunch*. Being members of an Irish battalion, the first priority as we stood readied on parade in the barn was spiritual absolution and Father Joe called us together for a prayer:

Hail glorious St Patrick, dear saint of our isle
On us thy poor children, bestow a sweet smile
In the war against sin, in the fight for the faith
Dear Saint, may thy children resist unto death
Ever bless and defend the sweet land of our birth
Where the shamrock still blooms as when thou
wert on earth
And our hearts shall yet burn, whatsoever we roam
For God and St Patrick, and our native home.

As the sermon ended a few gave themselves a final gee up repeating 'For God and St Patrick!'

'Was that the last rights we were just given?' I asked Dowler and Monahan.

'Aye, it sure sounded like them,' Dowler responded, 'I was expecting a few Our Fathers and a couple of Hail Mary's, but now we have to resist unto death.'

'Well, do condemned men get a last request?' joked Monahan, 'because I wouldn't mind a little bit more sleep?'

His humour was all the more unlikely given that he was one of 36 men tasked with entering the barracks to arrest the 500 or so mercenaries while they slept, knowing that many went to bed armed.

Our anti tank gun unit was assigned to surround the mercenaries' barracks and to open fire should the mercenaries choose to fight and to shoot any potential escapees. We would then assist in rounding up weapons and artillery and provide an armed escort once the mercenaries had surrendered.

Within a couple of hours we were lying on the dusty ground surrounding the factory-like billet a few miles north of Elizabeville. It was freezing cold and pitch black. As instructed, I was with the anti-tank gun unit near the front of the barracks with Dowler and John Conway. The remainder of 'A' Company that was not involved with entering the barracks had the building completely surrounded and there was a tense silence everywhere except for the whisper of last minute orders being relayed around the encirclement.

I lay there with my FN rifle at the ready, my heart beat thumping through every vein in my body with my primed finger readied on the trigger. It also occurred to me that if the mercenaries were former Foreign Legion troops then their motto was never to surrender arms, so we would probably be imminently faced with a shootout. I could suddenly remember every war film at the Picture House and every book and every battle I had ever read back in the Athlone barracks. I envisaged Kirk Douglas as Doc Holliday in the gunfight at the OK Coral and the great shootouts of the Wild West with Bert Lancaster and John Wayne. Dowler nudged me nodding over at Pakie Monahan's unit moving into position close to the doors of the barracks. Prendergast led the platoon into position with each main door manned with eight men, and two men covering each window.

As we had been briefed, on the stroke of 0400 hours our company commander Quinlan stood up in full range of the barracks and ordered Prendergast's units into the factory. The lights from armoured cars were suddenly lit up outside the barracks and Quinlan held a loud speaker to his mouth to address the mercenaries, just as they were rudely awakened by armed UN soldiers.

> This is the United Nations security force on whose authority we are acting to arrest all military personnel associated with the Katangan independence movement. We are a peace-keeping force but have been authorised to use arms in the event that you do not comply. The barracks have been surrounded with armed patrols to ensure you comply and to ensure your safe passage out of Katanga. If you do not comply we cannot guarantee your safety and you will be placed in military prison here in Katanga. The leader of the Katangan succession movement Moise Tshombie has also been arrested and you are required to give up your weapons and emerge out of the front doors only disposing of any weapons and artillery you may have at your disposal. You have two minutes to pack your personal possessions after which you are required to come out with your hands above your head

Outside the barn the night remained still, but we could hear the hectic commotion from inside the barracks with 'A' Company soldiers bellowing orders at the mercenaries, turning them out of the bunks with shouts of:

'Hands up! You're being arrested!'

With our eyes peeled on the front door, from our lair-like positions about 20 metres in front of the barracks, a few mercenaries began to emerge, some only partially dressed in long johns and carrying a pillow case of clothes in front of them. Most seemed bewildered and bleary eyed from the shock of being awoken and arrested mid-slumber, and a small pile of weapons including rifles and chicottes began to accumulate just outside the barracks door.

Quinlan carried on bellowing out the orders with his loud speaker:

'Line up, with your belongings laid out in front of you ready for inspection and stand to attention with your hands above your head!'

Just half an hour later, all the mercenaries had been rounded up and were stood in front of us. There had been two commando units comprising 450 men billeted in the barracks although none of their legendary mercenary officers was among them.

The transport planes roared their engines into life from the military airfield that was about a mile away and we formed a patrol to escort the mercenaries onto the planes, where they would be guarded and eventually dropped in Salisbury, Rhodesia.

The shock of being deported was beginning to hit some of the mercenaries and they began swearing at us in their various languages of French, Africaans and Flemish.

'Footsak jou bliksem!' [fuck off you bastard] shouted one as he was encouraged to keep up the pace although it was noticeable that many marched at the languished speed which I presumed must have been the fabled foreign legion march of 88 paces per minute.

We said nothing to antagonise them further, so apart from a few obscenities, threats and deathly stares, our whole operation was over within an hour and a half and we watched the transport planes jet off into the new-dawn sky.

I felt so proud to be in 'A' Company and how everyone had carried out their orders just as we had been instructed. It also struck me that our officers in 'A' Company like Prendergast and Quinlan had also been the first to put themselves in firing line not like the way I had read of officer types in previous wars where the poor bloody infantry were the only ones sent into danger. We discussed amongst ourselves that it was Prendergast who had been the first one through the doors of the barracks charging through the bunks turning the mercenaries out of bed, but he never even blinked with fear.

We returned back to Elizabethville after our successful operation and were briefed on the outcome of other parts of operation *Rumpunch*. Tshombie had been arrested but had escaped from house arrest just a couple of hours later. Only a couple of the mercenary officers had been arrested, the rest were still at large and said to be re-grouping under the direction of Tshombie who had gone into hiding. The UN issued an order to arrest and expel from The Congo anyone who they suspected of being a mercenary, i.e. who dressed in khakis and voeldsoens, or who didn't have official resident papers. As a result any remaining mercenaries quickly changed into civilian clothing and vanished into the white Congo society by hiding out in succession supporting towns. The other problem was that the Katangan gendarmerie was mostly comprised of native Congolese and the UN had no grounds to expel them

Operation *Rumpunch* had turned into a fiasco and our officers were livid at the way Tshombie was simply allowed to escape from his house imprisonment to re-establish the Katangan succession movement who could now claim that we acted militarily against them. Up until this point they had avoided challenging the UN militarily but *Rumpunch* had changed all that; we had, in the words of Julius Caesar, crossed the Rubicon.

CHAPTER NINE

Apache Country

Date: September, 1961
Location: Jadotville, The Congo
Status: Peacekeeper

'Forward, the Light Brigade!'
Was there a man dismay'd?
Not tho the soldier knew
Some one had blunder'd.
Theirs not to make reply
Theirs not to reason why
Theirs but to do or die
Into the valley of Death
Rode the six hundred.

Alfred, Lord Tennyson,
The Charge of the Light Brigade

AMID THE DISARRAY of *Rumpunch* the UN force in The Congo, which now numbered some 18,500 men in total, the largest operation ever undertaken by the organisation in its history, began to untangle. The full weight of the Katangan succession forces and pro colonial white-Africa media was now pitted against us. The UN command structure was also feeling the pressure when it emerged that Connor Cruise O'Brien had not sought authorisation from Dag Hammarskjöld for the operation and that the senior Irish UN officers in Elizabethville had not informed their UN military commanders of their mission. We also heard about a number of disagreements between the senior Irish UN officers and those in charge of us in 'A' Company. Our officers were apparently accusing their superiors of incompetence for letting Tshombie and other succession leaders escape so easily which had undermined *Rumpunch* and the whole operation to expel mercenaries, placing the entire UN operation in jeopardy.

Rumpunch had been a 'Pig's Ear' we heard, carried out without official UN remit or appropriate military protocol, allowing our key antagonists to re-invigorate their campaign against Congolese civilians and against us. Tshombie had been temporarily in the hands of the UN but was now using his capture and subsequent escape during *Rumpunch* to stir up resentment in the press and on radio broadcasts. I remembered what The County used to say to me when I was young: 'never wound a prince, it just makes him angrier,' and the white Belgian community's anger, fuelled by Tshombie's heroic escape and anti-UN PR campaign, was now becoming a very real risk to our safety.

Posters of Tshombie were becoming prominent on every telegraph pole in Elizabethville, and small barricades were being erected throughout Katanga to keep the UN out of Belgian controlled towns. The British, French and Belgian press had stepped up its personal attacks on the UN, most notably against Connor Cruise O'Brien. Calls for an independent Katanga had reached a new intensity as newspapers back in Brussels were reportedly screaming out the hijacked anthem of the mercenaries 'Le Rois! Le Lois! Le Liberte!' They portrayed their fellow countrymen, who they characterised as the oppressed ex-pat white Belgian population, as having their lives destroyed by a 'communist anti-colonial juggernaut.'

'And all because the UN seemingly couldn't organise a piss up in a brewery' was what we were saying amongst ourselves. The result of all the internal UN bickering was that 'A' Company was dispatched on 3 September to the town of Jadotville, about 80 miles north of where we were in Elizabethville. It felt like we were being sent as far away from HQ as possible, probably, we presumed, because the UNOC command didn't like being told that they had made 'such a bollocks' with *Rumpunch*.

Our new assignment made little sense when Prendergast told us that we were being sent to protect the white civilians of the Jadotville mining community. It made even less sense when he told us that 'A' Company was replacing two other UN companies who were recalled back to Elizabethville although they had only been in Jadotville for one week.

'Why would they want to swap us with two other UN units?' I asked Dowler and Pakie Monahan, to which they just shrugged.

We also couldn't understand why the white community of Jadotville needed such special consideration given that the native Congolese and particularly the refugees in the camp were the most at risk from the escalating turmoil. As we left Elizabethville, the camp was continuing to receive an influx of thousands every day with some estimating that there were now over 100,000 displaced people living within the sprawling slum, all dependent on the UN for food, water and protection.

We were told that Belgian politicians had lobbied back at the UN in New York, for a unit of UN peacekeepers to continue to guard Jadotville's civilians. The Belgian foreign diplomat Paul-Henry Spaak argued at the UN

General assembly that if the UN forces were intent on expelling their only means of defence, as they had shown during the unauthorised *Rumpunch* operation, then the white Belgian community would be exposed to brutal tribal warfare and at the mercy of communist troops from the north. As such, Spaak portrayed the mercenaries as security guards and threatened that if the UN did not provide similar levels of protection, then his government would have no alternative but to redeploy their own paratroopers to defend their ex-pat civilians.

We understood that 'ours was not to reason why', so we again packed our bags and set off from the Barn for Jadotville along the main Elizabethville Road but given the rising tensions, the front and rear of the column were to be kept on high alert throughout the journey. We were given ten days' supplies and some light military equipment but most importantly we were given our latest bag of mail from home. I was delighted to be handed a letter; something to read when I had a quiet moment to myself. Like everyone else I didn't want to open mine in front of the other soldiers in case it brought a lump to my throat. The platoon sergeant John Monahan told us that we would only be travelling at 15mph due to potential ambushes and also because of the threat of elephant or rhino traps that were becoming a regular feature in Katanga to disrupt main transport links. The traps were mainly created as part of the tribal war, an ancient defensive strategy that dug concealed pits around villages to capture rival invaders or rampaging wild animals. They were constructed by digging a huge hole, sometimes 40 foot wide and 20 foot deep and then lining the bottom with carved and spiked trunks from the bouma tree and coated in curare, intended to impale and poison any would-be attackers. The traps could easily swallow up the UN transport vehicles we were travelling in, holding up the rest of the column for enough time to leave us as an open target for random tribal attacks. The grim spectre of the Niemba massacre loomed large and was at the forefront of everyone's mind.

The convoy started out slowly into 'Apache country', the lawless 'Injun' territories of the John Wayne Westerns that I had watched with such enthusiasm back home at the Picture House. I dreamt back to those voyeuristic days when I had gazed longingly at the canvas, wagon train convoys travelling through the Wild West to the High Chapparal, vulnerable to attack from the apache braves. War was exciting back then as a child, when I was able to sit there chewing on my fizzballs and bulls-eyes, but now in the reality of a war-torn country, my heart was pumping with the same resonant wallop of adrenalin as we were on our way to Jadotville, peering out in search of any possible enemies.

Pakie Monahan had also been considering the probability of us running into an ambush and told us about a story he had heard of two cannibals sitting by an open fire:

'So one cannibal says to the other one,' he started, clearly building up to a gag, '"Them missionaries are always too fat and juicy, but them Irish UN fellas are too thin, dry and sunburnt". Then the other cannibal butted in, "Then why don't ya stop complaining and just eat the spuds!"'

A nervous laugh went round but Pakie hadn't finished.

'So the first cannibal says: "No, the missionaries have plenty of meat on them but I have tried everything to cook them properly, roasting, stewing and baking them but I still can't get them to taste right".

So the second cannibal asks, "What did they look like before you cooked them?"

And the first cannibal replied, "Well, this one was wearing a brown robe, was short and fat, and had a big bald spot on the crown of his head."

"Ah that explains it," interrupted the second cannibal, "ye'll have to friar them!"'

Again we laughed tentatively.

'I don't know what yer making gags up about cannibals for,' Dowler suddenly piped up as Pakie finished, 'how would ya like it if them Baluba mistook you for one of them juicy missionaries?'

'Ah now Sean,' Pakie immediately responded, 'they wouldn't be eating comedians like me; us comedians taste funny!'

Suddenly a piercing noise from above disrupted the light-heartedness, as we heard a Fouga jet overhead, the attack plane that we knew had been supplied to the mercenaries. It had been described to us as having the same menacing buzz of the German Stukas during the Second World War but were a decade more advanced. As we looked out, it was flying barely 50 feet above our convoy, a single pilot with two machine guns clearly at his disposal. We immediately readied our rifles in anticipation of an attack, but the Fouga just kept on flying. Our mandate remained that we could not open fire unless we were fired on, but just three minutes later the distinctive buzz of the Fouga had returned, again flying low over our convoy.

'Smile for the cameras,' Dowler blurted out as we crouched down in the truck with our guns ready, 'yer having yer photograph taken!' and the Fouga again whistled past us before disappearing once more into the sun-blurred horizon.

John Monahan took the situation more seriously and radioed ahead to Prendergast.

'Company Sergeant. This is platoon Sergeant Monahan. Low flying military aircraft flying too close to convoy, we are in position to defend ourselves; over.'

We then heard the muffled voice of Prendergast.

'Hold fire as per our instruction platoon sergeant,' he directed as the crackling radio obscured his obvious frustration 'but if this fecker even winks a strafing bullet in our direction, then blow the bastard's bollocks off. Over!'

'Will do Sarge. Over and out. Did yiz hear that lads?' Monahan asked us.

'Aye, loud and clear Sarge!' replied Dowler.

Sure enough the Fouga returned for a third time, lower than ever and passing directly over the rear of the convoy.

'Hold yiz fire lads!' John Monahan repeated 'It may be just a reconnaissance mission.'

'Aye, or just some feckin mercenary taking the piss,' whispered Dowler, knowing that the mercenaries knew we could only open fire if we were shot at first, as yet again the Fouga continued flying past before disappearing into the distant hills.

This time it didn't return and we put our guns down.

'Well they know we are coming to town anyway,' the Tiger blurted out. 'I hope they don't go putting themselves out; putting on a big welcome for us and all.'

The Fouga pilot, we presumed, probably had all the key information about the convoy he needed, the number of vehicles, details of our heavy armaments and an approximate number of men.

'I wonder if he's figured out that our anti tank gun unit doesn't have an anti tank gun!' I suggested sarcastically.

‘Ah, we’ll only be stationed up there for a week anyway, as that’s all the supplies we have,’ Dowler pointed out as we approached the strategically important Lufira Bridge crossing, ‘but if me and Michael were in charge of ordnance, we’d have thrown in a few extra packs of bacon and eggs for us all, but we’ve just got a load of these dog biscuits and bully beef tins to last us until we get back to the barn.’

The Lufira Bridge was the only crossing point of the Lulua river for 100 miles and was on the main Elizabethville to Jadotville road. We knew from our morning briefings that the bridge was strategically important to the UN and had been regarded as of equal importance to the Post Office and broadcast buildings back in Elizabethville. But we had not seen a UN patrol since we left the Barn which brought dismay to the officers of ‘A’ Company given that we were effectively cut-off once we were on its north side. Again we heard the crackling radio discussion between our officers, explaining that they would need to get HQ to secure the area given the escalating campaign against the UN, or we should remain on the south side of the bridge to protect such a vital position. The convoy stopped just short of the bridge to await further instruction.

After an hour or so, we were ordered to continue our advance and all appeared under control as the transport engines kicked back into gear. I looked down the Lulua River as we crossed the half mile wide bridge, a torrent of fast flowing water just 30 feet below our truck. The river had been dyed by the distinctive Katangan clay-red soil to become a dirty brown colour gushing, into mini-whirlpools and sweeping up anything in its path. Apparently the locals called this ‘the river of blood’ which was brought to the Congo by the white man who had disrupted the natural environment to mine out the earth's treasures. The beauty of African nature however remained abundant in the small tributaries and streams that fed into the mighty Lulua. Antelope grazed on the fertile river banks and huge pelicans glided along just a couple of feet above the richly abundant feeding waters beneath them. Probably the most beautiful bird I had seen in The Congo was the small hummingbird, its vivid array of colourful feathers flittering effortlessly in the glistening Congolese sunshine. I was transfixed for a moment in boyhood escapism watching nature's thrilling display of agility, which allowed the humming-bird to hover in the same spot above the reeds as if it were suspended in time; where war, politics, propaganda campaigns and most of all my age had no relevance.

'Why would anyone want to bring guns to such a beautiful place?' I asked myself as we proceeded up the 20 mile gradual ascent towards Jadotville, where the landscape slowly became dominated by dry undulating terrain and parched bushes and shrubs.

Just a mile or so before entering the southern end of Jadotville, the convoy stopped again. Our billeted accommodation was to be in designated villas formerly used by mine-labourers on the outskirts of the town and we would not be able enter the town itself until we had been cleared to do so by our officers.

Some asked if it was OK to just pop in to town to one of the bars for a drink but we were told that there was a similar situation to the white neighbourhoods of Elizabethville as the Jadotville population was hostile to the UN.

'Then what are we doing here protecting them?' a few asked at the same time, as Pakie Monahan summed it up by saying:

PS John Monahan (demonstrating anti-tank gun) with CS Jack Prendergast. September 1961. Picture courtesy of Phillip Sweeney.

'Either they're ungrateful feckers, or we're stupid feckers!'

'Or probably both!' Dowler responded. 'I don't know what in feck's name are we doing here protecting them if they don't want us around the place. Let them defend themselves!'

A few others gruffed their approval for Dowler's logical suggestion albeit in the knowledge that 'we were not to reason why' and 'orders are orders'.

Just the next day, after some of our officers had met with Jadotville's civil leaders, we found out that the city's hotels were playing host to a rising number of mercenaries, including many of those we had probably expelled during Operation *Rumpunch* just a week beforehand. They had been directly recruited and paid for by

Union Miniere which had its headquarters in the centre of the town. Its main mining locations for copper and uranium were in the surrounding area and accounted for over one-third of The Congo's GDP. The mercenaries were being flown in from Salisbury, the same airport to which they had been dispatched during *Rumpunch*, apparently arriving at Kamina, the military base retained by Belgium after independence, and entering Jadotville from the north. Although the UN still had a remit to arrest anyone on the 'chasseux blancs' the so called 'white list' distributed for the arrest of foreign agitators during *Rumpunch*, we were sure that we would not be able to walk in so easily at 4 o'clock in the morning and arrest them. To compound the threat, we heard that three units of Colonel Muke's Katangan gendarmerie comprising some 450 men had been assembled in Jadotville over the past week and were arming and training civilian militia and Lumba tribal members with antiquated but effective Martini Henry bayonets and Lee Enfield rifles, the same as those we had trained with back in Athlone. As our officers left Jadotville to return to the Purfina garage, a barricade was erected on the main road, manned by a few mercenaries, with a clear mandate not to allow any UN personnel in.

This did not sound good at all and many of us were wondering how the UN intelligence had been so lacking when it had been so thorough in its knowledge of mercenary operations beforehand, knowing each and every location of active commando units. Some suspected that our Elizabethville HQ must have known that the town was 'hostile' being that two UN companies were located here in the past week and would have submitted intelligence reports. They would surely have recorded that mercenary commando units were located in Jadotville, and that the city was heavily manned with Katangan gendarmerie. But UN HQ had not passed any of this intelligence onto us.

If we had been lured into a trap we weren't getting much help from our own side to get ourselves out of it and we were immediately ordered to set up a defensive cordon to secure the area, either side of the main Elizabethville – Jadotville Road, which included the Purfina petrol station, the villas and the surrounding exposed land. The cordon was ringed about 800 yards around an inner cordon which itself was set about 300 yards radius around the Purfina garage.

Guard posts were set up around the perimeter and the villas themselves were fortified with gun emplacements' and sand bags, with all doors and windows secured. The Purfina garage had disused mechanic workshops and slightly dilapidated offices attached which was selected as our HQ and canteen for our ten day assignment in Jadotville.

The defensive cordon that was put in place meant the whole of 'A' Company was on high alert and we would be on a rota of guard duty 24 hours a day. I was part of the support platoon which was required to guard the outer perimeter; two other platoons manned an inner perimeter which included the villas whilst a third platoon set up defences around the Purfina garage itself. I bunkered down directly in-line with the villas on rising ground to the west about 600 yards from the main road, finding a concealed spot conveniently located behind an anthill and next to some thick bushes and elephant grass. Initially my guard duty was from 1200 hours to midnight, not the best time as it included the blistering heat of the midday sun. Although I was sheltered by nearby bushes, small swarms of tsetse fly would converge around shrubbery from about

1630-1830 hours making the late afternoons even more uncomfortable. Dowler, Conway and our platoon sergeant John Monahan were all posted in the near vicinity and we all regarded the tsetse fly as 'horrible little feckers' with a biting sting like two wasps back home. The medical officer Joe Clune had set up his surgery back at the villas and gave us a small bottle of quinine that would at least numb the soreness, but the best defence was not to get stung at all, so I covered whatever exposed skin I could and tried to swat the tsetse fly away.

The town of Jadotville itself held a population of about 100,000 people of which some 15,000 were reportedly white, mainly Belgian ex-pats, most of whom having some connection to Union Miniere or their financiers, Societe Generale. Outside of the major cities, it had become the largest mining town in the copper belt as the main distribution hub for Katanga's most profitable mines and was regarded as the richest town in Katanga, given its prominent business connections and mining wealth. It was named after the famous Belgian engineer, Monsieur Jean Jadot who was credited with connecting up Henry Morton Stanley's old railway system with the lower Congo and Katanga in the 1920s after which a flourishing secondary and tertiary industry had become established in the town, with fine houses and hotels at its centre.

Many of the problems that plagued Elizabethville, like the growing refugee camp, did not affect Jadotville, largely because the surrounding area had been completely cleared of any political opposition allowing the white community to live an undisturbed colonial lifestyle where they didn't have the inconvenience of desperately poor black people on their doorstep. Therefore, they were able to carry on exploiting local labour as the black community was largely comprised of friendly tribal groups like the Lumba who remained markedly poorer than the whites but had seemingly accepted their lower status as they had been provided work as mine labourers and were given protection from enemy tribes through mercenary commando units. In many ways the Lumba had no choice but to accept the status quo because if white rule ended, they would likely be its biggest casualty given their collaboration with the white minority over decades of colonial rule.

We still had our radios that we had bought back in Tripoli and to conceal the light from the on/off switch at night, I hid mine down my trousers whilst I was on guard duty. Up here on the Jadotville plateau I could receive the BBC World Service and radio Brazzaville, which provided a little bit of music amid the news that was always dominated by increasingly fraught East/West relations and the growing possibility of a nuclear war.

I imagined The County straining his head to listen to the very same radio broadcasts which were always dominated by stories of impending doom. However, since we had been re-assigned to Jadotville the threats had become much more immediate. The town was just 15 miles up the road from the uranium mine of Shinkolobwe, and some predicted that this would be the most likely target should the USSR wish to ignite a military confrontation with the US by seizing or bombing its nuclear resource whilst at the same time facilitating a Russian-backed coup in central Africa.

Apparently, both Gizenga's communists and the new Nationalist government of Cyrille Adoula understood the risks of a nuclear bomb being used on Congolese soil and had forged an agreement to co-operate with each other to avert a nuclear crisis. The agreement between the East and West supporting factions left Moise Tshombie's colonial-supporting Katangan independence party isolated as Gizenga and Adoula were staunchly united in opposition to Katangan succession. Russia had however stated that the agreement was worthless without Katanga and would not support any agreement without the province's inclusion. On the day that we arrived in Jadotville, Gizenga and President Adoula were flying together in a show of unity to attend a conference of 24 non-aligned nations in Belgrade. The conference was called to agree on the wording of an appeal to both Kennedy and Khrushchev to meet without delay to avert World War Three and to 'establish a safe peace'.

We heard on the news that Kennedy and the UK Prime Minister Macmillan had already proposed to Chairman Khrushchev that both sides refrain from nuclear weapons testing that 'take place in the atmosphere and produce radioactive fallout.' But the appeal fell on deaf ears as Nehru ominously warned 'that once again the foul winds of war are blowing' after he delivered the non-aligned countries' appeal to Khrushchev.

'Don't be worrying yerself about all this nuclear talk Michael,' Dowler told me 'us Irish have been through Cromwell clearances, the famine and the black and tans; so we'll easily handle a bit of owld uranium. And anyway, winds are always feckin blowing somewhere in Africa, it's whether Offaly can beat Down in a couple of weeks to lift the Sam Maguire that ye should be worried about.'

'Aye Sean, but they're saying that Jadotville will be the next Hiroshima or Nagasaki,' I replied with a sense of realism well beyond my immature years, 'these weapons they're testing are 50 megatons or 30 times the power as those bombs that were used on Japan.'

Dowler said nothing for a moment, clearly absorbing the gravity of the situation 'Well then, Mick Casey had better have one of his most glorious days!' he exclaimed.

It was a trick that many in 'A' Company were becoming expert at, that when we were faced with overwhelming odds, they would completely switch the subject back to something about home.

The County had told me that there was a fabled legend in the All-Ireland that the greatest finals were an omen of impending crisis as 'the greatest all-Ireland in history' was played in hurling between Cork and Killkenny during a ferocious thunder storm, only equalled by the ferociousness of the game itself. The same day was remembered throughout Ireland as the day World War Two began.

'But it's in the back-line,' Dowler continued, 'of Paddy McCormack, Greg Hughes and John Egan where the game will be won for Offaly.'

It wasn't just Dowler who distracted himself with football. The two All-Ireland finals that traditionally took place in September were what all of 'A' Company were talking about after Down had surprisingly beaten Kerry and Offaly had beaten Roscommon.

So instead of fearful conversations about the terror that would be unleashed amid a looming World War Three, the biggest yelps could be heard in the Purfina canteen with:

'C'mon Leinster!' regularly heard from those, like me, not from 'The Faithful County' itself. Offaly's colours of green white and gold hoops, co-incidentally similar to the green, white and orange of the Irish tricolour adorned every kit-bag, making it look more like a St Patrick's day parade, and everyone who had a transistor radio tuned into the news from 'Paddy of Radio Brazzaville' to hear the latest team news.

I knew that my mother, who was a native of Offaly, would have her home county's colours outside the railway crossing house back in Edgeworthstown probably next to her Star-of Bethlehem plants, allowing my mind to drift back to my old life and job in an Edgeworthstown pub, with the people and characters busily anticipating the big game. It was those moments of warmth thinking about home and family that was keeping all of 'A' Company occupied whilst being on duty in one of the most dangerous places on earth. As the radio continued to crackle up predictions of a nuclear conflict from below my waist I knew that most back home in Ireland, with the exception of The County, would be completely oblivious to what was going on in The Congo.

With the tricolour so evident around the Purfina garage and the villas, the residents of Jadotville would have been in no doubt where this particular company of UN troops were from, but just a couple of days later the barricade that had been erected just a few days before became fortified and armed with mercenaries carrying light weapons. There was now no way for us to enter the town without igniting a confrontation. Next to the barricade there was also a small demonstration by local white civilians, holding placards displaying:

UN

X

NON
ENTRE!

It still didn't make sense to us. If these people didn't want us here to protect them, then we should be protecting those who really need our help, i.e. the desperately poor refugees who were being systematically cleared from their Katangan homes. But the demonstrations against us in Jadotville were apparently not as large as the 'anti-UN' rallies taking place back in Elizabethville and we were told over radio Brazzaville that the headline on the Irish Independent newspaper that day told of riots breaking out, demanding that the UN leave Katanga.

Anti UN Riots in Katanga

Headline: Irish Independent 07.09.1961

We no longer had any letters from home to supply us with news as this was being held back at our Elizabethville base until our operation in Jadotville was completed, so 'Paddy from Brazzaville' became our only connection to what the Irish papers were saying. We were not the only Irishmen in the area, however, as one of the mercenary commando units based in Jadotville was reported to be that of 4 commando, the infamous and brutal mercenary group led by 'the mad bloodhound' himself; Mike Hoare, whose notoriety could send a shiver down any soldier's spine.

In the distance we could hear the unmistakable crackle of gun-shots and we presumed 4 Commando was providing training as the shots were being fired in regular interludes and with a rhythm that made us suspect that it must be from a rifle range. I could tell that these were the Lee-Enfields, immediately recognisable by the clunking bolt action and high-pitched echo that resounded for about three seconds after the shot was fired. On hearing the sound of gunfire the officers of 'A' Company, after radioing

PJ Sweeney dug-in at his defensive post, September 1961. Picture courtesy of Phillip Sweeney

ahead their intentions, defied the barricade to make a trip into town to investigate the breach in UN terms.

On their return, the officers said nothing about what weapons were being used in the town as the local mayor had denied them access to inspect the so called civilian areas, but two platoons of 'A' Company were immediately told to dig-in by building trenches around the Purfina garage. Our platoon sergeant John Monahan told us that the commander of 'A' Company, Pat Quinlan, believed that the Katangan gendarmerie and the mercenary commando units were readying an attack on us, and from then on we would be placed on high alert.

'There's no more feckin about lads,' John Monahan ordered, 'these fellas are just waiting for the order to open fire. We have to be ready for them. From now on we're all on red alert round the clock. It's six hours' rota on armed guard down at the perimeter, then six hours setting up defences, then another rota of guard duty.

When yer back in the villas we'll be sleeping on the floor, or under the bed if possible; but no-one gets more than four hours sleep per day. Put away any non-essential items including yer football flags and keep yer personal supply of water full at all times.'

'Have we asked for re-enforcements Sarge?' asked Dowler, as all of us were aware that the Katanga gendarmerie and the mercenary units, reportedly billeted in the town had us outnumbered by at least five to one.

'Aye we have,' responded John Monahan, 'but they are not able to send any immediately.'

'What about re-supplies Sarge?' continued Dowler, 'we've only brought ten days' supplies with us on this mission and we only have three days left.'

'There are no supplies available either. Yer current rations will need to be halved except water, drink as much as ye can, ye'll need to.'

'Does this mean we are cut off Sarge?' questioned the persistent Dolwer.

'Aye, it does.' John Monahan replied bluntly.

We heard just a few hours later what the officers must have already known, that the Lufira Bridge had been blockaded by the gendarmerie and that UN vehicles were not being allowed to pass through. We were apparently ordered by Elizabethville HQ not to attempt a break-out and to remain at our posts in Jadotville until relief arrived. The order for us to remain apparently came from continued Belgian political pressure back at the UN in New York, who insisted that the population of Jadotville needed protection, even though our radio operators had reported that we were under siege by the same residents and not allowed to enter the town.

I looked at my watch. It was 1115 hours on 10 September 1961 and I had 45 minutes until I again went on guard duty.

As we prepared our packs of water, rations and quinine for another six hour shift down on the outer perimeter, the ever resourceful Dowler had acquired a pair of field glasses and was busy surveying the hills surrounding us, darting quickly from one window to the next.

'Look at this Michael!' he said handing me the glasses, 'what d'ya see?'

I looked through at the magnified landscape and could make out a small gun emplacement:

'Aye,' I said, 'I can see a couple of fellas with guns!' I replied.'

'Now look about 40 feet to the left,' instructed Dowler, 'd'ya see that?'

I could just make out the profile of a group of ten armed gendarmerie, who appeared to be busy in conversation. But then Dowler grabbed my arm and ushered me towards an adjacent window in the villa.

'Now, what d'ya see?' he asked.

This time I didn't need to be directed and I scoured the hillsides picking out the distant movement of small groups of armed gendarmerie and mercenaries who all appeared to be aiming their gun installations in our direction.

'Jaysus,' I said, 'we're feckin surrounded! D'ya think we should tell the officers?'

'They already know ya feckin eejit ya!' Dowler immediately responded. 'That's why Holy Joe gave us the last rites again at mass this morning. The officers have been radioing back to Elizabethville to let them know we're under siege but they're just telling us to hold our position.'

Guard duty took on a different perspective after that point; every rustle of a leaf was met with a nervy clasp of my FN rifle as we knew the mercenary and gendarmerie forces were focusing their crosshairs and manoeuvring into positions surrounding us. No shot had yet been fired, but everything else was set ready for an attack despite our status as peacekeepers and all it needed was an order by their commanders to commence hostilities. It was like war had been declared but the fight had not yet started, all part of the escalating phoney war that had begun when we were back in Elizabethville, the only thing apparently stopping an all-out conflict being our status as non-combatant peacekeepers.

The next day there was still no sign of re-enforcements or re-supplies and our dog biscuits and tins of bully beef were now considered a luxury as I carefully halved each portion to last an extra meal. I figured out that if I chewed for twice as long I could fool my stomach into believing I had had a full meal. My transistor radio was still hidden down my trousers from when I was posted down on the perimeter and it kept my growing hunger distracted with more solemn warnings of a military confrontation. The continuing tensions between East and West had The Congo and Berlin as the main flash points where armies were readied for action.

Radio Brazzaville was no longer informing us about the upcoming All-Ireland but was reporting on recent developments in America. The Kennedy administration had apparently given Russia an ultimatum that if there were any more interference to flights over Berlin, this would be regarded as aggressive action or an act of war. The report would then be followed quickly by a sports bulletin that Mickey Mantle was winning another world series for the NY Yankees, becoming the seventh player to hit 400 home runs and on target to break Babe Ruth's record. I could feel my anger beginning to boil at the inconsequential way that a pending global catastrophe was being reported in the same breath as a baseball game. But then the headlines hit far closer to home.

'And news from Katanga today is that Conor Cruise O'Brien has issued a warning for Moise Tshombie to surrender immediately or risk a military intervention by the UN to stop the succession.'

'Oh fuck the lot of ye!' I suddenly burst out almost by accident, disturbing the still Congolese night and causing a slight commotion in the guard posts around me, 'ye and yer feckin Micky Mantle!'

'What's up with ya?' whispered Conway.

'Nothing!' I replied harshly, 'just sick of all these bollocks playing with people's lives, including ours.' My ranting wasn't over and the build up of tensions over the past few days just came crashing out of my mouth like the perpetual victim whose blood suddenly boils over when he has finally had enough.

'It's alright for O'Brien to issue feckin warnings when he's sitting up there in Les Roches on his fat arse sipping afternoon tay; while we are feckin surrounded by the people he is threatening. And we're cut off from our own feckin useless UN, getting bitten to fuck by tsetse fly and eating half a dog biscuit every four hours!'

Dowler had heard my outburst from his guard post beyond Conway's and called over almost mockingly:

'What team did ya say was gonna win the All-Ireland Michael?'

'Oh fuck football!' I immediately responded as I continued ranting. 'What the fuck happened to all that bollocks we were told by our own government that we were not going to fight, just to keep the peace. I even told my mam I was just a feckin policeman. And here's these feckers sending us off to protect these rich white Belgian bastards while they are helping to besiege us.'

'Aye!' responded Conway, as he tried to pacify me, 'yer right Michael.'

My whole body was pumping with rage as I settled down again behind the anthill, my mind still furiously re-wording my adolescent fury with better-worded modifications that in my uncharacteristic outburst I was unable to articulate.

Before that moment I had never openly disagreed with anything or anyone in the army, as I was too concerned with maintaining a low profile should anyone suspect my age. But everyone in 'A' Company was becoming more tired, hungry and fearful of the ongoing siege and the inability or reluctance of the UN command back in Elizabethville to send re-enforcements or supplies.

As my temper calmed, I began to feel a little guilty that my outburst had been directed at Connor Cruise O'Brien since I had witnessed the pressure he was under in the press briefings back in Elizabethville to prevent a broader conflict including the possibility of nuclear war. With the western press still targeting him personally, I knew he was in an equally impossible position from a political perspective as we were, surrounded and under siege in Jadotville. Moreover, he seemed to be the only politician who was willing to stand up to the successionists who were causing more misery to the tens of thousands of refugees; all the other western European politicians just wanted to make the right sounding noises but secretly wanted to maintain the status quo of white colonial power. The reality was that they would lose too much money from European banks and mining companies should that status quo change.

More importantly however, as far as we knew, the UN did not have the authority to intervene militarily, only to prevent a civil war and to expel mercenaries on the white list. The UN mandate allowed us only to use force in the last resort. With the rhetoric being dialled up to include militarily imposing the UN demands, the mercenary and gendarmerie forces were effectively given a mandate to militarily defend themselves, which to them meant they could attack us.

The next day Radio Brazzaville was also reporting that the headline of the Irish Independent that day read:

> Irish unit cut off
>
> 12. 09.1961 Irish Independent

It recounted the fact that we, i.e. 'A' Company, were cut off and surrounded by 500 Katangan gendarmes although it made no mention of the presence of mercenary commando units.

The world was now seemingly aware of our plight in Jadotville as the article went on to describe us as being cut off behind enemy lines amid the growing stand-off between the UN and Katangan sucessionists. I immediately knew that The County would have read the front page of the Irish Independent and probably deliberated about telling my worrying mother, to which I concluded that he would have had no choice but to tell her as she would surely hear that 'A' Company were besieged from the inevitable gossip around Edgeworthstown.

'When are them re-enforcements due to arrive, Sarge?' Dowler again asked John Monahan after the Radio Brazzaville broadcast became common knowledge.

'We still don't know, we were expecting them yesterday.' Monahan replied. 'We have told them we are cut off but they're telling us to hold our position and that re-enforcements are on their way.'

'Well, it's just that we are going to run out of supplies by tomorrow night Sarge.' Dowler pointed out.

'Aye, we are aware of the situation and so is UN HQ' insisted Monahan with a firmness that suggested that he was becoming exasperated with the ineffective efforts of the Irish UN commanders in Elizabethville.

The next morning, 13 September 1961, I was due back on guard duty from 0800-1400 hours and I was busy ensuring my equipment was organised for another stint. Dowler, The Tiger, Sweeney and Pakie Monahan were all due to attend mass at 0700 which was still being held daily for all of 'A' Company except a skeletal guard duty, despite our high alert status and being under siege for the last three days. Dowler was joking that he had never been to mass before whilst holding a gun:

'I'll have to bring it with me to confession as well,' he joked 'he'll think twice about giving me too much penance when he sees I have one of these on my arm!'

I preferred to avoid mass as Father Joe was still ominously handing out the Last Rites to those that attended;

'One of these days he's gonna be right and ye'll all be on yer way to heaven,' I stated.

Well if yer not blessed, ye'll have to remain in purgatory,' retorted Dowler. 'And then yer poor owld mother will have to spend hours on the rosary to allow ya to join us angels up there in Heaven.'

Whatever the religious implications I found the last rites too foreboding as they had unnerved me during the *Rumpunch* operation. Pakie Monahan, however, was undeterred and piped up:

'Well, if Holy Joe can really turn water into wine, that's enough to keep me attending mass, whatever he says about yer rites.'

But I remained sceptical and with typical adolescent flippancy, I covered my religious guilt and apprehension by using one of the Oscar Wilde quotes I had often heard The County using:

> I think that God in creating man, somewhat overestimated his ability.
>
> Oscar Wilde

So I remained in the less threatening environment of the villa before I was to relieve Conway down on the outer perimeter.

But that morning did not turn out how we expected it to. Without warning, Father Joe's congregation and the rest of 'A' Company were called upon to withstand the greatest trial of their lives.

We were attacked.

CHAPTER TEN

The Hell of Jadotville

Date: September, 1961
Location: Jadotville, The Congo
Status: Active Service

IT WAS A HAIL OF bullets – an armed mercenary vehicle was heading straight for us, firing arbitrarily at anything in its way. The jeep came from the direction of the town and sped past us in the villas before heading straight towards the Purfina garage, blasting automatic rifles furiously with the randomness of a spray gun. Nobody knew where the bullets were landing but the shrieks from all around the cordon and the peppering bullet-thuds I could hear from around our sandbagged villa verandah suggested their aim was as indiscriminate as a frenzied rat-catcher's.

For a moment, I forgot everything in the confusion of bullets and shouting, my eyes darting round the villa looking for anything that could remind me of what I was supposed to do. If someone had asked me my name, I would not have been able to answer, my only human sense still working was my hearing; everything else was numbed by the piercing sound of screeching bullets. All around me everything was in disarray as if the mirror of my life had been smashed into a thousand splintered fragments. I was angry at myself for my own panicked reaction. We had been under siege for the last three days and I knew an attack could come at any time, but when it did, I didn't know what to do. Suddenly it all came back to me:

'I'm Pte Greene 809385! Grab my gun, my back-pack! And stop being such a fuckin eejit!'

It was John Monahan who first noticed the charging jeep and raised the alarm by firing shots and shouting at us all to take cover. Just a few seconds after, he burst through the villa door running towards the window, his gun thrust out in front of him, jabbing it forward and smashing the villa window to return fire. I instantly joined him next to the window as the armed jeep continued speeding up the road in the direction of the Purfina garage, with at least four mercenaries unloading their weapons indiscriminately at anything that was moving. They were headed for the daily Mass that was taking place, where the bulk of 'A' Company was assembled, including Dowler, Monahan and most of the officers. I knew they had brought their rifles to mass but like me they would never have expected to have been attacked without warning, although hopefully Sgt Monahan's warning shots may have just given them a fraction more time to take cover.

As the jeep got within 40 yards of the Purfina garage I could see the sparkle of gunfire emanating from within the garage itself, returning a peppering of bullets down the side of the jeep.

'They've been hit!' yelped a voice from the window next to ours.

One of the mercenaries suddenly clasped his shoulder as flesh and bone were sent splattering in all directions and he slumped downwards in the jeep, the other mercenaries busily tending to him while sporadically firing their small arms back at the Purfina. As the jeep began to drive away I could see some in 'A' Company running towards the road unleashing their FN rifles towards the jeep as the mercenaries sought to make their escape.

The first jeep was well out of range for us but suddenly another jeep started coming towards us from the direction of the Jadotville barricade. John Monahan kept firing from his vantage point of the villa window causing the second jeep to stop and turn back. Even if it made it past us in the villa it would surely have been a suicide mission to carry on towards the Purfina garage where most of 'A' Company was now prepared to repel another attack.

For a couple of unnerving minutes, the sound of angry bullets abated but it was an uneasy calm as we knew we were surrounded and there could easily be other points of attack at any moment. John Monahan knew there was no time to waste and shouted:

'Fill up any containers ye have and take yer forward defensive positions when I tell ya to!' as he continued to blast his rifle back towards the main barricade.

There were two other Privates in the villa, like me blundering about amid the upheaval, all of us ducked down, furiously filling any containers we had.

I picked up an old jug, my blue UN helmet, even some empty bully beef tins; anything that wouldn't leak and proceeded to fill them with water. The others started filling the bath and sinks as Monahan continued directing:

'Fill those buckets! Both fuckin taps!'

I couldn't fit both buckets in the sink so scooped whatever water my leaking hands could hold into the containers.

'Leave them taps running!' Monahan roared over, 'now, take up yer forward defensive position, I'm covering ya!'

Me and the two others immediately threw on our back-packs and rifles and scrambled towards the door.

The hail of bullets had stopped except for the odd blast being aimed back towards the town's barricade to where the second jeep of mercenaries had now taken cover. The first jeep had made its escape over hills to the south, but there was huge commotion around the Purfina garage with officers blaring out orders and soldiers running to their posts.

With one hand holding onto my helmet I ran towards my post beyond the anthill on the outer perimeter wishing I could just get through the first 100 yards or so, then maybe just the next 100. I must be out of range soon, I nervously calculated.

'Please God, don't let them shoot me!' I mumbled to myself as I desperately scampered over the undulating ground, which caused me to stumble at least three times, towards the safety of the bushes.

I could hear Conway's voice shouting out at me from within the dense shrubbery from where he had been on guard duty during the attack.

'Keep going Michael, I've got ye covered, ye've nearly made it!'

I jumped the final five yards, sliding on my stomach head-first into the brambles as half a mile behind me the commotion at Purfina was still being frantically sorted out. I knew I was safe here, hidden behind the ant-hill and the impenetrable camouflage of the bush.

'What the fuck is happening?' Conway called over.

I was still panting desperately 'I think they're erm,' I took another gulp of breath, 'I think they're commencing hostilities.' I finally managed to say using the only military terminology I could remember. 'Did yiz hear anything on the radio?'

'No fuck all!' Conway replied, 'Just looked up to see the armoured car speeding up the road firing guns and everyone diving for cover.'

'Aye,' I continued 'I think they must have known that we say mass at this time, so they tried to catch us off guard.'

'Was anyone hit?' Conway asked

'Must have been,' I presumed. 'There were so many bullets flying around, someone's bound to have been shot. And I know at least one of them mercenary feckers got hit as I saw his shoulder blown off.'

By now I had got my breath back and the major commotion back at the Purfina garage and around the villas had died down as most had reached their defensive posts.

In the distance I could see Dowler, John Monahan and about six others running, heads down towards our position, their guns and back-packs flapping loosely from either arm, as the machine gunners around the Purfina garage covered their run with random blasts in the direction of the Jadotville barricade.

As soon as they arrived, Monahan directed us to cover each area of ground that surrounded the outer perimeter.

'If anything moves out there, just feckin shoot it,' he said. 'And if it moves again, shoot it again.'

We continued to whisper loudly between ourselves about the sudden attack. Dowler said that he saw at least four men hit at mass, but he didn't know how severely.

'How about Pakie?' I asked, 'and Sweeney and the Tiger?'

'I don't know,' Dowler replied. 'The rest of us,' he continued, 'just fell to the ground and started firing back. We were half way through *The Lord is my Shepherd* when we heard this almighty crack of automatic rifles, from the direction of the barricade and the villas. We knew immediately they would be heading towards us. It's a good job we took our guns to mass or they'd have probably shot the lot of us.' Then with a glance up to the heavens he exclaimed: 'Thank you God!'

'So de ya still think Offaly will win the All-Ireland Sean?' I asked curtly.

I didn't receive a reply.

An hour or two went past with just the occasional sporadic pot-shot to and from the barricade on the main road leading into town but the atmosphere remained acutely tense; everyone wondering where the next major flare up would take place.

Suddenly a blast came from the bushes in front of us, it was a sniper.

Three of us opened fire into the bush, scattering the area with a shower of deadly bullets that nothing would have survived. We heard a stifled high-pitched scream that could only have been that of one of the Lumba boy soldiers followed by the resonant thump of a limp body falling from its vantage point.

We knew who we were up against, some of these boy soldiers were the most ruthless warriors in this Congo conflict, many brainwashed from boyhood to carry out pitiless murder and torture of their enemy that would have made an adult mind recoil in anguish. Encircling their enemy with sniper fire were the hallmarks of the notorious butcher, baker and candlestick maker gang before they finished off their enemy by hacking off body parts and mutilation.

There were another ten members of a support company who had joined 'A' Company for the assignment in Jadotville, bringing the number of men we had to 157. One of the engineers from the support company was a private called Bill Ready who was originally assigned as a driver but had ran out to the outer perimeter with John Monahan. He had been hit by the sniper's bullet. With the young perpetrator supposedly out of the way, we ran over to attend to Ready's injuries. He had been shot through his side but the same bullet had then travelled out through his stomach, then had re-entered through his inner thigh and out again through the back of his leg.

The blood was gushing out of him and he was writhing around in pain. I couldn't believe the utter devastation that a single bullet could cause. In the films at the Picture House, bullets always appeared to stop on entry like a resolute sandbag with death arriving within seconds but this bullet had passed through Ready like water, splattering human skin and blood everywhere. I could see that he hadn't been killed but he was very much in pain and he clearly was in desperate need of medical attention if he were to survive.

John Monahan immediately understood the danger and called over to us:

'Ok! Greene and Delayney, ye'll have to carry him back to Joe Clune back in the villas to get this treated.' It was typical of Monahan, no emotion, no overreaction, just another incident that required urgent attention.

'If two of ye carry him, one arm over each shoulder,' he continued, 'ye'll be able to run faster. But ye'll have to keep as low as possible; head over in the direction of the garage, the high ground will keep ye covered for the first 60 yards then turn towards the old outhouse in front of ye, its these 250 yards that are the most dangerous as ye'll be exposed to possible cross-fire. Once yer beyond this, ye'll be out of reach of enemy fire as our machine gunners can pick off any snipers that would be in range.

Then head down the couple of hundred yards straight to Clune's Villa requesting immediate medical assistance. I'll radio ahead.'

Without a moments hesitation Delayney and I arranged one of Ready's arms each over our shoulders and immediately began carrying him.

'Jaysus Ready, yer a ton weight,' noted Delayney after just ten yards. Ready wasn't able to respond, clearly in agony from his gunshot wound, but trying to take as much weight as he could on his other leg whilst stumbling along, almost losing consciousness. We staggered through the next 20 yards, repeatedly tripping over our own feet. As instructed we kept as low as possible but Ready and Delayney were both much taller than I was so the dead weight was almost falling down on top of me, like I was holding up a huge unwieldy bag of spuds and with Ready's long arms and legs making it even more cumbersome.

Although Delayney had joined the army at the same time as me and had gone through the same recruitment company, I hadn't really spoken to him much before, but ahead of us lay the perilous 250 yards of uphill open ground where we knew we had no fire cover.

'Lift his leg,' Delayney shouted over, 'we have to run fast!'

'Ya don't think I feckin know that already!' I responded, but it was no time to bicker like worried parents as Ready's ever fainter coughs reminded us he was getting weaker and was losing consciousness.

Our pace suddenly quickened to the point that Ready was being dragged between stumbles, desperate to reach the apparent refuge of the wooden outhouse. We were only about 40 yards from perceived safety when we heard another bullet whistling past about six inches from my chest and just an inch or two over Ready's head. It was so close that we could hear the revolutions of the bullet-casing zipping through the air.

'Another feckin sniper!' I shouted as a shower of bullets from the outer perimeter sprayed the dense shrubbery from where the sniper's shots originated.

We carried on desperately pulling Ready beyond the outhouse walls, resting him against a pillar as we gasped frantically to catch our breath. We couldn't be sure we were out of enemy range and we knew we had no time to lose, so within a couple of short nervous breaths we again picked up Ready by the arms and legs for the final few hundred yards before the villas. We were running sideways whilst trying to keep Ready's head from slumping back into a flaccid unconsciousness. The final stretch was slightly downhill making the task easier but both Delayney and I continued to stumble over Ready's flopping limbs, still bickering at each other as to who was doing the most work.

'Will ya lift him up!' I roared over at Delayney, 'I can't feckin carry him on my own!'

'And what in Jaysus' name de ya think I'm doin?' yelled an equally exhausted and frightened Delayney.

I could see PJ Sweeney manning the machine gun on the inner cordon and, on seeing us struggling with Ready's sagging body, he let loose a tirade of cover fire towards the bushes behind us. We had nearly made it. Surely, I thought, an enemy sniper wouldn't' dare give away his lair by firing a long-range shot at us now?

We must have dragged Ready's failing body the final twenty yards to the villa where the medical officer Clune had the door open and his surgery equipment ready for our arrival.

'Sgt Monahan radioed me ahead,' Clune pointed out as he helped lift Ready's body through the doorway. 'He looks in a bad way alright. We'll have to move him over to the Purfina garage after I've stopped the blood.'

My heart sank, I didn't have the strength or energy to carry him another 300 yards, but this was no time for self pity.

'Yes Sir!' I shouted while still panting for breath.

'No, I'll get Corporal Lucey to drive him over there in a jeep,' Clune noted, whilst bandaging Ready's middle, 'we need to get him there immediately.'

I almost collapsed in relief and exhaustion although keenly aware that I had to make it back to my post on the outer perimeter.

'We'll just carry him into the back of the jeep!' Clune ordered 'so, press down these swabs against his wounds.'

'Yes Sir!' Delayney and I again immediately answered.

This time we were helped by two other privates who were posted around Clune's villa, allowing us to share the burden of Ready's heavy frame.

One of the privates was called Kevin Knightly. He held Ready under both arms, taking the bulk of the weight as he walked backwards towards the waiting jeep. The three of us lifted whatever we could to keep Ready off the ground; a leg, an arching back whilst pressing down bloodied bandages.

'We'll take him from here now lads,' noted Knightly, as Ready was bundled into the back of Corporal Lucey's jeep which immediately sped away in the direction of the Purfina garage.

Delayney and I then took the same route back as the one we came, knowing we could be lined-up in the cross-hairs of an eager sniper as we sprinted over the exposed ground til we first reached the outhouse, a chance to catch a moment's breath. Just a couple of hundred yards more til the safety of the bush; crouching down, our heads dipped as low as our knees. Perhaps we'll make it back after all, I thought, my heart still palpitating until finally we once more had the cover of an anthill and bushes.

'Good job lads!' John Monahan directed over to us, 'lets just hope he's alright now.'

I retrieved my back-pack and started gulping from my water flask.

'Take it easy on the water Greene,' Monahan noted. 'They've turned off our water supplies, so each flask now has to last ye 24 hours at least.'

'Aye Sarge!' I responded professionally in Monahan's direction. No-one had to tell me what this meant with no water in the savage heat of The Congo. 'We're really in the shit now,' I muttered to myself.

We stayed on the outer perimeter for a few more hours, allowing the bush to absorb the worst of the midday sun, but the sporadic gunfire on the other side of the Purfina garage, less than a mile away from us continued in ten minute spurts throughout. The snipers around us must have sought a better vantage point or be lying low as the sound of crickets began their rhythmic chatter as the late afternoon was approaching and the deluge of tsetse fly descended once more.

With batteries running low on my transistor radio, I would only turn it on for the 20 minute 1800 hours news from radio Brazzaville to hear if the assault on us would be mentioned, and what the world might be doing about it. As I suspected, the attack had indeed been reported but my jaw nearly dropped open when I heard about the details:

> Good evening, this is radio Brazzaville with the
> news at 6 o'clock on Wednesday 13th September

1961. At dawn this morning, the UN launched an attack to round up foreign agitators to end the Katangan succession. The operation was called Operation *Morthor* and once again it is being reported that the mission did not have authorisation from the UN Assembly or the Secretary General Dag Hammarskjöld. Connor Cruise O'Brien has called the operation a success and that the 14-month Katangan succession is at an end. There was sporadic gunfire in Elizabethville today and casualties have been reported on both sides but the UN have regained control of the Post Office and surrounding buildings. O'Brien has again called on Moise Tshombie to surrender but in response Tshombie has declared that there will be no surrender and has called on Katangans to rise up and fight for their freedoms, although some have reported that he has flown out of the country.

I presumed that the report must have been in some way false about the UN initiating the offensive although I knew that Radio Brazzaville was not subject to the same propaganda pressure as those in The Congo, Rhodesia or South Africa. But it didn't make sense, why would the UN commanders back in Elizabethville, many of them Irish, launch an operation like *Morthor* when we were surrounded by mercenaries and gendarmerie; and then not even tell us? The broadcast continued:

In retaliation to Operation *Morthor* we have been given reports that the UN company that had been under siege for the last three days in the town of Jadotville was attacked by Katangan succession forces and that there have been many casualties on both sides following gun battles that have raged throughout the day. The Irish 35th 'A' Company of the UN is believed to be surrounded but holding out in an area south of the town. The foreign ministers of the US, France and Britain will hold a conference tomorrow to discuss the escalating crisis and have called on the USSR for restraint. Dag Hammarskjöld is believed to be flying into Leopoldville this evening to negotiate a peace agreement.

Others had heard the news broadcast as well, and some presumed that our officers must have been told that Operation *Morthor* was taking place. But Dowler was sure they couldn't have known:

'Jaysus,' he said. 'Some of them were standing next to me at mass this morning. Operation *Morthor* started at dawn two hours before, if they had known they wouldn't have been standing around with rosary beads waiting and praying not to get shot at.'

A little while later John Monahan confirmed it to us.

'We had no idea what they were planning back in Elizabethville lads,' whilst shaking his head in apparent disbelief.

The long Swahili night was approaching and Monahan warned us not to have any lights visible including those from cigarettes and transistor radios.

'It'll give yer position away,' he said. 'Stay vigilant and awake at all times, we are now in a war situation under war footings.'

It was a numbing realisation of our predicament. The last time Irish troops were placed under war footings in military law was during World War Two where we knew we could be shot for falling asleep on duty.

Dowler recounted a story back in 1943 when a guard in Athlone was discovered to be asleep manning the front gates to costume barracks. He was found by an officer and executed the next morning by firing squad. I didn't know if Dowler was telling an exaggerated tale but it unnerved me enough not to even consider a quick nap.

I had sat in the bushes that lined the outer perimeter of 'A' Company's defence all day since carrying Ready's injured body back to the villas. Daylight was beginning to ebb away and I knew it would be my last chance, before pitch darkness descended, to read my mother's letter that I had been given back in Elizabethville ten days beforehand. Just the quality of the Basildon Bond paper, which she would have had to save up to buy, suggested her growing anxiety at the escalating conflict. Back in Ireland I would have shrugged most of it off as uninteresting, but in the deadly situation we were now in, I longed for anything comforting. I had been stuck in an African bush for the last 12 hours and this was the only source of comfort available.

Dear Mickey

I hope you are well and looking after yourself over in The Congo. Everyone here at home is well, enjoying the long summer evenings. The farmers have all had a good year, we've had good weather to draw turf and for the hay.

The letter was eight pages long, telling me everything from the weather to what Mrs Flannigan had told her in the grocer's. She also told me that the CIE strike had finally ended and that my brothers Kevin and Franco along with the Dolly Dolan had set off for London to make their fortune. The last page of her letter read:

All the other boys still go to the Picture House on a Sunday evening. Little Phillip was telling me he saw the Guns of Navarone last week and came out telling everyone that it was just like his big brother Mickey in The Congo – he is very proud of you, as are we all.

We are also busy making plans to move over to London when you come home, probably moving to Kennington near Kitty and the twins. Your father thinks there is lots of work on London Transport. He has found someone to take in your dog Nasser, a farmer on the Granard Road, a good home with plenty of room for him to run around.

We've all been reading in the newspapers that the situation is getting more serious over there in The Congo and that the UN is being dragged into the troubles. Please don't get involved Mickey, you only have 2 months left of your tour of duty and we are all worried about you.

Remember you're not even old enough to be in the army yet and that all the others are older and bigger than you. Anyway, I know you're a good boy and will keep yourself safe.

Good Bye and God Bless

Mum, Dad and Philip

'But mam we're trapped,' I whispered softly as tears began to drop down off my face, smudging the ink on my treasured letter. I began to fold it away wondering if it would be for the last time. If she didn't already know, she would soon get to hear about our situation, and I could imagine her crying by the mantelpiece in front of our open hearth and pleading to my helpless father to somehow get me home. Tears continued to drip down my face as I knew that my mother would be hurting more than anyone, her mind equally trapped in a terrifying emotional siege of visualised danger.

No-one loved me like my mother and I recalled The County once said to me that:

> Whatever else is unsure in this stinking
> dunghill of a world, a mother's love is not.
>
> James Joyce,
> A Portrait of the Artist as a Young Man (1916)

'Oh mam, what have I done?' I whispered, 'I'm so sorry.'

As all of us in 'A' Company knew, there was no way out of Jadotville for us and no end of torment for our loved ones back in Ireland. We couldn't fight our way out because we were so heavily outnumbered with inferior arms and we couldn't give up because the chances of surviving a vengeful mercenary or gendarmerie prison were too remote. If it was 4 commando and Mike Hoare we were fighting against then we stood little chance as their reputations suggested they would more than likely have all of us executed. The other rumour that was circulating through 'A' Company was that the same mercenary who had shot Patrice Lumumba was directing another commando unit in Jadotville* and would have no hesitation in shooting what he regarded as pro-Lumumbaist UN soldiers. Our only real hope of getting out of this alive lay in a political solution where the old colonial-supporting

* *Heroes of Jadotville: The Soldier's Story* xvii

nations of Britain, France and Belgium could stop their covert support of an independent Katanga and pressurise Tshombie to stop the succession. Our only other hope it seemed was to defend ourselves until our promised re-enforcements and re-supplies arrived.

The Swahili sunset had drawn in quickly and we all sat at our posts in the bushes along the outer perimeter as the chill of night began to envelop us. We couldn't hear a sound, just the odd rustle of wind blowing through the bushes; but enough to keep us nervously on edge. It was a pitch-dark clear sky but that evening emerging in the distance I could hear the distinctive beat of the Lumba tribe's booming drums, presumably carrying out one of their ritual tribal dances. Against the moonlit blackness of the night-sky, I could see the flickering silhouettes of contorted tribal warriors projecting an oversized ghoulish dance with spear-like instruments around an open fire, or 'wakha-wakha' in Swahili, as the distant noise built up a more noticeable intensity.

'I presume that it's just a custom, almost like a celeidh dance back home,' I whispered loudly over to Conway who was posted just a few yards away. 'Except that them Lumba may be sacrificing a few hens or goats to keep their ju-ju man happy.'

Conway didn't say anything and we continued to sit there in the bushes listening to the pounding thumps of the beating drums. Dowler had also heard the pulsating throbs echoing and displayed against the dark night sky, but had reached a much more menacing conclusion as to what their rhythm was meant to indicate:

'That's a feckin war dance!' he whispered, 'them Lumba must be preparing some kind of attack.' I gulped as Dowler continued with his ominous assessment: 'Aye they're probably pumping themselves through with maji and smoking feckin pot as we speak,' noted Dowler, 'and this is not yer average horny goat weed. If they're smoking that dhagga shite they'll be so stoned, they wont even be able to feel an anti-tank gun if we blew it straight through them.'

He was interrupted by another exchange of gunfire from beyond the Purfina garage which now seemed to flare up every 15 minutes, almost as if to remind us that their bombardment would be continuous and we would be getting no respite that night.

'I think I'd rather we were attacked by Muke's gendarmes or the mercenaries,' I commented back through the bushes, 'at least they don't want to eat ya for breakfast when yer dead.'

'Wouldn't we all,' Dowler responded, 'but ours is not to reason why or how!'

I could see John Monahan in the distance moving quietly between posts on the outer perimeter. When he finally reached me, he had some new orders that we were making a pullback from our frontline at 2200 hours.

'We're retreating back to the inner perimeter Michael,' he said, 'we're too exposed out here and we want to consolidate our position around HQ.'

'Aye Sarge,' I responded.

'I'll send a message along the line when we are about to move so keep an eye out for it,' he continued. 'Take off all buckles, buttons or anything else that shines and put them out of sight in yer back pack. If there are snipers out there in the bush and they see something shining or flickering in the darkness, they'll just shoot at it. D'yiz understand?'

'Aye Sarge, will do.' I replied.

'When ye get to the inner cordon, we have to dig slit trenches. They'll be over there, beyond those small mounds,' noted Monahan pointing back towards an area in front of the Purfina garage. 'They'll be dug on rising slopes which will provide cover til ye have them ready. We'll show ye where to dig and will give ye the shovels when ye get there.'

As Monahan moved on, I immediately took off every buckle and dirtied the front of my boots with soil, stopping momentarily to contemplate as I noticed the dried blood from Ready's gunshot wounds. I didn't know whether Ready, nor if any of the others who had been shot at mass had survived, just that I needed to take every precaution and follow John Monahan's advice to keep myself alive.

The order came down the line as expected at 2200. Like many of the others on the outer perimeter I had taken off my shirt as there were too many buttons that could have potentially glistened to give away my position. We immediately set off from the safety of the bushes, crouched down and running as fast as we could over the open ground, stumbling slightly in the tufts of grass that we were unable to see in the dead of night. Some ran in a direct line but I tried to follow the same route I had earlier in the day when carrying Ready where I knew there was relative safety once I reached the outhouse. A biting cold breeze whipped around my naked torso as I recognised the dim outline of the path I had memorised, allowing myself to relax a little as I began the last 200 yard stretch down towards the villas.

We began digging straight away; furiously thrusting the short handled shovels into the rock solid ground that shook so hard in contact with the rich Katangan soil that it reverberated back up through our freezing bodies. There were three of us digging our trench: myself, Dowler and Conway and we now had no cover from bushes or shrubs, so a slit trench would be our only chance of cover on the inner perimeter. We could still hear bursts of gunfire on the other side of the Purfina garage, but the crackle of guns would light up the night sky for about ten seconds allowing us enough time to see what we were doing. After two hours of furious digging, our efforts had amounted to a trench of about six feet long but with a depth of only six inches. Just as John Monahan had described to us, we were protected by the rising mound of ground in front and Sweeney's machine gun station was ready to blast at anything that moved in the distant bushes.

'I hope these aren't our graves we're digging Sean,' I noted in the pitch darkness.

'Well if they're not, ye'll be able to get yerself a grand job over in London as a grave-digger,' replied a breathless Dowler.

It was an hour or so after midnight and the bitterly cold dampness of the descending dew leeched into our stiffening bones but we carried on desperately pounding the shovels as our hands became more bruised and blistered. I tried to make light of our predicament

'Is that yer ribs I can hear rattling Sean?' I asked.

'No they're my teeth, my ribs are frozen solid!' replied Dowler

I laughed and coughed at the same time: 'Feckin hell Sean, how the fuck did we end up here?'

'Aye if we'd stayed back in Ireland,' Dowler replied 'I would be dreaming of waking up in a few hours time in my warm bed, making myself two boiled eggs and three slices of soda bread dripping with butter, and all washed down with a cup of tay with two big spoonfuls of sugar.'

'What instead of a lovely dog biscuit?' I asked sarcastically, 'Jaysus Sean, I'd rather eat stones!' It was a moment of humour, allowing my face to enjoy a rare smile that allowed a little bit of warmth to feed my frosting body. But the indulgence of comedy was short-lived, as another blaze of gunfire flared around us. The sound of incoming bullets was getting noticeably louder which could mean only one thing, the mercenaries, tribesmen and gendarmes were getting closer, but this time the shots were coming from our side of the cordon, near the outer perimeter where only a few hours beforehand we had been bedded down in the dense shrubbery.

'We'll have to open fire.' Dowler immediately decided, and then the three of us crawled like alligators up the raised ground in front of the trench, and placed our FN rifles atop the highest point.

'On three we open fire!' instructed Dowler 'then get back down this mound as quick as ye can before them feckers let their guns loose on us! One!....Two!....Three!

Our guns blazed for about four seconds, lighting up our faces like lanterns before we scurried backwards down the slope towards the trench. The outer perimeter, where we suspected the gendarmes to be hiding, was out of range for our FN rifles, bringing us a little comfort as it meant we would also be out of range for them. From the shrubbery a few shots peppered back towards our position immediately initiating a constant barrage from our machine gunners situated about 30 yards to the right of us. Despite the darkness, both sides had achieved setting up their new lines of defence, the exchange of gunfire providing the best clue yet of each others whereabouts. From then on, the expanse of rugged ground in front of us, just out of range for both sides, would be regarded as no-man's land.

With dawn just a few hours away we knew we had to carry on digging the trench as the morning sun would expose our positions to the prying field glasses of mercenary commanders and longer range mortar bombing. Each thrust of the shovels continued to yield just a few measly crumbs of soil as we angrily scratched at anything we could to loosen the rock-hard earth.

As the awakening sun began to emerge over the Eastern hills, the chill of dew on our tattered clothes began to warm. Morning had arrived and we had dug about three foot down, only enough room for us to crouch down uncomfortably in the slit trench. We needed at least another two feet, to keep out of sight and to protect us from cross-fire as the enemy continued their offensive against us.

With the higher ground just in front of the trench, we continued digging on our knees but I calculated I had enough cover to stretch my legs for a moment to relieve the pressure on my overburdened joints. It was a decision that nearly cost me my life.

I suddenly heard an overwhelming crunching sound that echoed for a few startled seconds and I immediately fell to the ground, as the machine guns behind us offloaded another barrage into no-man's land. I was sure I had been hit and began shaking uncontrollably as my blue UN helmet was sent flying off behind me.

'I've been hit!' I yelped over to Dowler and Conway as I padded my head desperately in search of the bloody gushing wound I anticipated.

Dowler bounced over to inspect my head.

'I can't see any blood Michael!' he immediately responded 'a few scratches alright. How many fingers am I holding up?'

'Two!' I blurted out.

Dowler seemed to relax a little. 'Yer alright Michael, I can't see anything wrong with ya.'

The smell of cordite that lingered in the air convinced me there was a bullet out there that may not have had my name on it, but certainly knew my initials. I bent backwards to retrieve my helmet, the peak of which had been smashed open with a four inch fracture, leaving a crack down the front of my once treasured 'casques bleus', dividing the letters U and N.

'Look at this!' I shouted back at Dowler as I sought to verify my claims, but he had returned to the other side of the trench to continue digging.

'Look will ya!' I continued ranting, 'they've blown the feckin front of my helmet away!'

'It's probably just shrapnel!' responded an unconvinced Dowler, equally exhausted after a sleepless night of digging, 'but keep yer feckin head down in future, rather than standing up like a feckin meerkat, or we'll be writing deeply sorry letters back home to yer poor old mother!'

'Jaysus Sean!' I said almost exasperated, 'I nearly died!'

'Ye'll feckin die when we allow ya to die! Is that clear?' he suddenly burst out. 'Not feckin before, and certainly not until we're out of this fuckin mess! D'yiz hear me?'

'Aye Sean! I replied somewhat taken aback, 'I hear ya.'

'Now pick up that feckin shovel!' he commanded, 'stay on yer feckin knees, carry on feckin digging and stop asking me feckin stupid questions!'

It was that moment of stark reality that shook me into the realisation that from now on I could have no fear. If I died; then so be it. If I lived; then likewise so be it, but right now I was just another wide-eyed trapped animal trying to fight and survive in this most precarious and brutal game of military warfare, although what we were fighting for I still had no idea.

We had been under siege for the last four days and in a raging gun battle for the last 24 hours, running for our lives, carrying the injured, shooting indiscriminately into bushes with the threat of snipers firing back impeding our every movement. Some would have described it as being at the gates of Hell itself and many in 'A' Company had already been shot. We didn't know yet if they had died or would pull through but it was that bullet which had passed within an inch of my youthful brow that had crushed any idealism I once had.

I had heard about near-death experiences back home, and how some who survived had described their perceptions of everything around them as being crystal clear, completely impenetrable and sharply focused from then on. Every sensory experience they explained was heightened as they levitated beyond their mortal anxieties to enter a trance-like feeling of being re-incarnated into a new body. I wondered if this was happening to me as everything around me appeared serene but bursting with vibrancy: much bigger, louder, almost lucid and all displayed in brilliant colours. It was how I remembered the childhood sensation of imagining life in an invisible body, observing the mad pantomime of the world of grown-ups under a cloak of concealment. That single bullet had nearly deprived me of all my dreams, and my family of a son, an uncle and a brother, I rationalised. But instead of cowering or running for cover as I had done when carrying Ready through no-man's land, I suddenly felt more alive than I had ever felt before, adrenalin pumping through every inch of my body in the realisation that the men around me needed my support at every moment and I needed theirs if we were to stay alive. There could be no more harking back with boyhood reverie to my comfortable home in Ireland and grand evenings watching films about the Wild West at the Picture House. This was a real war that my intently focused eyes and consciousness were furiously filming. It was the men in 'A' Company who were my closest family now; and if even just one of these forsaken band-of-brothers should perish in this god-forsaken jungle, a little bit of all of us would die with him.

This wasn't me that was going mad, I decided, it was the world and its so-called leaders. From now on there could no longer be any peripheral distractions that could divert my attention, I had to remain calm and focused on surviving; all that mattered was in front of me in the here and now; as if my concerns about the past and future suddenly vanished.

I knew that it was not in Dowler's character to rebuke me; in peacetime he would no doubt have reacted differently; a happy-go-lucky shrug of his shoulders or a cheeky tap on his nose that indicated he had everything under control. War is not the kind of situation where normal humans expect to find themselves thrust into. This was no place for 'a decent sort of fella' like Dowler who, under normal circumstances, would do anything for anyone. It was also no place for someone like me, an underage impostor who didn't even like guns. Neither Dowler nor I were the kind to panic or make a fuss, but war brings out those parts of our nature that we never intend the outside world to see, exposing our fears and failings in the most humiliating and dangerous arena.

John Monahan arrived in the trench a few moments later:

'Are yiz alright lads?' he asked 'I saw a few bullets whistling past here, did any of yiz get hit?'

'No Sarge,' I replied deliberately before Dowler and Conway had a chance, 'except maybe a few bits of shrapnel.' I showed him the peak of my helmet to clarify what I meant.

'Fuckin hell!' he responded, 'that's a bit too close. Ye'll have to stay down for a couple of hours til any remaining snipers have been flushed out. There may still be a few out there who crept up during the night, but they can't stay low for long as they've no cover. So, just sit here for a while til I tell ya to start digging again. This trench isn't deep enough yet to provide ye with sufficient cover.'

'Aye Sarge,' we all responded as Monahan crawled away to check on others in the platoon, typically unconcerned about his own life and the possibility of remaining snipers.

'So, we might as well just sit back and enjoy the fine weather!' Dowler quipped, seemingly trying to break the frosty atmosphere of our previous exchange.

'Aye, this is what we call back home a "biblical" day, Sean.' I replied.

The morning sun was gradually maturing to unleash its awesome power as if God himself was shining a celestial beam over this little pocket of strife in Africa. More immediately we knew the blazing sunlight would turn our trench into a dry and fearsome furnace for at least five hours. We still had two days' supply of water left, surely enough to last us until we were re-supplied from Elizabethville, which we were expecting imminently. We mixed a little of the water with freshly dug soil and smeared it over our exposed skin providing our only means of protection from the sun's blistering rays, then sat back wearily in the trench.

As ordered, I hunkered down and watched John Monahan and CS Prendergast running from trench to trench, organising and co-ordinating our defence. They could have ordered us, the expendable PBI (Poor Bloody

Infantry), over the top, but instead risked their own lives at every moment: totally in command of the situation, completely professional and utterly fearless.

'They must be some brave old lions themselves,' I considered to myself.

I could also see many familiar faces in distant trenches and noticed The Tiger, Pakie Monahan, PJ Sweeney, Danny Hegarty and others busily going about their duties setting up defences and manning defensive posts along the circular inner cordon. It struck me that they were all working away with the calmness and efficiency of people who had just emerged on the other side of their own near death experience. Although, we had all come from very different pasts, many with young families of their own, for the time being at least, none of us could afford to lament about happier times; with such imminent danger lying all around us. So despite having had no sleep, my body and mind felt the exhilaration of being more awake than it had ever done before, even if none of us could have foreseen that we would remain under fire and vividly awake for another three nights or a further 70 hours of continuous combat.

A little while later Dowler called over:

'What are they saying on the radio, Michael?'

'They're saying that the UN operation has been a success although Tshombie has refused to surrender Sean,' I replied.

'Well, while they're out celebrating, I hope they remember to send us a few more dog biscuits,' noted an increasingly frustrated Dowler, 'because this doesn't feel like much of a success from where I'm sitting.'

Within the trench that we had been digging, the earth was a bit cooler, but the midday sun could not be avoided and for the next few hours, the sun's rays beat down relentlessly from directly overhead. Anything metal including our FN rifles was too hot to touch with naked flesh and even the triggers could only be handled through a protective rag. My smashed UN helmet provided a little shade at first but soon began to feel as if it were melting on my head.

Dowler joked that you could fry an egg on it – if we hadn't run out of eggs.

'We'll have to go buy ourselves some new hens!' he joked, 'we'd be able to have them fried boiled or scrambled out here.'

I laughed again as sweat streamed excessively down the sides of my face, the acidity of which stinging my eyes but providing my parched lips with a little moisture as my body sought to replenish its lost salt from wherever it could.

Every object around me was boiling as the unremitting heat set about devouring everything, and we could feel our arms and faces being consumed by burgeoning blisters. What little food we had left would surely perish soon, so I scooped out a four inch cubby hole in the side of the trench to hide away my remaining dog biscuits.

It seemed inconceivable in this heat that my bladder was telling me that it needed to have a piss; surely I couldn't afford to lose any more body fluid. But the call of nature doesn't always listen to logic, so rather than letting such valuable fluid evaporate on the trench floor I started to soak my vest in precious moisture.

'I read this somewhere in one of the World War One books,' I called over to Dowler and Conway as I unfolded the vest to ensure it all got covered, 'it helps to keep the body temperature cooler.'

'Well, just as long as ya don't go shitting yerself!' Dowler responded.

But I was long past worrying what people might say; the piss-soaked vest provided a cooling effect on my whole body, refreshing and energising, which I also used to pad down my scalding face and arms.

'So, did that work then Michael?' Dowler and Conway questioned curiously.

'Would ye believe me if I told ye that it felt better than a night with Brigitte Bardot?' I immediately responded, as the piss-soaked vest clang like a wet curtain onto my chest and back. I knew it wouldn't be long before they too would be enjoying the experience.

Within a minute the gunfire had started again and we clambered up the mound to fire back, demarking a territory that rational men understand no-one should enter. But yesterday's no-man's land had already become today's cemetery and I could count at least 15 lifeless bodies strewn across the ground in various prostrate positions, most of whom having advanced during the night in the mistaken belief that they had the cover of darkness to protect them. Some lay strewn around with gaping mouths and staring eyes where death had been delivered instantly to the head. Others were clenching their ruptured guts that spewed between their hands as death had slowly consumed them; the whisky and blood that had poured from their mouths now lying congealed on the ground around them. I could distinguish some of our fallen enemies by their attire; a couple of older and probably drunken mercenaries with their dishevelled clothing lay close to one another. One had forgotten to tie the laces of his veoldskin boots, his open shirt buttons probably glistening in the moonlight that caused him to be cut down as an easy target. I wondered whether the other mercenary lying close to him with one arm reaching out, had been trying to save him. There were other clusters of bodies; groups of two or three uniformed gendarmerie and many young Lumba warriors who normally wore shorts and a t-shirt but had dressed according to their ancient tribal custom for battle wearing the hides of the fiercest jungle animals. Some were still adorning their grand headdresses as they lay lifeless underneath their leopard and tiger pelts scattered between the rigor mortised carcasses of smaller terrain animals that had been caught in the cross-fire or been used as target practice during the night.

There was no time for pity or remorse, regardless of how young or old our adversaries were, they had caged us in and been trying to kill us. If they hadn't been stopped, we would be the dead, nameless and quickly forgotten soldiers lying dead in that barren plateau of land on the outskirts of Jadotville.

As ordered we offloaded a series of blasts of our FN rifles towards the bushes and scurried quickly back to the cover of the trench. We thought if we kept low we would be safe but with the last round of fire we had clearly given away our position too easily. Within a minute, a massive blast erupted, and a mound of ground to the right of us was sent cascading into the air as a mortar bomb crashed down within 12 feet of our trench. It arrived with a menacing hiss-like moan before unleashing a thunderous vibration that reverberated through the earth around us. We ducked down as debris rained down, clattering on our helmets, but more worryingly the juddering ground made every one of our limbs and facial features quiver with imminent rupture. I could feel the pressure in my eyes almost bursting, and I checked nervously that my fingers and my ears were still attached, not to mention that my bollocks hadn't been blown off. If we were any closer or had been outside of the trench, we would no doubt have been decapitated. Even without the instruction of John Monahan we knew we had to start digging deeper to make the trench more secure, again furiously scraping at crumbs of loose baking hot red soil for the cherished protection that lay deeper in Mother Earth.

Within a minute, another mortar-bomb had smashed down, this time a little further away but with the same shuddering blast that caused a second shower of earth to scatter all around us. Almost before the debris had time to settle, both Prendergast and John Monahan appeared even though there was barely enough room to fit two more men in the trench.

What the fuck were they doing here? I thought to myself. Did they not know or care about the power of these bombs? It seemed they didn't.

'Stay low lads!' shouted Prendergast as he and Monahan began directing with their arms towards our machine gunners and defence posts before a tirade of gunfire and mortars were returned towards our enemy on the outer perimeter. To better gauge their success, they then immediately ran towards another nearby trench.

'And shoot straight lads!' ordered John Monahan as he was heading off, 'we have them now!'

They must be invincible, I thought to myself, as the bombardment continued all around them. Conway too, immediately clambered up the mound to return fire:

'C'mon on then yiz bastards!' he roared as he offloaded his FN rifle, inspiring myself and Dowler to do the same. It didn't matter about giving away our positions; the only way to die was to die fighting, just as John Monahan and Prendergast were prepared to do.

The sudden burst of activity caused a commotion in the bushes and within seconds, small clusters of tribal warriors launched a charge into no-man's land towards us, whilst yelling and hollering like young Tarzans. They were probably high on dhagga or maji and been told that our bullets would evaporate like water when it came into contact with their immortal bodies. I readied myself to shoot as they sprinted over the open ground running directly towards us.

'I don't want to do this, but I have to protect my brothers' I told myself as my finger anxiously rested on the scalding trigger, 'and those that I fight I do not hate'* I muttered imagining what The County may have said in the same situation. But I did hate them, not only for trying to kill us but for everything they were fighting for: colonial white rule, greed, money and power. And besides, I knew that if I didn't shoot them, there was no other way to stop them killing us.

The Lumba charge had only covered about 40 yards before their advance was abruptly cut short by a burst of machine gun fire from beside us, the running warriors collapsing like dominoes until they too lay prostrate in the open burial ground in the wasted patch of earth we called no-man's land.

On seeing his tribal fellows cut down, I could see a young Lumba warrior trying to retreat back to the bushes. With his back to us, I could make out the awesome sight of a large black-mane, like I had read about the famous Katanga lions, something I thought I would never see in Africa. The glistening big-cat tresses, that were once so imperious in these primeval forests made the limbs on which it hung look even thinner, like those of a young boy. It was as close as I would get to ever seeing one

---

* Quoted from *An Irish Airman Foresees His Death* William Butler Yeats, 1919

of these magnificent creatures in real life but within a couple of seconds the spindly legs of the young Katangan lion had crumpled underneath him like matchsticks, peppered by machine-gun bullets, his human arms flailing in his last gasp of life.

I immediately flipped over on my back, breathless and nauseous. I wanted to avoid watching the great writhing lion and all its human potential being slain in front of me, but could still hear the screams of the other fallen casualties scattered throughout no-man's land, wailing like ghostly banshees in the early afternoon sunshine. The cries of those dying an audible death in front of us, was suddenly too much for me to stomach and before my hand was able to reach my mouth I was vomiting uncontrollably as I slid back to take cover in the trench. That lion was probably just another underage adventure seeker like myself I pondered as I retched another impulsive vomit over the ground around me. I wasn't the only one whose stomach hadn't been designed to withstand such appalling scenes. I had seen Dowler vomiting the same way just an hour or so before, so like he had done, I just wiped my mouth, said nothing and crawled back up the mound while still gagging back another mouthful of puke. There was no time for sympathy or to be off-colour, I just had to continue fighting.

Then another lull in gunfire, but a kind of deathly calm where the ghoulish yells become even more audible as the grim reaper makes his final selection. Dowler, Conway and I remained up on the mound for a few more moments watching out for the faintest movement from the distant bushes but none came as even the native birdlife in the distant bushes seemingly froze in fear.

'I didn't get a chance to ask Prendergast or Monahan again whether the re-enforcements or re-supplies were on there way,' noted Dowler as we all returned back to the trench in the lull to continue digging.

'Jaysus Sean,' I replied, 'I think we have more chance of seeing the venerable Dr Livingstone.'

'Aye!' Dowler scoffed, 'and no-one except Henry Morton Stanley has seen him for the last 80 years.'

We had to keep talking about inane subjects. Just like our stomachs, the human mind would not be able to deal with pondering about what we had seen in no-man's land, let alone the reality of our predicament.

'I can see now why they called Stanley the breaker of rocks' I pointed out, 'this feckin ground seems to be made up of solid stone.'

'Aye, and all the men that were killed breaking out a railway line for him,' replied Dowler 'and now here's us trying to break out the same ground with people trying to kill us.'

As my piss-soaked vest began to dry out, the temperature in the trench again became unbearably hot, too scorching and energy sapping for any vigorous digging. Our pace slowed until we could barely labour our shovels into the rock-hard soil.

In the distance we could begin to hear the familiar sound of an aircraft slowly getting louder as it flew towards us. We all stopped digging, wondering whether this was our longed for supplies or re-enforcements, but didn't want to risk cheering in case we were being let down again. Still closer it flew as the sound became even more familiar until Dowler suddenly erupted:

'It's the feckin Fouga, get yer heads down!'

We immediately ducked low in the trench as the distinctive buzz of the Fouga got within 500 yards and just a couple of seconds later was unloading strafing machine gun fire from under each wing. The bullets created a corridor of flying earth within 30 feet of our trench that was beating a path directly towards the Purfina garage. It was the very same Fouga Magister jet that had watched us so closely arriving on the road to Jadotville ten days beforehand, barely 50 feet above the ground, menacingly tilting its wings as its deathly buzzing engines focused on its target and took it straight over our heads.

Many of those in nearby trenches fired their FN rifles back towards the plane which was more like firing pea-shooters at a flying tank. Our trusted FN rifle was invaluable on the ground but it certainly was not an anti-aircraft gun. However, a few bullets scraped the plane's silver paintwork, not enough to bring it down but maybe enough to let its mercenary pilot know that although we were sitting ducks, we were armed, and all we needed was one lucky bullet.

I had only seen machine gun strafing from a jet once before in Hitchcock's *North by Northwest* when Cary Grant is repeatedly chased by a crop-duster biplane 'where there ain't no crops,' and as the Fouga buzzed away into the horizon I knew it would be back. It was barely a mile away when it started its turn, with wings pointed out like a horizontal angel banking round a sharp bend, revving its engines as it gained speed and started heading back towards us. This time myself, Dowler and Conway were also ready to open fire although it seemed to be remaining higher in its approach, probably because of the unexpected shots it took on its last passage.

'A little bit closer,' muttered Conway, 'and a little bit lower and I'll get ye right between the feckin eyes!'

Conway wasn't the only one who was determined to shoot it down. Just 50 yards in front of us, a private by the name of Paddy Gilday was standing atop his trench with a Gustav semi-automatic gun lodged in his hip, with one hand over the trigger and the other on the barrel. He was yelling at the mercenary pilot:

'Right ya feckin bastard! Lets see what ye've got!' beckoning the plane to head towards him and he began firing straight at the oncoming Fouga, with the force of unloading his magazines while standing up making him stagger and lose his balance.

I couldn't believe my eyes. Although Gilday, like me, was still only a private he was probably the oldest man in 'A' Company, I presumed in his late 40s or early 50s, but he didn't seem to have a nerve in his body.

Despite his incredible bravery, it was obvious that Gilday was dangerously exposed and would be cut down within the next 20 seconds if he stayed where he was. As the pilot readied his weapons for the final turkey shoot, Gilday's old drinking buddy, Shinners McInerney, who was probably the second oldest man in 'A' Company, also leapt up to his feet to join Gilday, firing wildly in the Fouga's direction. Suddenly everyone in the 30 or so trenches on the inner cordon clambered out of their defences and started firing desperately towards the oncoming Fouga. The machine gunners too began discharging their magazines and a cloud of bullets filled the air, like a swarm of rhythmic swallows chasing after their aerial target, until the Fouga pilot was so peppered that he had to alter his attacking course or risk being shot down.

It felt like the 'I'm Spartacus!' moment from the Picture House when The Dolly Dolan leapt out of his seat, as all of 'A' Company jumped up to defend Gilday and McInerney who were both still wearing the Irish Tricolour of Offaly's All Ireland team pinned to their shirts. Some started whooping as the Fouga abruptly changed direction and headed off over the Eastern hills with those on the other side of the inner cordon continuing to fire as it made its escape. The exhilaration was incredible – all for one and one for all! If Gilday and Shinners McInerney were willing to put their lives on the line for one of us then so was everyone else for them.

Some punched the air with delight and relief and I could feel my pumped up heart repeatedly crashing with adrenalin against my ribcage as shots aimed in our direction began to re-emerge from the distant bushes, but these were tame in comparison with the strafing jet, with most falling short of our trench. We turned around to fire back over the cemetery of no-man's land to re-establish our forward defensive position.

Prendergast and John Monahan were busily running between defensive posts, shouting orders and waving their arms furiously to direct points of attack, whilst probably trying to quell everyone's enthusiasm for Gilday's and McInerney's defiant stand.

A few moments later John Monahan again arrived at our trench.

'Remember to keep yer heads low lads,' he commanded, 'stay in yer trenches as much as possible even if the enemy tries to flush us out, yer much more likely to survive. That feckin Fouga will surely be back although he won't be flying as low next time, but we have to get these trenches at least two foot deeper.'

Despite the intense heat we had to carry on digging, as the mortar bombing from the outer perimeter continued to judder through our spines.

Conway said he was concerned he had lost the hearing in his right ear after he had been too slow to duck down when the last mortar hit.

'What?' asked Dowler.

'I said,' repeated Conway, 'I think I've lost the hearing in my right ear.'

'What?' replied Dowler again, by which time Conway realised that Dowler was taking the piss out of him and he would just have to carry on digging with or without his right ear.

Even with obstructed hearing, the sound of chucking propellers in the distance became easily audible about 20 minutes later. A large black spot like a giant fly was heading straight for us but we couldn't make out its objective or even whose side it was on: perhaps it was another enemy machine gunner or maybe it was a special mercenary commando unit that was being dropped in against us. The last thing we suspected, so soon after the Fouga's strafing attack, was that it may be someone coming to our aid.

Dowler suddenly erupted:

'Look the cavalry is coming!' as the letters U and N became distinguishable on its side.

Prendergast and John Monahan waved their arms around desperately to prevent any of the trenches shooting at the incoming helicopter; shouting out,

'Friendly aircraft! Don't shoot!'

A furious round of gunfire was however unleashed from the outer perimeter as the mercenary and gendarmerie forces also realised which side the helicopter was on. But it continued flying towards us, the bullets pinging loudly off its fuselage, as the dusty ground around was whipped up by the force of the propellers creating a cloud of red powder.

'They'll never survive this,' I noted with resignation 'nothing could get through that hail of bullets.' But the helicopter carried on towards the ground near the

Purfina garage where it slowly made its descent, landing out of view from our trench.

Our very own Santa Maria convoy had managed to land but a gunfight like no other ensued as the trenches and machine gunners on the North Eastern side of the Purfina garage tried to defend the landing against a barrage of mortars and shots from the outer perimeter.

'Them feckin mercs know they're bringing in supplies!' Dowler exclaimed as the battle raged on the other side of the cordon but out of our view. I could see other men in 'A' Company running from the Purfina garage towards where the helicopter would have landed, clinging onto their helmets amidst the maelstrom of dust and wind being whipped up by chucking propeller blades.

'I'm telling ya Sean,' I repeated, 'no-one could have survived that shower of bullets. Oh, them poor feckin pilots – how they continued to land through all those bullets is amazing enough.'

Five minutes or so went past, and still the gunfight raged on the other side of the Purfina garage. Our side of the defensive cordon was relatively quiet, save for a few minor exchanges, as both sides awaited the brutal outcome of the latest round of distant combat. We hoped desperately that our side would prevail. We knew we couldn't afford to lose, having nearly run out of food and water. Our hopes were resting on that helicopter to keep us supplied until our re-enforcements arrived.

An hour or so later John Monahan again returned to our trench:

'Did the helicopter pilots get killed Sarge?' I immediately asked, fully expecting the worst outcome.

'No, they are alive and well, they have a couple of bullet cuts and scratches alright, but they're fine otherwise,' he replied.

I was amazed – how could they have survived that onslaught of bullets with just a few scratches. But Monahan had other more ominous news.

'However, they had no supplies on them and their helicopter is non-operational, they're now stuck here with us.'

Although Monahan's voice remained factual and non emotive, I could feel my heart sinking with each word that emerged with his last statement.

'But Sarge,' I asked, 'I thought they were bringing in supplies?'

'So did we,' Monahan replied, 'but all they had were a few jerry cans of water and they have been contaminated with oil. Although they had been told we were under siege, they said they thought they were on a peacekeeping mission and didn't expect to get caught in a gunfight.'

'Well them fellas back in Elizabethville knew because it was on the radio four days ago that we were under siege,' interrupted Dowler. 'They know we need supplies but yet they gave the helicopter nothing to bring in.'

'Aye,' I confirmed, 'and if they didn't know they were gonna come under fire, well that makes 157 of us then Sarge, because no-one told us we'd be caught in a two day gunfight either, and with no end in sight.'

John Monahan obviously felt he needed to explain a bit more about what was happening given our obvious annoyance.

'It seems they hadn't been given any supplies from HQ in Elizabethville to bring to us except for the contaminated water. But it doesn't matter now, they're alive and so are we. We'll just have to make do with what we've got.'

'And, did the helicopter pilots say anything about our re-enforcements Sarge?' Dowler asked.

'Nothing, they didn't know anything about them,' noted Monahan, 'but we know yer running out of food. From tomorrow morning Bobby Allen will have a bite for ya in the canteen, once at dawn, once at dusk. But ye'll have to keep rationing the water as we've nearly run out.'

As Monahan again set off to inform the other trenches of the bad news about the helicopter's lack of supplies, we could soon hear overhead the familiar buzzing sound of the Fouga jet returning to taunt us. Although he was remaining at about 1000 feet altitude to avoid being fired on, the mercenary pilot had re-armed his plane with larger bombs. On his first pass over our defensive cordon, he dropped two bombs when he was directly over the Purfina garage but their momentum meant that they exploded way beyond the outer perimeter and may have actually killed or injured some of his fellow mercenary forces. However, we knew it was only a matter of time before he got his eye in and within a couple of hours he would no doubt be back. By the time he returned however, we hoped we would again be protected by the darkness of the Swahili night.

Our trench was by now nearly five feet deep, our hands raw and bleeding from digging all night and all day, but thankfully as the sun began its rapid departure the intense heat finally abated. I knew from the dipping angle of the sun that it was time to tune into Paddy from Brazzaville at 1800 hours to get an update on what the outside world was hearing:

> Good evening, this is radio Brazzaville with the news at 6 o'clock on Thursday 14th September 1961.

UN troops have continued with their offensive to stop the Katangan succession and today launched an attack to re-take the post office building in Elizabethville amid bloody scenes as pockets of Belgian colonial resistance took up arms against them. An Irish peacekeeper killed in action in Elizabethville yesterday has been named as Private Gaffney. The situation in Elizabethville today has been described as calm and Connor Cruise O'Brien has declared that the UN is now in control of Katanga.

However, there have also been reports of many killed in the town of Jadotville where the Irish 35th 'A' Company of some 150 men remains under siege holding out against superior succession forces. Some reports have suggested there could be at least 100 men dead with the Irish radio reporting that there have been five Irish peacekeepers killed in bitter fighting at Jadotville.

There was no agreement by the foreign ministers of US, Belgium, Britain and France attending a three day conference in Washington as to how best to end the fighting in Katanga. Despite protestations from the US foreign secretary Dean Rusk, Britain has joined France in denying access to its African airspace for UN relief planes to fly over. Dag Hammarskjöld has indicated that the relief planes are desperately needed for humanitarian purposes and for continued UN operations in The Congo. He has pleaded with the foreign ministers to allow relief flights to continue, but so far this permission has not been granted.

Irish Independent

Grave Report From Strife-Torn Congo

FIVE IRISH SOLDIERS KILLED

Bitter Fighting At Jadotville In Katangan Drive

Kaunda Greets Britain's Move

Russia Agrees To Talks In U.S.A.

Hurricane Death Toll Rises

To-day

Luftwaffe Blundered Into Berlin

Move To End TV Bogey

The Irish Independent, courtesy of www.irishnewspaperarchives.com

After his arrival in Leopoldville this morning, Hammarskjöld has called on all sides involved in the current military confrontation in Katanga to agree a proposed ceasefire. Sir Roy Wellensky of Northern Rhodesia has defied the remit from the international community and has offered direct military support to Moise Tshombie's succession forces. He has also told representatives of European nations that it is their duty to protect European nationals. Foreign Minister Paul Spaak

> of Belgium has welcomed any assistance to help innocent Belgians caught up in the conflict. Meanwhile President Kennedy has stressed that Soviet restraint is of the 'utmost importance'.
>
> In other news it is reported that a judge in Jackson Mississippi has handed down four-month gaol sentences to fifteen church ministers who had attempted to dine together in a segregated restaurant.

'They're saying on the radio that five of us have been killed already,' I called over almost dumbfounded to Dowler and Conway.

Neither of them said anything but I knew the news would have hit them like a sledgehammer. We had no idea what was going on back in Elizabethville but it sounded like UN troops had come under fire yesterday and this morning and perhaps was the reason why they were not able to re-enforce us here in Jadotville for the last two days. Like me, neither Dowler nor Conway knew Private Gaffney but we presumed he was just like us, and had simply been caught in the wrong place at the wrong time. More immediately the reports said that men in 'A' Company were dying here in Jadotville. We had no idea who they were. I presumed that Ready must have been one of the five casualties being talked about on the radio. The reports of peacekeepers being killed made our circumstances even more urgent but we hoped that as the situation in Elizabethville had calmed it would surely become a priority to send re-enforcements to us.

Whatever was happening in the outside world, it seemed that Dag Hammarskjöld was the only powerful voice of reason amongst the world leaders and was probably our only hope of this siege ending peacefully. All the other leaders of the western world it seemed were just trying to look at new ways for the white-man to retain power over formerly enslaved and colonised people. It was obvious that western European nations had too much vested interest to simply hand over their colonial riches, they needed the tax money from their corporations in their former colonies to retain the economic bounty that had helped establish their newly created national health, welfare and education systems, which if dismantled would result in political humiliation. Hearing that the French and UK governments would not be allowing UN relief planes to use their African airspace was just another tactical manoeuvre to covertly impede the demands of the international community to end colonialism and self determination. Wherever in the world former colonies threatened to break away from the long arms of European governments, as it was throughout Africa ever since the Suez crisis in 1956, the entente cordiale remained as steadfast as ever.

It seemed that the political and legal systems of the free world were intent on white domination at any cost and all the governments of Western Europe were concerned about was power, the plight of white people and retaining their wealth. They didn't care about brutalising and starving Africans, they didn't really care about freedom and they certainly didn't care about us.

I had my last few drags of my Sweet Afton cigarette butt that I had been saving especially behind my ear until nightfall, the last time I would be able to smoke until the morning.

'Do ya know what I'm gonna do Sean when this war is over?' I noted pulling on my last drag of my treasured cigarette.

Dowler again didn't respond, probably still maudlin over the news broadcast that there may already be five of 'A' Company dead.

'I'm gonna go onto one of those film-sets with Gregory Peck, David Niven and even John Wayne himself, and I'm gonna tell them what a real war is like: digging, shooting, more digging, dying bodies crying for help, puking-up, digging, strafing from a jet, waiting around, even more digging, mortar bombing and dying of thirst, then more feckin digging. And then I'm gonna sit in a chair and direct all them bollocks politicians to act out a real feckin film, as I sit there smoking these lovely Sweet Aftons until they admit that they are just a bunch of feckin selfish, greedy bastards, who don't give a fook about anyone except themselves. But then I will just carry on smoking and playing the fiddle until the lot of them burn.'

'Is that one of them hippie fags yer smoking Michael?' Dowler asked, as I finished my nonsensical ramble.

'I wish it feckin was Sean,' I replied, 'and I hope their film-set is swarming with these tsetse fly, and they bite the livin Jaysus out of them.'

I angrily took another swinging swat at the swarm of tetste fly around me and stubbed out the last of my Sweet Afton butt on the trench floor, making sure every ember was extinguished as the slightest flicker of light in the fast approaching darkness could give away our position. I then gathered up any clothes that I had placed on the side of the trench that had avoided them getting them covered in piss, as I would need any spare clothes to protect against another freezing night.

Dowler still had his field glasses and was peering beyond no-man's land and the outer perimeter, where we could see in the distant hills small fires being set all around us. It was immediately obvious to all of us that the encirclement of flames in the darkness would also provide the Fouga jet pilot with an illuminated ground target when he delivered his next round of bombs.

'I wonder what that owld towny of ours, Sir Henry Hughes Wilson, would make of the position we're in Michael?' Dowler commented, 'd'yiz think he would have sent us over the top?'

'I don't think Sir Henry would have left one of his units cut off,' I replied, 'and not try to re-enforce or re-supply them.'

We presumed that the field commanders in charge of 'A' Company back at the Purfina garage were probably pondering the same question as to why we hadn't been re-enforced, but given our desperate situation they were probably trying to figure out what our next tactical manoeuvre should be.

Even me, probably the youngest and most inexperienced soldier in 'A' Company, understood that our options, without assistance from those in Elizabethville, were very limited. I borrowed Dowler's field glasses to peer at the darkened horizon and all I could see were silhouettes of bushes and hills, dotted amongst which was another ring of whaka-whaka open-fires, billowing smoke. The tribal drums however played to a different rhythm this evening, there was no energetic dancing visible in the night sky as there had been yesterday and the vibrant beat of the previous evening had slowed to a melancholic funeral procession pace, with only one beat every two or three seconds. This was how the tribal people communicated their emotions and intentions throughout this jungle nation as the slower resounding beat also seemed to have a determination to avenge their loss which clearly indicated to the rest of the jungle community; that revenge and more death would follow. I reckoned there must have been already 60 people killed that day but they would have no bodies yet to bury or cremate, as their fallen comrades were still lying rotting in no-man's land in front of our trenches. Occasionally in the distance we could hear wailing as the extent and identity of those that had not returned probably became clear to the victims' families. Eerily, we could also hear the sound of cavalry bugles that we suspected were being played by the mercenaries in slow-paced 'last-post' processional sequences, the tunes that ominously belonged to the mercs' former employers: the French Foreign Legion.

We knew these Wild Geese were the same as those that had fought alongside the Pied Noir, becoming the OAS in the Algerian war. They were notorious for avenging the killing of one of their own by killing at least ten times that number, be they adversaries or unlucky civilians who happened to get in their way. As former Legionnaires it was in their training and code of honour that their missions were sacred, that they should give up their lives if necessary and never to surrender arms.

Even more ghastly were the customs of our other adversaries sitting around those distant hill-fires. The Lumba warriors believed they had to cannibalise those that brought death to their tribe to free angry spirits from the pain of death. None of us dared to speak about the likelihood of such a macabre ending when our end surely came but it was clear to us that both the mercenaries and Lumba would stake us out for as long as it took even if that meant another night and day of fighting.

The distant hill-fires smoldered all night as the tribesmen, gendarmes and mercenaries prepared themselves for another attack on us the following morning.

We could do nothing except sit here waiting to defend ourselves in the trench until re-enforcements arrived. I jealously contemplated that the gendarmes and mercenary forces would have the comfort of their glowing fires to keep them warm during the night and could even imagine them covered with blankets and having a nice night's sleep under the stars. They were safe out there in those hills: no barrage of gunfire every 20 minutes and out of our range. They had also probably just enjoyed a hearty stew, bread and butter and a cup of tea with a whisky nightcap to send themselves off to sleep, I considered.

As I had read back in Athlone, war is rarely an equal contest but everything, it seemed, was stacked against us as we endured our second sleepless night of watching, waiting and avoiding the inevitable sporadic attacks from guns, mortars and bombs.

'Please God,' I said to myself, 'let our re-enforcements arrive soon.'

Myself, Dowler and Conway discussed sombrely amongst ourselves that we would struggle to stay awake for another long night as nothing in our soldier's training had ever prepared us to spend 50 hours with no sleep.

'We can last for one night,' I suggested, 'but I don't think we'll be able to stay awake for two full nights.'

But we knew this was very different to our training: it was war itself, and as we were still being attacked there would be no rest allowed. It remained at the forefront of our minds that under war footings it was considered a court martial offence to be found asleep on duty.

Our thoughts of rest were soon interrupted as we were quickly reminded that the Katangan succession forces had no intention of even letting us think about rest, as a three minute long bombardment blasted gunfire from all around the outer perimeter. Just ten minutes or so later and the Fouga jet had returned overhead, although again remaining high in the night sky. This time he dropped his bombs into no-man's land scattering dead human and animal carcasses into the air. It was like this all night, gunfire every 20 minutes and a bombing raid every couple of hours. Down in the trench, we were reasonably safe from the gunfire but knew that a direct hit from a bomb or mortar would blow our weakening bodies to bits. We also had to be careful of snipers creeping up through the darkness into no-man's land, so every hour or so we would direct a barrage of fire indiscriminately into the waste ground in front of us to stop or at least deter any would be approaches.

The waiting for something to happen seemed endless as the long Swahili night and partially-full moon inched its way over us. After just a few hours, it was almost a relief to hear a barrage of distant gunfire which we knew would fall short of our trenches, stimulating our eyes to bolt open once more and providing a sudden shot of adrenalin to help us stay awake.

To pass the time, I tried to recount the old pub story about The County, the one I had heard told with such passion by the town Seanachai's back in Edgeworthstown where he had led the tiny county of Longford out at Croke Park against the mighty Meath. But my weary mind could only manage a monosyllabic few sentences that eventually tailed off without an ending. It had been a vain attempt to help us stay awake but my mind was running out of vigour, my body was freezing and neither Conway nor Dowler had the energy to listen. Then it was back to endless hours of waiting in a state of exhausted wakefulness, interrupted only by bursts of bullets, then more silence and the occasional mortar bomb.

About every 30 minutes we could hear the sound of a bullet whistling past over the trench. I thought longingly about writing a letter home to tell my mother that I was still having a great time out here on holiday in Africa watching a great film down at 'le cinemoi' under a clear night sky. But I knew I would not be able to as even thinking of the words 'home' and 'mother' made me choke back tears. Besides, it would have been impossible to write as I had left my writing pad back in the villa and we could have no lights on in the trench. It was just us lying in the darkness peering up into the vast Congolese sky above us lit up by ten thousand stars. For a moment it almost sounded enchanting but we were surrounded by a massively superior armed mob of professional soldiers and tribal warriors intent on killing us. I edged uneasily into the earth, and wondered why I didn't dig this trench a little deeper when I had the chance. I lay shivering, the night bitterly cold between 0200-0400 hours when the freezing dew descended down the trench into every part of our bodies.

To generate a bit of warmth I started to dig further into the side of the trench with my helmet to try to create a larger cubby hole but all I could muster was a groove barely a few inches deep, scant reward for two hours of digging. We had been taught how to make a bivouac in basic training, how to use twigs, leaves, bushes or anything that nature offered to make a bed, but none of that was available here, just my sodden uniform and the trench walls to keep the worst of the cold at bay.

My once impeccable uniform and what kit I still had with me were filthy. Back in Athlone they would probably put me on a charge, I considered, but war was not about having shiny boots and polished buttons like the tale of Private Fortescue I had heard so many times in the recruitment company. This war was about lying in your own shit through extreme temperatures, and trying to remain hidden while waiting for something to happen that may just keep us alive.

'Right, on three lads,' instructed Dowler, 'one, two, three!'

We all jumped up to spray bullets into no-man's land.

'Bang, bang, bang, bang' then immediately back down the side of the trench for a ten second lull during the inevitable return of fire before Dowler again counted to three and up we jumped again for more senseless shots over the parapet 'bang, bang, bang, bang.'

The return fire was getting more distant.

'They must be retreating and perhaps we had foiled another attack,' we told ourselves before our optimism was cut abruptly short by closer range attackers. Then another round of counter attack fire before settling back to the monotony of counting stars, staring at other galaxies and wondering why the one we inhabited was so feckin mad that we had to go round shooting at each other all night.

We remained awake and eventually morning had nearly arrived, serenaded by a riotous dawn chorus of squawking birds and shrill insects. It never lasted long before it was soon cut short by peppering gunfire. The beauty of nature had tried to reassert its majestic influence, only for insane humans to send it all scampering for cover. Our tins of bully beef were empty but the first shimmer of the orange sun to the east meant it was time to run over to the Purfina HQ as John Monahan had instructed us the previous night, for one of our two meals we were being rationed that day. We were all desperately keen to get out of the trench after two nights of digging, but being the lowest ranking of the three of us in the trench, Dowler then Conway would go before me.

Conway set off as Dowler arrived back and he seemed enthused.

'Ready is alive!' Dowler stated with obvious joy in his voice. He knew how important this news would be to me and carried on: 'Aye, I saw him lying down over in the Purfina garage, all bandaged up like an Egyptian mummy, but he's alive all the same.'

'Oh Jaysus, that's great news.' I replied. 'So who are the five that are dead then?' I asked.

'I don't know,' Dowler responded a little bemused 'I didn't see any dead people over there, lots of activity and officers shouting at one another, but none dead.'

I was eager to see this for myself and when Conway had returned, I sprinted as fast as my ducked posture would allow over to the Purfina garage. In my eagerness I had not secured my tin water-cup and billy tray and they rattled loudly behind me causing another volley of shots from the outer perimeter to let loose behind me.

As Dowler had described the HQ, back at the Purfina garage was a hive of activity. I could see our officers arguing amongst themselves with orderlies, medical staff, the priest and quartermasters all hurrying around. But everything had retained a soldierly order, neat stacks of ammunition, spare FN rifles and most notably, all were wearing clean pressed uniforms. I was embarrassed at the state of my appearance with my muddied face and arms and my blood and puke stained uniform, which had become shredded and stunk of sweat and piss. Standing by the canteen tables there was even some welcome warmth emanating from the two big pots of food that was being handed out by the company cook Bobby Allen, so I warmed my frozen, raw and blood-spattered hands against the boiling stoves.

'How are ya Bobby?' I opened, 'we heard on the radio that there was some terrible news and that five of us had been killed?'

'No, none dead yet, that I know of anyway,' Bobby replied with his typical buoyancy, as he splodged a quarter ladle full of vegetable stew into my billy tray, 'but there's a few in there that'll need a little luck to pull through alright,' as he gestured with his eyebrows over to the medical room.

I looked over and could see the top half of Ready's bandaged body against the far wall behind the door. Dowler was right, he was very much alive. He turned his head round for a moment and I acknowledged a nod in his direction, but his frowning and tightened face suggested he could see no further than the pain he was in, as his head slowly returned to its former straight upright position.

'Now, make the most of this food ration will ya?' Bobby continued, 'we've only got two more rations left, and there doesn't seem to be any sign of more arriving from Elizabethville.'

'I think they'll be sending the supplies today Bobby,' I suggested optimistically. 'It's quietened down in Elizabethville now so they'll be able to send help to us.'

'Well I hope yer right Michael,' replied Bobby, 'because they've been saying for five days now that they're on their way.'

I finished the few vegetables and potatoes in my billy tray, savouring each bit of precious moisture that soothed my charred and blistered lips, even licking the inner tray edges in case I had missed any. I was in no hurry to leave the safe, clean, orderly and covered environment of the Purfina garage but I knew I had to return to the disgusting post of the slit trench where in just a few hours time there would be another five hour furnace with no cover from the relentless African sun. I quickly used the latrine at the back of the Purfina garage but before I set off back to join Conway and Dowler, Bobby Allen ushered me over once more.

'And here Michael,' he whispered dipping his hand into a bag concealed under the table, 'there's a packet of cigarettes for ya.'

'Oh tanks a million Bobby!' I replied gladly, 'these things'll keep me going for sure.'

I was delighted to get the cigarettes even though they weren't Sweet Aftons as I had nearly run out of those I had brought with me from Elizabethville. It gave me a spring in my step and I set off with renewed energy back to join Dowler and Conway. At least today we wouldn't have to dig into the rock solid ground and could get some cover from the sun under the trench walls.

'Bobby was telling me that everyone is alive,' I pointed out enthusiastically as I jumped back into the trench with Dowler and Conway.

'Aye, its grand news alright,' replied Dowler, 'did ya see Ready?'

'Aye, I did Sean, he's still bad I think, but they reckon he'll be fine. Actually he looks a lot better and cleaner than ye two,' I nodded at both Dowler and Conway. 'Here; Bobby gave me an extra packet of cigarettes,' I stretched out my hand to offer them over, 'would yiz like one?'

Conway gladly accepted but Dowler declined saying,

'No, ye know I don't smoke, and I'm not gonna start now, now that we're so close to the Pearly gates with all of them young angel girls waiting for me. But Bobby gave me this tin of peaches,' he stated gladly, 'we'll have a slice each.'

He began carefully opening the peaches and handed a slice over to me and Conway, both of us eagerly accepting the peaches and putting them straight into our salivating mouths. The thick juice of the peaches sluiced around from jaw to jaw for about ten seconds before we had to bite through and swallow, trying to savour each drop of the fruity wetness. But again that moment of quiet luxury was disturbed by another burst of gunfire, and it was back to the brutal business of fighting for our lives.

Between rounds of return fire Dowler suddenly asked,

'Did they tell ya when ye were back in the Purfina, that the re-enforcements didn't get through?' Neither Conway nor I said anything, hardly wanting to believe what Dowler was about to tell us. 'Well apparently Prendergast was heard saying that the relief column got held up at the Lufira bridge and were then ordered by the Irish commanders in Elizabethville to turn back.'

'But they will be trying again to get through to us, surely?' I protested.

'Well they don't think there is any chance of them trying to re-send re-enforcements again because HQ back in Elizabethville are now refusing even to answer their radios to our SOS calls.'

'What, they're not going to send any supplies or any help? Ya can't mean they'll just leave us here to get slaughtered?' I asked in disbelief, 'but we don't stand a chance, what are we supposed to fight with?'

'I don't know,' replied an equally bemused Dowler.

I didn't know what to think, but was overcome by an intense feeling of worthlessness; that our own Irish commanders in Elizabethville did not regard us as worth helping or worth saving. Any hope we had of the siege ending and getting out of this alive seemed to be quickly disappearing.

'Can I ask ye both a question?' I asked a few minutes later, 'what the fuck are we fighting for, because for the life of me, I can't feckin think of it?'

'We're fighting for Ireland Michael,' Dowler immediately responded.

He was right of course: we were fighting for our country and every Irish boy's collective memory of those brave nationalists and rebel heroes of centuries past, who fought for Ireland to become such a proud independent country. All of those grand tales of those that had died came flooding back; Robert Emmet, Padraig Pearse, James Connolly and Kevin Barry; household names in Ireland's unstinting memory of the fallen that had once sacrificed their lives for the Emerald Isle.

I remembered the way my heart would pound against my chest when I heard how those Irish heroes would remain resolute in the face of the executioner and how they stood proud, not cowed in fear to give their lives for their fellow countrymen. As a boy I dreamt of being associated with such bravery but it now dawned on me, in the face of our own imminent demise that the senior Irish officers back in Elizabethville didn't care about their own soldiers who were fighting for their country, just the power structures that kept them in the rank of senior officers. It was obvious that the order to recall the relief column and to refuse to answer their radios was just another part of a petty argument that had worked against 'A' Company since we arrived in The Congo. But this was no longer like our initial peacekeeping days when we were given sub-standard digs in the barn or when we were given the menial jobs of cleaning and washing up in Leopoldville during the recent election. We didn't know whether it was due to a personality clash between the senior officers and those officers in charge of 'A' Company, but one thing I was sure about; this continued cowardly, small-minded and grudging power game had resulted in 157 of us being cut-off and abandoned. If there had been a disagreement it had nothing to do with most of us out here on the Jadotville plateau but they were playing with all of our lives and condemning us to a slaughter. When I heard that they were now refusing to answer their radios when we were calling for help made my blood boil over. I blasted another round from my FN rifle, my teeth gritted with hatred both for the enemy in front of me and for those in our own army back in Elizabethville who regarded our lives as so valueless that they had deserted us.

'Ye never get to hear the stories of the Irish feckers that abandoned their own in the history books back in Ireland,' I stated with obvious frustration. 'All we ever heard about was how brave the Irish were and how the English were to blame for everything that went wrong in Ireland!'

'But I still needed to fight to protect the other men in 'A' Company,' I told myself 'and I still need to protect those poor refugee people who also stood no chance against these colonial forces just like their fore-fathers stood no chance against slavery and Leopold's agents. The harrowing images I had seen back in the Elizabethville refugee camp reminded me that this was not a noble enemy rather another version of what Roger Casement called a 'colony that was a scandal before the whole world.'

There were other important reasons to fight; to stay alive so that my own family suffering back in Ireland may see me again or at least be proud of what I fought for. I may have become disillusioned fighting for those apparently distinguished Irish officers back in Elizabethville; and ashamed to be fighting under the same flag as them, but I had plenty of reasons to carry on fighting.

'Oh, and we're apparently fighting to keep the peace!' I told myself sarcastically.

For the next few hours as the sun scorched down on our baking trench none of us spoke. I prayed for some cloud to pass over us, not only to protect against the burning sunlight but also to provide cover from the Fouga jet. Additionally, with another freezing night only a few hours away, a bank of cloud could hold in some of the day's warmth but as I looked longingly into the heavens there was not a single wisp of cloud in the sky. All day it seemed we had just been going through the motions of intermittent bouts of return fire, maintaining our precarious safety by preventing the enemy entering no-man's land. Ultimately, we knew it was futile, without re-enforcements there was no way we could expect to halt the enemies advance for much longer. We were at a standstill and within a day or so at best, we would be overrun as the sheer number of enemy forces would inevitably count against us. But even more immediately than re-enforcements, we knew we had almost run out of the most vital supply in the unrelenting heat of The Congo – water.

I no longer pissed over my clothes to keep cool; instead I drank it. With barely any water left in our rations and my head throbbing from the heat and dehydration I abandoned any respectable behaviour and social etiquette I may have once had. As the battle dragged through its third day, my body was telling me to get any moisture it could to stay alive and if that meant drinking my own piss, then so be it.

'Well ye have to die some way.' I said with resignation as another mortar bomb landed close to us that afternoon.

Dowler too was no longer revolted at the extent I was prepared to go to just to get some moisture in my body and told me that he too would lick the sweat off Ghandi's sandals if he thought it would quench his thirst.

I laughed at the thought of it, but after that exchange again there was no more conversation between us in the trench, all of us just maudlin at apparently being abandoned, until the time came to tune in the radio, for the evening news at 1800 hours to find out what the outside world was hearing.

> Good evening, this is radio Brazzaville with the news at 6 o'clock on Friday 15th September 1961.
>
> To all of our Irish listeners, we have some grave news to report relating to the Irish peacekeeping company that had been holding out under siege in Jadotville. As many as 57 or over one third of the company have allegedly been killed already in three days of fighting against succession forces. Those still alive remain under heavy bombardment including mortars and aerial bombing. A ceasefire has not been possible and the Irish Foreign Affairs Minister Frank Aitken has said he will fly out today to The Congo today to broker an agreement amid growing discontent and criticism at home to explain why Irish peacekeepers are being used in a combat mission.

It was almost as if we were listening to a news report about some other army, in some kind of parallel universe, a disaster that was surely happening to other poor forsaken soldiers; but then another crackle of gunfire beyond the Purfina reminded us that this was most definitely us they were talking about. The news-report continued:

> Today in Dublin, the Taoiseach has expressed his profound shock and horror at the reports and has offered his condolences and prayers to the families. We have to repeat that these reports are as yet unconfirmed.
>
> Moise Tshombie has reportedly left the province of Katanga and is believed to have set up his headquarters in Ndola in Northern Rhodesia where he has been promised the full support of the Northern Rhodesian government and military. With the backing of Sir Roy Wellensky, he has stated that there will be no end to the succession campaign and that all external military personnel and equipment occupying Katangan soil or airspace including the UN are now targets for the succession offensive.
>
> The United States has again expressed their deep concern over the continued fighting in Katanga and has urged all sides to make every effort to reach a cease-fire, while the Soviet Union has declared it will not stand by and allow western imperialism to impose their will on African people who are demanding an end to colonial exploitation.

CITY SPECIAL

Irish Independent

• *Heavy Losses Announced* • *Reports Of 57 Dead Unconfirmed* • *Mr. Aiken For Congo To-day*

IRISHMEN STILL HOLDING OUT

Mortared And Bombed By Katangans

President Dissolves The Dail

23 Irishmen Captured

Taoiseach's Statement

"PROFOUND SHOCK AND SORROW"

A Fateful Week-end

To-day

LATE NEWS

Katanga State Dies In Hatred And Bloodshed

O'Brien And Tshombe To Hold Talks

BOMB SENT TO DR. ADENAUER

£4315

FOR YOU AT AGE 55

The Irish Independent, courtesy of www.irishnewspaperarchives.com

With relations between the superpowers reaching a new low, President Kennedy has said that the United States yesterday renewed nuclear testing, the first such test in three years, by setting off a small underground explosion in the Nevada desert. Kennedy said that the decision to resume testing was taken reluctantly because the Soviet Union had without warning, but after a great deal of preparation, resumed testing in the atmosphere.

I knew the same headlines would be dominating the papers back home including the Irish Independent the next day. Heaven forbid what The County and my mother would make of what they were hearing about Jadotville and the growing likelihood of a nuclear confrontation.

It seemed almost unbelievable that our battle in this god-forsaken plateau of Jadotville was now being directly linked to an imminent Cold War nuclear confrontation. We knew Russia was waiting in the wings to defeat the Katangan succession, which if successful would ring-fence The Congo's resources for the gain of western European governments and businesses. We knew that Khrushchev himself knew all about sieges as he was the General in charge of the Russian army that broke out during the siege of Stalingrad but if we and the UN failed to break the siege of Jadotville, the consequences could be catastrophic. To avoid a Russian-backed Communist invasion with the inevitable consequence of a nuclear war, the Congolese parliament led by Cyrille Adoula not surprisingly voted to invade Katanga in retaliation to Moise Tshombie's declaration of an all-out war. With a civil war having been formally declared and with the situation spiralling out of control, finally it seemed that the Irish government and Taosieach had sat up and realised what was happening to Irish troops that had been sent to keep the peace.

'He's not the only one who is in shock and horror' I noted after the Radio Brazzaville news, 'but I'll tell ye now, one day the world will find out all about how the so-called colonial empires treated these African people. And I'll tell ye something else; when the Taoiseach and the people of Ireland finds out what happened here in Jadotville, and the war we've been thrown into, he'll surely condemn them feckers in Elizabethville for their role in abandoning us.'

Although we were stunned at what the outside world was hearing about 57 of 'A' Company being killed, we didn't immediately believe the radio headlines as they had been proved false when they reported that five of us had been killed the previous day. However, it seemed inconceivable that the amount of bombs and bullets had not killed at least some of 'A' Company. Maybe, I considered, our officers over at the Purfina HQ may not want us to hear the full extent of our casualties as it would be bad for morale. 57 dead did seem too many as they would not be able to hide all of those bodies and prevent the news from reaching those of us in the front line but it didn't make sense that the radio reports could be so misinformed.

Without knowing who or what to believe, it was the first question that everyone was asking when they returned to the Purfina garage canteen for their evening rations at the end of the third day of fighting:

'Is it true,' I asked the cook Bobby Allen, 'that 57 of us are dead?'

'Well I don't know of any dead yet,' Bobby replied as he delivered a noticeably smaller splodge of ration into my billy-tray, 'unless they're not telling me something.'

As Bobby continued talking, I eagerly scouted my eyes all around the Purfina garage for evidence of any deaths, maybe covered bodies or mounds in the ground but could see nothing. Everyone I could see seemed to be very much alive, lots of dried blood and bandaged wounds but still alive. Despite the continuous shelling and broken windows, the Purfina HQ still looked remarkably clean inside with officers professionally going about their business; talking through our defence and possible points of attack on maps laid out on makeshift tables.

I was re-assured that in spite of the overwhelming odds we were facing, our officers in charge of 'A' Company still had everything under control; a solid dug-in defensive cordon that had already withstood three days of constant onslaught. But how long could it last? How long would it be before there was a direct hit from a mortar or the Fouga jet accurately delivering a bomb? None of us knew what the future held as I was left wondering how those huddled men gathered round the maps had even managed to defend us thus far. Although I had only come over to the Purfina garage for my evening food ration, I left with something that every soldier needs; the knowledge that the officers directly in charge and the men around him were the best there is. Like most, I didn't care that much about food, the hunger had long worn off and we only needed water to stay alive. But without water, however brilliant the men in 'A' Company were, it was becoming more obvious that we might all be dead soon anyway.

'I only have enough food and water for one more ration tomorrow morning,' pointed out Bobby Allen, 'but I've heard the other side have sent terms through for a ceasefire.'

'Ah that's grand Bobby,' I replied, forgetting completely about the meagre ration, 'we don't need food especially if they are discussing a ceasefire, Jaysus that would be great alright.'

As the third night of the battle descended like a giant dark canopy over Jadotville, I discussed with Dowler and Conway the possibility of the upcoming ceasefire. Although we didn't know anything about what was being discussed, any hope of this battle ending was worth contemplating. Without details of our own ceasefire to talk about, we spoke about the Christmas day truce during the First World War when the British and German soldiers on the front line exchanged gifts and had a game of football on Christmas day 1914.

'As they have a few Irish mercs on their side, perhaps we'll have a game of Gaelic?' suggested Dowler. 'But they'll have to take them headdresses off them tribal fellas, I'm not playing football against a feckin hyena!'

'Aye Sean,' I responded. 'They wouldn't stop laughing at ya!'

Our hopes of a swift end to the battle and even a game of football in a ceasefire were short-lived as the talks, we were told collapsed. We speculated as to why but knew we would get no answers from our officers as they would avoid any talk of ceasefire negotiations as they could bring either disappointment or false hope. But with everyone so desperate for news, stories have a habit of filtering through to every man even on the front line. Apparently, our officers could not accept the terms of the ceasefire as it required us to put down our arms unilaterally, effectively leaving us at the mercy of Muke's gendarmerie and the mercenaries. As neither of them had the most honourable reputation, it was a risk that our officers felt they couldn't take. Additionally we heard that they managed to get a radio message through to UN HQ in Elizabethville with the order finally coming back from the Irish commanders that we should fight on until re-enforcements arrived.

I sighed deeply as the third night of the battle began just as the previous two, with the Lumba warriors and mercenaries setting their fires in the hills all around us. Tonight however our mood was much more subdued; the news of the failed ceasefire negotiations and of our own commanders in Elizabethville not sending re-enforcements so far and telling us to fight on until re-enforcements arrived had made us finally realise there would be no end of the battle for us: it would be a 'batteile du jour' – a fight to the death. We were no longer fooled into believing what Elizabethville was telling us, that re-enforcements might arrive within a few hours – we knew they had no intention of sending help after they had recalled the relief column.

Resigned to another long night of battle we could hear the familiar distant beat of the Lumba drums and wailing from their ju-ju man that would no doubt continue for another few hours at least as they mourned that day's losses and prepared another attack on us in the morning. We knew the Lumba had total belief in the power of ju ju to overcome evil situations just as we were praying to our only possible saviour, God, for some kind of divine intervention.

So, after my usual round of bullet-interrupted *Hail Mary*s and *Our Father*s, I settled down for another freezing night, packed in against the trench walls, looking longingly into the African heavens.

Last night I counted about 1,400 stars to pass the time but this night, the more I stared into the moonlit atmosphere the more stars began appearing. We were packed in a slit trench and surrounded by hundreds and possibly thousands of enemy troops. I felt terribly lonely, and soon lost count of stars between bouts of return fire. I knew it would not be long before the battle to stay awake began to dominate my thoughts for the third successive night.

We knew that sleep remained a court martial offence, and I discussed with Dowler and Conway the possibility of getting some rest without John Monahan and Prendergast finding out:

'Perhaps we could have two of us remain awake while one gets an hour's sleep?' I suggested.

Both Dowler and Conway liked the idea of contemplating a short nap, knowing that just as the human body needs water to survive, the human mind needs some kind of rest to remain sane.

We were also aware however that tactics for armed warfare adopted by most armies, including the mercs and gendarmes against us, many of whom having completed their training in the French Foreign Legion or Belgian military, liked to attack at night as it was the time when human beings were by nature least suspecting.

Eventually we decided that we wouldn't risk a sleep regardless of what happened to our minds because the other men around us in 'A' Company were lying awake in slit trenches maintaining the defensive cordon. How would we have reacted if we found out that they had taken a nap and possibly let the cordon be breached endangering all of our lives?

So, the night again ticked slowly by as all around us our enemies, as well as the wild jungle animals rested. With nature fast asleep in the surrounding hills and bushes, the absolute silence caused our heads to lollop around until we again propped them up against the side of the trench. The heavy night air enveloped our faces causing our eye-lids to eventually close as our senses began to drift away. For a split moment, I must have nodded off but was suddenly startled by the thunderous crash of another mortar that shook my unsuspecting and tranquil body so hard I thought my eyes would pop out.

'Jaysus!' I yelped, 'that feckin mortar scared the livin jaysus out of me!'

Dowler and Conway were both equally stunned into action and I suspected that they too may have succumbed to their drooping eyelids and waning senses, but none of us said anything; just carried on loading a fresh round of magazines into our FN rifles, all eager to prove we were wide awake by launching the next round of return fire.

Shortly before the Swahili sun rose again on the fourth morning of the battle, we ran over to the Purfina for what we knew would be our last ration. There was a pint of water for each trench that would need to last the whole day. We knew it would not be enough and judging from the forlorn faces all around the HQ, so did everyone back at the Purfina garage. But it was all that was left and after that there was nothing.

It turned out that during the night we heard that the officers in charge of 'A' Company had agreed to a short cessation in fire which would formally last an hour providing enough time for the mercs and gendarmes to gather up the fallen enemy soldiers in no-man's land.

John Monahan arrived in the trench a few minutes before the hour's cessation was to begin.

'We are just talking to them at the moment about a permanent ceasefire,' he explained, 'but this is only a short ceasefire so that they can collect their dead and injured, before their hostilities against us will resume. We are still under war footings.'

Prendergast shouted over to all the trenches on the stroke of 1100 hours the order to temporarily halt the battle.

'Men of 'A' Company: ceasefire!'

'Oh thank Jaysus for that, it's over for while at least,' noted Dowler.

It was more a short respite than a feeling of relief as none of the men of 'A' Company moved from their trenches, suspecting the enemy of watching our movements for when the battle inevitably resumed.

Dowler and Conway both peered out of our trench, watching guardedly as the dead were cleared up in front of us. I knew the sight of the dead bodies being picked up and blood dripping from dismembered limbs would make me puke again so I stayed low preferring to stare at the trench floor.

'What's happening?' I asked them.

'Not much,' responded Dowler, 'just a few poor owld bastards being swept up.'

'But, is there any chance that the ceasefire will continue on past the hour?' I asked optimistically.'

'No, I don't think so,' responded Dowler with disappointing certainty.

'Why? Are they busy shining their bayonets for the next round of battle?' I asked.

'Aye,' replied Dowler. 'That and the four feckin horsemen of the apocalypse are busy pulling on their jodhpurs and fastening up their saddles out in the far bushes.'

'Oh, so we're fucked then?' I remarked.

'That we are Michael,' sighed Dowler, 'that we are.'

Being that so many of our enemy had been killed in the three previous days of battle; all around us were the remnants and smell of death. I knew many of the bodies in no-man's land were strewn over vast areas but I was pleased to hear that in this most gruesome place where a human could expect to find themselves there was still the honour of a lull in the fighting to collect the dead. There would be no way that all of the spattered body parts would be recovered in such a short time, but they would gather what they could to give those brave dead warriors in no-man's land the final dignity that every human deserves. But it wouldn't be long before what remained of this human mess spread over the Jadotville plains around us would eventually be cleared up by scavenging jungle animals and birds.

The temporary ceasefire didn't last its designated hour; it lasted for 46 minutes and about 30 seconds, just enough time for the last gendarmery medical units to scoop up a few more wasted human remnants. The ceasefire was broken first by the re-emergence of the Fouga jet that subsequently inspired a round of gunfire from an eager trigger-happy mercenary unit on the outer perimeter:

'Vive le Guerre!' [Long Live War!] roared the lone desperado, as he offloaded a volley of shots from the bushes on our side of the perimeter, as the ominous echo of both resounded around the hills around us.

My eyelids dipped in both disappointment and resignation, but no-one in 'A' Company returned fire as there had been no encroachment into no-man's land, honouring our side of the ceasefire agreement until the final second.

'There's no honour amongst thieves,' Dowler noted with disillusionment. 'Ye can't even trust them mercs to abide by the rules of warfare.' We weren't surprised however, rules may have had a place back in the recruitment company or around plush tables in Geneva or New York but there was little room for rules in African jungle warfare. If our enemy sensed an opportunity against us we knew they would take it, a chance to kill before being killed is in every human's natural instinct. But we were fighting for the UN and Ireland, so had to remain true to the accepted conventions our government had agreed, although I am sure there wasn't a man on the defensive cordon that did not want to fire back once the ceasefire had been breached. Had we been a bunch of stateless professional hired hands that could overlook the conventions of warfare, the battle would have immediately restarted. But we waited. Then precisely on the turn of the hour we blasted a shower of magazine bullets towards the outer perimeter from where the ceasefire shots emanated. The battle to defend ourselves in Jadotville had clearly resumed.

As noon inched into the early afternoon hours, the blazing afternoon heat had become familiar but remained deeply uncomfortable. Our water ration was running out too quickly with just half a cup left for the remainder of the day and night. We were well into the battle's fourth afternoon and hadn't slept for the last three nights. I could feel my body failing, my throat as dry as the Katangan soil around me and my skin bloodied and blistered from the intense daytime sun.

I struggled to look down and aim my FN rifle but knew I had to clamber up and fire indiscriminately into no-man's land when I heard a crackle of gunfire. I was in a trance playing a game of desperate animal-like survival where the only emotion I had left in me was hatred.'

'You're eyes are full of hate 41!' I told myself remembering what the Roman Consul Quintus Arrius said to Ben Hur 'That's good. Hate keeps a man alive. It gives him strength.'

I needed strength from any source available and continued to talk to myself mostly from my memory of Hollywood films to boost my failing senses as the sun beat down relentlessly into the trench. My bullet-cracked UN helmet was the only thing preventing the sun from scalding directly down onto my scalped head, but was itself wilting from the intense heat.

Sweat started to pour profusely down my face.

'Its's feckin raining!' I suddenly yelped with excitement.

'What are ye feckin talking about?' asked a bemused Dowler.

'Look Sean,' I said, showing him the moisture on my face, 'I'm telling ye, it's a monkeys wedding!' referring to the evening downpours we used to occasionally get in the barn back in Elizabethville.

'There's no rain here Michael,' Dowler pointed out 'look there's not a cloud in the sky.'

'I'm telling ya Sean,' I insisted, 'it's a monkeys wedding! Merci beaucoup! Merci beaucoup!' And I held my face up to the sky to let the alleged rains wash over my face.

'Michael listen to me!' Dowler said abruptly, 'ye're feckin hallucinating!'

At that moment I collapsed.

I remember vaguely hearing my mother's voice whispering in my ear:

'Yer alright little Micky the Bun, I'm not going ta let ye die, I'm watchin over ya,' before I started to regain consciousness and the next thing I knew I was lying on the trench floor with Dowler propping up my head while Conway poured our last ration of water into my parched mouth.

They both appeared worried and I noticed that Conway looked at Dowler and started tapping his forehead just above his right eyebrow to indicate he thought I was going delirious.

'Am I dying Sean?' I asked wearily.

'Michael, I told ye before;' he replied sternly, 'we're not going to let ye die!'

Gradually, the cup of water allowed me to become re-orientated again to my surroundings; as the familiar sound of bombs and bullets welcomed me back to the land of the so-called living.

But that was it; we were now completely out of water, Dowler and Conway having sacrificed their share to allow me to regain consciousness.

They would probably never realise how grateful I was for that single cup of water.

We had now not only run out of water, but the batteries for my radio had also finally given up, so there would be no evening news for us to listen to. Additionally there were no rations left back at the Purfina garage so another night of battle followed the days fighting with no break.

I don't remember much about the fourth night of the battle, my eyes remained open but my brain was anything but awake. I lost the feeling in some parts of my body as the cold caused my mind and senses to shut down. Remarkably, given they had given up their last ration of water for me a few hours earlier, Dowler and Conway still had more energy than I had. I tried to follow their actions, returning fire when we crept up the side of the trench, then back down again like crazed sleepwalkers. I lamented my lack of years that had probably made me more vulnerable than they, and wondered why I had been so foolish to volunteer for a job that could only be survived by mature battle hardened men. I was embarrassed by collapsing and hallucinating and thought I had in some way let others down. There was no doubt, I was way out of my depth but this was not like last Christmas having a drink with The County when I had been sick trying to prove I could drink like a man, this time being out of my depth meant lives depended on it.

The night eventually passed but there was still no point running over to the Purfina garage in the morning. It was the fifth day of the battle and we had long given up hope of re-enforcements or re-supplies and there was nothing more to eat or drink. Even if they had any rations back at HQ, I no longer had the energy to make it over to the garage canteen, my legs had become too weary. Without water we all just sat forlornly against the side of the trench knowing we were slowly dying:

As the sun rose again over to the East, I could hear a distant tune being sung faintly from one of the trenches but many of the other trenches immediately joined in as if they were trying to hold up our exhausted bodies for one last rendition of the Irish national anthem: aptly titled *A Soldier's Song*.

Soldiers are we, whose lives are pledged to Ireland.

Gunfire from the outer perimeter threatened to stifle its last performance, but the rhythm and harmony in the voices never faulted, and indeed came back still stronger and louder until a resounding chorus could be heard from the trenches all around the Purfina garage.

Some have come from a land beyond the wave.
Sworn to be free, No more our Ancient sire land
Shall shelter the despot or the slave
Tonight we man the gap of danger
In Erin's cause, come woe or weal
'Mid-cannons' roar and rifles peal
We'll chant a soldier's song.

Some sang the anthem in Gaelic but whatever language was used, the words never seemed to have so much meaning as it did that early dawn African morning of Sunday 17 September 1961.

'That must have been The Tiger wanting to sing his last song.' I suggested croakily.

I could see Conway and Dowler both turn their heads away as if they didn't want me to see their tears as I again opened my mother's letter to hold it one last time against my face. Not since I had been shot through the peak of my helmet on the second morning of the battle had I allowed myself to think about the life I had enjoyed back in Ireland but with time obviously running out for us, I wanted my dying memories to be filled with thoughts of home. I decided I would watch the last movie reels of my life flashing in front of me in an imaginary heaven; smoking a Sweet Afton cigarette and it would be hennessy balls, fizzballs and bonbons for my last make-believe meal. If I just propped myself up a bit against the trench walls, I considered, it would feel just like I was watching this epic movie from the most luxurious seats at the back of the Picture House in Edgeworthstown, complete with velvet arm-rests looking down watching the final scenes of the young red-legs fighting nobly til they met their end.

'It's feckin biblical!' I muttered below my breath.

A minute or so later Dowler spoke to both Conway and I with muted optimism.

'Well lads, I'll see yiz in heaven,'

'Aye! we will Sean!' we responded, 'it was a pleasure knowing ye both.'

'Yep th-th-th-that's all folks!' quipped Dowler as if he were imitating Porky Pig's quip-ending to a Loony Tune cartoon.

A faint smile stayed fixed across my face. If I had to die I could wish for no better way to do it. All of my child-hood Picture House dreams had come true, dying after one of the greatest defences in military history. Better still, it was all filmed in an exotic African location and I was surrounded by the bravest men that Ireland would probably ever produce. We may just be another bunch of idealistic young adventure-seekers that were destined never to return to Ireland's shores but I was so proud to be one of them.

When the singing from the other trenches had stopped we all sat back in the trench, our heads lapsed back against the sides in one of those frequent moments of eerie battlefield silence when birdsong reclaims its rightful place as the futility of war becomes so apparent. I remembered what Kevin Barry said before he was executed: 'it's nothing to give one's life for Ireland. I'm not the first and maybe I wont be the last,' before the exhausted but relentless gunfire from distant bushes began again.

I had wanted to enjoy my final moments and had barely any energy to stand up let alone returning to the fight, but I again clambered up the trench to fire another round of bullets into no-man's land. My two dog-biscuits I had stored away in my grooved out cubby-hole were useless without water and I was down to my last magazine of bullets. Our batteile du jour was nearly over, just a few more blasts from our FN rifles to delay the inevitable endgame and soon enough we would be overrun and shot dead where we lay; which would at least save us from dying from thirst.

Then, all of a sudden John Monahan arrived again in the trench. We knew he had no more supplies to give us but he had arrived with some astonishing news.

'We've arranged a ceasefire lads, the battle is over!'

I daren't show any joy, the pain of disappointment this time would be just too much to bear, but I couldn't help the balls of tears welling up with relief in my battle-weary eyes. Before they dropped embarrassingly down my cheeks, I quickly padded my face with my ragged shirt and wondered again if I were hallucinating.

'In 15 minutes,' Monahan continued in a hurried tone, 'Prendergast will give the call to ceasefire, and commandant Quinlan will exchange a truce at the roadblock with the Gendarmerie and the mayor of Jadotville.'

It seemed almost inconceivable – perhaps we were going to survive after all.

'Is it really over Sarge?' checked Dowler guardedly.

'Aye, it's really over,' confirmed Monahan.

'Does that mean we will be allowed to get some rest?' asked Dowler, as if he were testing the authenticity of Monahan's statement.

'Aye it does,' replied Monahan. 'As soon as Quinlan has signed the document, stand yer weapons down, we will no longer be on war footings from that point.'

'Now Michael' Dowler noted triumphantly and with an energy that defied his failing voice 'didn't I always tell ya there was a God.'

'Well whatever prayers ye do say at that mass of yours Sean,' I replied 'just keep feckin saying them; just for the next 15 minutes anyway.'

I counted through each minute that went by in my head and sure enough about 15 minutes later Prendergast gave the long-awaited order:

'Men of 'A' Company – Ceasefire!'

Immediately, all around the Jadotville plateau fell silent, but it was an uneasy distrustful silence that we all knew had the potential to re-ignite at the twitch of a rogue finger.

A minute later we peeked over the parapet of the trench to watch our Commanding Officer Pat Quinlan along with the Company Sergeant Prendergast walking purposefully and proudly down to the road block where the mayor of Jadotville was holding up a white flag of truce. From our trench I could see the mayor's facial features which I studied to gauge his integrity. He had a neatly trimmed moustache that wrapped around the corner of his lips, which menacingly pointed downwards – reminding me of the evil Fu Manchu in the film *Yellow Peril*. Although he was a prominent member of the Jadotville civilian community; the mayor had the cold eyes and sinful face of the devil himself. I knew immediately that we couldn't trust him.

As the assembled leaders spoke for a minute over paperwork, various life forms started to appear from their hiding places: trenches, bushes, anthills, outhouses or whatever lair they had found over the last five days of battle. Most were humans re-emerging from their animal like existence into normality, but were gradually joined by small creatures and birds as the vibrant sound of jungle life slowly and hesitantly began to re-establish itself.

Thousands of exhausted and suspicious eyes from both sides were focused on the roadblock where the truce was taking place. I could see Quinlan talking directly to the Gendarmes leader – Colonel Muke, or Old Stoneface. Beside them stood an old merc who I presumed to be one of the notorious commando leaders, Mad Mike Hoare, Bob Denard or Jaque Schramme, busily discussing the paperwork. Sometimes I could see them nodding, then making gestures with their arms then shaking their heads. Like all the other desperate eyes anxiously concentrated on the proceedings down at the roadblock, I was watching for the slightest gesture that might tell me what was happening.

Just a minute or so later; Quinlan and Prendergast were on their way back towards the Purfina garage, signalling to more junior officers and NCOs that the ceasefire treaty was in place. John Monahan immediately gave the order to us to stand down our weapons.

What had seemed completely implausible just half an hour beforehand was now a reality; we could actually start thinking of home and mother, and the lives that we believed we had lost but now remarkably lay ahead of us.

After eight days of being under siege, including five blistering hot days and four long nights of continuous fighting, we were finally allowed some rest – the battle of Jadotville was really over.

CHAPTER ELEVEN

Home wasn't quite home any more

Date: December, 1961
Location: Edgeworthstown, Ireland

'Hello mam,' I uttered quietly as I walked through the door of our railway crossing house back home in Edgeworthstown.

'Micky that isn't you?' she murmured back as she stood up from tending to the open hearth, 'oh, Lord Bless us and save us, it is surely,' and she immediately came over to the door and gave me a tentative stroke of my cheek as if to verify that it was really me who was standing in front of her.

I could feel her apprehension and the look in her eyes held the same fear as when I had set out for The Congo some six months beforehand.

'Oh my boy has come home,' she proclaimed, as she gradually regained her motherly familiarity and she hugged me still tighter as her worst fears gradually lifted.

'Praise God for his mercy,' she continued, 'we knew he'd listen to our prayers,' as tears streamed down her face.

She seemed much smaller, but most noticeably her face had aged and had become sallow from the anguish of the last few months.

'Yer looking well, mam.' I commented but she just shrugged it off as if she knew I was just being polite.

'Now Micky,' she stated as she regained her composure. 'We'll get ya something to eat. What would ye like? We have lots of sausages and yer favourite; boxty, but first I'll get ya a nice cup of tea with two big spoonfuls of sugar.' She was speaking to me like the boy she had raised and chastised many times, making up for that period of my adolescence she thought she had lost.

'Aye, tea would be grand,' I replied, as I took a seat in The County's usual chair in the corner of the room.

'Yer father will be home shortly,' she noted, 'he's been really looking forward to seeing ya ever since we heard ye were being released from prison.'

I knew that both my mother and The County would have followed every snippet of news about us in The Congo, my mother travelling down to Athlone each day during our imprisonment to hear first hand any announcements from the army information officer. They had also been informed from representatives of The Red Cross and Amnesty International that we were being treated well enough in prison and would not be executed.

As she prepared a fresh pot of tea she told me that a gasp went round the assembled mothers and wives in Athlone when they were told that all 157 Jadotville men were still alive after the battle, with the wounded receiving medical treatment and out of immediate danger.

'It was such a relief Micky to hear that ye were all still alive,' she commented, 'especially after all the newspaper reports that suggested at least 57 of ye were dead. Many of the mothers just couldn't believe it. But I knew ye were alive Micky, and that God in his mercy would spare ye.'

'Thanks mam,' I replied, 'we knew ye'd be praying for us.'

'But then,' she continued, 'we didn't know what would happen to ye in prison and in some ways that was the worst part. One minute ye were being freed, next there was another threat against ye.'

'Ah, we were all just happy that the battle was over mam,' I replied downplaying the threats to us in prison, 'just surprised that we had become prisoners at all.'

'Ah ye made it home safely Micky,' she replied, 'that's what's important,' and she handed me a cup of steaming sweet tea, something I had dreamt of so many times when in The Congo but especially when we were prisoners.

This was the happy ending we had all dreamt of: a return to simple normality. We would have been happy enough at mere survival let alone being able to enjoy the simple things like a cup of tea that perhaps we had once taken for granted.

'Aye mam,' I replied. 'It's great to feel the cool rain once more. It was very hot out there in The Congo ya know, but as ya can see, I did get a great sun tan,' I noted rolling up my shirt sleeves.

'So I hear all the other boys are well too? How's Sean? And Pakie?' she asked, 'and they're both glad to be home no doubt?'

'Aye they're all grand mam,' I answered. 'Sean will be giving me a lift back to Athlone later.'

Thinking of others in 'A' Company caused my mind to drift back to remember the casualty count when the battle of Jadotville finally finished and the ceasefire was announced. The relief that was slowly being felt at surviving tempered by the absolute shock that we would become prisoners of war and what the future held.

The ceasefire on the last day of the battle had indeed been a ruse and, as I suspected from his malevolent demeanour, the mayor of Jadotville was its instigator. When the mercs realised what little supplies we had left, they amended the wording of the agreement and called it an honourable surrender. Realistically it would have been impossible for us to fight on any longer without water and our Commanding Officer Quinlan made the inevitable decision to accept the altered terms as we simply had nothing left to fight with. The decision undoubtedly spared the lives of those of us who were probably only hours away from death in the stifling heat of the trenches as the mercenary and gendarmerie forces prepared to overrun us. Instead they took us prisoner but we were keenly aware that our captors had the worst possible reputations, and perhaps many of us believed our lucky survival would prove only a temporary respite. We considered what options we still had left, perhaps an escape or a breakout, but the chances of continuing survival whichever route we considered appeared very slim. The officers in charge of 'A' Company ordered us to abide by the agreement and insisted that we would be protected by the ceasefire and honourable surrender they had signed. But the daily taunts from beyond the barbed wire surrounding us threatening our execution and subsequent cannibalisation convinced us that our legal agreement in the lawless and seditious Heart of Darkness in Central Africa was valueless.

With the UN leader Dag Hammarskjöld having been shot down and killed en-route to Ndola to negotiate an end to the Jadotville siege we became morbidly pessimistic about our hopes for survival. Unbeknown to us, his death did bring about a change of policy from other world leaders looking to distance themselves from accusations of complicity and direct blame. Seemingly in shock at the death of a world statesman, Britain and France immediately opened their African airspace for humanitarian purposes but more importantly, the Soviets and the US dialled down their aggressive rhetoric towards each other averting a possible nuclear confrontation in The Congo. The press barons of the colonial nations portrayed a situation depicting their politicians as acting honourably in their citizens' best interests and continued to criticise the UN for sparking off a war by intervening to end the succession. It made popular reading in European capitals to talk about the plight of white ex-pat nationals and to let the tainted UN representative, Connor Cruise O'Brien, bear the brunt of the criticism for initiating the offensive without the specific and unambiguous authorisation of the UN assembly. To us it seemed simply inhuman that human value was solely dependent on having white skin and to completely ignore the hundreds of thousands of native African refugees who were at imminent risk of death as a direct result of the actions of European governments and businesses. It remained just an inconvenient truth that the reality of colonialism and corrupt government had been the cause of such human atrocity, so the press barons continued to direct their journalists to write stories that, to us exposed their true motive: to retain, through corporate collusion, The Congo's vast riches for white European gain.

The head of the succession movement, Moise Tshombie, remained a master of propaganda, and Dowler noted sarcastically,

'Soon he would have to get a picture of himself with a crown of thorns while hanging on the cross to get people to pray for him.' To which Pakie Monahan replied:

'But have ye noticed it's only the white fellas that are praying for him; nobody would be praying for him down at the refugee camp, just cursing the bastard along with his Belgian, French and British supporters for doing the work of the devil.'

When his forces took us prisoner, Tshombie soon realised that it would be a publicity disaster for the succession movement to have us executed and that, had he done so, he would instantly incur the wrath of the US who became much more supportive of the UN after Hammarskjöld's death. To gain the sympathy of the US, Tshombie called his succession a fight against the threat of communism and that The Congo should also be able to enjoy being part of the free world through capitalism, whilst his own pockets were being handsomely lined by the Societe Generale and Union Miniere. Unlike the execution of Patrice Lumumba, Tshombie wasn't implicated directly in Hammarskjöld's death, but all of us in 'A' Company were sure it was one of the mercenary pilots he was paying that shot down the fated plane. We were also convinced that it was probably the same Fouga Magister jet that had strafed and bombed us for five days in Jadotville. By keeping us alive in prison, Tshombie claimed the moral high ground by compassionately allowing us peacekeepers to live while so many of his loyal gendarmes had been killed fighting for the Katangan state. But there was another motive behind him keeping us alive: he could use us a valuable bargaining counter to further his succession demands.

Each day in prison ticked by slowly until finally on 25 October 1961, after a few last minute threats and arguments, Tshombie granted our release as part of a prisoner exchange for mercenaries listed on the chasseux blancs that had been arrested throughout the UN offensive to end the succession.

The feeling of imminent relief was incredible but our last bus journey to Elizabethville remained subdued in case it turned out to be yet another false dawn. As we approached the town we could see other UN patrols and slowly we began to sense that we were among our own and almost free. We started to shake hands with each other and many became unusually emotional at the prospect of imminent release:

'Thank you Sean,' I said to Dowler, then, 'thank you John, thanks Pakie,' as I busily began expressing my gratitude to everyone around me. I knew it was them, every one of the men who fought at Jadotville who had kept me alive; and that in many ways, I owed them all my life.

With all the gratitude being shown, Dowler said that it felt like being back at mass when the priest embarrassingly directs everyone to offer each other the sign of peace. A full Mass with communion had continued every day we were in prison, thankfully without another recitation of the Last Rites but every one of us including me attended. I had never prayed so diligently in my life, my mind never once distracted as it always had when I was a child, to thoughts of Johnny Cash in his black shirt singing *Don't Take Your Guns to Town*.

Pakie Monahan vowed that he would never skip mass again after God had answered his prayers and the Tiger noted that he too would become a much more regular churchgoer after the miracle of us all surviving Jadotville and prison.

'And I think I'll start by joining the choir when I get back,' he stated, 'a few of them gospel songs in the style of Elvis Presley to give thanks to the Good Lord above,' which caused my first smile to sweep across my face in six weeks.

With our release getting nearer, all the familiar character traits were beginning to re-establish themselves throughout 'A' Company, although the personal qualities were a little more well-intentioned and virtuous than before.

'And,' Monahan piped up, 'instead of reading all about dirty French actresses in the evenings, I'll only be reading the good book!'

'Well ye can give me all yer pictures of Brigitte Bardot then,' I offered. 'After Jadotville I think life is too short. And seeing as ye'll not be needing them magazines anymore, I'll have them off ye.'

'Ya can feck off and buy yer own!' he told me with an air of mischief, 'them magazines deserve to remain in a good god-fearing home.'

As our conversations reverted to their former humour; those exchanges normally reserved for free men, I stood up to breathe in the fresher air that comes with freedom, which only a prisoner can really appreciate. But as our liberty inched closer, it turned out that it wouldn't be the homecoming many of us were expecting.

Buoyed by the very thought of being amongst our own, we waited eagerly to get off the bus that had brought us to Elizabethville. But as we smiled and greeted anyone in our gaze we were met with disapproving looks, shaking of heads and nods of condemnation in our direction. There were no hand-shakes between one-time friends and messmates and when we stood down off the bus, we were met with silence and we walked forlornly to our billet accommodation back in the Barn, with barely any hint of acknowledgement.

We were completely bemused and I commented to Dowler,

'What the fuck is happening here? It seems like they don't want to see us.'

'The Lord moves in mysterious ways Michael,' he replied, 'sometimes maybe a little too mysteriously.'

The inexplicable atmosphere continued, with the canteens and bars going uneasily quiet when anyone in 'A' Company walked through the door. What we didn't know at the time was that our six weeks in prison provided a window of opportunity for the more senior Irish army commanders in Elizabethville to compile their reports. Those that we believed had abandoned us in Jadotville had proved to be particularly diligent in constructing their military documentation which told of a compelling tale of their heroics and our capitulation. The original radio logs of every correspondence during the siege that detailed requests for re-enforcements or re-supplies had been surreptitiously rewritten. The radio logs would surely have ensured the court-marshall of the Elizabethville commanders but the amended logs apparently said that Jadotville wasn't a battleground and there was only a minimum of force pitted against us compared to that used against them in Elizabethville. They alleged that 'A' Company surrendered too easily even though they claimed that scarce re-enforcements and re-supplies were on the way to help us, many risking their lives to come to our aid but that the surrender came too soon and their efforts had been in vain. Our defeat had put the UN and those senior Irish UN commanders in a weakened negotiating position that allowed the succession to gain momentum. Their hard won gains in Elizabethville that had achieved so much had been rendered useless, as they implied that our officers had made the wrong decision and we had turned tail and fled. This was a propaganda campaign like no other we had seen up to that point, a deeply personal and unjustifiable attack on every soldier in 'A' Company but probably most unfairly against the valiant commander of 'A' Company, Pat Quinlan.

None of us could believe that such a falsified account of Jadotville had been supplied.

'It certainly doesn't fit with anything that I remember about it,' I stated.

'Aye, nor I,' commented both Dowler and Pakie Monahan.

'They are probably just trying to cover their own arses,' I suggested, 'to cover-up the facts about what happened in case they get court marshalled for feckin abandoning us.'

Our platoon sergeant John Monahan had also found out something else since our release.

'After the Force Kane relief column failed,' he told us scornfully, 'it turns out that they didn't even raise another request to send re-enforcements, and there was us getting fired on in the trenches and relying on them as our only hope.'

'That's why they weren't answering their radios,' I concluded, 'and now they have to change their story or they'll be hung when they get back to Dublin.'

'Ah they won't get away this,' announced Dowler with his typical optimistic air, 'the truth will surely come out.'

There were clearly two versions of events circulating about what happened in Jadotville but the rank and file soldiers in the rest of the 35th Battalion had clearly only heard about the military reports submitted by the Elizabethville commanders; that we had not put up a fight and surrendered too easily. The result was, that the day that 'A' Company was released from prison, was a shock as great as any we had faced up to that point.

The cold shoulder and silence we were met with on the day of our release eventually broke as some began openly accusing us of cowardice for surrendering so soon. When it was explained to them by those who endured Jadotville what the battle was really like; being surrounded and attacked by more than 3,000 enemy forces, mortar bombing, jet strafing and possibly more than 300 enemy dead, many simply didn't believe it. We tried to explain that we were under siege for eight days while the actual battle didn't stop for five days with no sleep and that we eventually ran out of food, water and ammunition. But some said that it couldn't be true as none of us had been killed and that we had just refused to fight on. They were quick to point out that whilst they were risking their lives in Elizabethville, we chose to look after our own skins; that they would never surrender so easily and would have chosen instead to die to the last man. They accused us of holding up the little white feather to avoid getting involved in a fight and that we weren't worthy of being called soldiers; some even said we didn't deserve to be still alive. Possibly most hurtful of all, they said we had let our country down as we heard more about their own bravery during Operation *Morthor* in Elizabethville. Supported by the official version of events, it was as if they only wanted their own fight to be talked about, that there wouldn't be enough recognition for everyone who had fought in The Congo and that theirs was the only viable war story that should come out.

It was a very different account of the battle of Jadotville than we had all witnessed and we heard that the officers in charge of 'A' Company quickly provided an 'on-the-ground' military report of events surrounding Jadotville. We knew this account would have included accusing their superiors in Elizabethville of failings and mistakes which compounded the threat to us given our precarious position of being under siege. I instinctively knew from my days in the recruitment company back in Athlone that the hierarchy of the army would protect officers of higher rank who had already submitted the 'official' version of events. I took a little comfort however when I recalled what happened to Corporal Haydn during the 'farting on parade incident' where he suddenly vanished, to where I never found out, but much depended on what the army chose to accept and what they believed would be the best account for the Irish army's reputation.

Although there were no witnesses to support the Elizabethville commanders, the army command most often stuck by seniority and by the original details to avoid back-pedalling. It was made more complicated by the fact that it was the army commanders themselves who were being implicated in wrongdoing, which if proved could lead to them being discredited with possible charges arising as a result.

With senior military careers seemingly at stake, the division grew between those that served in Jadotville and those that didn't, but the whispering campaign against us which was supported by the official version of events gained momentum and filtered down to affect every soldier.

There were many arguments and brawls as a result, with some drunkenly taunting us with ripped white sheets or little white feathers that they had deliberately plucked from a nearby farm hen.

'Here!' one said over towards a quartet of Jadotville soldiers sitting at a table the other side of an Elizabethville bar about a week after we had been released, 'I would like to have an argument ye, but stop! I surrender!' and they would throw their bar towels on the floor to ridicule us. Sure enough another argument would break out with the Jadotville soldiers similarly accusing them of cowardice for abandoning us.

I was still careful not to attract too much attention because of being underage, and I remained quiet throughout the mockery, preferring to avoid confrontation that could have caused people to look more closely at my details, but I could see the harm that the false accusations was having. I satisfied myself that I should be grateful for being alive, that I could see my family again back home in Ireland and that within six months or so I would be able to leave the army. For others though it would not be so easy; some had envisaged a military career or at least another full contract. The army was in many ways their life, so they tried desperately for the truth to be told about what really happened in Jadotville.

Some of those in army command however had too much to lose from the truth getting out and the mockery continued until by the time we arrived home to Athlone, the 157 men who endured Jadotville had become figures of contempt and derision.

The first thing I wanted to do when I arrived back in Ireland was to go to Edgeworthstown, a place that was safe and dependable, away from the savage propaganda campaign that was being waged against us. As I sat sipping tea in The County's seat in the corner of the room my mother continued to make nice conversation about our ordeal, busily fussing over me and bringing me slices of currant bread.

'Yer brothers Kevin and Franco have moved over to London,' my mother began explaining. 'Aye Kevin has found some work on the trains and Franco is on the buses. The Dolly went over with them but decided to move up to Scotland as he heard about a job on a farm. I think he prefers to be outside in the country air.'

My face warmed as I could imagine my brothers and the Dolly embarking on their journeys probably aboard the Princess Maude and my heart began to beat once more with the vivacity of youth, thinking again of a future, another great adventure maybe also to London, that had so nearly been stolen from me.

A little while later The County arrived back home. I stood up to offer him his usual chair but he declined as he shook my hand like grown men do, with a tight grasp and looking directly into my eye, he said,

'Thank God yer home son, it's grand to see ya.'

'Thank-you dad,' I replied.

He told me he was pleased to see that Dag Hammarskjöld had been posthumously awarded the Nobel Peace prize the week after we were released from prison, and that it was ultimately a victory for the UN that had saved the world from a nuclear catastrophe.

'So Micky,' he noted, 'are ya goin ta tell us all about it?'

For a moment I was stuck for words and hadn't prepared myself to relive the siege all over again let alone within earshot of my mother, but as I began recounting some of the events, words just began to pour out.

'Oh dad,' I said, 'we helped the local people build their refugee camps and they were the friendliest fellas ye could wish to meet. Most of them however were starving but they still wore a little freedom box around their necks which Lumumba had given them but apart from that, they had nothing, everything taken away from them by greedy white European men who bribed a few politicians and paid the press to cover their crimes. But then I saw the most fantastic wild animals and birds in the world: elephants, rhinos, huge pelicans, hummingbirds and monkeys. Every day we awoke to the blazing sunshine and the sound of the jungle dawn chorus. It was the most colourful place I had ever seen, no film at the Picture House or magazine pictures could ever compare.'

I could tell The County was enthralled but for now he just chided me,

'What, it was even more fantastic to look at than the fine cattle we have in Edgeworthstown?' he quizzed sarcastically.

'Aye, dad,' I continued. 'I even got to see one of the famous black-maned lions of Katanga.' My train of thought was abruptly interrupted by the image of the flailing lion's arms I had seen on the second day of the battle. The silence was however only momentary as The County beckoned me to continue.

'What about what happened in Jadotville?' he pressed, 'we were very worried about ya ye know, yer brothers and sisters thought ye were a gonner.'

'Aye Jadotville was rough alright,' I conceded briefly as I became more conscious of my mother listening to my account.

'We heard down in Athlone that the commanders let yiz down?' noted The County as he began to quiz me more closely.

'Well I don't know the details of what happened dad,' I replied, 'but we were cut off and had run out of everything: bullets, food and we had no water left at all. When no re-supplies arrived, even eight days later, we eventually agreed to a ceasefire, although they later called it an honourable surrender.'

'Some of the other parents and wives of those that fought in Jadotville are very angry about all of this, son,' The County suggested as I began to sense his rising indignation; 'they're saying that they just deserted ye and left ye for dead?'

Again I didn't want to say too much in front of my mother who had clearly been agonising over the same stories over recent months.

'A lot of bad things happen in war dad.' I finally replied.

But The County's anger would not be quelled so easily.

'Well the people of Ireland will judge them for what they did to our sons!' he stated as his normal reserve gave way to outright resentment, 'as sure as God is my witness, they'll surely answer for this.'

I looked away to avoid The County's direct angry stare, and to avoid any more questioning although he clearly had many more questions burning inside him.

In the window I could see the latest candle my mother had lit for me every night I had been away. It had nearly burnt out, the wax having gathered around its base like a disregarded ball gown. My eyes drifted back around the living room where once had been so much life and fun, and I thought back to the time we were all celeidh dancing and the train smashed through the crossing gates. But the vibrancy and exhilaration of those childhood days were long gone. Even our excitable dog Nasser with his thumping tail resounding against the bare stone floor had found a new home. It was as if the house had become consumed by the events of Jadotville; a bitterness that I knew would linger amid a futile quest to get some answers, all ravages of war that most rarely contemplate.

It is never just the soldiers involved that bear the scars of battle; anger and fear continue to rage in the minds of parents, wives, children and loved ones, permeating every aspect of their hitherto innocent lives. I was still waking violently most nights, grasping for my illusory FN rifle and roaring at my phantom enemy, but I never knew that the anguish of constant agitation, nightmares and drenched pillows had extended back home to affect my parents as well.

I heard that other members of 'A' Company who fought in Jadotville were suffering even worse, relying more and more on the comfort of alcohol in desperate denial that they had become a grown man who needed to wear a nappy at night. The convenient diagnosis made by our critics was that the men of Jadotville had gone a bit soft in the head or were 'a bit touched' adding to the isolation and resentment against the outside world, which we felt was forsaking us again.

Reliving it all at home, my innocent haven, I began to feel a tear welling up in my eye but thankfully my mother changed the subject.

'As all of yer brothers and sisters have moved over to London, Micky, except for young Phillip, we've decided we'll be going over as well in a few months' time, will ya be coming with us Micky?' she began asking tentatively. 'I mean will ya be leaving the army and coming over to London with us?'

I considered it for just a moment.

'I will surely,' I gladly replied, 'I will surely.'

It was time for all of us to look forward rather than back, to start thinking of a new life when I left the army, the career in music or films I had envisioned. It was what I had originally joined the army for; to get enough money to make it over to London, where I could get lots of decent work and dance in the great dance halls of Cricklewood and New Cross.

Soon, the afternoon had passed and it was time to head back to Costume barracks in Athlone where I had to serve the last few months of my army service contract. Dowler had bipped his horn and parked his car outside our house to give me a lift.

'How did ya get on? He asked as I sat down in the passenger seat, 'I'll bet yer mother was delighted to see ya?'

'Aye Sean,' I replied. 'Apparently all my brothers and sisters thought I was dead.'

'Aye that's what mine thought too,' he quickly burst in, 'and there was us having a grand old time getting a bit sunburnt in Jadotville where there was hardly a battle at all.'

I laughed at his obvious sarcasm.

Back in Athlone, I rejoined the ordnance division and kept a low profile as I had always done but continued to follow the unfolding accounts surrounding the events of Jadotville. The Irish UN envoy, Connor Cruise O'Brien, was still the target of Western colonial media whose influence had impacted many commentators in Ireland. His extra-marital dalliance with the daughter of the finance minister, Maire MacEntee reflected badly on the government which was keen to appear morally untainted. The government was also facing increasing criticism for sending Irish troops into a war situation, given Ireland's status as a neutral country. The defence department was questioned as to why Irish troops were so ill-equipped and why Ireland had to play such a leading role amongst the non-aligned nations.

When the government was asked directly about Jadotville, they only referred to the official version of events, that it was considered a minor standoff with minimal force used. The idea of neutral Irish troops being involved in such a bloody battle, or that there were 300 enemy soldiers killed was clearly a major embarrassment for the government, let alone the accusation that senior officers in the Irish army had abandoned a Company of young Irish soldiers to what could have been another Niemba massacre. The politicians soon realised that by sticking to the official version of the events, that it was our fault for surrendering too soon and downplaying the attack on us, was far more palatable for their political careers.

We were told that the commander of 'A' Company, Pat Quinlan, had submitted to the Irish defence ministry the full military account of what took place on the ground in Jadotville which we knew would tell the truth of what happened. The stage was set: did they believe the witness reports of what really took place or the accounts of those senior officers being implicated in wrongdoing whose report was compiled from Elizabethville?

The day came about three months after our return from The Congo when the Ministry of Defence published its commendations and honours list for those who had served a tour of duty in The Congo. We gathered in the barracks to hear the wireless announcement being broadcast direct from the Dail in Dublin. I looked around at the faces of Dowler, the Tiger, Pakie Monahan and PJ Sweeney gathered around Dowler's bunk to listen to the radio: all anxious to hear what the final reckoning would be. I knew The County too would be straining his head to hear the wireless back home in Edgeworthstown, eager for some kind of acknowledgment from the nation's leaders of the wrongdoing that almost cost him a son. With such raw emotion waiting on his every word, I was willing with all my heart for the defence department spokesman to lift the false accusations and ongoing stigma of Jadotville by acknowledging Quinlan's report which would go some way to stop the whispering campaign against us.

'This will put an end to all them barrack room barristers,' I noted optimistically.

'That's right Michael,' replied Pakie Monahan, 'but some of them are not going to like what they're about to hear.'

'Aye, the truth hurts alright,' I finished before a 'shush' went round as the TD was about to open his statement.

He began as we expected talking of the many great achievements of those Irish UN officers and soldiers that served so bravely in The Congo; who had answered their young nation's calling to so proudly and honourably represent the people of Ireland. He then went on to list some specific operations including *Rumpunch* and *Morthor* warmly congratulating and commending the commanders in Elizabethville for their bravery and determination in the face of such danger. He listed many individual personnel who would be invited to Dublin to receive special commendations for outstanding service to the nation and to the UN, taking perhaps 20 minutes to call out each person's name. But despite the recommendations contained in Cmdt Quinlan's report, Jadotville was never mentioned and no soldier in 'A' Company who took part in the battle of Jadotville would receive an honour.

As the TD wrapped up his statement, many in Dublin could be heard on the wireless clapping but I could see the faces around me visibly dropping.

'Did he feckin forget to say something?' I asked openly.

'Aye,' noted Monahan 'but he didn't forget them others in charge of us in Elizabethville. Perhaps he just wants Jadotville to remain under the carpet.'

'Well in all the books I read about war they always said that what a soldier sacrifices in the name of his country should never be forgotten, but they have just delivered the final coup de gras.' I quickly realised however that my protestations were pointless so I immediately conceded. 'Oh, I suppose it's easier for them this way.'

'Well let them go to Dublin to collect their medals,' Monahan noted, 'but when they walk up on stage and the band starts playing, they'll never be able to sing 'The Soldier's Song' like we did that last morning in Jadotville.'

Although I was leaving the army just a month or so later, I knew exactly that the army and governments attempt to sweep the events of Jadotville under the carpet would mean for those who fought there. The so called young and proud nation of Ireland was busy trying to wash its hands of us, supposedly in the name of the people that elected them. Perhaps, I concluded, they believed the reputations of a few senior officials were worth it, but the cost, I knew would be too much for some, especially some of the officers and career soldiers, as the whispering campaign against those in 'A' Company was destined to continue.

Just a minute or so later I left the room and started walking around Costume Barracks and noticed another group of eager raw recruits being given their orders by belligerent corporals over by the barrack square. Although I was now 17, I was still younger than all of them unless of course they too had forged their birth certificate. I thought back to my time as a trainee in the recruitment company, imagining again hearing the derisory comments Havistock-Brown would make about the army hierarchy. Never once did those comments undermine the belief I had in this proud nation, its great history, the rebel heroes and its many martyrs. But all of that had been shattered by what I had just heard on the radio, when Ireland's leaders had wrongly and so cruelly disowned its own brave sons.

As I walked a little further, I noticed CS Prendergast and PS John Monahan walking between buildings probably having just listened to the same radio broadcast. Ireland probably didn't deserve such noble men fighting on their behalf I concluded, who were, along with many others in 'A' Company, the bravest men I would ever meet.

I eventually left the army in April 1962, joining my mother, The County and my young brother Philip emigrating over to London. The conflict in The Congo continued for a few more years, but as Belgium and the other colonial powers bordering The Congo gradually released their oppressive stranglehold, the Katangan succession movement eventually faded and an uneasy, corrupt power structure heavily funded by the CIA was installed. Media attention switched to Vietnam and Cuba for the next round of Cold War antagonism, where once more, human casualties took second place to political ascendancy.

I shared a flat with my parents in Kennington during our first year in London where I found work with The County on the railways.

We often spoke about politics, various war zones around the world and the hypocrisy and misinformation of journalists and politicians motivated solely by winning the propaganda war and re-election. While they filibustered and manoeuvred for personal gain, some like Dag Hammarskjöld and many innocent civilians, like so many in The Congo, made the ultimate sacrifice.

As well as being my father, I also became great friends with The County, drank pints with him down at the pub and put the world to rights many times. I had grown up very fast in The Congo, and I never felt like a boy again.

I was eager to find another Picture House in London which reminded me of the one in Edgeworthstown as war films had once again become de-riguer in 1962 with *Lawrence of Arabia* and *The Longest Day* the biggest grossing films that year. The Picture House in Lewisham was where I had my first date after I had met a young girl called Annie-Kate Mulligan the previous week at the Galtymore dance-hall in Crickelwood, dancing to the country and celeidh tunes of Larry Cunningham and The Mighty Avons.

The County and Katleen Greene in their London flat, in the 1970s

Annie had told me she had been watching and reading about the battle of Jadotville after she met my brothers Kevin and Franco out in New Cross in the midst of the battle. They told her one night that they heard I had been killed and were only awaiting final confirmation. She said she prayed for me and my poor suffering mother every night on hearing the accounts and was so relieved and delighted when she read that all 157 men who fought at Jadotville had miraculously survived the whole ordeal.

Two years later in April 1964, Annie-Kate became my wife. We had two sons and now in 2012 we have five grandchildren. I never had the career in music and films that I had once envisioned with all my typical youthful idealism and instead I became a regular carpenter. In many ways I have everything I ever wanted but over the 50 years since Jadotville, a little part of me still thinks about the men of 'A' Company that so inspired me.

Annie-Kate Mulligan and Michael Greene, London, 1963

Despite many subsequent investigations and independent reports, including by the Irish military, which finally authenticated Cmdt Quinlans's account and uncovered the truth of what happened to 'A' Company, successive Irish governments believed that the events of Jadotville were probably best kept under the carpet.

Keeping it where it had been conveniently swept half a century before may have avoided some embarrassment in the corridors of power but denied a nation a reliable account of a truly remarkable sequence of events.

The stories to which I bore witness included such inconspicuous heroes: Shinners McInerny, Paddy Gilday, Eric Thors, Bjone Hovden, Sean Dowler, Pakie Monahan, Mick Tighe, PJ Sweeney, John Conway, Danny Hegarty, Sgt John Monahan, Sgt Jack Prendergast and Cmdt Pat Quinlan; just some of the names in 'A' Company that Ireland never got to hear about. Whilst none of them went looking for a battle, they were caught up in a military defence against overwhelming odds; and unbelievably they all survived. Even back then as an underage teenager I could understand the real heroism being played out in front me and I was determined that one day, others would finally get to hear about it.

Eventually in November 2005, after much lobbying from many quarters, the Irish government unveiled a plaque in costume barracks Athlone in memory of those that fought in Jadotville and endured the subsequent imprisonment. The plaque now sits proudly beside two UN armoured cars near the officers' mess, not far from the same barracks square where it all began for me when I joined as a trainee soldier in 1959. A few years later in 2010, The Taoiseach, Brian Cowan formally exonerated the men in 'A' Company who fought in Jadotville of any wrongdoing and spoke proudly of their brave service to Ireland.

On my holidays to Ireland a few years ago, I took a trip with Sean Dowler down to Athlone to see the plaque.

He greeted me with his usual enthusiasm.

'Now Michael,' he proclaimed, 'ye'll have more medals on yer chest than Idi Amin himself!'

'Aye Sean,' I replied, 'anyone would think that I gave away my last cup of water.'

His response was a wry smile. Having remained in the army and based in Athlone for the rest of his career, Dowler told me that Jadotville had always remained the first topic of conversation amongst the Jadotville veterans.

'We spoke about it every day,' he told me, 'and I'll tell ya now, there are many names engraved on that brass plate Michael, who would have loved to have been around to see this.'

'Hmm,' I acknowledged with a little compunction that perhaps the acknowledgement came too late.

'Tell me Michael,' he suddenly blurted mischievously, 'when ye went over to London, did ya ever become that grave digger?'

'Aye,' I laughed, recalling vividly the rock hard soil on the Jadotville plateau where we had dug our slit trenches.

'Just that I always told the lads,' Dowler continued mockingly, 'that was what ye wanted to be when ye grew up.'

'No, I feckin didn't!' I replied knowing he was taking the piss. 'I dug enough holes during those days to last me a lifetime. So instead, Sean, I became one of them film moguls.'

Dowler looked at me with a premature smile, fully aware that I too was having the craic.

'Yep,' I continued teasingly. 'I wanted to make epic films about biblical battles for young fellas, like when me and the Dolly were kids, to watch from their velvet cushioned seats with arm-rests at the back of their local Picture House.'

Dowler laughed. 'Ah, that's why ye have lots of money then Michael, I'll have to let you buy the lunch so, seeing as ye've been making all these epic films.'

'Aye Sean,' I replied. 'But none of them films was as good as the one we both watched in Jadotville; that was the finest film I ever saw.'

'Yer right Michael,' pondered Dowler, 'twas surely.'

Michael Greene, Sean Dowler: August 2008

Afterword

Since 1961, none of the recommendations for honourable active service and outstanding valour has been approved by the Irish Ministry of Defence or the Irish Government, for any of the 157 Officers, NCOs and men who served as part of 'A' Company at Jadotville, The Congo.

> God my men were fine….Ireland never reared better sons. They would have died to a man if I had decided to continue. They never wavered …no man ever got the loyalty I did from those boys. When things were darkest they were aways smiling.

Comdt Patrick Joseph Quinlan. Company
Commander 'A' Company 35th Infantry
Battalion African Congo 1961 ONUC
Exerpt from certificate of service 2006

Jadotville veterans October 2011 attending 50th Anniversary of the battle at Costume Barracks, Athlone. Michael Greene and Sean Dowler centre of middle row.

Bibliography

Brundage, W. Fitzhugh, 'LYNCHING IN THE NEW SOUTH: Georgia and Virginia, 1880-1930, Urbana and Chicago, University of Illinois Press 1993.

Conan Doyle, Arthur, 'THE CRIME OF THE CONGO' Doubleday, Page & Co., New York 1909.

Conrad, Joseph, 'Heart of Darkness' Penguin Classics, London 2007.

Cottrell, Peter, 'THE ANGLO-IRISH WAR: The Troubles of 1913-1922' Osprey, Oxford 2006.

Crouch, Barry A., 'A SPIRIT OF LAWLESSNESS: White Violence Texas Blacks, 1865-1868 Journal of Social History 18, Winter 1984.

Devlin, Larry, 'CHIEF OF STATION CONGO' Public Affairs, New York 2007.

Doyle, Rose, with Leo Quinlan, 'HEROES OF JADOTVILLE: The Soldier's Story. New Island, Dublin 2006.

Franklin, V. P., 'BLACK SELF-DETERMINATION: A Cultural History of the Faith of the Fathers' Lawrence Hill & Co. Westport, Connecticut 1984.

Foden, Giles, 'MIMI AND TOUTOU GO FORTH: The Bizarre Battle of Lake Tanganyika' Penguin, London 2004.

Foley, John, 'NO WHITE FEATHER' Book Republic, Dunboyne, Meath 2011.

Godwin, Peter, 'MUKIWA: A White Boy in Africa' Picador, London 2007.

Golding, William, 'LORD OF THE FLIES' Faber and Faber, London 1954.

Goldsmith, Oliver and William J. Rolfe, 'SELECT POEMS OF OLIVER GOLDSMITH' Harper and Brothers, New York 2005.

Hammarskjöld, Dag (Translated from Swedish L. Sjoberg & W. H. Auden), 'MARKINGS' Random House, New York 1964.

Hanson, Neil, 'THE UNKNOWN SOLDIER: The Story of the Missing of The Great War' Corgi, London 2007.

Hennessy, Maurice N., 'THE WILD GEESE', The Devin-Adair Co., Old Greenwch, CT, 1973.
Herge, 'TINTIN IN THE CONGO: The Adventures of TinTin' Egmont, Glasgow 2005.
Hoare, Mike, 'CONGO WARRIORS' Paladin Press, Boulder, Colorado 2008.
Hoare, Mike, 'THE ROAD TO KALAMATA: A Congo Mercenary's Personal Memoir' Leo Cooper, London 1989.
Hoare, Mike, 'CONGO MERCENARY' Paladin Press, Boulder, Colorado 2008.
Hochschild, Adam, 'KING LEOPOLD'S GHOST: A Story of Greed, Terror and Heroism in Colonial Africa' Pan Macmillan, Basingstoke 2000.
Huxley, Aldous, 'BRAVE NEW WORLD' Vintage Books, New York 2007.
Hynes, Samuel, 'THE SOLDIERS' TALE: Bearing Witness to Modern War' Pimlico, London 1998.
Joyce, James, 'A PORTRAIT OF THE ARTIST AS A YOUNG MAN' Penguin Classics, London 1992.
Keogh, Dermot, with Andrew McCarthy, 'TWENTIETH CENTURY IRELAND: Revolution and State Building' Gill & MacMillan, Dublin 2005.
Kipling, Rudyard,'THE COMPLETE WORKS OF RUDYARD KIPLING (1865-1936)' Delphi Classics 2011.
Lee, Harper, 'TO KILL A MOCKINGBIRD' HarperCollins, New York 1960.
Litton Helen, 'THE IRISH CIVIL WAR: An Illustrated History' Wolfhound Press, Dublin 2006.
MacDonald, Alan, 'A LACK OF OFFENSIVE SPIRIT: The 46th (North Midland) Division at Gommecourt, 1st July 1916' Iona Books 2008.
Mandela, Nelson, 'LONG WALK TO FREEDOM: The Autobiography of Nelson Mandela' Little Brown and Company, London 1994.
Meisler, Stanley, 'UNITED NATIONS: The First Fifty Years' Atlantic Monthly Press, New York 1995.
Meredith, Martin, 'THE STATE OF AFRICA: A History of Fifty Years of Independence' Simon & Schuster, London 2006.
Morel, E. D., 'RED RUBBER: The Story of the Rubber Slave Trade Flourishing on the Congo, on the Year of Grace 1906' University Press of the Pacific, 2005.

Mitchell, Angus, 'CASEMENT' Haus Publishing, London 2003.
Nzongola-Ntalaja, Georges, 'THE CONGO: From Leopold to Kabila, A People's History' Zed, London 2007.
O'Brien, Conor Cruise, 'TO KATANGA AND BACK: A UN Case History' The Universal Library, New York 1966.
O'Brien, Conor Cruise, 'CONFLICTING CONCEPTS OF THE UNITED NATIONS' Leeds University Press 1964.
O'Donoghue, David, 'THE IRISH ARMY IN THE CONGO 1960-1964: The Far Battalions' Irish Academic Press, Dublin 2006.
Orwell, George, 'NINETEEN EIGHTY FOUR' Signet Classics, Penguin Group, New York 1961.
Power, Declan, 'SIEGE AT JADOTVLLE: The Irish Army's Forgotten Battle' Maverick House, Dunshaughlin, Meath: 2005.
Richardson, Neil, 'A COWARD IF I RETURN, A HERO IF I FALL; Stories of Irishmen in World War 1' The O'Brien Press Ltd, Dublin 2010.
Shaw, George Bernard, 'JOHN BULL'S OTHER ISLAND' Penguin Books, London 1984.
Turner, Thomas, 'THE CONGO WARS: Conflict, Myth & Reality' Zed, London 2007.
Twain, Mark, 'KING LEOPOLD'S SOLILOQUY: A Defence of His Congo Rule' Warren Co USA 1905.
Urquart, Brian, 'HAMMARSKJÖLD' W. W. Norton & Co, New York 1994.
Walker, Martin, 'THE COLD WAR' Fourth Estate Ltd, London 1993
Wilde, Oscar, 'THE WORKS OF OSCAR WILDE', Abbeydale Press, Enderby, Leicester 2000.
Wrong, Michela, 'IN THE FOOTSTEPS OF MR KURTZ' Harper Collins, London 2001.

The following websites were retrieved in June 2012 unless stated:

'Leopold II, E.D. Morel and the Congo' www.bouncingballs.com/timeline/people/nr_leopoldmorel.htm
'France admits Algerian Campaign was 'war' BBC http://news.bbc.co.uk/1/hi/world/africa/365868.stm Retrieved 2008-11-16
'Patrice Lumumba, and the Independence of the Congo from Belgium' http://www.dlwaldron.com/Lumumba.html Retrieved 2009-08-14

'Heart of Darkness: the Tragedy of the Congo, 1960-67' http://worldatwar.net/chandelle/v2/v2n3/congo.html Retrieved 2008-11-16
'MEMORY OF CONGO: The Colonial Era' Jean-Luc Vellut http://www.congo2005.be/geheugen/brochureEN.pdf
Remembering the Forgotten Heroes of World War I – Courtesy of The Longford Leader http://www.irishidentity.com/extras/hidden/stories/armistice.htm Retrieved 2010-02-21
The Irish Soldiers in WWI http://www.irishcultureandcustoms.com/ACalend/VetsWW1.html Retrieved 2010-02-21
'IRELAND' http://www.greyfalcon.us/Ireland.htm The Associated Press Dec 30th 2005. Retrieved 2010-02-21
'The Irish in the Somme' http://news.bbc.co.uk/1/hi/northern_ireland/5125854.stm Retrieved 2009-09-18
'Irish Military History and the Victoria Cross' by CSV Media NI http://www.bbc.co.uk/history/ww2peopleswar/stories/22/a6084722.shtml
Congo Massacre Survivor: Army must tell real story
http://www.independent.ie/national-news/congo-massacre-survivor-army-must-tell-real-story-516794.html Jerome Reilly Nov 5th 2000. Independent.i.e.Retrieved 2009-03-14
Jonathan Swift 1667-1745 http://www.poetsgraves.co.uk/swift.htm Retrieved 2011-12-12
The Irish Slave Trade – The Forgotten White Slaves http://www.thetruthseeker.co.uk/?p=49619 John Martin
Wendell Phillips http://www.britannica.com/EBchecked/topic/456585/Wendell-Phillips Retrieved 2011-11-08
Ku Klux Klan History http://www.adl.org/learn/ext_us/kkk/history.asp?LEARN_Cat=Extremism&LEARN_SubCat=Extremism_in_America&xpicked=4&item=kkk Retrieved 2010-08-19
Rubber http://www.newworldencyclopedia.org/entry/Rubber Retrieved 2010-03-15
The 1916 Rising Personalities and Perspectives http://www.nli.ie/1916/pdf/4.2.pdf Retrieved 2011-02-21
W. B. Yeats 'An Irish Airman Foresees his Death' http://www.thebeckoning.com/poetry/yeats/yeats.html

Film Bibliography

'AROUND THE WORLD IN EIGHTY DAYS' Dir. Michael Anderson, Michael Todd Co.(1956).
'THE LONE RANGER' Dir. Stuart Heisler, Wrather Productions (1956).
'A REBEL WITHOUT A CAUSE' Dir. Nicholas Wray, Warner Bros. (1955).
'SEVEN BRIDES FOR SEVEN BROTHERS' Dir. Stanley Donen, Loew's, MGM (1954).
'THE THREE MUSKETEERS' Dir. George Sidney, Loew's (1948)
'THE DEFIANT ONES' Dir. Stanley Kramer, Curtleigh & Stanley Kramer Prods. (1958).
'CARMEN JONES' Dir. Otto Preminger, Carlyle Prods. (1954)
'BATTLESHIP POTEMKIN' Dir. Sergei M. Eisenstein, Goskino (1925).
'RIO GRANDE' Dir. John Ford, Republic and Argosy Pictures (1950).
'FORT APACHE' Dir. John Ford, Argosy Pictures (1948)
'SHE WORE A YELLOW RIBBON' Dir. John Ford, Argosy Pictures (1949).
'THE COCOANUTS' Dir. Robert Florey & Joseph Santley, Paramount Prods. (1929).
'A PICTURE OF DORIAN GRAY' Dir. Albert Lewin, MGM, Loew's (1945).
'DIAL M FOR MURDER' Dir. Alfred Hitchcock, Warner Bros. (1954).
'FROM HERE TO ETERNITY' Fred Zinnemann, Columbia Pictures (1953).
'SANDS OF IWO JIMA' Dir. Allan Dwan, Republic Pictures (1949)
'SAMSON AND DELILAH' Dir. Cecil B. DeMille, Paramount Pictures (1949).
'THE MISSISSIPPI GAMBLER' Dir. Rudolph Mate, Universal Intl Pictures (1953).
'BABY FACE NELSON' Dir. Don Siegel, Fryman Enterprises (1957).
'LASSIE COME HOME' Dir. Fred M Wilcox, MGM, Loew's (1943).
'BEN HUR' Dir. William Wyler, Warner Bros. (1959).
'GENEVIEVE' Dir. Henry Cornelius, J. Arthur Rank Org & La Societe des Films Sirius (1959).
'THE MUMMY'S CURSE' Dir. Lesley Goodwins, Universal Pictures (1944).

'BABETTE GOES TO WAR' Dir. Chistian-Jaque, Iena Productions (1959).

'SPARTACUS' Dir. Stanley Kubrick, Bryna Productions (1960).

'THE MAN FROM LARAMIE' Dir. Anthony Mann, Columbia Pictures & William Goetz Prods (1955).

'THE WIZARD OF OZ' Dir. Victor Fleming, MGM, Loew's (1939).

'THE AFRICAN QUEEN' Dir. John Huston, Romulus Films, Horizon Pictures (1951).

'THE QUIET MAN' Dir. John Ford, Republic & Argosy Pictures (1952).

'THE HUSTLER' Dir. Robert Rossen, Rossen Films, Twentieth Century Fox (1961).

'MISFITS' Dir. John Huston, Seven Arts Productions (1961).

'GENTLEMEN PREFER BLONDES' Dir. Howard Hawks, Twentieth Century Fox (1953).

'THE SEVEN YEAR ITCH' Dir. Billy Wilder (1955).

'OCEAN'S ELEVEN' Dir. Lewis Milestone, Dorchester, Warner Bros. (1960).

'THE MAGNIFICENT SEVEN' Dir. John Sturges, Mirisch Company, Alpha prods. (1960).

'THE SEARCHERS' Dir. John Ford, Warner Bros. C.V. Whitney Pictures (1956).

'THE GREAT IMPOSTER' Dir. Robert Mulligan, Universal Intl. Pictures (1961).

'INVASION OF THE BODY SNATCHERS' Dir. Don Siegel, Allied Artists, Walter Wanger Prods. (1956).

'THE SEARCH' Dir. Fred Zinnemann, Praesens Film, MGM (1948).

'THE STRANGER' Dir. Orson Welles, International Pictures, Haig Corp. (1946).

'THE HOUND OF THE BASKERVILLES' Dir. Sidney Lanfield. Twentieth Century Fox (1939).

WHITE KING, RED RUBBER, BLACK DEATH' Dir. Peter Bate. Periscope Productions & BBC (2003).

'UNTAMED' Dir. Henry King, Twentieth Century Fox (1955).

'THE FOUR FEATHERS' Dir. Zoltan Korda, London Film Prods. (1939).

'OHM KRUGER' Dir. Hans Steinhoff, Tobis Filmkunst (1941).

'BOY ON A DOLPHIN' Dir. Jean Negulesco, Twentieth Century Fox (1957).

'TARZAN THE APE MAN' Dir. W.S. Van Dyke, MGM (1932).

'MOGAMBO' Dir. John Ford, Loew's (1953).
'AN AFFAIR TO REMEMBER' Dir. Leo McCarey, Twentieth Century Fox, Jerry Wald Prods. (1957).
'LA DOLCE VITA' Dir. Federico Fellini, Riama-Film, Gray-Film, Pathe Consortium Cinema (1960).
'THE SCARLET PIMPERNEL' Dir. Harold Young, London Film Prods. (1934).
'THE GUNFIGHT AT THE OK CORRAL' Dir. John Sturges, Paramount Pictures, Wallis-Hazen (1957).
'THE GUNS OF NAVARONE' Dir. J. Lee Thompson, Columbia Pictures, Highroad Prods. (1961).
'NORTH BY NORTHWEST' Dir. Alfred Hitchcock, MGM (1959).
'THE ADVENTURES OF DR. FU MANCHU' Republic Prods, Studio City TV Prods. (1956).
'LAWRENCE OF ARABIA' Dir. David Lean, Columbia Pictures, Horizon Pictures (1962).
'THE LONGEST DAY' Dir. Ken Annakin & Andrew Marton, Twentieth Century Fox (1962).